Creation

The Story of Beginnings

Michael Scharf Publication Trust
Yeshiva University Press

MAGGID

Jonathan Grossman

Creation

The Story of Beginnings

The Noam Series

Translated by Sara Daniel

The Michael Scharf Publication Trust of
Yeshiva University Press

Maggid Books

Creation: The Story of Beginnings

First English Edition, 2019

Maggid Books
An imprint of Koren Publishers Jerusalem Ltd.

POB 8531, New Milford, CT 06776-8531, USA
& POB 4044, Jerusalem 9104001, Israel
www.maggidbooks.com

Cover art: *4 Seasons,* by Ofra Friedland (ofrafriedland.com)
Courtesy of the artist

ISBN 978-1-59264-503-9, *hardcover*

A CIP catalogue record for this title is
available from the British Library

Printed and bound in the United States

The Noam Series
is dedicated to the memory of

Dr. Noam Shudofsky *z"l*

by his family and friends

Noam loved the study of Tanakh
and enabled generations of students to
"Understand and discern, to listen, learn and teach, to observe, perform and fulfill all the teachings of the Torah with love."

Contents

Foreword

In Jewish tradition, *peshat* or "plain sense" exegesis is often regarded as a gold standard for interpreting the Hebrew Bible (*Tanakh*). Much ink has been spilled defining *peshat* exegesis. By now it is clear that *peshat* is not simply "the literal sense." After all, the Bible – like any literary work – often employs figurative language. Is *peshat* the "original intention"? Is it the way the text was understood by its original audience? Is it the sense determined through philological analysis? How does *peshat* relate to midrash? These questions can hardly be answered in this context. Yet they are relevant to consider when reading Jonathan Grossman's *Creation: The Story of Beginnings*, which to my mind illustrates the potential richness of *peshat* interpretation in a contemporary setting. Firmly rooted in the multi-faceted tradition of *parshanut hamikra* (Jewish Bible interpretation), this work also engages fully with modern scholarship while opening new avenues in understanding the cultural-religious significance of the Hebrew Bible. Through Grossman's insightful and often creative literary analysis, we are made to appreciate ethical and theological dimensions of the first eleven chapters of the Torah in the spirit of "the way of *peshat*" prized in Jewish tradition.

For some readers it may be surprising to associate *peshat* with theology, ethics, or even contemporary applications of the ancient text of Scripture. It may also seem unusual to characterize *peshat* as a creative form of interpretation. All of these are features are typically associated with midrash. Indeed, Jonah Fraenkel, a contemporary scholar of rabbinic literature, avers that *peshat* is a type of interpretation largely devoid of creativity since it aims to reveal only the original meaning of the Bible. On the other hand, *derash* or *darshanut* is innovative by definition, as it connects Scripture to new ideas with contemporary religious relevance. As noted by James Kugel, the Rabbis of the midrash did not view the Bible as a book of history, but rather a "Book of Instruction" for readers in all ages, teaching them how to behave and think – in ways not necessarily connected to the original meaning.

Yet recent scholarship of the tradition of Jewish interpretation has shown that there are seventy faces to *peshat* – which, in fact, calls for exegetical creativity and innovation. The great *pashtan* Rashbam reports that his grandfather Rashi was revolutionary in introducing a *peshat* program within Ashkenazic learning. More importantly, Rashi also acknowledged "the *peshat* interpretations that newly emerge every day" (*hapeshatot hamitḥadeshim bekhol yom*) – further interpretive innovations within his circle of students and beyond. (See Rashbam's commentary on Genesis 37:2.) As Rashbam, and perhaps even Rashi before him, came to learn, other schools of *peshat* interpretation had already emerged in faraway centers of Jewish learning in the Muslim East, in Spain, and in the Byzantine orbit. The multiplicity of *peshat* rather than its singularity was already evident in the formative medieval period – and continues to this day.

Indeed, modern critical theory questions the very notion that "the text itself" ever has a singular meaning. As the British literary critic Frank Kermode has remarked, "the plain sense…must be of the here and now rather than of the origin," since "the body of presuppositions which determines our notions of the plain sense is always changing." The plain sense thus depends on the imaginative activity of interpreters who provide Scripture with a variety of contexts, some imposed by authority and tradition, others by the need to make sense of the ancient text in a different world ("The Plain Sense of Things," *Midrash and Literature*, ed. G. H. Hartman and S. Budick [New Haven 1986], 190–191). While *peshat* exegesis aims, in some sense, to illuminate an original meaning, it also necessarily bridges chronological and cultural gaps between the Bible and its readers.

Both the classical tradition of Jewish *peshat* interpretation and modern critical theory inform Jonathan Grossman's *Creation: The Story of Beginnings*. This rich and highly learned volume also incorporates midrashic material, modern Bible scholarship, and contemporary Jewish thought. Grossman extracts new meaning from the biblical text, drawing upon the words of the sages and the great medieval commentators, such as Ibn Ezra and Nahmanides, both of whom recognized the symbolic dimensions of the opening chapters of Genesis. Grossman lays the theoretical groundwork for his readings of Genesis 1–11 by discussing the representational nature of the Creation, Eden, and Flood narratives, which "depict…the raw materials, the basic elements, of our familiar world as they come into being." In the opening chapters of Genesis, as Grossman observes, we witness "a world where primal boundaries have not yet been stabilized, where giants walk and terrorize all around." These chapters are "the stuff of myth and legend, of a wild prehistorical age, where heaven seeps into earth, and men live for centuries alongside giants. The world has not yet been tamed into the familiar, natural, mostly realistic setting of the rest of the Bible." Maimonides advanced this sort of approach in the twelfth century, drawing upon rabbinic learning and Greco-Arabic philosophical and literary conceptions; Grossman offers a twenty-first-century account using the tools made available by contemporary scholarship and the rich Jewish tradition.

According to Grossman's reading, the opening narratives of Genesis depict humanity gradually achieving independence from God – a theme that continues throughout the Book of Genesis, as Grossman himself has argued in earlier published works. While the lineage of Abraham becomes the focus of Genesis from chapter 12 onward, its first chapters "are universal stories, and there is therefore room for comparison between biblical etiology and parallel stories from the ancient Near East that depict the creation of the world and humanity." Within these stories Grossman finds universal messages in the Bible relevant for all of humanity.

A fine example of Grossman's insightful reading of the biblical narrative relates to the Garden of Eden episode, which endows the familiar story with new meaning through literary-structural analysis. According to Grossman, it is a "story of autonomy achieved by rebellion," through which every person stakes his or her own path, becoming "aware of his or her own body and its mortality." Grossman cites Sigmund Freud, who describes how an individual achieves freedom from the authority of his parents at the cost of the pain of independence. Within this reading, the serpent represents an internal voice aroused within mankind – bringing him out of the innocence of childhood into turbulent adolescence. Placed at the Tree of Knowledge, the serpent invites Eve to become "like God, knowing Good and Evil." Were it not for the serpent, Eve would not have even taken notice of the forbidden tree. The serpent induces her to perceive its bold, bright colors – and succumb to their temptation.

Adam and Eve believed that rebelling against God by eating the forbidden fruit would bring them independence, autonomy, and control over their own lives. Their punishments, however, reveal the harsh truth adolescents inevitably learn as they become adults: freedom comes at the cost of the heavy – sometimes even crushing – burden of adult responsibilities. Rebellion leads to a new sort of enslavement, not the absolute liberation initially imagined. Informed by the perspective of modern psychology, Grossman offers the following paraphrase of the biblical text:

> Woman will long for man, and he will rule over her; man will toil away at the earth, and reap in sorrow for the rest of his life. Woman's freedom is handed over to others; man no longer controls the ground that he must work and keep, and it will bring forth thorns and thistles along with man's hard-earned bread. The serpent's promise of godlike power and freedom is eclipsed by the daily struggle of survival this freedom exacts.

And as Grossman concludes:

> In this narrative, maturity is presented as a painful process.... Knowledge comes at a heavy price, shattering the child's world

> of blissful ignorance. The rebellious teenager leads himself to a world tainted with sin and burdened with toil, but the ground is waiting for him, waiting for him to break the crust of the soil and tease out its fruits....
>
> In this way, the Garden of Eden plays a dual role in the narrative: it is a physical site, the source of four mighty rivers and the setting of humanity's first drama, but it also functions as a symbolic site that every person passes through over the course of his or her development.

Grossman here echoes Nahmanides, who wrote that "the Garden of Eden exists somewhere in this world," along with "the four rivers and the Tree of Life and the Tree of Knowledge," since "everything appearing in Scripture in the Creation section is true in its literal sense." Yet Nahmanides goes on to say that "the matters are twofold in meaning": they "all are literal (*kemashma'am*)... true and firmly established, but also are written to convey a wondrous mystery (*sod*)" (*Kitvei Ramban*, Chavel ed., II:295–297). Nahmanides in the thirteenth century evinced the symbolic meaning of the Creation narrative through Kabbalah. Grossman does so using tools provided by contemporary scholarship and thought – both Jewish and non-Jewish.

The serpent in the Garden has long been identified with the "evil inclination" (*yetzer hara*) in Jewish (and Christian) tradition. Grossman's nuanced reading of this myth-like creature is based more directly on Rabbi Abraham Isaac HaKohen Kook's depiction of the "evil inclination hidden deep in the depths of the soul" as "a bone-rotting envy that drenches any hint of light in dismal darkness." This "is *envy of God*," as "humanity envies God for His infinite joy, His absolute perfection. This envy," continues Rabbi Kook, "distorts reason and plunges sense into darkness.... It results in utter heresy" (*Shemona Kevatzim*, 1:129). Grossman takes this "heresy" as a reference to Nietzsche, for whom the ideal man (*Übermensch*; "over-man" or "super-man") must break the shackles of religion, effectively replacing God. Yet Rabbi Kook's characterization implies a spark of light in this darkness, since the desire to be "like God" is a creative force that at once is the source of rebellion and idealism. As Grossman writes:

> Moved by the serpent's words, the woman sees the tree through new eyes. It is now seen as a source of temptation, hiding a promise within. This promise is the promise of "becoming like God." Each and every teenager effectively aspires to be like God, to be unlimited, all powerful, unstoppable, and, at the same time, perfect, magnanimous, idealistic.

This psychological insight about the teenage spirit speaks to us vividly in the twenty-first century and infuses the Garden of Eden narrative with new and contemporary significance.

The Torah was given at Sinai over three thousand years ago. The Genesis narratives held profound religious meaning for their original audiences living in the ancient Near East. Two thousand years ago the *Tanakh* would become a source of support, inspiration, and guidance for the Jewish people throughout their long exile. In modern times, with the advent of the State of Israel, the *Tanakh* relates to the Jewish people, both in its homeland and in the Diaspora, in yet other new ways. Representing the best of modern Israeli scholarship, Grossman's literary-theological analysis exemplifies what Rashi referred to as "the *peshat* interpretations that newly emerge every day."

Mordechai Z. Cohen
Professor of Bible and Associate Dean
Bernard Revel Graduate School of Jewish Studies
Yeshiva University
Jerusalem, 20 Av 5778

Preface

Chapters 1–11 of Genesis are as mysterious as they are familiar; a secret dimension always seems to be hiding beneath their well-known surface. These primordial tales of beginning are both seed and root of everything that follows after, and they offer a glimpse of what was before – of the how and why of existence itself.

A book devoted to a literary analysis of these stories, therefore, can hardly avoid delving into issues of theology, psychology, philosophy, and religious experience. While these questions do accompany the narrative analysis in this work, I have attempted to extrapolate them from the text itself and the subtle hints in its narrative design. This methodology is born from the simple – some might say naïve – motive of unearthing the narrative's own intentions: to detect, with the limited tools and capacity of the interpreter, the text's own cues, and to be guided by them. At the same time, my adherence to the text is also due to more practical limitations; a deep philosophical exploration of the first few verses of the Creation narrative could easily fill more pages than the present work. For these reasons, the reader may sometimes be left with the impression of a rough sketch rather than a full-blown landscape. Please consider the following discussions an invitation to deeper exploration of each biblical scene.

Genesis 1–11 paints the challenging portrait of a lost world, a once-mighty world swept away by the sins of humanity and built anew. The literary structure of this section draws a parallel between the old world and the new world, a parallel that invites close scrutiny of humanity's role in the world and its relationship with its environment and God. The very notion of a first divine attempt and its failure designates humanity's free will as the crowning glory of this section. Humanity has the power to do as it sees fit, and God Himself is forced to shape history through these actions. Yet at the same time, this section hints again and again at the limits of human power, at how pushing the boundaries too far brings about self-destruction. Through this piercing tension the world progresses; it may even emerge that the key to progress is enclosed in a husk of sin, so that new paths are breached as the sinners themselves are destroyed by inevitable punishment.

This book was written in memory of Dr. Noam Shudofsky (1933–2005), an accomplished man whose entire life was devoted to the world of Jewish education, both formal and informal. Noam began his career as a Bible teacher and advanced to become the administrator of the Ramaz School of Manhattan for approximately forty dedicated years. He was extraordinarily devoted to the students, faculty, and administration. His love for the Bible did not wane even after he was no longer actively teaching, and he was especially drawn to the literary approach of Bible study, an approach embraced by this work. Judaism was an inextricable part of his identity, and he held that every person must fulfill himself not only in an intellectual sense, but in life itself. And indeed, Noam was deeply involved in the international Jewish community with a love for the State of Israel. His intense efforts – both overt and covert – for the plight of Soviet Jewry, who were persecuted solely because of their Judaism, deserve special mention. Writing this book in his memory was a singular privilege for me, and I was also privileged to become acquainted with his entire family, people whose lives are deeply rooted in love of Torah and love of humanity, and imbued with humility and devotion.

This past year saw the passing of Dr. Shudofsky's beloved wife, Nechi, and it is with sorrow that we devote this book to her memory as well. Her warmth and generosity enveloped me from our first encounter, and I am glad that I was able to present her with this book in its original Hebrew.

With great pleasure, I wish to thank everyone who helped bring this book to light, from its first conception to its final design. First and foremost, I wish to thank my dear friend Binny Shalev, who made this journey together with me, a journey that taught me so much about humility and kindness. We were accompanied on our journey by Rabbi Dr. Itamar Eldar, whose contributions to the ideas expressed in this work were indispensable.

Translating a work of literary analysis is a complex task; literary analysis requires careful attention to each word and its nuances and connotations, and the challenge of rendering an analysis written in one language into another language speaks for itself. To my great pleasure, Sara Daniel undertook this task, and did it well. I am grateful for her literary sensitivity and keen knowledge of Bible study, and I thank her with all my heart.

I am privileged to send this book out into the world through Maggid Books, as part of their Maggid Tanakh Companions series. Matthew Miller and Rabbi Reuven Ziegler have brought about a revolution in Tanakh study, setting new standards for the rare, often incompatible combination of accessibility and caliber in the world of Jewish publishing. I thank them both for their dedication and ambition, and I hope Maggid Books will continue to soar.

This book has been published through the cooperation of Maggid Books and the Michael Scharf Publication Trust of Yeshiva University Press. This reflects the work's ambition to speak in two dialects, appealing to scholars and *Ohavei Torah* alike. These worlds do not contradict each other; on the contrary, at their best they enrich each other.

Special thanks go to Rabbi Dr. Stu Halpern, the Senior Advisor to the Provost of Yeshiva University, who oversaw this book's publication from Yeshiva University's end. His expertise and broad experience made every consultation a creative, original learning experience, and I thank him for his friendship and partnership. My appreciation is also extended to Dr. Mordechai Cohen for his foreword to this book. His broad, profound experience in Jewish Bible interpretation is like none other, and I am honored that his words serve as a gateway for my own.

My sincere thanks also go to Maggid's dedicated publication team: assistant editors Shira Finson and Tomi Mager, whose generosity and professionalism guided this book's publication from start to finish; and to Aryeh Sklar and Debbie Ismailoff, who worked diligently and thoroughly on the book's language editing and proofreading – I am indebted to them for their careful attention to detail.

Last but not least, of course, thanks are due to my wife and children, who accompany me on every journey into the world of reading, writing, and study, who so patiently and so fruitfully hear out every thought and dilemma, who color every ordinary day with joy.

יבואו כולם על הברכה.

Jonathan Grossman

Tishrei 5779

Introduction

REALITY AND SYMBOLISM

Everything follows its beginning,"[1] quotes Rabbi Haim Vital in the name of Rabbi Isaac Luria, the Ari, and even without delving into deep kabbalistic secrets, we intuitively feel its truth in many realms of our lives. The root of something reveals much about its nature, and exposing its point of origin often illuminates its entire process. This is certainly true when we shift our gaze to how the world came into being, indeed how being itself began. These primeval narratives reveal the nature of the world and its purpose, and the nature of humanity and man's role in the world. At the same time, they reveal those first primordial conflicts and failures that are imprinted deep, deep within the world's formation and being.

The primordial nature of these narratives affects their style and design. The first eleven chapters of Genesis are clearly distinct from the rest of Genesis and the Bible as a whole, in regard to their content, style, and atmosphere. Beginning with God's revelation to Abraham in chapter 12, the narrative takes on the classic biblical historical style. Abraham, Isaac, and Jacob are realistic, fleshed-out characters, whose lives resemble the paths our own lives take. While most of us, of course, are not approached by God, or even

1. Rabbi Ḥaim Vital, *Etz HaḤayim*, 4:4.

visited by angels, such interactions are a normal part of the biblical narrative, and they are an integral part of the more routine aspects of the forefathers' lives, such as birth, marriage, and death. This kind of biblical realism is not present in Genesis 1–11. These narratives present an entirely different biblical reality. For example, when the serpent opens up its mouth and speaks to the woman in the Garden of Eden, she is not surprised, and casually responds. In contrast, when Balaam is addressed by his donkey, the narrator explains that this is a miracle, that "God opened up its mouth," and Balaam recoils in shock, just as we would if we were to witness it ourselves. The serpent's capacity for speech, however, seems part of life in Eden, and loss of speech is not mentioned as part of its punishment, which implies that the text views its uncanny ability to speak as nothing unusual.

Nahmanides notes this phenomenon and views it as proof that the serpent is also a symbol of something mystical:

> Know, believe, that the Garden of Eden is within the Land, and so is the Tree of Life and the Tree of Knowledge, and from there the river flowed out and separated into four rivers we are familiar with, for the Euphrates is in our own land and within our own borders, and the Pishon is the Nile of Egypt, as the sages say. But while they are on earth, they all have heavenly counterparts, which are their elemental counterpart, as it says, "Let the king bring me into his chamber".... These are the chambers of Eden, from here they said, the work of the heavens is like the work of the Garden of Eden (Song of Songs Zuta 1:4). The rivers are parallel to the four heavenly camps, from where the powers of earthly rule are drawn... and the serpent does not have the power of speech today, and if it had in the first place it disappeared with its curse, for it was the fiercest curse of all! But all these are double entities, truly revealed and secret together.[2]

Nahmanides emphasizes that not only can the serpent be read as a mystic symbol, but also the rivers, and the entire narrative.

---

2. Nahmanides on Gen. 3:22.

While the sages made various attempts to identify the Tree of Life and the Tree of Knowledge as actual species, suggesting that the forbidden fruit was either the citron, the fig, wheat, or grapes, the most straightforward reading is that of Ibn Ezra:

> Many hold that the Tree of Knowledge was a fig tree, as they "sewed fig leaves." However, if this was so, it would have read this way: "And they sewed the leaves of the Tree of Knowledge." Many also say that it was wheat. I believe that these two trees were inside the Garden of Eden, and cannot be found anywhere else on earth.[3]

As we will see below, Ibn Ezra is generally wary of charging the text with symbolism, but his approach towards the Tree applies to the wider context of the story, which is painted in the bold, bright colors of ancient myth.[4] This is a vastly different palette than the realistic shades of the rest of the Bible.

This is true not only of the Eden narrative, but of the rest of the stories in this section. The Creation narrative depicts the raw materials, the basic elements, of our familiar world as they come into being; the Flood narrative paints a world immersed in primal waters, a world where primal boundaries have not yet been stabilized, where giants walk and terrorize all around.[5] This is the stuff of myth and legend, of a wild prehistorical age, where heaven seeps into earth,

3. Ibn Ezra on Gen. 3:6.
4. On symbolic readings about the Eden narrative, see the comprehensive discussion of Terje Stordalen, *Echoes of Eden: Genesis 2–3 and Symbolism of the Eden Garden in Biblical Hebrew Literature* (Contributions to Biblical Exegesis and Theology 25: Leuven, 2000), 81–104. This is recognized in traditional commentary; see Deborah Schechterman, "The Doctrine of Original Sin in the Jewish Philosophy of the Thirteenth and Fourteenth Centuries," *Daat* 20 (1988): 65–90; T. Horowitz, "The Garden of Eden Story (Genesis 3) – Reality or Parable? – an Interdisciplinary Debate," *Sha'anan* 9 (2004): 39–88.
5. It is worth mentioning that in ancient Near Eastern records, the ages of ancient kings who ruled before the Flood are much more advanced than the ages recorded in the Bible. In those records, kings lived around thirty thousand years, and some even lived as long as 72,000 years. The difference between the Sumerian royal dynasties

and men live for centuries alongside giants.[6] The world has not yet been tamed into the familiar, natural, mostly realistic setting of the rest of the Bible.

This does not mean, of course, that the first chapters of Genesis are tantamount to the myths of the ancient world. In fact, a comparison with myths from other cultures reveals yawning disparities, not only in content but in moral and theological premise and atmosphere.[7] Yet, these first stories should be read as a unique biblical genre in themselves, as stories that predate and illuminate familiar history, its premises, and its purpose.

This paradigm has several implications. I especially wish to focus on the question of interpreting these stories as vehicles of symbolic meaning. This substantial question can be applied generally to the rest of the Bible as well: When should something be read as a symbol for a more abstract concept?

This question is exemplified in a fascinating midrashic debate about the Burning Bush, in the form of a dialogue between R. Yehoshua b. Karha and "a certain non-Jew":

> A certain non-Jew asked R. Yehoshua b. Karha, "Why did the Holy One, blessed be He, decide to speak to Moses from within a bush?"

---

and the biblical genealogies is that Genesis presents the names of people, not rulers, and Genesis' purpose is religious, not political, as claimed by Kenneth A. Mathews, *Genesis* (NAC: Nashville, 1996), vol. 1, 98.

6. While Nahum Sarna is correct that the description of the tributaries of the rivers flowing out of Eden – Euphrates and Tigris – give a realistic sense (Sarna, *Understanding Genesis* [The Heritage of Biblical Israel Series 1: New York, 1966], 25), there is much more actual real geographic information provided in the rest of the Bible, which highlights the meta-territorial, unrealistic nature of Eden even more (compare in Yairah Amit, "Biblical Utopianism: A Mapmaker's Guide to Eden," *USQR* 44 [1990]: 11–17). Moreover, the names and descriptions of the other two rivers lend a fairy-tale quality to the episode.

7. See a general survey of connections and disparities in Mathews, *Genesis*, vol. 1, 86–101. Yehezkel Kaufmann devoted impressive efforts to the essential differences between pagan myth and Genesis 1–11 (Kaufmann, *The Religion of Israel* [Jerusalem, 1953], vol. 1, 303–350), and see further below.

> He said to him, "Had it been from a carob or sycamore, you would have asked the same question. But as I cannot leave you without an answer, why from a bush? To teach you that there is nowhere without Divine Presence, even a bush."[8]

The fact that the Midrash places this question in the mouth of a non-Jew undermines its legitimacy. R. Yehoshua's initial response cautions against loading symbolic meanings onto narrative elements. Yet his next statement is somewhat confusing. Why does he feel compelled to further answer him if he believes that the bush does not necessarily have symbolic meaning in itself? Moreover, his answer is a typical midrashic didactic answer, one without any show of contempt for the questioner. And strangest of all, this midrash is part of a series of midrashim where various sages ask the very same question as that non-Jew and propose various answers, and the midrash itself goes on to list *eight* different explanations that charge the Burning Bush with symbolism. To cite just two of them:

- R. Yoḥanan: Just as the bush serves as a fence for a garden, Israel serves as a fence for the world.
- Another option: Just as a bush can flourish only with water, Israel can flourish only with the Torah, which is called water, as it says [regarding the word of God], "All who are thirsty, come to the water" (Is. 55:1).

The logical flow of this midrash, therefore, has a keen effect, where the initial impression is that this question lacks legitimacy, but is then swiftly echoed and thereby legitimized by Israel's own sages. While the question of when and whether narrative elements can be ascribed a symbolic meaning exceeds the scope of this discussion,[9] in the context of Genesis 1–11, this issue has special weight. I wish to recall Nahmanides' interpretation of the serpent in Eden in light of the polar debate between medieval commentators.

8. Exodus Rabba 2:5.
9. See further in Jonathan Grossman, *Text and Subtext: On Exploring Biblical Narrative Design* [Hebrew] (Tel Aviv, 2015), 15–33.

Rabbi Obadiah Sforno begins his commentary of the Eden narrative with a declaration that the serpent is merely a metaphor:

> The serpent is the devil, the evil inclination.... For some entities are described in ways that are similar to it, just like the king is called a "lion," as it says, "The lion has come up from its copse" (Jer. 4:7), and dangerous enemies are called "poisonous serpents," as it says, "I am about to unleash poisonous serpents against you" (Jer. 8:17). In the same way, the Omnipresent refers to the enticing Evil Inclination as a "serpent," because it is similar to the serpent, whose benefit is minimal and whose harm is great.[10]

Following the sages, Sforno identifies the serpent with the devil, with the evil inclination. Note, however, that he is not merely claiming that the evil inclination is *like* a serpent. Rather, he considers the serpent an actual metaphor, and its narrative a parable. Just as a king is referred to as a lion, or an enemy is likened to a snake, without any real lions or snakes involved, the evil inclination is referred to as a serpent in this narrative, without any actual serpents present in the scene. The advantage of this reading is that it easily justifies the serpent's human speech and intelligence, and the fact that it lures the woman to sin, since real serpents do not speak any human language, nor lure people to sin.

In contrast to Sforno, the Ibn Ezra writes:

> Some say that the woman understood the language of animals... while others said it is the devil. But then how can they explain the end of the scene? How will "the devil" crawl on his belly, and eat dust? And what is the point of the curse "He will strike your head"?... Rather, it seems to me that things are as they are, and the serpent originally walked upright, and He who made humans sentient beings also made it a sentient being. As the verse itself testifies, it was craftier than any other creature, just not as much as a human.[11]

10. Sforno on Gen. 3:1.
11. Ibn Ezra on Gen. 3:1.

Ibn Ezra is opposed to the idea that the serpent is an embodiment of the evil inclination, and he supports his position with the fact that the actual serpent – the familiar snake that crawls on its belly and bites people – is cursed at the end of the story. Why would such a curse be relevant if the serpent were merely a symbol of the evil inclination?

This dispute is a good example of the deliberation that accompanies the reading of the Eden narrative, and the first eleven chapters of Genesis in general. Do the regular rules of allegory apply, or does the unique mythical nature of these narratives invite a reading more heavily inclined towards symbolic understanding? Even those who believe that the historical narratives (beginning with Abraham) should be read as historical accounts with minimal symbolic weight must admit that the question is more complex when applied to Genesis 1–11.

I believe that a certain compromise can be reached between Ibn Ezra and Sforno. Sforno is correct that these narratives have substantial metaphorical weight; the creation account is not merely a historical event, but reflects a fundamental approach to reality. We will yet explore how the story of Eden takes place in every generation, within every individual. From this perspective, it is an archetypal narrative that certainly tends towards the allegorical. Yet these primeval stories are not merely theological allegory. If this were the case, its allegorical nature would presumably have been more obvious. And, with the exception of the Eden narrative, there are no scenes of a fantastical nature. These narratives function on the premise that they actually took place.

The solution lies in a simple semantic substitution with great implications: rather than the term "parable" or "allegory," the appropriate term to use is "symbol." Unlike a parable, which dissipates with interpretation, the literary symbol remains substantial, adding another layer of significance on top of the literal meaning of the text. To claim that the Burning Bush is a symbol does not negate its actual existence – its leaves and branches, its color and shape, its form. It only means that this bush, beyond its botanical existence, also represents certain abstract ideas. The same is true of the first eleven chapters of Genesis. To paraphrase the aforementioned words of Nahmanides, while these narratives take place on earth, they *also* have heavenly counterparts. Each historical event, and each element of these narratives, express certain abstract concepts as well.

One of the boldest philosophers in this context is Rabbi Abraham Isaac HaKohen Kook. Discussing the relationship between the biblical narratives and parallel stories from the ancient Near East, he writes that they should be considered symbolic ideas more than actual historical events. As he responds to Dr. Moshe Seidel, who often consulted with him about philosophical and ideological issues:

> In regard to this, I believe that anyone with proper sense should know that even if there is no truth whatsoever in [the new studies about the formation of the biblical text], there is no need to deny their actual questions, because it is not the Torah's purpose to relate simple facts and events that took place. The main part is its content, its inner reflection about its ideas, and this can be elevated yet further wherever there is an apparent contradiction we are encouraged to overcome. Most of these ideas have already been stated by the medieval commentaries, and above all in *Guide for the Perplexed*, and today we are prepared to develop these ideas further.
>
> It makes no difference whether there was an actual golden age when humankind exulted in all the physical and spiritual goodness, or whether reality began from the bottom, from the lowest level of being and continually rises. All we need to know is that there is the ultimate possibility that humanity, even if it reaches utter greatness, can lose everything if its ways are corrupt, and can bring evil upon itself and many generations that follow, and this is what we can learn from the reality of humankind in the Garden of Eden, its sin, and its expulsion.[12]

12. *Letters of Rabbi A. Y. Kook*, 163–164. Letter 91 is also written to Seidel about the relationship between the biblical creation account and modern scientific discoveries. See Rabbi Tamir Granot's analysis and explanation of this letter (Granot, "Torah and Science according to Rav Kook, Letter 91," *HaMeir LaAretz* 65 (2007): 403–435). See also Rabbi Kook's *LeNevukhei HaDor*, ch. 32, and many other excerpts in Dr. Yoshi Farjun, "Wisdom and Science Are Yours: A Collection of Annotated Sources," in *People of Faith and Biblical Criticism*, ed. Y. Brandes, T. Ganzel, and C. Deutsch (Jerusalem, 2015), 19–161.

The understanding that the genre of these stories is close to myth shapes our reading, and may also influence the interpretation of specific verses. An apt example is the definition of "day" in the creation narrative. John Day, a noted Bible scholar, challenges the claim that the creation narrative is merely symbolic:

> Moreover, the text clearly speaks of creation in seven, or rather six, days, and since each day has an evening and a morning it is hardly plausible that we should interpret the days as geological periods, as some apologists have sometimes supposed.[13]

However, while he is correct that the first narrative in the Torah is a description of actual events rather than a mere parable, his claim that each day represents a regular twenty-four-hour period is misguided.[14] If this narrative were part of the historical narrative of Genesis 12 and on, he would be correct. There is no justification for interpreting, "Be prepared for the third day, for on the third day the Lord will descend before all the eyes of the people upon Mount Sinai" (Ex. 19:11), as a symbol for three stages of preparation before the revelation at Sinai. Here, three days means three days. Even if these three days have further symbolic meaning,[15] their primary meaning is a simple chronological description. Given that the creation narrative is rooted in the symbolic sphere, however, each "day" may well be a stage in the process of the "six days of creation" leading up to the Sabbath, without necessarily entailing the actual passing of time. I concur with the reading that each "day" marks

13. John Day, *From Creation to Babel: Studies in Genesis 1–11* (LHB/OTS 592; London: Bloomsbury, 2013), 3. See also Terence Fretheim, "Were the Days of Creation Twenty-Four Hours? Yes," in *The Genesis Debate: Persistent Questions about Creation and the Flood*, ed. R. Youngblood (Nashville, 1986), 12–35.
14. R. C. McClone, *The Genesis Debate: Persistent Questions about Creation and the Flood*, ed. R. Youngblood (Nashville, 1986), 12–35; Bruce K. Waltke, "The Literary Genre of Genesis, Chapter One," *Crux* 27 (1991): 2–10.
15. Such as the following interpretation: "As the Creator warned them before drawing near to Mount Sinai – 'Be prepared for the third day,' that is, that they should prepare themselves through their deeds, to break and subdue the Evil Inclination ... so that they will then be ready to receive the Torah" (Rabbi Abraham Dov of Ovruch, *Bat Ayin on the Torah*, on *Parashat Mishpatim*).

a certain "period."[16] This is certainly supported by the fact that three "days" pass before the creation of the celestial bodies that dictate Earth's diurnal course. While day and night are defined on the first day, with the creation of light, the passing of each day is described with the phrase "And there was evening (*erev*) and there was morning (*boker*)," words that denote the movement of the setting sun (*maariva*) marking the onset of night, and the rising sun lighting up the dawn.[17] How can these phrases have literal meaning before the creation of the sun and moon?

We will yet discuss the significance of a week of days leading up to the Sabbath. The week necessarily consists of days, but this does not of necessity mean that the sky was created in twenty-four hours, on the second day of creation. What is important is to distinguish between various stages of creation and to define them as "days" that comprise a "week," as a chronological paradigm to perpetually recall how the world came into being.

This example, of course, is but a window into the vast sea of deliberations that accompany these chapters. On one hand, the Tree of Life certainly functions as a symbol, but on the other hand, the shame of nakedness is real, as are the clothes that cover it up. Our task is to navigate these stories by walking the fine line between symbol and reality, which is to appreciate the symbolic interpretation as a convenient, sometimes obvious solution, while recognizing the historic reality that the narrative seeks to illuminate. The boundary between symbol and reality is diaphanous, and we will flit back and forth as we attempt to explain reality and, at the same time, give it meaning.

---

16. Unlike Fretheim, "Days of Creation." He also discusses the approach that the days are symbolic. See especially the articles edited by David Hagopian, *The Genesis Debate: Three Views on the Days of Creation* (Mission Viejo, CA, 2001); Walter M. Booth, "Days of Genesis 1: Literal or Nonliteral?" *JATS* 14 (2003): 101–120; James Edward Smith, *In the Beginning: Commentary on Genesis 1–3* (Morrisville, NC, 2016), 89–90.
17. On the connection of the word "*boker*," "morning," with sunlight, see August H. Konkel, "*Boker*," *NIDOTTE* 1: 711. He proves this from several texts, such as, "Early in the morning (*baboker*), as the sun begins to shine (*kezaraḥ hashemesh*), raid the city" (Judges 9:33); "They abused her all night long, until *morning*, and sent her off at daybreak. The woman came back towards *morning* and collapsed at the entrance of the man's house where her master was, until first light" (Judges 19:20–21). About "*erev*," evening, see Konkel, ibid., 715–717.

IS GENESIS 1–11 AN INDEPENDENT UNIT?

In order to focus on these chapters, we must first assume that they form a distinct, cohesive section. Unlike the Abraham cycle or the Jacob cycle, which each revolve around a single protagonist and are thus easily defined, Genesis 1–11 rushes through the first two millennia of world history, with no single central character or narrative, yet everyone who divides up the book of Genesis defines the first eleven chapters as a separate section. This is undoubtedly related to their unique character, the prehistorical atmosphere that ends with the birth of Abraham. This section, therefore, can be seen as an introduction to Abraham, or as an introduction to national history.

The definition of this section as an independent unit does not negate profound connections between this unit and the rest of Genesis. On the contrary, it leads up to the Abraham cycle and the ancestral cycles that follow with perfect continuity. This is generated, first and foremost, through chronological synthesis, with chapter 11 ending with the birth of Abraham. Other factors also contribute to this unit's cohesion within the rest of Genesis, despite its distinct character. I wish to point out several components that will inform our discussion throughout the rest of this book.

1. **Theological development:** I will propose that a process connected to character development and divine providence unfolds throughout Genesis.[18] From this perspective, the first eleven chapters of the book are an integral part of this process. In these first narratives, we see humanity gradually achieving independence, something that continues to be developed throughout Genesis.[19] This idea also has implications for the inner process of chapters 1–11 and its literary structure.

---

18. See especially in Robert L. Cohn, "Narrative Structure and Canonical Perspective in Genesis," *JSOT* 25 (1983): 3–16. In this context, he divides the book of Genesis into five distinct stages: The World of Eden/Noah and the Flood/The Abraham Cycle/The Jacob Cycle/The Joseph Narrative.
19. This is especially salient in the Joseph cycle, where human responsibility is given much room. There, it is within human power to interpret dreams (see Jonathan Grossman, "Different Dreams: Two Models of Interpretation for Three Pairs of Dreams

2. **Unifying themes:** The most salient structural marker of Genesis is its division according to "*toledot*."[20] This introduction ("these are the *toledot*") arranges the book into subsections according to the work's central characters. There are five such introductions in the first eleven chapters of the book (from the *toledot* of heaven and earth to the *toledot* of Shem) and another five in the rest of Genesis (from the *toledot* of Terah to the *toledot* of Jacob).[21] According to this formula, the book of Genesis is arranged in one cohesive sequence of *toledot* subsections.[22]
3. **Ancestral cycles responding to chapters 1–11:** Some claim that the blessings Abraham receives present a solution to the failures and curses described in chapters 1–11.[23] If this claim is too extreme,

---

[Genesis 37–50]," *JBL* 135 [2016]: 717–732.). Compare to the words of Cohn: "The rebellious abuse of freedom in Eden gives way to the faith of Abraham, the boldness of Jacob, and the wisdom of Joseph. In [each] scene, the divine director retreats from the stage permitting his actors to shape their own world" (Cohn, "Narrative Structure," 15).

20. Translator's note: Translating the word "*toledot*" is problematic in itself as it seems to mean both "descendants" and "history" in different contexts. As an extensive discussion of its function throughout Genesis exceeds the scope of this book, I will often use the Hebrew word (in transliteration), "*toledot*," rather than presenting a literal translation.
21. The formula, "these are the *toledot*" is mentioned twice in Esau's list (36:1, 9), so the question is whether the correct number is five or six. On this division, its characteristics, and the readings it encourages, see Victor P. Hamilton, *The Book of Genesis, Chapters 1–17* (NICOT: Grand Rapids, 1990), 2–11 (and the references there to further studies).
22. See also Thomas Desmond Alexander, "Genealogies, Seed, and the Compositional Unity of Genesis," *Tyndale Bulletin* 44 (1993): 255–270. He adds that the description of lineage and the recurring motif of descendants is woven throughout the book, unifying it. Ian Hart proposes reading the first creation narrative (ch. 1) as a prologue to Genesis which is based on three main principles: creation in six days, humankind created in the image of God, and Sabbath. He holds that these three motifs are developed throughout Genesis (Hart, "Genesis 1:1–2:3 as Prologue to the Book of Genesis," *Tyndale Bulletin* 46 [1995]: 315–336).
23. Thomas W. Mann, "All the Families of the Earth: The Theological Unity of Genesis," *Interpretation* 45 (1991): 341–353. For blessing and curse as a wider theme in Genesis 1–11, see Karolien Vermeulen, "The Art of Blessing and Cursing in Genesis 1–11: Stylistic Patterns and Their Ideological Motivation," in *Doubling and Duplicating in the Book of Genesis: Literary and Stylistic Approaches to the Text*, ed. E. R. Hayes and K. Vermeulen (Winona Lake, 2016), 113–128.

a subtler formulation may be more convincing: Abraham's election is presented as a reaction to the world before the Flood, an attempt to create a different kind of humanity. This is especially salient in regard to the contrast between Abraham and the Tower of Babel narrative. Some even claim that the narratives in 1–11 are reflected later in Genesis (not only as thematic developments, but as actual analogies).[24] I find this less convincing, but if we combine this claim with the idea of theological development throughout the book, then it is clear how the first section of Genesis anticipates, and is the nucleus of, the entire work.

THE STRUCTURE OF GENESIS 1–11

While there is clear dialogue between Genesis 1–11 and the rest of the book, the first section still stands as an independent unit with its own literary structure. Some have proposed that these chapters are arranged in an interwoven structure of narrative sections interspersed with genealogical sections (or, at least, the mention of birth):[25]

- Creation: 1:1–2:3
    - Genealogy (the *toledot* of heaven and earth): 2:4
- Adam and Eve: 2:5–3:24
    - Genealogy (Eve's sons): 4:1–2
- Cain and Abel: 4:3–15
    - Genealogy (Cain's line): 4:17–22
- The Song of Lamech: 4:23–24
    - Genealogy (Seth's line): Ch. 5
- The Flood: 6:1–Ch. 9
    - Genealogy (The Dispersion of the Nations): Ch. 10
- The Tower of Babel: 11:1–9
    - Genealogy (Shem's line): 11:10–26.

This structure, of course, sees genealogy as a key component in this section. Narrative fills in the spaces between births and genealogical lists, explaining

24. Isaac M. Kikawada and Arthur Quinn, *Before Abraham Was: The Unity of Genesis 1–11* (Nashville, 1985).

25. Ibid., 60.

who these characters are and what they do, but the main objective of this section is a book of *toledot* that explains how the world's population evolved until the birth of Abraham. I find this structure unconvincing (the Song of Lamech, for example, can hardly be extricated from Cain's genealogy) and unlikely to have been intentional, but this analysis does reveal a central theme of this section, which is the intensive focus on birth and genealogy.

I believe that the most convincing literary structure is proposed by Gary Rendsburg and Jerome Walsh,[26] albeit with minor changes of my own. They propose that these chapters are arranged in two parallel halves:

a. The creation of the world, the creation of humanity (chs. 1–3)
b. The sons of Adam and Eve and Cain's curse: "Cursed are you" (4:1–16)
c. The technological development of humanity (Cain's line – 4:17–26)
d. Seth's line: ten generations from Adam to Noah (ch. 5)
e. The fall – the sons of God. Walsh refers to this as "blurring the boundaries between heaven and earth" (6:1–8; and we can also add: "people of the name").

a1. The destruction of the world, and its re-creation (6:9–9:17)
b1. The sons of Noah and Canaan's curse: "Cursed is Canaan" (9:18–29)
c1. The ethnic development of humanity (ch. 10)
e1. The fall – the Tower of Babel. Walsh refers to this as "blurring the boundaries between the divine and the human" (11:1–9; and we can also add: "Let us make a name for ourselves").
d1. Shem's line: ten generations from Noah to Abraham (11:10–26)

The basis of this two-part division is, of course, connected to the "plot," namely, the Flood that destroys the world recalibrates reality, wiping out creation from the face of the earth, and all begins anew. Thus, it follows to

26. Gary A. Rendsburg, *The Redaction of Genesis* (Winona Lake, 1986), 7–26; Jerome T. Walsh, *Style and Structure in Biblical Hebrew Narrative* (Collegeville, 2001), 112.

compare the two halves of the section. Indeed, as this structure reveals, there are many parallels between these halves, which even correspond in a fixed sequence, albeit with an inversion between the final two components (d–e/e1–d1). Walsh proposes that this inversion is related to how both halves end. In the first half, there is a blurring of boundaries between heaven and earth preceding the utter destruction of the Flood, while in the second half there is continuity despite the blurring of boundaries, representing continuity and hope for the future. This is expressed through the ten generations that conclude this section and lead directly to the next *toledot*, of Abraham's birth and God's revelation to him.[27] As we will yet discuss in the analysis of Shem's list and its comparison with Seth's line, the text indeed colors the final genealogical list in this section in shades of hope and optimism.

Stable and convincing, this basic structure stands, even if there is room to debate the particular delineation of units and their specific titles.[28] The titles given to these units can shape the apparent strength of these parallels, and they certainly reflect what the interpreter in question perceives as the narrative's central objective.

Rendsburg and Walsh present the section's structure as proof that the diachronic divisions drawn up by modern scholars are irrelevant, given that the entire section follows a cohesive, convincing narrative structure. These claims have not gone unanswered, and based on the following two challenges posed by diachronic scholars[29] I wish to suggest a few slight improvements to this structure.

1. If the two halves are compared, there is not perfect symmetry between them, given that the final two components are inverted. To those who reject this structure because of this imbalance, Rendsburg's claim that there is no choice but to incorporate Shem's line at the end of the unit in order to reach Abraham is

27. Walsh, *Style and Structure*, 113.

28. This challenge must be addressed by anyone who argues for an artistic structure. See Nathan Klaus, *Pivot Patterns in the Former Prophets* (Jerusalem, 1984), 6; David A. Dorsey, *The Literary Structure of the Old Testament: A Commentary on Genesis-Malachi* (Grand Rapids, 1999), 33–34; Grossman, *Text and Subtext*, 236–41.

29. Zipora Talshir, "The Unity of Structure in Genesis I–XI – Research on the Verge of Midrash," *Shnaton* 11 (1987): 131–138.

unconvincing.[30] This claim, however, can be challenged. The striking asymmetry may play an important role in the overall narrative objective (see Walsh's claim above).[31] Moreover, as I will propose shortly, this structure can be emended slightly to create perfect symmetry between the two halves.

2. A further claim against this structure is that some of the unit's titles are imprecise. Referring to both the act of the sons of God and the Tower of Babel as "the fall" is not convincing. There is no human agency in the incident with the sons of God, so it can hardly be considered a human "fall." If we look for a story of human failing, then the sin of Eden certainly falls under this category, yet in the proposed structure, the Eden narrative is included within "the creation of humanity" and does not even receive its own title and definition. A similar claim can be made about referring to Cain's line and the dispersion of the nations as "technological development" and "ethnic development," respectively. These titles are not strictly accurate descriptions of these sections, and are obviously used in order to generate similarity between them.

In order to address these objections, I will adopt the basic division proposed by Rendsburg and Walsh, but with certain changes to the exact delineation and definitions of three of the smaller units. Even if these differences seem negligible, they will have dramatic significance for the analysis and understanding of the narratives.

The above structure places the "technological development" of Lamech's three sons (ch. 4) parallel to the "ethnic development" of Noah's three sons (ch. 10). While we will see that there are certainly justified parallels between the two sets of three sons, following chapter 10 there is even more explicit technological development: the Tower of Babel. In fact, the text even emphasizes humanity's new technological capacity: "'Come, let us make bricks and burn them thoroughly.' And they had brick for stone and bitumen for mortar" (11:3), before the actual

30. Rendsburg, *Redaction*, 8, 19.

31. See also David W. Cotter, *Genesis* (Collegeville, MN, 2003).

focus on the construction of the city and its tower. Moreover, as I will discuss, despite the popular reference to these verses as the "Tower of Babel" narrative, there is actually less emphasis on the tower itself. As such, it is not strictly accurate to define this narrative as "the blurring of boundaries between heaven and earth." For this reason, I perceive the story of the city builders in chapter 11, rather than chapter 10, as a more suitable parallel for the description of the sons of Lamech.

A second problematic issue is the inclusion of the Eden narrative (chs. 2–3) as part of the "creation of the world." While both narratives describe the birth of the world and humanity, these accounts are completely different in nature, and markedly separated within the text itself. I therefore find it more convincing to consider the Eden narrative an independent sub-unit, and its content of sin and curse easily marks it as a component parallel to the story of Noah's drunkenness.

The third change I wish to make is to their definition of the incident of the sons of God. Rendsburg and Walsh consider it an independent unit, defined as an episode of "the blurring of boundaries between heaven and earth," in parallel to the Tower of Babel narrative.[32] There is certainly room to compare these episodes, as we will discuss in context, but more importantly, this brief, obscure incident does not stand as an independent unit, and it is more logical to read it as an integral introduction to the Flood narrative.[33]

My final premise is that the story of Noah's drunkenness functions as a dual narrative, encompassing both the story of Noah, and the story of his sons. In this way, it is in dialogue with two consecutive narratives

---

32. Dorsey also placed the two narratives in parallel but focused on a different parallel element, the divine intervention that prevents incompatible connections – between heaven and earth (in the story of the sons of God), and between humanity as a whole, which is not spreading out over the world as it should (Tower of Babel). See Dorsey, *Literary Structure*, 55.

33. For various reasons, Emil Kraeling and Guy Darshan reached a similar conclusion (Kraeling, "The Significance and Origin of Gen. 6.1–4," *JNES* 6 [1947]: 193–208; Darshan, "The Story of the Sons of God and the Daughters of Man [Gen. 6:1–4] in Light of the Hesiodic *Catalogue of Women*," *Shnaton* 23 [2014]: 155–178), and presumably this view was shared by the hand that divided the Pentateuch into chapters, who opened the Flood narrative with this incident (ch. 6).

in the first half of the section, as I will discuss at length in context, with both the Eden narrative, and the story of Cain and Abel:[34]

Act One	**Act Two**
a. (ch. 1): The world's creation	a. (6:1–8): Introduction to the world's destruction (7–9:17): The world's destruction and re-creation
b. (chs. 2–3): The Garden of Eden: eating from the Tree of Knowledge, nakedness and covering	b. (9:18–29): Noah's drunkenness: drinking wine, loss of knowledge, nakedness and covering
c. (4:1–16): Cain and Abel, and Cain's curse	c. (9:18–29): Shem, Ham, and Japheth, and Ham's-Canaan's curse
d. (4:17–26): The sons of Adam and Eve (Cain's line and Seth)	d. (ch. 10): The sons of Noah (the lines of Shem, Ham, and Japheth)
e. (4:17–24): Cain and Lamech: technological development, the building of the city of Enoch	e. (11:1–9): The Tower of Babel: technological development, the building of the city of Babel
f. (ch. 5): The line of Seth: from Adam to Noah	f. (11:10–26): The line of Shem: from Noah to Abram

This structure also sees the Flood as the cutoff line between the two halves of Genesis 1–11, between the old world and the new. As we will see in our

34. A similar structure is proposed by Matthieu Richelle in "La structure littéraire de l'Histoire Primitive (Genèse 1,1–11,26) en son état final," *Biblische Notizen* 151 (2011): 3–22. He bases his structure on the *toledot* formula and places the story of the sons of God as the end of the first section, unparalleled in the second. He perceives this episode as "Crise paroxystique" (ibid., 17).

analysis of the Flood narrative, the destruction and re-creation of the world shares close linguistic and thematic connections with the world's creation in chapter 1: "The parallel structures thus underscore the roles of Adam and Noah as uniquely first men commanded to 'be fruitful and multiply, and fill the earth' (1:28; 9:1)."[35]

The similarities between the two "creations" of the world obviously also highlight the disparities between them, as I will discuss in context. According to this structure, the second "act" opens with the sons of God (which serves as an introduction to the Flood narrative): "And it was when humans (*ha'adam*) began to increase in number over the earth and daughters were born to them" (6:1). This verse transports the reader from the perspective that all people are descended from a single family, which accompanies the reader throughout the first half, to the concept of "humanity." The "*adam*" mentioned in this verse is not a reference to Adam himself, but to humankind. As the human population grows, things begin to spin out of control. The Flood washes this chaos away, and the world begins anew.

The opening of this second act is essentially a fulfillment of God's blessing to humanity at creation: "Be fruitful and multiply, and fill the earth and subdue it" (1:28), and now, "humans began to increase in number over the earth."[36] But this fulfillment leads to grave disappointment, a world of disorder and evil.

Noah's drunkenness and the Eden narrative (components b) are the first two accounts of humanity's actions following the world's creation/re-creation.[37] In both episodes, we will see, the protagonist eats or drinks from a fruit tree, leading to the acquisition, or loss, of knowledge. The motif of nakedness and covering is salient, and significant, in both narratives, and in my analysis of the story of Noah's vineyard I will

35. Cohn, "Narrative Structure," 5.

36. See more about this reading direction in Laurence A. Turner, *Announcements of Plot in Genesis* (JSOTSup 96: Sheffield, 1990), 28. After the Flood, God will repeat His blessing of "Be fruitful and multiply" to Noah, but, as we will see, this blessing will have several important differences.

37. As proposed by Dorsey. He refers to the Eden narrative as "Adam's sin" and the story of Noah's drunkenness as "Ham's sin" (Dorsey, *Literary Structure*, 55). In this way, he conveys that the sinner Ham should be paralleled to the sinner Adam.

discuss the precise parallel between the narratives, the disparities between them, and how this comparison illuminates both episodes.

As mentioned, the story of Noah's vineyard also focuses on Noah's sons, sibling rivalry, and dominion and slavery ("Cursed be Canaan, a servant of servants shall he be to his brothers" [9:25]).[38] These themes place this scene in parallel to the story of Cain and Abel (component c), especially based on my analysis of God's words to Cain (4:6–7). The story of Noah's drunkenness is therefore parallel to both the Eden narrative and the struggle between Cain and Abel, the world's first father and his sons and the new world's first father and his sons.[39]

As I alluded to above, components d–e are not entirely distinct. The description of Lamech's sons and their revolutionary professions can certainly be read as one unit, and in parallel, the dispersion of the nations in chapter 10 and the etiological description of how it began in chapter 11 can also be read in sequence. Nonetheless, it is also justifiable to read them as distinct units, and in this way, the second half of Genesis 4, which describes the two different branches that stemmed from Adam (Cain and Seth), is parallel to the description of the three different branches that emanated from Noah in chapter 10 (Japheth, Ham, and Shem – component d). These are both descriptions of family growth without focus on the chosen line (in contrast to chapters 5 and 11, Seth's line and Shem's line). Note that the description of Seth's son that concludes chapter 4, "And Seth too had a son, and he named him Enosh" (4:26), is repeated in the next

38. In chapter 4, Cain is described as a "worker of the ground" (4:2), similarly to Noah, who is referred to as "a man of the ground" (9:20) after the Flood. See Rendsburg, *Redaction*, 14.

39. As stated, according to Rendsburg – who bases his structure on that proposed by Jack Sasson – the curse of Canaan is parallel to the story of Cain and his curse (Sasson, "The 'Tower of Babel' as a clue to the Redactional Structuring of the Primeval History [Gen 1–11:9]," in *The Bible World: Essays in Honor of Cyrus H. Gordon*, ed. G. Rendsburg [New York, 1980], 211–219). Rendsburg makes the interesting observation that referring to Cain's and Abel's offerings as a *minḥa* creates a dialogue with the name *Noaḥ* (Rendsburg, *Redaction*, 14), just like Cain's unquoted statement to Abel in this story (4:8), which is parallel to Ham's words to his brothers, which are not actually mentioned to the reader.

chapter: "Seth lived 105 years and begat Enosh" (5:6). This reinforces the premise that Enosh's birth at the end of chapter 4 is part of the story of "the family of Adam," while chapter 5 focuses on the chosen line that will produce Noah.

In both halves of Genesis 1–11, the descriptions of the chosen line are preceded by stories of human technology (component e). In Act One, Cain's family fulfills this role. Cain himself builds the first city (4:17), and the sons of Lamech display extraordinary innovation and creativity: "And Adah gave birth to Jabal; he was the father of those who live in tents and raise livestock. His brother's name was Jubal; he was the father of all who play the lyre and pipes. As for Zillah, she too had a son, Tubal-cain, who forged all kinds of tools of copper and iron" (4:20–22). Despite their astounding creativity, this family line is the subject of harsh criticism, and history marches on with a different branch, the line of Seth. Similarly, the record of Shem's line is preceded by the Tower of Babel narrative, the story of human technology and the grand plans for a mighty city. Like Cain's line, its builders are nonetheless doomed to failure. Soon, God will abandon Mesopotamia and choose the land of Canaan.

Both sections end with a list of ten generations that lead to the next biblical frontier (component f). At the end of the first act, Noah, the first star of the second act, is born; and at the end of the second act, Terah and his three sons step on to the stage, the harbingers of a new biblical era.

What can we learn from this narrative design? How does this structure contribute to the meta-objective of the first unit of the Bible? We will focus on individual narrative objectives as we analyze each component, but for now, I wish to focus on the fundamental principle that this structure illuminates.

The basic division of Genesis 1–11 into two halves invites comparison of the prediluvian and postdiluvian worlds. The first world did not endure, and the world's creation had to be reenacted differently. Indeed, the second half echoes the elements of the first half, giving a strong impression of a second attempt. The ideal world of the first creation did not turn out as planned, and the Creator had to make do with a contingency plan. While not strictly ideal, this new plan was more successful given the circumstances.[40]

Although simple, this idea is also unspeakably audacious, with two extreme theological implications for the biblical approach towards God's relationship with the world. The first touches upon the issue of free choice as a meta-principle in biblical thought. The second asks: why is the world so far from ideal?

Above all, the basic idea of a failed first creation that requires the Creator to renew the world differently teaches about the biblical emphasis on free choice. Time and again, the premise of these narratives will be that it is up to humans to determine the course of the future. This is salient through the contrast between chapter 1 and chapter 2. In chapter 1, God speaks and the world becomes; "Let there be light" instantly produces light. The success of creation is constantly reiterated in the refrain, "And God saw that it was good." What a painful disparity there is between this divine refrain and the second creation and its aftermath, when divine command cannot determine the course of human action.[41] Human beings have free will, and they do not always act in accordance with divine will. Adam and Eve eat from the forbidden fruit. God's words to Cain do not prevent Abel's subsequent murder. These decisions will affect the course of history. The genesis of the world unfolds through the tension between divine will and human will, to the extent that God regrets the course set by humanity and wipes out the world to begin anew.[42]

The second principle that arises from the understanding that the world is not ideal is that history reflects a process, that history is not just

40. The sages already hint to a similar reading in the famous midrash that the world could not meet the high standards of creation, as Rashi (on Gen. 1:1) mentions in the beginning of his commentary on the Torah: "God created – it does not say 'The Lord created,' as at first it occurred to Him to create the world with the attribute of Judgment. He saw that the world could not exist, so the attribute of Mercy joined with the attribute of Judgment, as it says, 'On the day that the Lord God made the earth and the heavens.'"

41. Beverly J. Stratton, *Out of Eden: Reading, Rhetoric, and Ideology in Genesis 2–3* (JSOTSup 208: Sheffield, 1995), 134.

42. On the biblical revolution of human free will, see Joshua Berman, *Created Equal: How the Bible Broke with Ancient Political Thought* (New York/Oxford, 2008).

a series of sporadic, coincidental, unconnected events. Rather, there is an ultimate purpose to the course of history, that gradually, painstakingly, reality will reach an ideal state, and that once-lost paradise will be regained. There is still a promise of utopia, of a divine garden where animals do not kill each other, where man and woman live in harmony. The parallel structure of Genesis 1–11 is not a chiastic structure that reflects tragic, irreparable reversal, but a classic structure that often conveys a two-step process.[43] The ideal state of the beginning of the first half is not negated; it is simply not yet fulfilled. In this way, Genesis 1–11 serves as an introduction to the entire Bible, as a blueprint for the course of history.

Repentance Preceded the World's Creation

In other words, reality is moving and evolving towards its point of origin. The world was created with Adam and Eve living in the Garden of Eden, without death, without suffering, with complete harmony between them and their surroundings. After their expulsion from the garden, and moreover, after the Flood, the human's relationship with the world changes. We will explore this change in human status at length, but for now, I will point out the most drastic change. After the Flood, Abraham is elected to lead the world back to its ideal state through God's name. This is not merely the election of a leader; this is a profound change in human order. After the Flood, nations are born, and the world evolves and develops through these nations.

This pattern of failure and a new path to *tikkun* is woven throughout Genesis 1–11. The Eden narrative revolves around this theme, where man and woman fail to meet Eden's standards and they must leave the garden, but the conclusion of the narrative hints that with the establishment of the Tabernacle and the cherubim, man will once again walk alongside God. The Tower of Babel narrative assumes that linguistic diversity is the result of divine intervention, and a return to one universal language is also anticipated in messianic prophecies: "For then I will change the speech of the peoples to a pure speech, that all of them may call on the name of the Lord and serve Him with one accord" (Zeph. 3:9). After the Flood, the once-vegetarian world was divided into

43. See Grossman, *Text and Subtext*, 256–263.

predators and prey, but there are messianic visions of a return to a world where animals are no longer eaten (see especially Is. 65:25). As we will see, the general sense that accompanies Abraham's election is despair of the old world and hope that change and rectification will transpire through Abraham and his covenant with God, that through Abraham, "all the families of the earth will be blessed" (12:3).

In light of this pattern, it emerges that the world is heading not to an unknown destiny, but back to its beginning. The optimistic vision of the future guides the world throughout history back towards its familiar primal origin.[44] Similar to Plato's theory of forms, the shadow of Eden is imprinted upon the universal subconscious. The fact that the distant future is embedded within the distant past renders it possible, within reach. This is no wild apocalyptic vision without any relation to reality. On the contrary, redemption is rooted deep within the nucleus of reality. Similar to Franz Rosenzweig's idea that creation anticipates revelation and redemption, Genesis 1–11 contains the fruits of the ancient past that, in turn, bear the seeds of the imminent future.

GENESIS AND THE ANCIENT NEAR EAST

Given that Genesis 1–11 describes the beginning of creation and the birth of humanity, its horizon transcends nationality. While the course of history depicted in the Bible gradually narrows its focus to the line of Abraham, its first chapters are universal stories, and there is therefore room for comparison between biblical etiology and parallel stories from the ancient Near East that depict the creation of the world and humanity.

Over half a century ago, one scholar coined the scholarly obsession of comparing biblical narratives to other narrative traditions as "parallelomania,"[45] and some noted that this "mania" was especially

44. Joseph Dan perceives the world's purpose in its very beginning: "From the moment the first verse in Genesis was stated, the foundations for apocalypse were laid.... If there is a beginning, there is also an end" (Dan, *Apocalypse Then and Now* [Tel Aviv, 2000], 19). I concur that there is free will from the beginning of the world which already anticipates its purpose. However, the unit's structure shows that this is not merely an assumption derived from the world's creation, but from the development of the plot itself.

45. Samuel Sandmel, "Parallelomania," *JBL* 81 (1962): 1–13.

rampant in regard to Genesis 1–11.[46] The perpetual scholarly search for comparisons between Genesis 1–11 and other Mesopotamian creation myths is often exaggerated. It is actually difficult to find legitimate parallels between the biblical creation account and the Babylonian creation epic *Enuma Elish* or other Babylonian myths. While the Egyptian creation myth is more closely related,[47] the disparities remain significant, and only specific parallels can be justified. While other Mesopotamian myths share certain elements that are found in the Eden narrative (especially the Babylonian myth of Adapa, who refuses the food of immortality), such as the creation of humans from clay, these are specific motifs rather than grounds for comprehensive comparison. Such parallels with the story of Cain and Abel are very weak, and even though the Tower of Babel narrative has many Mesopotamian characteristics, there are no parallel plots to be found in Babylonian literature, only certain shared motifs.[48]

The only biblical narrative with substantial Mesopotamian counterparts is the Flood narrative. The main elements of the plot can also be found in the story of *Atrahasis*, the Akkadian flood myth, and the story Utnapishtim tells Gilgamesh in the *Epic of Gilgamesh*.[49] The scholarly consensus is that these flood myths spread from ancient Babylon towards the west during the Amarna period in the fourteenth century BCE.[50] It thus makes sense that the Israelites were familiar with these myths before they heard the biblical account, and it thus makes sense to focus on the differences between these myths and the biblical version, and whether it contains any polemic subversion. Even given this fascinating premise, many have rightly commented that there are still

46. Mathews, *Genesis*, vol. 1, 86.

47. Moshe Weinfeld, "God the Creator in Genesis 1 and in the Prophecy of Second Isaiah," *Tarbiz* 37 (1968): 105–132.

48. On the connections that exist between the Tower of Babel narrative and the ancient Near East, see below in my analysis of the episode.

49. On the Flood narrative as documented by Brusus (a Babylonian priest from the third century BCE) and its parallels to the biblical Flood, see Day, *From Creation to Babel*, 99–102.

50. Wilfred G. Lambert, "A New Look at the Babylonian Background of Genesis," *JTS* 16 (1965): 299–300.

substantial disparities between the biblical Flood narrative and other flood myths, both theologically and on the level of plot. The same holds true of the vast range of motifs and themes common to biblical narratives and other ancient traditions.[51]

Again, with the exception of the Flood narrative, it is difficult to find ancient material that can substantially be compared to Genesis 1–11, and the most precise formulation of the connection between biblical narratives and other narratives from the ancient Near East may be that some central themes of Genesis 1–11 can also be found in other ancient myths of the beginning of the world and humanity. The premises of these stories, such as the assumption that the world was actually created, are common to many cultures, but these are alternate descriptions rather than works that sustain textual comparison. It is thus no wonder that some saw these parallels as evidence of a "common universal memory": "The proposal, however, is not of a common text or an original story or a cultural continuum, but rather a common universal memory."[52]

Rav Kook wrote of these common motifs:

> When the idea of prophecy is understood in its proper depth, we will also understand its relationship to science and knowledge… and thus we will find that many concepts in the Torah, both in the laws and the narratives, are certainly present in the works of the great leaders of the ancient nations.[53]

Even if this is not a strictly literary parallel, and even if one text is not in intentional dialogue with another, the common motifs encourage exploration of their function in the biblical narrative based on their function in other ancient texts. In this way, we can point out how the biblical perspective differs from other prevalent perspectives in the ancient world. While I will discuss specific motifs in context, for now I wish to point

51. See, for example, throughout Simon B. Parker, *The Pre-Biblical Narrative Tradition: Essays on the Ugaritic Poems Keret and Aqhat* (SBL 24: Atlanta, 1989).
52. Mathews, *Genesis*, vol. 1, 87.
53. Rav Kook, *LeNevukhei HaDor*, ch. 32, 167–169. See similar chapters of Rav Kook in Farjun, *A Collection of Sources.*

out the fundamental disparity between the premises of these ancient myths and those of Genesis 1–11. Many have pointed out that the idea of monotheism is the main biblical revolution, and the introduction of monotheism is certainly one of the salient themes throughout the Bible. Even if this principle is not central in the patriarchal cycles,[54] it is certainly a major idea championed throughout the rest of the Bible.[55]

However, even more then monotheism, a completely new concept of divinity is presented in the biblical text. To quote Yehezkel Kaufmann's response to Preuss' claim that the Witoto tribe's belief in their god Naimuena is another example of early monotheism:

> Naimuena is nothing but a pagan god in all respects. This god is the head of a pantheon, a god who was born ... this god dies and goes down to the underworld, and from there he sends forth water to fertilize the earth. He is associated with fertility. He makes the forest sprout up from his own saliva, and the trees and plants from his own urine.[56]

This comment is crucial to the understanding of the biblical revolution. The essential difference between biblical divinity and pagan divinity is not a factor of how many gods rule in the world – one or many – but of an entirely different paradigm of the concept of divinity. In the Persian religion of Zoroastrianism, for example, it is believed that there are only two forces at play (Ahura Mazda and Angra Mainyu in the case

54. As fiercely claimed, for example, by Menachem Haran, *Ages and Institutions in the Bible* (Tel Aviv, 1973), 5–6.

55. Even pointing out local historical attempts to establish monotheistic beliefs does not negate the revolutionary nature of the biblical innovation in this context. The most famous attempt of the latter is that of the German Egyptologist Jan Assmann, who proposed that the Egyptian king Akhenaten was the harbinger of monotheism, as Akhenaten declared not only that the god Aten was the "supreme god," but that he was the only god (Jan Assmann, *Moses the Egyptian: The Memory of Egypt in Western Monotheism* [Cambridge, 1997]; this idea was famously developed by Sigmund Freud). However, given that thousands of pagan images besides those of Aten were discovered in his city, it is now assumed that the king declared Aten as the head of the pantheon but did not negate the pantheon itself.

56. Kaufmann, *The Religion of Israel*, vol. 1, 322–323.

of Zoroastrianism), but these two forces can also be considered as part of the general "pagan concept." According to Zoroastrianism, Ahura Mazda, while not actually created, is not fully omnipotent. That is, the existence of these gods are subject to external conditions, and they themselves form an essential part of life and the world.[57] In contrast, the biblical God's unique nature is His essential being. He is extrinsic to the world and its rules.

The ancient world perceived their gods as part of reality, and this is evident in their creation myths. This is especially salient in Babylonian creation myths, where the heavens and earth are formed from the corpse of the defeated goddess Tiamat, and humankind is formed from the blood of Kingu, Tiamat's son, whose arteries are slashed to obtain his blood. In this sense, the gods were an almost physical presence in human life, and they are characterized as such. They quarrel and fight, they require sustenance, and they give birth. Similarly, the Babylonians believed that humans could turn into gods or demigods, that a state of divinity was achievable by man. This motif is a fundamental component of many ancient Mesopotamian myths, such as the myths of Tammuz, Lugalbanda, and Gilgamesh, who are all humans who became gods or demigods.[58] This potential transition is even reflected in the Sumerian language, whose nouns are divided into two separate grammatical categories: one for gods and humans, and one for animals and inanimate objects.[59]

Such fusions do not exist in the Bible. A person cannot become a god, and is never granted immortality. Even Moses, referred to as "the man of God," is only described so in the same verse that mentions his

---

57. Thus, it is no coincidence that in later parts of the holy writ of Zoroastrianism, gods from the pre-Zoroaster era suddenly feature. The dualistic, abstract tendencies of this religion easily made way for other gods, which remained deities of a pagan, anthropomorphized nature, even during the Zoroastrian revolution itself (see further in Shaul Shaked, *Encyclopedia Biblica*, s.v. "*Peras – HaDat HaParsit*," vol. 6, 609–615).
58. Gilgamesh was also considered the judge of the underworld, and a demigod, given that his mother was the goddess Ninsun. See Kaufmann, *The Religion of Israel*, vol. 1, 340–341.
59. See more about this phenomenon in Samuel Noah Kramer, *Encyclopedia Biblica*, s.v. "*Shomer*," vol. 7, 544.

future death (Deut. 33:1). The only narrative that seems to allude to the blurring of boundaries between the human and the divine – the sons of God who take the daughters of man – ultimately retains the barrier between deity and mortal. On the contrary, it is this very episode which leads to the limitation of the human life span.[60]

CHARACTERIZATION: GOD AND HUMAN

In Genesis 1–11, there is almost no penetration into the characters' thoughts. This is not surprising, given that it is also true of most of the biblical narrative. Here, however, not only are their thoughts and emotions concealed from the reader, but there is almost no direct speech. To prove this point, it suffices to present *all* the direct quotations from the four main human protagonists of this unit:

1. Adam: He names "woman" (2:23) and responds to God after he eats from the forbidden tree (3:10–12).[61]
2. Eve: She responds to the serpent (3:2), to God after her sin (3:13), and names Cain and Seth (4:1, 25).
3. Cain: He answers God after Abel's murder (4:9, 13–14).
4. Noah: He responds to his sons' actions by cursing Canaan and blessing Shem and Japheth (9:25–27).

Even considering the general paucity of speech in biblical narrative, the characters' silence in this section is extreme. Throughout three intense chapters, before, during, and after the Flood, Noah opens his mouth just once, only to promptly close it again and step off the biblical stage.

On the other hand, these chapters are not entirely devoid of speech, or even thoughts. The characters' silence is complemented by God's relative effusion. Creation is a series of divine statements, and in

60. Umberto Cassuto, "The Episode of the Sons of God and the Daughters of Man," in *Biblical and Oriental Studies*, vol. 1 (Jerusalem, 1973): 17–28.

61. Stratton traces the process of the reading experience of the creation narratives, and claims that part of the reading consciousness accompanying the story is surprise at the lack of communication between God and man: "[The reader] may also observe and wonder why God has not yet spoken in the Genesis 2–3 story to this man whom God created" (*Out of Eden*, 32).

the Eden narrative, a full thirteen verses are God's direct speech. In the story of Cain, God makes two substantial speeches, the first after Cain's offering is rejected (4:6–7), and the second after Abel's murder (4:9–15). The contrast between God and the human characters is especially salient in the Flood narrative, when Noah silently obeys all of God's lengthy orders (6:13–21; 7:1–4; 8:15–17; 8:21; 9:1–7; 9:8–17). These narratives are full of God's speech to Himself and to others, including orders and punishments, blessings and curses, and promises and covenants. Yet, throughout these stories, His human audience is almost silent. The only narrative in which there is balance between human speech and divine speech is the story of the Tower of Babel. There, humans make two consecutive speeches in the brief, nine-verse narrative:

- And they said to one another, "Come, let us make bricks and burn them thoroughly" (11:3).
- And they said, "Come, let us build us a city and a tower whose top will reach heaven, and let us make a name for ourselves, lest we be scattered over the face of the whole earth" (11:4).

In contrast, God also makes two statements after He witnesses the construction of the city:

- And the Lord said, "Look, they are one people and with one language, and this is what they have begun to do. Now nothing they intend to do will be impossible for them" (11:6).
- "Come, let us go down and there confuse their language, so that they will not understand one another's language" (11:7).

The balance between human and divine speech here is logical, given that the main theme of this narrative is human language and communication. God's response is that humans will no longer be able to understand each other's language.[62]

62. Joseph Blenkinsopp proposes that for the sake of comparing God's speech in the narrative to the humans' speech, God uses the plural tense "let *us* go down," and thus God is presented as parallel to the united body of humanity (Joseph Blenkinsopp, *Creation,*

Given the ratio of divine speech to human speech in these chapters, it emerges that God is its main actor. This is true of other biblical narratives, but unlike those of a more historical nature, here the relationship between God and His world is based on a stark hierarchy of divine intervention in the world.[63]

This premise is consistent with the theory I will develop below, namely, that over the course of the book of Genesis, divine providence evolves from a salient, active force to a subtle Hand that works behind the scenes. This is especially evident in the final episode of Genesis, the Joseph story.[64]

And indeed, in the first eleven chapters of the book, God is wholly active. He brings the world into being and gives names to each creation, He plants a garden and walks about in the cool of the day, He refuses to accept Cain's offering but responds to him personally, He shuts the door of Noah's ark before unleashing the Flood upon the earth, He goes down to see the city of Babel under construction and muddles the workers' language. This overt intervention gradually winds down over the course of Genesis, with the most obvious cut-off line between Genesis 11 and the patriarchal cycles that begin in Genesis 12 (which sees a similar but more subtle process). This gradual change has profound theological significance for questions of God's relationship with the world and divine providence. It is no wonder, therefore, that Genesis 1–11 sees several episodes that are deeply concerned with the boundaries between heaven and earth, such as God's concern that after eating from the forbidden fruit, humanity would indeed be "like God," or the allusions in the brief story of the sons of God intermingling with the daughters of man, or the divine interruption of the building of a "tower whose top reaches the heavens."[65] At the same time, human characterization

---

Un-Creation, Re-Creation: A Discursive Commentary on Genesis 1–11 [London/New York, 2011], 164). As he emphasizes there, even though the human voice is heard in this tale, there is no actual dialogue with God (in contrast to the Eden narrative or Cain's exchange with God).

63. In the words of Cohn, "With God so much in the forefront, human character relationships do not develop" (Cohn, "Narrative Structure," 5).

64. Cohn, "Narrative Structure."

65. See especially below, in context of the use of the plural for, "Let *us* make man" (1:26).

also undergoes a stark change between Genesis 11 and the Abraham cycle. We know nothing about Adam and his life outside of Eden, we know very little about Cain, who murdered his brother, and despite almost four chapters describing the Flood and its aftermath, we hear Noah's voice only once. There is a rapid shift from human protagonist to human protagonist in the first eleven chapters of Genesis. In contrast, the Abraham cycle focuses fully on a single character, his family, and the events that befall him. This allows for developed characterization and identification with the protagonist. Moreover, it reflects interest in a particular human, interest both literary and theological. In the Abraham cycle, there are several episodes in which God plays no part at all (such as Lot's rescue from captivity in Genesis 14) and other narratives of a striking political-national nature (such as Abraham's covenant with Abimelech in ch. 21).[66]

In parallel to the broader process of the book of Genesis, a similar process takes place over the course of chapters 1–11. God is obviously the sole player in the creation story of chapter 1; He alone invents reality and brings it into being. As we will see in our analysis of the Eden narrative (chs. 2–3), the central theme is humankind's "maturation," man and woman's transformation to autonomous beings who converse with God for the first time and even stray from His instructions. It is no coincidence that the serpent's temptation focuses on the illusion that man and woman can become "like God" by eating from the Tree of Knowledge (3:5).[67] In this sense, humanity achieves certain independence in the second story of Genesis. In the next generation, Cain takes initiative and offers up an offering to God from his own free will. This offering

66. I have discussed the absence of God in the story of Lot's rescue elsewhere (Grossman, *Abram to Abraham: A Literary Analysis of the Abraham Narrative* [Bern, 2016], 90–94), as well as the realistic-political atmosphere of Abimelech's covenant and its contribution to Abraham's characterization (ibid., 290–299).

67. Some argue that this is also the central theme in the story of *Atrahasis*: humanity exceeding its boundaries (expressed through humans making too much noise in the story and disturbing the gods' rest), with the gods putting the humans in their rightful place. See Robert A. Oden Jr., "Divine Aspirations in Atrahasis and in Genesis 1–11," *ZAW* 93 (1981): 197–216. Even if this is one theme in the story, it is certainly not central, as it is in the Eden narrative.

is not ordered by God, but is a voluntary act that expresses independence and free moral choice. This initiative eventually leads to murder, which is an expression of the dangerous side of this free will. I will yet point out the profound connection between the story of Cain and the story of Eden. Beyond this connection, there is a crucial difference between Adam and Eve and their son Cain. Adam and Eve hang their heads and silently accept their punishment, while Cain speaks up and responds to God's decree. Whether his response should be understood as a solemn expression of regret, or as a complaint at the severity of his punishment,[68] his reaction differs from that of his parents. His exchange with God after his sentence leads to a certain sign "so that no one who found him would kill him" (4:15). The Midrash draws attention to this disparity from another angle:

> "And Cain went out from the Lord's presence." From where did he go out?.... R. Hama, in the name of R. Hanina son of R. Isaac said, "He went out happy, as it says, 'He is coming out to meet you, and when he sees you his heart will be glad'" (Ex. 4:14). He met Adam, who said to him, "What was your decree?" He said to him, "I repented and made reconciliation." Adam slapped his own face, "Such is the power of repentance, and I had not known."[69]

Humanity's role develops further by the end of Cain's line in chapter 4. There, the human is presented as the key to a complex cultural world of science and art, and at the end of the chapter, with the birth of Seth's dynasty, there is even religious development: "Then people began to call on the name of the Lord" (4:26). Even if, as some have noted, this description is in dialogue with Abraham's calling on the Lord's name (12:8), Abraham does so as a result of God's revelation to him, while

---

68. On the exegetic debate of how to understand Cain's words in v. 13, see Cherry, *Torah through Time*, 94–95. This is also related to the meaning of the word *"avoni"* in the verse – does it mean sin or punishment? (For further examples of passages where the meaning is unclear, see Robert Gordis, "Commentary on the Text of Lamentations [Part Two]," *JQR* 58 [1967]: 25.) Ed Greenstein sees intentional ambiguity in the use of this word (Edward Greenstein, "Wordplay, Hebrew," *ABD* 6: 969).
69. Genesis Rabba 25:13.

the worship of Enosh's generation is presented as a voluntary human initiative.[70] As we will see, these developments are complex, but in light of my current argument, this undoubtedly marks a new stage in human development and initiative.

While the precise identity of the "sons of God" in chapter 6 requires careful analysis, regardless of whether these beings are human or divine the story conveys a sense of violated boundaries, of upheaval and the loss of order.

If so, the world's development from creation, until the Flood that brings its destruction, sees the gradual rise of human independence. From being sheltered under the trees of God's garden, huddled under the wings of the *Shekhina*, eating from the Tree of Life, humanity begins its journey towards autonomy and independence. This autonomy gives rise to culture, art, science, and religion, but also to violence and destruction, for "the inclination of the human heart is evil from its youth" (8:21). As we will see in our analysis of the Flood narrative, the difference between the prediluvian world and the postdiluvian world hinges on this very point. After the Flood, humanity becomes God's partner in the world's re-creation, and its role changes in the world. While the crown, the privilege granted to humanity with creation, is taken away, there is hope and an expectation that the crown will be restored through human action and responsibility.

Genesis 1–11 reflects a complex process that unfolds in each individual unit and over the course of the entire section. It is not merely a "prelude" or an "introduction" to the book of Genesis. While it does lead up to the story of Abraham and the chosen people, it tells the story of the first attempt to build a world, of the distant past that anticipates the distant future.

70. Markus Witte, *Die biblische Urgeschichte: Redaktions und theologiegeschichtliche Beobachtungen zu Genesis 1,1–11,26* (Berlin, 1998), 198.

The Creation: Humanity and Nature (1:1–2:3)

Is chapter 1 of Genesis a "story"? Some readers may consider this a question for theoreticians, without any relevance for their own understanding of the chapter. Yet, this question has theological implications. Chapter 1 is a series of chronological events, with a protagonist, and in this respect, we can refer to it as a "story" or "narrative." However, a story usually contains some kind of conflict that its characters must deal with, and chapter 1 in Genesis admittedly seems to be devoid of any such conflict. No obvious points of conflict arise or are resolved over the course of the plot, not even for those who consider its opening verses, "the earth being unformed and void, with darkness over the surface of the deep" (v. 2), as a hint to the evil forces that "the good God will vanquish and drive away."[1] Even if these forces represent a certain primordial evil, there is no real suspense; God obviously triumphs over void and chaos. In other words, there is no real plot. Some argue that chapter 1 is not an independent narrative, but an introduction to a narrative which does

1. Weinfeld, "God the Creator," 121.

contain conflicts (sin, murder, and flood, for example). Nonetheless, the rest of the narratives in this section are also independent units, and chapter 1 is certainly structured as a unit that stands alone.

Like most other stories, our chapter opens with an exposition of sorts (though this definition is contingent on how verses 1–2 are defined), and the chapter draws to a dénouement, to a happy end, in the form of the Sabbath. Yet, what takes place between this opening and this ending seems to be entirely devoid of conflict; there is nothing for the protagonist to resolve.

This unique "plot," of course, is no coincidence. Rather, it is the faithful reflection of a chapter that marches along to the refrain that "all is good." Unlike other ancient Near Eastern creation accounts (and even other creation narratives found in the Bible itself), the first chapter of Genesis paints a harmonious picture without struggles or shadows.[2] No gods argue among themselves, the sea does not attempt to engulf the Divine Creator, and sea monsters and serpents are created along with the rest of the animals. Rather than conflict, the most striking feature of this narrative is its flawless organization, its perfect order, and its natural, seamless flow.[3] This design is evident not only in the actual plot, which presents a reality in which the world is formed out of God's words, but in the very feel and fabric of the words, and

2. See, for example, Jon D. Levenson, *The Love of God: Divine Gift, Human Gratitude, and Mutual Faithfulness in Judaism* (Princeton and Oxford, 2016), 122–123. Israel Knohl disagrees with Kaufmann and believes that Genesis 1 should be read as a representation of a creation that makes order out of existing chaos that reflects "a primeval entity that preceded Divine creation." He believes that "The primeval elements mentioned in Genesis 1:2 (chaos, darkness, deep) all belong, to some degree, to the dark side" (Knohl, *Biblical Beliefs* [Jerusalem, 2007], 16), which existed before creation. However, he does emphasize that "in contrast to the battle myths of the ancient Near East and its parallels in the Bible," there is no echo of a struggle between good and evil, or any other struggle, in Genesis 1 (ibid., 17).
3. Recently, Scott Noegel suggested to understand the term "earth" in verse 1 as meaning "the underworld." He based this reading on other instances in the Bible in which "earth" is "the underworld," and also on Mesopotamian and Ugaritic texts. Thus, he suggested that the first two verses should be translated as follows:
"(1) In the beginning God created the heavens and the underworld. (2) And the underworld was void and waste, and darkness was over the face of the deep, and the spirit of God hovered over the face of the waters" ("God of Heaven and Sheol: The 'Unearthing' of Creation," *Hebrew Studies* 58 [2017]: 119–144). This is a

in the special narrative rhythm.[4] The formulaic repetition that shapes the units of the story ("that it was good", "and there was evening and there was morning"), the division into days, the repetition of "and God said" at the beginning of each day, along with other repetitive elements – all generate a sense of structure and order. This conjures up the image of a stable, harmonious natural world as the physical manifestation of divine wisdom, a world which is entirely "good."

This statement has profound theological significance, significance which may be polemical when read against other Mesopotamian creation stories rife with tension and battle, as well as significance that counters claims that the world is a capricious world without rhyme or reason. In this chapter, natural order is an expression of divine wisdom, which implies that the very fact that the world was created assumes that its creation was the result of free choice, and even implies that it has purpose. For some, order is next to godliness:

> Holiness means keeping distinct the categories of creation. It therefore involves correct definition, discrimination, and order... Morality does not conflict with holiness, but holiness is more a matter of separating that which should be separated.[5]

While I am not sure that I identify with this approach,[6] it nonetheless reflects something that emanates from the creation narrative, which is that the pristine order of the chapter – which represents world order – has religious significance.

---

challenging and intriguing reading, and if it is correct, the story of creation turns God into the Creator of "the underworld" as well, and even this world is presented in the narrative as part of the orderly world created in Genesis 1.

4. I discuss this at length in Grossman, *Text and Subtext*, 114–115.
5. Mary Douglas, *Purity and Danger: An Analysis of Concepts of Pollution and Taboo* (London/New York, 1996): 54–55.
6. Douglas believes that according to the Bible, impurity is related to disorder; something that deviates from regular order arouses impurity. This approach is criticized by Anna S. Meigs, "A Papuan Perspective on Pollution," *Manuscripta* 13 (1978): 304–318. See also Jacob Milgrom, *Leviticus 1–16* (AB: New York, 1991), 718–736.

If narrative purpose is indeed inherent in the narrative structure, then it is crucial to expose this structure. Yet, a careful analysis of the story reveals more than one possible structure, and as I will show, each structure encourages a different understanding of reality, and of the relationship between the creations. I will explore three different divisions of this chapter, which are implied in the text itself, and I will focus on two components that demand special attention – the textual attitude towards the lights, and towards the human's place in the world.

THE FIRST DIVISION: "WITH TEN ACTS OF SPEECH, THE WORLD WAS CREATED"

Each set of creation is introduced with the anaphoric opening, "And God said." Dividing the text according to this phrase, we get a higher-resolution structure than the more classic division point of days. Medieval commentators argue whether the phrase "And God said" describes an actual statement (Ibn Ezra), or whether it is an abstract expression of thought and will (Nahmanides). Either way, the intensive repetition of this verb is not coincidental, as the sages already noted in *Pirkei Avot*:

> By ten acts of speech the world was created. What does this teach us? Could not the world have been created by a single act of speech? It is to exact punishment from the wicked who destroy a world created by ten acts of speech, and to reward richly the righteous who sustain the world created by ten acts of speech.[7]

In addition to the opening refrain, which describes the creative divine acts of speech, the description of each creation concludes with another statement. After every act, God gazes down approvingly at His new creation: "And God saw that this was good." I will address the meaning of this evaluation below.

---

7. Avot 5:1. The Mishna's count includes two "acts of speech" uttered on the sixth day that do not introduce actual creations: "God blessed them and God said to them, 'Be fertile and increase, fill the earth and master it'" (v. 28); and "God said, 'See, I give you every seed-bearing plant that is upon all the earth'" (v. 29).

The acts of speech, and God's stamps of approval following their creation, appear as follows:

And God said:	Let there be light (v. 3)	And God saw that the light was good (v. 4)
And God said:	Let there be an expanse in the midst of the water, that it may separate water from water (v. 6)	
And God said:	Let the water below the sky be gathered into one area, that the dry land may appear (v. 9)	And God saw that this was good (v. 10)
And God said:	Let the earth sprout vegetation: seed-bearing plants, fruit trees of every kind on earth that bear fruit with the seed in it (v. 11)	And God saw that this was good (v. 12)
And God said:	Let there be lights in the expanse of the sky to separate day from night (v. 14)	And God saw that this was good (v. 18)
And God said:	Let the waters bring forth swarms of living creatures, and birds that fly above the earth across the expanse of sky (v. 20)	And God saw that this was good (v. 21)
And God said:	Let the earth bring forth every kind of living creature: cattle, creeping things, and wild beasts of every kind (v. 24)	And God saw that this was good (v. 25)

And God said:	Let us make man in our image, after our likeness (v. 26)	
[God blessed them and God said to them:	Be fertile and increase, fill the earth (v. 28)]	
And God said:	See, I give you every seed-bearing plant that is upon all the earth (v. 29)	And God saw all that He had made, and found it very good (v. 31)

This sequence reveals the gradual evolution of creation, from the most basic introduction of time and space through flora, fauna, and humanity.

As mentioned, this division results in the highest resolution division of creation, as each group of new creations is introduced with its own act of divine speech. Most of these groups are largely cohesive, and its members intuitively fall into the same category. For example, fruit trees and grasses are created with the same speech act, as are all land animals, from insect to mammal. Similarly, the sun, moon, and stars are also created with a single divine pronunciation.

There are exceptions to this intuitive grouping, however. The biggest surprise in this context is the inclusion of water creatures and birds in one category: "Let the waters bring forth swarms of living creatures, and birds that fly above the earth across the expanse of sky" (v. 20). Birds and fish are not an obvious combination. According to modern taxonomy, birds and fish are two distinct classes, and this divergence is alluded to in the divine blessing, "Be fertile and increase, fill the waters in the seas, and let the birds increase on the earth" (v. 22). The distinction between filling the seas and increasing on the land reflects the significant difference between them, but the question remains: Why aren't there two separate speech acts for the fish and the birds?

This merging points to an essential connection between these two categories.[8] On the second day, God separates "water from water"

8. As opposed to Hermann Gunkel (*Genesis – Translated and Interpreted,* trans. M. E. Biddle [Georgia, 1997], 111), who perceived this as a forced combination as a result of the number of days.

(v. 6), meaning the seas and the skies are both perceived as sources of water. This distinction is not merely metaphorical, as the verses describe an actual body of water in the sky: "God made the expanse, and it separated the water which was below the expanse from the water which was above the expanse" (v. 7). If so, both birds and fish can be considered "water creatures." Indeed, each move their wings or fins in a similar way through their own watery blue expanse, and each are granted an extra dimension of movement denied to land creatures.

This idea is echoed in biblical law. Three sets of dietary laws are discussed for three different categories of animals in Leviticus 11: land creatures (Lev. 11: 2–8); water creatures (11:9–12); and birds, or creatures of the sky (11:13–23). Some have proposed that "[T]he clean animals are those that conform to these standard pure types. Those creatures which in some way transgress the boundaries are unclean."[9] Regardless of this theory, the discussion of impurity from dead animals in the second half of Leviticus 11 focuses on a single category. That is, only dead land creatures cast those who touch them into a state of impurity, while dead sea creatures or dead birds (according to Leviticus) have no such impurity. This is not because fish were not widely available in the land of Israel,[10] but rather because birds and fish do not share a living sphere with humans, and therefore their death does not arouse impurity. "Water" creatures are differentiated from land creatures, and the deaths of birds or fish do not result in the impurity associated with human death.[11]

As mentioned, the opening statement of each section is mirrored by a repeated closing formula: "and God saw that it was good." A creation cannot be evaluated until its completion; once the creation is complete, the Creator evaluates it and perceives its perfection. Only after this critical appraisal, which also lends autonomy to each completed creation,[12] does God move on to the next stage of creation, and pronounce the

---

9. See Gordon J. Wenham, *Leviticus* (NICOT: Michigan, 1979), 169.
10. Regarding this premise and its proofs, see Milgrom, *Leviticus 1–16*, 660.
11. The relationship between sky and sea is multifaceted, as is evident from the tension of the sky's creation according to the different divisions of the chapter, as I will discuss below.
12. See further in Eliezer Schweid, *The Cycle of Appointed Times: The Meaning of Jewish Holidays* (Tel Aviv, 1984), 53.

next speech act. Therefore, if there is further need for the distinction or naming of a creation, the concluding "*ki tov*" ("that it was good") is postponed until the end of each process. For example, the waters that gather to one place (v. 9) are not deemed "good" until after the dry land and body of waters are named (v. 10).

One creation deviates from this rule:

1. God said, "Let there be light"; and there was light. (v. 3)
2. God saw that the light was good. (v. 4)
3. God separated the light from the darkness. (v. 4)
4. God called the light Day, and the darkness He called Night. (v. 5)

God declares that the light is "good" immediately after its creation, before it is separated from the darkness, and before light and darkness are named day and night. This indicates that the differentiation between light and darkness is different from the two other differentiations that take place in this chapter, that of the separation of the upper waters from the lower waters (vv. 6–7), and that of the great lights which differentiate between night and day (v. 14). The separation of upper waters and lower waters – of sky and sea – is a physical differentiation which defines and shapes space. The skies are above, the waters are below. Using the lights to differentiate between day and night, in contrast, defines time rather than space. When the sun sets and the stars begin to glow in the darkening sky, the time called "day" is over and the time called "night" begins.

But how can we understand God's differentiation between light and darkness? Based on the fact that the sun and moon were created only on the fourth day, some readings propose that the light created on the first day is not light as we know it, but rather an abstract divine light, the qualities of which are discussed in kabbalistic literature.[13] This

---

13. Mark Smith, "Light in Genesis 1:3 – Created or Uncreated: A Question of Priestly Mysticism?", in *Birkat Shalom: Studies in the Bible, Ancient Near Eastern Literature, and Postbiblical Judaism Presented to Shalom M. Paul on the Occasion of His Seventieth Birthday*, ed. Ch. Cohen et al. (Winona Lake, 2008), vol. 1, 125–134. This may have been the sages' intention of their explanation that the light created on the first day was kept for the righteous in the future (Genesis Rabba 12:6). Some drew a connection between two different kinds of light – actual and symbolic. Rabbenu Baḥya on

reading, however, is problematic in context. The creation of light is preceded by a divine act of speech, and is followed by the formulaic pronunciation that God considered it "good." The creation of light and its differentiation from darkness is the only act that takes place on the very first day of the world's existence. It is problematic to interpret this light as something abstract that does not actually exist in the world. Moreover, the light created on the first day is clearly different from the light of the sun and moon. The world is filled with light that does not come from the sun, such as firelight, lightning, and electricity. The light created on the first day is the essence of light, the very concept of light, as in, the idea and existence of illumination.

If so, what is the meaning of the differentiation between light and darkness in verse 4? Umberto Cassuto explains that this act has no bearing on the entity of light, but rather serves to define darkness:

> It was not the Creator's intention that there should be perpetual light and no darkness at all, but that the light and the darkness should operate consecutively for given periods and in unchanging order. Consequently, God divided the one from the other, that is, He separated their respective spheres of activity.[14]

In other words, the creation of light was complete *before* light was differentiated from darkness. This step was necessary not for the existence of light, but for the existence of the concept of darkness. Darkness dissipates with the appearance of light. Darkness can exist only when light is limited within time and space. The subtle chiastic order of the naming of

---

Gen. 1:3 writes, "According to *peshat* there were two lights: the first – the light used in this world, the light of the sun and the moon; the second – the light reserved for the righteous in the future. And it is known that the light used in this world is taken from the light reserved for the righteous in the future."

14. Umberto Cassuto, *A Commentary on The Book of Genesis: From Adam to Noah*, trans. Israel Abrahams (Jerusalem, 1961), 26. Nahmanides' interpretation (on Gen. 1:4) is similar: "And God separated between the light and the darkness – this is not the darkness mentioned in the first verse, which is fire – this refers to the absence of light. For God set the measure for the light, that [darkness] would be absent so long as it was there."

light and darkness reflects how they were named simultaneously: "God *called* the *light* Day, and the *darkness* He *called* Night" (v. 5).[15] Light can exist without darkness, and this illuminates how God could perceive that "the light was good" before the act of differentiation. This act was necessary in order to enable the existence of darkness, but it has no bearing on the existence of light in itself.

This idea also sheds light on another anomalous detail in this verse. Every act of creation concludes with the statement, "And God saw that this was good" (vv. 10, 12, 18, 21, 25), with the exception of the creation of light, where "God saw that the light was good" (v. 4). It is light, and not darkness, which God perceives as good. Light is God's creation here, and light is what God is evaluating.[16] As mentioned, the creation of light is complete before darkness is differentiated from light. The sole purpose of this differentiation is to give darkness its place.

Tracing the pattern of the concluding formula, "and God saw that this was good," reveals two other anomalies.

The Water Cycle

The first anomaly, alluded to above and widely noted in research, is the absence of "*ki tov*" ("that it was good") following the creation of the sky, when the upper waters are separated from the lower waters. One reasonable, prevalent explanation is that the arrangement of the waters is not yet final at this stage, that the Creator appraises that the waters are "good" only after they are gathered to certain areas alongside dry land.

This argument, however, is not without its flaws. If each act of creation opens with a new statement of "God said" and concludes with "God

15. On how chiastic structure can function as an expression of simultaneity, see Robert S. Kawashima, *Biblical Narrative and the Death of the Rhapsode* (Bloomington, 2004), 59–60.

16. See also Claus Westermann, *Genesis: A Continental Commentary*, trans. J. J. Scullion (Minneapolis, 1985–1994), vol. 1, 113. Nahmanides (on Gen. 1:4) notes this deviation and explains it differently: "He added 'the light,' for if it had said just 'and God saw that it was good,' it would have referred back to the heaven and earth, even though their existence had not yet been decreed, for they did not yet stand thus. However, from the matter creation on the first day, the sky was created on the second, and on the third the dust was separated from the water to form the land, which was called 'dry land,' and then their existence was decreed, and God said that they were good."

saw that this was good," then why is a new divine act of speech necessary if the separation between water and dry land is only a continuation of the separation of the waters? If the answer to this question is that the first stage of creation focuses on the sky, which then receives its name (as opposed to the waters), while the second stage of creation that takes place on the third day focuses on the arrangement of the waters, then our question still stands: Why doesn't God perceive that the sky is good on the second day?

We can read this pattern as a reflection of the complex relationship between the upper and the lower waters. On one hand, sea and sky are separate entities. The separation of upper and lower waters and the definition of boundaries between land and water are two momentous steps, each worthy of their own divine act of speech. Yet sea and sky are profoundly connected, as documented in modern science, that seawater evaporates into steam, which rises up, cools down, forms clouds, and rains back down onto the earth. The blue of sea merges into the blue of sky as the upper waters and lower waters are in a constant state of negotiation, drenching the land from above and from below.[17] Only after creating all the elements of this intricate cycle does God step back and conclude, "*ki tov*."

Humanity and Free Choice

At first glance, the second anomaly is surprising. God does not perceive that humanity is "good." The fact that the creation of humanity receives special attention in the text, as we will discuss below, makes this omission all the more surprising. Some apply the conclusion of creation in its entirety, "And God saw all that He had made, and found it very good" (v. 31), to the conclusion of the creation of humanity, which precedes it.[18] Others note that this formula appears seven times in the narrative, a symbolic number that testifies to the perfect harmony of creation, and suggest that this statement is omitted from the last act of creation in order to maintain this numeric harmony.[19]

---

17. About 78 percent of rainwater that falls on dry land comes from evaporated ocean water. Water evaporates from the ocean and from freshwater sources and returns to them in the form of precipitation, rivers, and groundwater.
18. Nahmanides on Gen. 1:31. See also Levenson's discussion in *Love of God*.
19. Tyndale House Publishers, *Genesis 1–12* (NLT Study Bible: Illinois, 2008), 24.

Both suggestions, however, are problematic. On the sixth day, the creation of land animals is concluded with the usual formula (v. 25). It would be illogical to assume that this formula is omitted from another creation on the same day for the sake of numeric harmony. Moreover, the final statement could theoretically have applied equally to all the creations of the final day, but the creation of animals receives its own "*ki tov*." Why, then, does it seem that human status is presented as secondary to animal, vegetable, and mineral?

The key to this mystery seems to lie in humanity's unique character. Eliezer Schweid writes in his analysis of Rosh HaShana:

> Of every creation on every day, it is said, "God saw that it was good"…. Whatever is consistent with divine will is granted existence and endurance. These words are also stated about humanity, with all the more emphasis. Humanity, created in God's image, acts according to its own will and consideration, and for this reason, a person is worthy of being examined anew each time. Upon creation, he too was good, by his very nature, and was blessed. But as soon as he used his free will, he sinned.[20]

While the idea of human free will indeed informs these verses, it is because of this free will – unlike Schweid's claim – that God does *not* look down and perceive that humanity was "good." God cannot determine whether His new creation is good, because humanity has the power of choice and free will. Whether the creation of humanity will emerge as something good, neutral, superfluous, or even harmful, remains to be determined by humanity's actions and decisions. Had God immediately perceived that humanity "was good," His evaluation of humanity a few generations later would have been a grave contradiction, when it says: "The Lord saw how great was man's wickedness on earth, and how every plan devised by his mind was nothing but evil all the time. And the Lord regretted that He had made man on earth, and His heart was saddened" (6:5–6). There, God "sees" humanity in action, and His evaluation is completely different. Rather

20. Schweid, *The Cycle of Appointed Times*, 53.

than its being "good," humanity's "wickedness on earth" was "great," and rather than rejoicing in the creation of humanity, God feels deep regret and disappointment.

The absence of "*ki tov*" following the creation of humanity hints to the potential danger of a creature with free choice, created in the image of God with the ability to choose between good and evil, without nature compelling him to act one way or another. This reading turns the tables completely. The concluding statement, "And God saw all that He had made, and found it very good," not only fails to compensate for the lack of "good" following humanity's creation, but it may not be referring to humanity at all. Creation as a whole is "very good," referring to its individual creations and the symbiosis between them, but a question mark hovers over one particular creation. Perhaps humanity will be a part of this harmonious system, or perhaps it will upset the balance and bring everything crashing down.

Parallel Acts of Speech

The nine "acts of speech" of creation can be divided into two groups. The first opens with the creation of light, and the second begins with the creation of the lights:[21]

(1) God said, *"Let there be light"*; and there was light. God saw that the light was good, **and God separated the light from the darkness.** *God called the light Day, and the darkness He called Night.*	(5) God said, "*Let there be lights* in the expanse of the sky *to separate day from night*… And God set them in the expanse of the sky to shine upon the earth, *to dominate the day and the night,* and **to separate light from darkness.** And God saw that this was good.

21. Gunkel, *Genesis,* 120. Many have noted this structure, but in the context of the division according to days. Indeed, the division into days retains this structure – but this division is more salient when tracing after the creative acts of speech. See further below.

(2) God said, "Let there be an expanse in the midst of the water... and it separated *the water which was below the expanse* from the water which was above the expanse. And it was so. God called the expanse Sky.	(6) God said, "Let the *waters bring forth* swarms of living creatures, and birds that fly above the earth *across the expanse of the sky*"... And God saw that this was good.
(3) God said, "Let the water below the sky be gathered into one area, that the dry land may appear." And it was so. God called the dry land *Earth*, and the gathering of waters He called Seas. And God saw that this was good.	(7) God said, "Let the *earth* bring forth every kind of living creature: cattle, creeping things, and wild beasts of every kind".... And God saw that this was good.
	(8) And God said, "Let us make man in our image, after our likeness"... [(9) God said to them, "Be fertile and increase, fill the earth and master it.]
(4) And God said, "Let the earth sprout vegetation: *seed-bearing plants*, fruit trees of every kind on earth that bear fruit with the seed in it." And it was so.... And God saw that this was good.	(10) God said, "See, I give you every *seed-bearing plant that is upon all the earth*, and every tree that has seed-bearing fruit".... And God saw all that He had made, and found it very good.

The light in section (1) is parallel to the creation of the lights (5). This connection is not merely thematic. Both verses share a similar style and language, that the light that becomes "day" and the darkness that becomes "night" on the first day reappear on the fourth day, with similar language. The second divine act of speech creates sky and water, while the sixth act of speech fills this sky and water with creatures.[22] Similarly,

22. Rabbi Mordechai Breuer proposed placing the creation of the lights in parallel to the creation of heaven and earth together, as the lights hang in the sky. He also sees the sea and the land in parallel to water creatures and birds, and the creation of

the land is created with the third "And God said," and populated with the seventh. There is even a parallel between the final acts of speech in the first and second halves, that the seed-bearing plants created with the fourth act of speech are designated as food for humans and animals with the tenth act of speech.

This division reveals that the first acts of speech create the world's setting – time and space – whereas the bustle of life begins in earnest with the second set of speech acts. Then, the sun and moon begin their celestial dance. Goodly creatures fill the water, the sea, and the land, and humans walk the shore for the first time. All these are the world's inhabitants, the "residents" of the sky, the sea, and the land.[23] In the same vein, the fourth and tenth groups of creations fit in with this scheme. Plants and trees are created as part of the world's environment, but they remain untouched until living, moving animals appear on the scene, eating their fill and scattering their seeds from place to place.

This neat structure is disrupted by the creation of humanity, which has no parallel.[24] This may point to humanity's unique place in the world, which is also expressed with the gravity of the majestic plural, "Let us make man." This festive tone, in addition to the unprecedented announcement of a certain impending creation, draws the reader's attention to the importance of this particular creation. No such announcement is made prior to the creation of anything else ("*vayehi*," "let there be," is not a preliminary announcement, but rather functions as a speech act).

Effectively, the fact that humanity lacks a parallel element of creation in the first half of the narrative invites an even more dramatic conclusion. The missing counterpart of humanity's creation in the first

---

vegetation in parallel to land animals and humanity (Rabbi Mordechai Breuer, *Pirkei Bereshit* [Alon Shvut, 1998], vol. 1, 78–81). Gunkel deliberates about the following arrangement:

light – sky – land and sea // the lights – fish and birds – land animals and humanity (Gunkel, *Genesis*, 120).

23. See, for example, Gordon J. Wenham, *Genesis 1–15* (WBC: Waco, 1987), 6–7; Kikawada and Quinn, *Before Abraham Was*, 78; David Tsumura, *The Earth and the Waters in Genesis 1 and 2: A Linguistic Investigation* (JSOTSup 83: Sheffield, 1989), 42; Hamilton, *Genesis*, 125.

24. Walsh, *Style and Structure*, 105–106.

section is completed in the description of its creation: "And God said, 'Let us make man in our image, after our likeness'.... And God created man in His image, in the image of God He created him; male and female He created them" (vv. 26–27). Light is the setting for the lights, water and sky are to be home for birds and fish, but the basis for the creation of humanity is God Himself, people created in His image and His likeness. We will develop this idea further in our discussion of the third division of the chapter.

The relationship between the two halves of creation can also be formulated thus: the first set of creations, the "environment," is subjected to the dominion of the later set of creations. This is most salient in regard to the celestial bodies, which will control the movement of light and darkness: "God made the two great lights, the greater light to *dominate* the day and the lesser light to *dominate* the night, and the stars ... to *dominate* the day and the night" (vv. 16–18). Given that many ancient peoples related to the sun and moon as gods, the biblical emphasis on the sun and moon's "domination" can be perceived almost as a reckless endorsement of their mistake. This expression appears only three times in this chapter, and all three instances refer to the sun and moon's dominion over day and night.[25] This language, however, may be read as a polemic against this pagan stance, and I will develop this argument below, in my discussion based on the division into days, where this parallel is retained. There remains much to be said about the creation of the lights. For now, I will note that this division highlights their unique character. In any case, the celestial lights' dominion over God's first creation marks the beginning of the second section of the narrative, in which the new creations take possession of their earlier counterparts. The second half of the narrative ends with vegetation being designated as food for animals and humans: "God said, 'See, *I give you* every seed-bearing plant that is upon all the earth, and every tree that has seed-bearing fruit; they shall be yours for food. And to all the animals on land, to all the birds of the sky, and to everything that creeps on earth, in which there is the breath of life,

25. The word "*memshala*," dominion, does not feature again in this chapter. In the story of Eden, the man is granted "dominion" over his wife (3:16), and Cain receives the possibility of *memshala* over his brothers (4:7). I will discuss both instances in context.

[I give] all the green plants for food'" (vv. 29–30). The phrase, "See, I give you," is an indication that the later creations, people and animals, now have the rights to possess and use the earlier creations, plants and trees. Moreover, God's final creation, humanity, is given the right to rule over everything else (v. 26). The transition between the first and second half of creation thus marks the shift from habitat to inhabitants, from raw material to entities who will use and control this material.[26]

To divide creation according to divine acts of speech is to view creation in its highest resolution. Each group of creations is brought to life with its own act of speech, each passes under divine scrutiny, and each has its own status. But while each is "good" on an individual basis, the sum of their parts is "very good," and there is meaning to the particular sequence of their creation. The first group of divine speech acts creates the raw material, the environment, which will be dominated and used by the later creations. The first half of the speech acts paints the scenery, while the second half introduces the actors that will bring the setting and props to life.

THE SECOND DIVISION: A WEEK OF DAYS

Ten acts of speech, reflecting eight to nine groups of creations, are pronounced within six days, such that some groups of creations are created on the same day.[27] Nonetheless, this division still retains symmetry, [28]

26. Animals are somewhere in between. On one hand, they are inhabitants of the land, and they are permitted to eat any vegetation that grows upon it. On the other hand, they are given to humanity's dominion.
27. Amit proposes that despite the inconsistency between the number of creations and the number of days, they can be perceived as a single cohesive unit. The tight organization of creation within six days and the assignment of the seventh day as the day of rest at the end of the process is an indication of preconceived intent, which would not be the case with a week of creation that spread out over seven or eight days – with this arraignment, the sacred nature of Sabbath is emphasized (Yairah Amit, "Creation and the Calendar of Holiness," in *Tehillah le-Moshe: Biblical and Judaic Studies in Honor of Moshe Greenberg*, ed. M. Cogan, B. Eichler, and J. Tigay, 13–19 [Winona Lake, IN, 1997], 16). She is correct that this discrepancy is not an indication of later redaction, but the tension between the number of days and the number of creations still persists.
28. This has been noted by many. See a full discussion in Elizabeth Hayes, "Whose World? Whose Time? A Text World Theory Examination of the Style and Message

as the two days with two sets of creations (the third and sixth days) are parallel to each other:

1: Light	2: Sky (water and sky)	3: Dry land and greenery
4: The lights	5: Water creatures and birds	6: Land animals and humans (greenery is designated as food)

The creation of dry land and greenery on the same day is easily justified. Just as the waters that cover the seabed are included within the definition of the "sea," the greenery that covers the land is included within the definition of "land." This is especially clear from the naming of the dry land and the water on the third day: "God called the dry land Earth, and the gathering of waters He called Seas" (v. 10). The "gathering of waters" is the part of the world that is covered in water, and it is referred to as the "sea." In parallel, the text goes on to describe how the land is then covered in greenery. So the "sea" is land covered with water, while dry land, the *yabasha*, is land covered with vegetation.[29]

The creation of both animal and human on the sixth day is justified from a scientific-zoological perspective, though this juxtaposition has interesting moral and theological implications. First of all, both human and land animals are categorized as land dwellers, in contrast to creatures of water and sky. In a certain sense, the parallel structure of the days is based on living space. As a foil to the opening state of chaos and void, the first and fourth days describe the organization of the "heaven," while on the second and fifth days, the Creator deals with the "water," and on the third and sixth days, the "land" is set in order. From this perspective, it makes sense for all land dwellers to be created on the same day. Yet this division hardly mitigates the surprising observation that the difference

of Genesis 1:1–2:25," in *Doubling and Duplicating in the Book of Genesis: Literary and Stylistic Approaches to the Text,* ed. E. R. Hayes and K. Vermeulen (Winona Lake, 2016), 145–165.

29. Although vegetation also reproduces it is not blessed by God. Plant reproduction may be a more integral part of their natural life cycle than that of animals or humans (Gunkel, *Genesis,* 111). This may be reflected in the fact that in the creation narrative, plants are defined more as part of the scenery than as a form of life.

between water animals (created on the fifth day) and land animals (created on the sixth day) is far more acute than the difference between land animals and humans. That is, water creatures and land animals are created a whole day apart, while land animals and humans are grouped together as land dwellers. This division can hardly be dismissed as a technical distinction related to habitat.

The closely juxtaposed creation of animal and human bears significance for the status of both humans and animals. The notion of human superiority is challenged by this etiological affinity with animals, which is supported only from a biological perspective. On a cellular level, the human cell is identical to those of other land mammals, to the extent that in some cases, the vital organs of certain animals can be effectively transplanted into humans. What is more, humans and animals have far more in common, for what is life but a struggle for survival, food, and propagation of the species, from the moment of birth to the moment of death? This description applies equally to all living creatures, and from this perspective, a person is nothing but a sophisticated animal. This is only amplified by the fact that God designates vegetation for both human and animal consumption, and indeed, human and animal digestive systems are strikingly similar. As noted in Ecclesiastes, "For the fate of man is the fate of cattle; the same fate awaits them both, the death of one is like the death of the other, and their spirits are the same, and the preeminence of man over beast is nothing, for it is all but shallow breath.... Who can say that the spirit of a man rises up while the spirit of a beast sinks into the ground?" (Eccl. 3:19–21). From this perspective, it is only fitting that human and land mammals were created on the same day. Both draw the same breath, their hearts pump blood around their body. Inside, their systems are almost identical.

This similarity also has bearing for the status of animals. The fact that animals are not given over for human consumption when the world is very young imparts a strong message about the status of animals and their relationship with humanity. According to the developing doctrine of Genesis 1, animals, especially land animals, are also "living creatures," and the idea that these living creatures could be considered human food is not even suggested following the world's birth. Moreover, these living creatures are also burdened with a certain responsibility. They are to be held accountable if they ever kill a human (Gen. 9:5), as they must not harm someone who was created in God's image. The surprising fact that this moral discourse does not exempt animals from responsibility reveals a certain attitude towards animals, that they too are creations of the sixth day, and they too bear certain moral responsibility. Even if these words in chapter 9 only function symbolically, as an extension of God's words to humankind, they demand attention. It is worth noting that there is also biblical condemnation of killing animals for food (rather than for sacrificial purposes): "Bloodguilt shall be imputed to that man; he has shed blood; that man shall be cut off from among his people" (Lev. 17:4). The connotations of "he has shed blood" leave no room for doubt that the text perceives the slaughter of animals as murder, as bloodshed, as Rashi notes on that verse: "As though he had shed human blood, which costs him his life."[30] Animals must not kill people, but nor are people encouraged to kill animals without cause.

This idea is keenly reflected in the close proximity of animal and human creation. The division of creation into days sets animals and humans side by side, gently blurring the boundaries between them. Animals, like humans, pulse with lifeblood, and their deaths do not go unpunished.

At the same time, as noted, the close connection between the animal and the human rings with the pessimistic tones of Ecclesiastes, and were this the full picture of human existence presented in this chapter, then the biblical introduction of humanity would be none but a dreary portrait of physical, animal mortality. This tone, however, is balanced by other divisions encouraged by the text, which I will explore shortly. Before moving on, however, I wish to point out the center of gravity of this division into days – the holiness of Sabbath.

The Seventh Day

The division of the creation narrative into days culminates, of course, with the establishment of the Sabbath. As Rashbam already noted:

30. See further in Jacob Milgrom, "A Prolegomenon to Lev. 17:11" *JBL* 90 (1971), esp. 154–155.

> This is a classic biblical technique – to present and explain a matter which is unnecessary to the immediate context, but serves to illuminate something that will be explained further on.... This entire section, concerning the six days of creation, was written by our teacher Moses to explain to you what God said when the Torah was given, "Remember the Sabbath day and keep it holy".... Moses related [the account of the six days of creation] to Israel to inform them that the word of the Holy One, blessed be He, is true, [saying,] Do you believe that this world has always been as you see it now, full of all good? It was not so, for, "In the beginning, God created..."[31]

Rashbam argues that the entire purpose of the creation narrative is to justify the commandment of observing the Sabbath, which would be given to Israel in the future. Creation is compacted into six days and concluded with a seventh day as a model for the Israelite's working week. Through this pattern, through working for six days and resting on the seventh, we are reenacting the week of creation and imitating the divine. This model is the underlying objective of the creation narrative. Rabbi Mordechai Breuer makes a similar observation in his own unique style (even if he then deviates from this argument):

> Contrary to popular opinion, the seventh day is not considered sacred because the creation of the world was completed in six days. Rather, the reverse is true. The creation of the world was completed in six days in order to fulfill the sanctity of the seventh day.[32]

This suggests that there is special significance in the world's creation in six days, for God's rest must take place on the seventh day.[33] Ancient

31. Rashbam on Gen. 1:1. See also Weinfeld, "God the Creator," 109.
32. Breuer, *Pirkei Bereshit*, vol. 1, 76.
33. Attempts to find record of a seven-day week in the ancient Near East have proved fruitless. See Gotthard G. G. Reinhold, "Die Zahl Sieben als Zahl der Vollendung: Der Sabbat – Antworten auf die Frage nach seinem Ursprung," in *Die Zahl Sieben im Alten Orient*, ed. V. Golinets et al. (New York, 2009), 27–34.

exegetical traditions have already pointed out the significance of the number six in the ancient world. Philo, for example, writes:

> And he says that the world was made in six days, not because the Creator stood in need of a length of time (for it is natural that God should do everything at once, not merely by uttering a command, but by even thinking of it), but because the things created required arrangement. A number is akin to arrangement, and, of all numbers, six is, by the laws of nature, the most productive.... It was fitting therefore, that the world, being the most perfect of created things, should be made according to the perfect number, namely, six.[34]

From a mathematical perspective ("by the laws of nature"), Philo is convinced that the number six has a unique, perfect quality that is lacking in other numbers. Six is indeed the smallest perfect number, equal to the sum of its divisors. 1 + 2 + 3 = 1 * 2 * 3 = 6. The number six is also harmonious from a geometric perspective (there are six sides to a cube, and six points in the Star of David), and six is also the largest "all-harshad" number. The number six, or its multiple sixty, has profound presence in modern life, in all things circular or cyclical. For example, a circle has 360 degrees, an hour has sixty minutes, and a minute has sixty seconds. These figures are based on the Babylonian mathematical system, which revolved around the number sixty (and, of course, the arithmetical qualities of this number, which allows for convenient subdivision),[35] and the biblical year consists of twelve months, despite the difficulty this creates when synchronizing the solar and lunar calendars.

In the context of our discussion, however, the literary symbolism associated with this number is even more important than its mathematical qualities. Due to its centrality in ancient times, the number six pops up again and again in ancient Near Eastern narratives. There are countless examples, but it suffices to mention that Enkidu (Gilgamesh's close

34. Philo, *Philo of Alexandria Writings*, ed. S. Daniel-Nataf (Jerusalem 1991–2012), vol. 2, 17.
35. Some believe that as the Babylonian year consists of 360 days, they used the number sixty as their base number. Mayan culture also ascribed importance to the number sixty.

friend) is ill for twelve days before he dies,[36] that Gilgamesh must traverse a dark tunnel that stretches for twelve parasangs in order to reach Utnapishtim,[37] that the 120 oars that were consumed by the Sea of Death were each 60 cubits long,[38] that the ship he built was 120 cubits long, 120 cubits wide, 120 cubits tall, with six decks,[39] that Gilgamesh tells his boatman Ur-Shanabi to gaze upon his city, Uruk, saying, "Sixty myriad cubits of city, sixty myriad cubits of garden, sixty myriad cubits of clay-pits,"[40] that six years of famine are described in the story of *Atrahasis*,[41] and that Ereshkigal plagues Ishtar with sixty diseases.[42] The number six and its derivatives (twelve, sixty, thirty-six) appear hundreds of times in ancient Near Eastern literature, testifying to its symbolism as a whole, harmonious number. The number six seems to function similarly in the Bible. To name just a few examples, in Genesis 6:3, humans are allotted 120 years of life, and in Genesis 17:20, God blesses Ishmael in relation to the number twelve, "As for Ishmael, I have heeded you. I hereby bless him. I will make him fertile and exceedingly numerous. He shall be the father of twelve chieftains, and I will make of him a great nation."

The creation of the world in six days, then, is a declaration that the world is a perfect paragon of natural law, harmonious and whole.[43] However, the story of creation does not end after six days. Rather, in a surprising twist, the narrative persists for one day more: "On the seventh day God finished the work that He had been doing, and He ceased on the seventh day from all the work that He had done" (2:2). Many have protested that the work of creation ended on the sixth day, while the

---

36. Shin Shifra and Jacob Klein, *In Those Distant Days: Anthology of Mesopotamian Literature in Hebrew* (Tel Aviv, 1996), 249.
37. Ibid., 260.
38. Ibid., 269–270.
39. Ibid., 278.
40. Ibid., 288.
41. Ibid., 111–113.
42. Ibid., 372.
43. Menachem Kahana has demonstrated that the sages also used the number six or sixty in a similar fashion. Based on his research, he has suggested that the arrangement of the Mishna into six orders, and within which are sixty tractates, is no coincidence. See Kahana, "The Arrangement of the Orders of the Mishna," *Tarbiz* 76 (2006): 29–40.

seventh day marks the day after creation. The Septuagint, the Samaritan Pentateuch, and the Peshitta, for example, all emend "the seventh day" to "the sixth day," and solve the problem that way, but this change is unconvincing, as the sixth day has already drawn to a close, and focus has shifted to the seventh day.[44] In any case, the Masoretic version demands explanation. One dominant solution, raised by rabbinic literature, is that the concept of rest was created on the seventh day, so that God's work was only truly finished on the seventh day. On the level of *peshat*, the idea that "work" is equivalent to "rest" is problematic, as this verse explicitly refers to the cessation of work, rather than to "rest." It seems that we have no choice but to accept that in this verse, the biblical text deviates from its usual "up to and including" style, and in this case, uses language that is "up to but not including." That is, creation ended on the seventh day, because nothing was created on this day. If this is the case, the question arises as to why the text deviates from its usual style, and deems the seventh day as the final day of creation. This seems to be related to the essential nature of the transition between the numbers six and seven, between the immanent tension of six days of active creation and the conceptual design of a seven-day week. Indeed, to the onlooker, the world seems whole and harmonious, a self-evident world that follows natural law, a natural world that was created in six days. Yet the creation story shows that these natural laws are the product of a supernatural, divine hand. Divine will and wisdom shaped this world, and they explain how it came into being. The story of the world's purpose, of how the world came into being, does not begin with the world itself, but from somewhere beyond, from God, as well as God's will, intentions, and acts of speech. The world was created in six days, and one more. This "extra" day is a sign that this natural law is the result of divine will.

Sabbath, the culmination of the first six days of creation, unparalleled by any other day,[45] brings the narrative to a dramatic climax with its lyrical, festive tone (2:1–3):

44. Gunkel, *Genesis*, 116.

45. Amit correctly notes that the fact that the world was created in seven days does not necessarily entail the sanctity of the seventh day. The model of the "rising number" where the final component is the most special is common in the Bible (and outside

> The heaven and the earth were finished, and all their array.
>
> On the seventh day God finished the work that He had done, and He ceased on the seventh day from all the work that He had done.
>
> And God blessed the seventh day and declared it holy, because on it God ceased from all the work of creation that He had done.

The first two sentences of these verses open with the verb root C-L-H, meaning "finished." The syntactic subject of the first sentence is "heaven and earth," that their creation is complete. The subject of the second sentence is God, who is the One who completed His work on the seventh day, and the next verses refer to Him. The second stage, which also focuses on God, also consists of two sentences in two stanzas. The first stanza focuses on the cessation of the act of creation, or, to be more precise, the cessation of "work," as the text refers to it. This focus is evident enough in the content of these lines, but is further highlighted by the epiphora in this stanza, which serves as a festive refrain: "the work He had done." God finished His work on the seventh day, and on this day, He ceased, "*shavat*." At this point, the definition of Sabbath is negative. It is Sabbath because nothing happened; nothing was created on this day. Some might claim that this description of God's cessation from work is a sly jab at the Babylonian creation epic *Enuma Elish*, where the gods can rest only after they have created humanity to help them with their work.[46]

---

of it), but it still does not mean that the final day is necessarily sacred (Yairah Amit, *Hidden Polemics in Biblical Narrative* [Tel Aviv, 2003], 224–225, and see also Amit, "Creation and the Calendar of Holiness," 18–20). Indeed, the number "seven" in itself symbolizes perfection in the Bible and in the ancient Near East (alongside the number six). See further in Gotthard G. G. Reinhold, ed., *Die Zahl Sieben im Alten Orient: Studien zur Zahlensymbolik in der Bibel und ihrer altorientalischen Umwelt* (Bern, 2008).

46. The role of the human in the second creation narrative is more complex, and some argue that man is characterized as the keeper of God's garden, similarly to the characterization in *Enuma Elish*. See David Jobling, *The Sense of Biblical Narrative: Structural Analyses in the Hebrew Bible* (JSOTSup 39: Sheffield, 1986), vol. 2, 17–43, who even claims that God can be perceived as the "negative character in the story, as He took the human for the upkeep of His garden"; Edward Greenstein, "God's Golem: The

The second stanza infuses the Sabbath with positive content. The verse's opening, "And God blessed," is an indication that this is a new stanza, which imbues the day with its own unique meaning. With this blessing, Sabbath becomes unique unto itself, not just because nothing is created on this day, but because it is a day of blessing and sanctity. Here, blessing and holiness fills the void of cessation. This second stanza mentions only the cessation of work as the reason why the day is so special ("because on it God ceased from all the work of creation that He had done"), rather than as the day's essential definition. The seventh day marks the end of God's work, and at this end, the Sabbath is holy and blessed.

Whether or not Rashbam's claim that the creation narrative was solely designed as an explication of the Sabbath is exaggerated, the six-day division of creation is certainly required in order to lend proper weight to the seventh day. Were it not for the need for narrative momentum, the Creator could have created the world within minutes, or even in an instant. Spread out over a working week, the creation of the world reflects the course of the human workweek, and God's day of rest serves as the basis for every person's rest on this day. This is also reflected in the language of the Ten Commandments (Ex. 20:8–11). The concentric structure of the mitzva of the Sabbath emphasizes the *imitatio Dei* manifest in this commandment:[47]

A. Remember the Sabbath day and keep it holy.

> **B.** Six days you shall labor and do all your work, but the seventh day is a Sabbath of the Lord your God:
>
> > **C.** You shall not do any work – you, your son or daughter, your male or female slave, or your cattle, or the stranger who is within your settlements.

Creation of the Human in Genesis 2," in *Creation in Jewish and Christian Tradition*, ed. H. G. Reventlow and Y. Hoffman (London and New York, 2002), 219–239. Some argue against this, even in regard to chapter 2.

47. On this structure, and the possibility that the mitzva of the Sabbath has a similar structure in *Parashat Va'etḥanan*, see Martin Prudky, "The Two Versions of the Sabbath-Commandment: Structural Similarities," in *Stimulation from Leiden*, ed. H. M. Niemann and M. Augustin (BeAT 54: Frankfurt am Main, 2006), 239–255. He notes further similarities between the two commandments of Sabbath in the Ten Commandments.

B'. For in six days the Lord made heaven and earth and sea, and all that is in them, and He rested on the seventh day;
A'. Therefore the Lord blessed the Sabbath day and hallowed it.

This symmetrical structure generates a parallel between what is required of the people (A-B), to "keep the Sabbath holy" by refraining from any weekday work, and God's course of action during the week of creation (B'-A'). The central axis (C) is the commandment itself, "You shall not do any work." Thus, the working week is a reflection of the week of creation. Like God, people labor for six days, and cease their work on the seventh day. The close affinity between human and God is encouraged by the language of the text. God is said to "rest," even though this verb is more suited to describe human needs after an intense week of work. Through this shared rest, this commandment brings the human celebration of Sabbath closer to the ways of God.[48]

The end of the creation narrative in Genesis is in clear dialogue with the mitzva of Sabbath in Exodus. The law pronounced on Mount Sinai decrees, "Therefore the Lord blessed the Sabbath day and declared it holy," and this harks back to the end of the creation narrative: "And God blessed the seventh day and declared it holy."[49] Through this connection, a person's division of his or her week into productive working time and rest time essentially emulates God's creation of the world, elevating both work and rest. In this sense, Sabbath observance is considered equivalent to all the other mitzvot in the Torah, because the six working days – the time of productivity and creation – form a pattern that echoes the divine rhythm of creation.

The premise that the creation story forms the basis of *imitatio Dei,* so that a person essentially imitates God by working for six days and resting on the Sabbath, also illuminates other difficulties in the text:

48. For another explanation of "God's rest" in light of evolutionary theory, see Malcolm Schrader, "God Rested on the Seventh Day," *JBQ* 41 (2013): 130–134.

49. Some have even argued that the differences between the formulation of the mitzva of Sabbath in the Ten Commandments stemmed from the attempt to connect the mitzva in Exodus with the creation narrative (Gerald Klingbeil, "The Sabbath Law in the Decalogue(s): Creation and Liberation as a Paradigm for Community," *Revue biblique* 117 [2010]: 491–509).

1. I have already hinted that the idea of creation taking place over seven days is somewhat surprising. After all, why is creation a gradual process, when God could have created the world in a few moments? This becomes yet more surprising when a careful reading of the verses reveals that God is active during the day but does not work during the night. This can be extrapolated from the formulaic, "and there was evening and there was morning." Rashbam's reading seems to be the most cogent,[50] that this formula is a continuation of the narrative, rather than a summary of the twenty-four-hour period of day and night that constitutes a whole "day." That is, after light was created on the first day, the narrative goes on to describe the evening of that first day ("and there was evening"), which is followed by the break of the second day ("and there was morning"), which marks the end of the first day, at which point "one day" has passed. According to this reading, night follows day, which concurs with the modern notion of day and night (Sunday night follows Sunday), and contradicts the ruling of the sages that the day begins at sundown (Sunday begins with Saturday night, whereas the night that follows Sunday day is considered Monday night). Rashbam's view seems to provide the most logical analysis of these verses, as well as other verses in the Bible,[51] and its implications for the

---

50. Despite Ibn Ezra's fierce opposition to this interpretation. See Yosef Green, "When Does the Day Begin?" *JBQ* 36 (2008): 81–87.
51. I concur with Milgrom that Ex. 12:28, which states, "In the first month, from the fourteenth day of the month at evening, you shall eat unleavened bread until the twenty-first day of the month at evening," proves that the day usually begins at dawn. Otherwise, adding "at evening" would have been superfluous. This seems to be a unique issue for the Festival of Matzot (which also occurs with Yom Kippur). See Jacob Milgrom, *Leviticus 23–27* (AB: New York, 2001), 1967. On a broader biblical scale, however, the issue is admittedly more complex (for example, the fact that impurity lasts until the evening [Lev. 22:6–7] implies that the day ends at sundown). See more on this complexity in J. Amanda McGuire, "Evening or Morning: When Does the Biblical Day Begin?", *Andrews University Seminary Studies* 46 (2008): 201–214. Effectively, Rashbam's explanation solves another specific difficulty in the creation narrative: Many have questioned how the first day can be summarized, "and there was evening and there was morning," as on this first day, the evening could not have

characterization of God are dramatic, in that God works during the day, ceases at night, and resumes His work the following morning. This description is somewhat unsettling. What of the idea that "the Guardian of Israel neither slumbers nor sleeps" (Ps. 121:4)? However, this too allows humanity to imitate God through the natural rhythm of their lives. God works for six days and rests on the seventh day, and God works throughout the day and ceases to work during the dark of night. This serves as a paradigm for the human working week, and through this pattern, God's creation in His image can emulate and identify with its Creator.

2. No less surprising than the notion of God ceasing work during the night is the intensive repetition of the word "*melakha*," "work," during the description of the seventh day: "On the seventh day God finished the *work* that He had been doing, and He ceased on the seventh day from all the *work* that He had done… because on it God ceased from all the *work* of creation that He had done" (2:2–3). God's creation is not referred to as "work" even once during the first six days of creation, which makes sense, as "work" raises connotations of labor and toil. People may labor and toil, but this can hardly be said to apply to God, and many have commented that this anthropomorphism deviates from the general tone of the chapter.[52] This is anthropomorphism indeed, but rather than a deviation, it is part of the narrative objective. God is characterized as a working man, where for six days He toils away, stopping only at night, and on the seventh day, He rests. The combination of "*asa*," "do," and "*melakha*," "work," also serves to connect this narrative with the mitzva of the Sabbath in Exodus, where it appears twice: "Six days you shall labor *and do all your work*, but the seventh day is a Sabbath of the Lord your God:

occurred before the first day when light and darkness were created (see the medieval commentaries on this verse). According to Rashbam, this is not an issue, as he holds that the beginning of creation began with light – day, and only afterwards the evening began: "and there was evening, and there was morning" (the morning of the next day).

52. See, for example, Westermann, *Genesis*, vol. 1, 170. He also links this to the mitzva of Sabbath.

You shall not *do any work*." As Yairah Amit rightly notes, "The reader of biblical literature, who is familiar with these expressions, cannot read the text in Genesis 2:2–3 without connecting the narrative to the mitzvot of the Sabbath and to the inaction that characterizes this day."[53]

3. The six days of creation functioning as a model for the Israelite working week may also solve another textual conundrum. The name "Sabbath" is entirely lacking from the verses in Genesis, even though the creation narrative is deeply concerned with the naming of concepts that shape and define reality. The creations of each day are named on their respective day, such as "day" and "night," which are created and named on the first day. Yet on the seventh day, there is no naming of the concept known as "Sabbath."[54] It seems that while the seventh day is blessed and sanctified with the world's creation, the special name "Sabbath" is bestowed upon it only when Israel begin to keep the Sabbath. Israel must acknowledge the Sabbath as a holy day in order for the day to be fully realized in all its sanctity, in order to fulfill its essence. This is salient in Exodus, with the descent of manna (Ex. 16). At first, it emerges that Sabbath belongs to God. God rests on the Sabbath, and does not send manna down to Israel: "Today is a Sabbath of the Lord; you will not find it today on the plain. Six days you shall gather it; on the seventh day, the Sabbath, there will be none" (16:25–26). Immediately after, however, Sabbath is also given to the Israelites, "Mark that the Lord has given you the Sabbath; therefore He gives you two days' food on the sixth day.… So the people remained inactive on the

53. Amit, *Hidden Polemics*, 225–226.

54. Some have claimed that this is due to a hidden polemic in the description of the seventh day against Near Eastern pagan rituals that were similar to the name "*Shabbat*." Cassuto and Amit believe that the text does not use the word "*Shabbat*" as it recalls the Mesopotamian *shabbatu* (Umberto Cassuto, "The Sequence and Arrangement of the Biblical Sections," in *Biblical and Oriental Studies*, vol. 1 (Jerusalem, 1973), 7–16; Amit, *Hidden Polemics*, 225–229). Cyrus Gordon is convinced that the text wished to avoid association with the planet Saturn, *Shabtai*, which was worshipped at that time (Gordon, "The Seventh Day," *UF* 11 [1979]: 299–301).

> seventh day" (16:29–30). The seventh day is referred to as "Sabbath" in the context of transferring responsibility for its keeping from God to Israel. Exodus 31 also hints to this transferal of responsibility. It is because "in six days the Lord made heaven and earth, and on the seventh day He ceased from work and was refreshed" (31:17) that Israel must now "keep the Sabbath, observing the Sabbath throughout the ages as a covenant for all time" (31:16). The seventh day is blessed and sanctified at the dawn of time, but its holiness is realized only once Israel begins to observe the seventh day, imitating the Creator through resting. Only then does the seventh day become "Sabbath."

Rashi takes this a step further and explains that the holiness and blessing of the seventh day becomes relevant only when Sabbath leads to an encounter between God and the new nation of Israel. He writes on the words, "Blessed… holy": "He blessed them through the manna, as all week long a portion descended for each person, and twice the amount descended on the sixth day. And He sanctified it with manna, for none descended on that day. This text is written with reference to the future."[55] According to this reading, the Sabbath is blessed and sanctified only once the manna begins to descend for Israel, once Israel learns of the significance of the Sabbath through the patterns of the manna's descent. In the words of Rashi, "This verse is written with reference to the future."[56]

Ibn Ezra offers a different angle. He writes that the blessing of the Sabbath relates to the special qualities of the day itself:

---

55. Rashi on Gen. 1:3. He also connects the continuation of the section about Sabbath in Genesis with the mitzva of Sabbath in the story of the manna: "From all the work of creation that He had done" – the work that would have been done on the Sabbath, He doubled on the sixth day instead" (on Gen. 2:2–3).

56. Radak's interpretation is similar: "And God blessed it and made it holy when He commanded the Israelites to cease work on that day and make it holy. 'And He made it holy' – so that it would be holy and distinct from the rest of the days, because the Israelites cease work on that day. And thus it is the sign between them and God that they are holy through observing the Sabbath, which is testimony that the world was made new, and to inform all that the world is not ancient, for the Blessed God created it from new in six days, and ceased work on the seventh day."

> "And the Lord blessed." The meaning of the blessing is "special additions." On this day, the body is given renewed strength, while the mind's mental and intellectual capacity is increased. "And He sanctified it." He did not do any work on that day, as He did on its counterparts.

Ibn Ezra explains that even before Israel came into the world, Sabbath was a day of blessing and holiness. The special quality of the day is expressed through inaction, by not doing regular weekday work, and this distinction is a fulfillment of its holiness. The blessing that accompanies this day is, to Ibn Ezra, mystical. On the seventh day, the body's physical strength is renewed, and a person's understanding is clearer and deeper than usual.[57]

A third possible direction is that the blessing of the seventh day does not lie in the blessing granted to people, as Ibn Ezra holds, but in the very essence of the day itself. This is reflected in the biblical notion of time, in which the quality of certain times shapes reality, rather than the other way around.[58] This is not expressed in every biblical list of festivals (in fact, there are places which reflect a different perspective),[59] but in the list of festivals in Leviticus 23, the date itself is what defines each day as a "sacred occasion." The "sacred occasions" of the seventh month are sacred because they take place in the seventh month, and their holiness necessitates a cessation from work. It is no coincidence that the list of festivals in Leviticus 23 begins with Sabbath, the first and foremost of the holy days. Its very definition as a holy day goes hand in hand with the prohibition of work.

---

57. This direction was adopted by Westermann, who proved that this is the meaning of the blessing of the seventh day in light of other mentions of the word "blessing" in the chapter, like in the blessing "be fruitful and multiply" to the water creatures and to humanity (Westermann, *Genesis*, vol. 1, 172). See also Amit ("Creation and the Calendar of Holiness," 14–20), who perceives cohesion of the whole chapter through these blessings, and reads the Sabbath as the narrative climax (in contrast to I. L. Seeligmann, "Etiological Elements in Biblical Historiography," *Zion* 26 (1961): 141–169.
58. For different approaches about the formation of time in the Bible and its significance, see U. Simon, *Time and Space.*
59. Such as Ex. 23 and 34, and Deut. 16.

Regardless of whether the holiness of Sabbath is intrinsic to the day, or only fulfilled with Israel's observance, the holiness of the seventh day in the creation story paves the way for the mitzva of the Sabbath later in the Torah. Through this seven-day cycle, a person who works for six days and rests on the seventh is emulating his or her Creator. Before we take this discussion about the importance of *imitatio Dei* through this pattern of the Jewish workweek, I want to point out other complexities in the chapter that can be illuminated through the idea that in the first narrative of the Torah, God is characterized as a person who works for six days and rests on the weekend.

Creation through Speech and Creation through Action

Modern scholars are fiercely divided about the relationship between two modes of creation in this chapter: the creation of the world through speech, and the creation of the world through action. Some hold that these two modes of creation complement each other, while others argue that they pose stark contradictions. Jürg Hutzli, for example, detects two layers in the creation story. The first, more basic story, includes all of creation, and depicts creation through speech, while another partial narrative layer incorporated into the chapter describes God's creation through action.[60] Even if there is no concrete proof of two separate stories being intertwined within a single chapter, the careful reader cannot disregard the presence of two distinct narrative veins and the apparent tension between them.

Let us begin with the creation of light, which is "creation through speech": "God said, 'Let there be light,' and there was light" (v. 3). God's almighty power is manifest in this instant act of creation; to bring

60. Jürg Hutzli, "Tradition and Interpretation in Gen 1:1– 2:4a," *JHS* 10, article 12. This is the prevalent position in classic scholarship; see, for example John Skinner, *A Critical and Exegetical Commentary on Genesis*, 2nd ed. (ICC: Edinburgh, 1930), 8; Maurice Lambert, "A Study of the First Chapter of Genesis," *HUCA* 1 (1924): 3–12; Julian Morgenstern, "The Sources of the Creation Story: Gen 1:1–2:4," *AJSL* 36 (1919/20): 169–212. Rabbi Yehuda Rock adopts this reading, although he formulates it according to Rabbi Mordechai Breuer's "Aspect Theory." See Rock, "Knowledge and Labor in the Creation – Two Aspects of the Creation Story in Chapter 1," *Megadim* 25 (1996): 9–34.

something into existence, all He has to do is express His will. A mere utterance brings something into existence: "Let there be light," and "there was light." This first act of creation is instantly fulfilled through mere speech, so the process of the second act of creation is somewhat surprising: "God said, 'Let there be an expanse in the midst of the water, that it may separate water from water.' *God made the expanse, and it separated the water which was below the expanse from the water which was above the expanse.* And it was so" (vv. 6–7). The verse reads seamlessly if we skip the italicized words, as in, "God said, 'Let there be an expanse...' And it was so." Yet this act of creation also incorporates God's action: "And God made the expanse." The creation of the celestial bodies is even more puzzling: "God said, 'Let there be lights in the expanse of the sky to separate day from night; they shall serve as signs for the set times – the days and the years; and they shall serve as lights in the expanse of the sky to shine upon the earth.' And it was so. *God made the two great lights, the greater light to dominate the day and the lesser light to dominate the night, and the stars*" (vv. 14–16). Here, God "makes" the lights only after the report of their creation through speech, "And it was so," but the repetition is still palpable. This sense of repetition accompanies most of the creation described in this chapter, with the aforementioned exceptions of the creation of light and the exposure of dry land, which occur only through an act of speech: "God said, 'Let the water below the sky be gathered into one area, that the dry land may appear.' And it was so" (v. 9). With the exception of these two creations, the rest of creation contain two descriptions, once following divine speech and a second time following divine action.

I believe that this repetition can be read as part of the biblical anthropomorphism of the Creator, as a way to encourage humanity to follow in His path. Creation through speech is the backbone of this chapter; the verb "said" reverberates throughout the narrative and binds it together from beginning to end. But the idea of creation through speech builds a barrier between God and humanity, between God's creation of the world and human creation in the world. A person cannot create a new entity through speech alone; his words must be fulfilled with actions. To this end, the idea of creation through action is introduced alongside creation through speech. Though God *can* create through speech alone, as is clear from the first creation, the creation of light, divine creation through action accompanies most of God's acts of speech. This structure, of the combination of the verb "said" with the verb "made" or "create," establishes God's omnipotence while simultaneously inviting humanity to emulate its Creator.

The idea of *imitatio Dei*, though, is especially imparted through the mitzva of the Sabbath. The observance of Sabbath retroactively defines a person's week as a week spent following in the ways of the Creator. If a person makes and works and creates, just like God does, why is it that the first six days of the week are recognized as following in the ways of God only with the cessation of work on the seventh day? The answer may lie in the fact that in a comparison between human achievements and divine achievements, human achievements always fall short. Despite the extent of human creativity and wisdom, the disparity between human and God is too wide to bridge. Yet through cessation of work on the seventh day, through passive inaction, a person can be exactly like God, in not doing, just as God is not doing. Only by taking a break from action, from inadequate human ambition, from repeated attempts to achieve something, a person can truly emulate his or her Creator. Whether a person's weekly struggle is to achieve a new revolutionary breakthrough or to put food on the table, the non-action of resting on the seventh day achieves true solidarity with God. Through this shared non-action, the human can aspire to the divine and grow closer to God.

The division of the narrative into days highlights how the first six days lead up to the seventh day as the gravitational center of creation. Six days of work followed by the Sabbath serve as a model for the human working week, of six days of work and a seventh day of rest. By emulating this pattern, and resting on the seventh day, all seven days of the week become a tribute to God and His creation.

Two Parallel Trios of Days: The Celestial Lights

There is a distinct transition between the first and second halves of creation. Some refer to the first three days as "regions," and to the second as "corresponding inhabitants."[61] These names are not fully accurate,

61. Kikawada and Quinn, *Before Abraham Was*, 78.

as the light of the first day can hardly be defined as the "living area" of the lights created on the fourth day. To explain the latter relationship, it makes more sense to focus on the movement of the new entities. Thus, the creations of the first three days are immobile settings, while the later creations have the capacity for motion.

How does the narrative perceive and present the first creations of the second half of creation, the lights? In the ancient world, most pagan cultures worshipped the sun, moon, and stars, and looked to them as deities. Even thousands of years later, the celestial bodies were perceived as living beings. Maimonides' description, based on Aristotle's writings, sufficiently proves this point:

> All the stars and heavenly spheres possess a soul, knowledge, and intellect. They are living, enduring beings who recognize He who spoke and brought the world into being. Each and every one, according to its size and status, praises and glorifies its Creator, like the angels. And just as they recognize the Holy One, blessed be He, they have self-awareness, and they are aware of the angels above them. The stars and sphere possess lesser knowledge than that of the angels, and greater knowledge than that of humans.[62]

Maimonides based these writings on Aristotelian physics, which differentiates between linear movement – which characterizes the natural movement of the bodies that move beneath the lunar sphere – and the circular movement of the celestial bodies, which is not a natural movement and therefore must be the result of will and intent.[63] Within this paradigm, the circular movement of the heavenly spheres indicates that they are conscious beings.

The symmetrical structure of the chapter and the division into days reveals that the lights are given a special place in the biblical account, albeit a completely different one from their role in pagan cultures. The creation of the celestial bodies is the first component of the second half

62. *Mishneh Torah,* "Laws of the Foundations of the Torah," 3:9

63. See Isaac and Klein, "Introduction to the Book of Knowledge: The Thought of Maimonides against the Backdrop of General Jewish Thought," ch. 5, http://www.daat.ac.il/daat/mahshevt/haguto/5-2.htm.

of creation, of moving, living creatures. There is no explicit vivification of the lights, but their inclusion within this group brings them closer to the world of the living.[64]

The special status of the lights, however, is not merely reflected in their position within the narrative structure. The narrative space devoted to the celestial bodies far exceeds that of any other creation, even humanity. This is already evident from a brief count of how many verses are devoted to each creation:

Light – 3
Sky – 3
Dry land – 2
Vegetation – 2
The lights – 5
Water creatures and birds – 3
Land animals – 2
Humanity – 3
The designation of plants as food – 2

The Bible devotes approximately twice as many verses to the creation of the lights as it does to any of the other creations, but the special attention they receive is not merely quantitative. Their creation is arranged in a concentric literary structure (vv. 14–18), a structure far more sophisticated than the depiction of any other creation:

A. God said,

B. "Let there be lights in the expanse of the sky to separate day from night;

C. they shall serve as signs for the set times – the days and the years;

D. and they shall serve as lights in the expanse of the sky to shine upon the earth."

E. And it was so. God made the two great lights, the greater light to dominate the

64. See especially Johannes Meinhold, *Die biblische Urgeschichte: Mose 1–12* (Bonn, 1904), 40.

day and the lesser light to dominate the night, and the stars.

D'. And God set them in the expanse of the sky to shine upon the earth,

B'. to dominate the day and the night, and to separate light from darkness.

A'. And God saw that this was good.

The transition between the first and second half is clear. The structure invites comparison between plan and execution, between divine intent in the first half, and the actual result in the second half. The opening and conclusion of the creation of the lights (A-A') are standard: God speaks, and God approves. In the second parallel components (B-B'), the lights are assigned the task of differentiation. They will separate the day from the night, and they will separate light from darkness. Indeed, the reader has already associated day with light and night with darkness from the first day.

Component C has no parallel, and this omission stands out sharply, given the substantial repetition of the rest of the structure. The lights are created to differentiate between day and night, and to illuminate the earth, and these plans are fulfilled; but do they fail to dictate the set times of the days and years? I believe that this omission reflects that at the time of their creation, the lights did not yet serve as indications of set times. The lights shine upon the earth and differentiate between day and night from the moment of their creation, but they cannot serve as "signs" until people are created. They will hold this significance only once people begin to use the lights to define and determine the calendar ("days and years") and the dates of their festivals ("set times").[65] On the fourth day, before humans walk the earth or gaze upon the sky, this aspect of their creation is not yet fulfilled.

The plan that the lights will hang in the sky and illuminate the earth (D) is carried out precisely (D'). The central component that marks the transition from idea to fulfillment relates the actual creation

65. It seems that "signs" simply means the setting of dates (following Gunkel, *Genesis*, 110, for example) rather than astrological signs, as some propose.

of the lights with the surprising addition of the idea of "*memshala*," "domination," which bursts onto the scene. This word also echoes in the second half of the structure; the lights were intended for "separation" between day and night, but now they "dominate the day and the night" in addition to differentiating between them. Rule and domination are generally associated with humankind ("fill the earth and master it; and rule the fish of the sea"), but here, the lights are also granted authority, even if only on a semantic level: "The greater light to dominate the day and the lesser light to dominate the night" (v. 16), and, "to dominate the day and the night" (v. 18). Elsewhere in Genesis, this root is mostly associated with human rule and domination, such as, "Your longing shall be for your husband, and he shall rule over (*yimshal*) you" (3:16), or, "Shall you rule over us? Will you indeed dominate (*mashol timshol*) us?" (37:8), or, "He has made me a father to Pharaoh, lord of all his household, and ruler (*moshel*) over the whole land of Egypt" (45:8). At least one other instance, however, lends this word a more general sense of responsibility: "And Abraham said to the senior servant of his household, who had charge (*hamoshel*) of all that he owned" (24:2). Presumably, the celestial "domination" functions in this sense, in which their appearance in the sky and the light they cast will determine the passage of day and night.[66]

Yet, the implications of this root are not so easily dismissed. After all, the head of the Egyptian pantheon was the sun god (Ra, Amun-Ra, or Aten/Aton, in his various aspects), who was considered the creator and judge, all-knowing and all-seeing. In Mesopotamia, the sun god (Utu, in Sumerian) was the god of justice, protector of the poor and downtrodden. The Ugaritic sun goddess, Shapash, was associated with the underworld, to the extent that she was considered the "Queen of the Underworld."[67] This pagan fascination with the sun may certainly be in dialogue with certain biblical accounts where the sun is overpowered, such as the plague of darkness, where the sun is blotted out soon before Israel is released from

66. The verses in Psalm 136 can also be understood in this sense, although other readings cannot be ruled out: "The sun to rule by day, His loving kindness is for ever. The moon and stars to rule by night; His loving kindness is for ever" (Ps. 136:8–9).
67. See further in Karel van der Toorn, "Sun," *ABD* 6: 237–239.

Egypt,[68] or Joshua bringing the sun to a halt during battle (Josh. 10:11),[69] or the sign given to Hezekiah, where the shadow recedes backwards on his sundial (II Kings 20:8–11).[70]

The moon also held a central place in ancient pagan cults. The moon god, Sin, was worshipped in ancient Ur and Haran, and his Canaanite counterpart was Yarikh/Yareaḥ/Yaraḥ (vocalization differs, but in any case, the name is linked to the Hebrew word for moon, "*yareaḥ*"). He was believed to have powerful influence over animal and soil fertility.[71] Scholars believe that an ancient Hurrian text describing the union of the moon god with the moon goddess, Nikkal, was a ritual prayer for fertility and family safety.[72]

Ancient belief in the sun and moon is also evident in the Canaanite names of ancient towns, such as Beit Shemesh ("House of the Sun"), or Jericho (derived from "*yareaḥ*," the name of the moon god). Based on the names of towns in ancient Canaan, W. F. Albright concludes that moon worship was prevalent in Canaan in the second century BCE, but diminished somewhat in the first century BCE.[73]

---

68. For a broader discussion, see Jonathan Grossman, "The Structural Paradigm of the Ten Plagues Narrative and the Hardening of Pharaoh's Heart," *VT* 64 (2014): 588–610.
69. Compare to Robert Eisler, "Joshua and the Sun," *The American Journal of Semitic Languages and Literatures* 42 (1926): 73–85. On the reading of Joshua's prayer as a kind of incantation based on the broader connection between the celestial bodies and the battle outcome – without any specific desire to lengthen the day – see John Walton, "Joshua 10:12–15 and Mesopotamian Celestial Omen Texts," in *Faith, Tradition, and History: Old Testament Historiography in Its Near Eastern Context*, ed. A. R. Millard et al. (Winona Lake, 1994), 181–190.
70. Assuming that the movement of shadow reflects a change in the position of the sun. Bustenay Oded suggests that the sun did not move from its axis, and the sign is that in spite of this, the shadow receded (Oded, "Hezekiah's Illness and Isaiah's Wonders," in *Olam HaTanakh: II Kings* [Tel Aviv, 1994], 180). See the differences between the versions in Kings and Isaiah in this context (and other contexts) in Rimon Kasher, "II Kings 20:1–11–Isaiah 38:1–22," *Shnaton* 7–8 (1983–4): 75–89.
71. See further in M. Plessner and J. Licht, *Encyclopedia Biblica*, s.v. "*Yareaḥ*," vol. 3, 837–839.
72. Ronald E. Clements, "*Yareaḥ*," *TDOT* 6: 355–362.
73. W. F. Albright, "Was the Patriarch Terah a Canaanite Moon-God?", *BASOR* 71 (1938): 35–40.

The Bible explicitly grapples with this phenomenon. For example, Deuteronomy 4:19 warns, "And when you look up to the sky and behold the sun and the moon and the stars, the whole heavenly host, you must not be lured into bowing down to them or serving them," and Deuteronomy 17:2–3 states, "If there is found among you … bowing down to them, to the sun or the moon or any of the heavenly host …" Despite these explicit prohibitions, there is evidence that worship of the sun and moon did make its way into Israelite culture, as Jeremiah prophesies: "At that time – declares the Lord – the bones of the kings of Judah, of its officers, of the priests, of the prophets, and of the inhabitants of Jerusalem shall be taken out of their graves and exposed to the sun, the moon, and all the host of heaven which they loved and served and followed, to which they turned and bowed down" (Jer. 8:1–2, and see also Job 31:26–28). This is also clear from the description of Josiah's reform; Josiah removes all the vessels that were used to serve "all the heavenly hosts" from the Temple, and puts an end to the worship of "those who offer sacrifice to Baal, to the sun and moon and stars, and to all the heavenly hosts" (II Kings 23:4–5). From the description in that same chapter, verse 11, a solar cultic ritual seems to have been well developed: "He put down the horses that the kings of Judah had devoted to the sun, from the entrance of the House of the Lord to the chamber of the eunuch Nathan-Melekh, in the precincts; and as for the sun chariots – he burned them with fire." This also seems to be the case in Ezekiel: "There, at the entrance to the Temple of the Lord, between the portico and the altar, were about twenty-five men, their backs to the Temple of the Lord and their faces to the east; they were bowing low to the sun in the east" (Ezek. 8:16).[74]

In light of all this, it seems surprising, even reckless, that the first chapter of Genesis should lend any semblance of authority to the sun and moon. Yet the text still uses this root, with all its connotations of rule and domination. This language challenges the argument that the creation of the lights is a covert polemic against the pagan belief that the

74. The prevalence of these cultic rituals in Israel is hard to determine. See further in J. Glen Taylor, *Yahweh and the Sun: Biblical and Archaeological Evidence for Sun Worship in Ancient Israel* (Sheffield, 1993).

lights themselves were gods. Many support this claim with the observation that the words "sun" and "moon" are absent from the narrative,[75] which is surprising given the gravity of names and naming in this chapter. The refusal to call the "greater light" and the "lesser light" by their names can be read as a belittlement of their importance, as it reduces them to their roles as lights and nothing more.[76] Yet this still fails to address the use of the root M-SH-L – if the biblical creation account seeks to undermine the sun and moon as deities, then why is the expression "dominate" used to describe their role?

I believe that the biblical description of the lights' creation presents an alternative paradigm to the prevalent pagan perception of the lights as gods.[77] The description of their creation by God, and the emphasis on their practical function, topples them from their pedestal. Yet the large amount of narrative space devoted to them, and the surprising use of the root M-SH-L, celebrates, rather than challenges, their importance. Rather than deny the glory of the sun and moon, the text harnesses this glory and characterizes the sun and moon as God's emissaries in the world, preparing the ground for celestial tributes to God's grandeur. Psalms 19:2–7 states:

> The heavens declare the glory of God, the sky proclaims His handiwork....
>
> He placed in them a tent for the sun, Who is like a groom coming forth from the chamber, Like a hero, eager to run his course.

---

75. See, for example, in Gerhard von Rad, *Genesis*, trans. J. H. Marks, 2nd ed. (OTL: London, 1963), 53; Sutzkover, "Name-Giving."

76. Wenham, *Genesis*, 21; Bill T. Arnold, *Genesis* (NCBC: Cambridge, 2009), 42–43; Hamilton, *Genesis*, 127–28; Mathews, *Genesis*, vol. 1, 154. At the same time, the opposite can be suggested. Instead of being called by name, they are replaced with the extremely complementary "two great lights." Cassuto does not see this omission as detrimental in any way, as he holds that it is clear to the reader what celestial bodies are being referred to (Cassuto, *From Adam to Noah*, 45).

77. Taylor makes a similar claim about the creation of the lights (Taylor, *Yahweh and the Sun*), as does Tsumura about the creation narrative in general (Tsumura, *The Earth and the Waters*).

> His rising-place is at one end of heaven, and his circuit reaches the other; Nothing escapes his heat.

Or see Psalm 148:1–3:

> Halleluya! Praise the Lord from the heavens, praise Him from the heights....
>
> Praise Him, sun and moon; praise Him, all shining stars.

It is also worth noting that in Genesis, the root M-SH-L sometimes functions as an expression of secondary authority. Abraham's servant may be in charge of his household, but he is obviously subject to Abraham; Joseph may rule over Egypt, but he is second-in-command, the deputy of Pharaoh. The sun's light is brilliant and life giving, and the moon's glow illuminates the darkness, but they are secondary to the light and power of God. Rather than undermine their power, the biblical text acknowledges the importance of the sun and moon in the ancient world, yet at the same time firmly puts them in their place as God's emissaries, as powerful forces that govern day and night yet remain subject to God along with the rest of His creations. This division emphasizes the importance of the lights, but as we will see, a completely different picture emerges through a different division of the narrative.

Separating Light and Darkness

The act of "separation," so dominant in the creation of the celestial bodies, also supports the narrative's division into two sets of three days. The idea of separation is central to the creation narrative in general, appearing five times (for the sake of comparison, this root does not appear again in the book of Genesis), and some even claim that there is an etymological connection between "*havdala*," "separation," and the verb "*livro*," "to create," which may be associated with "cutting" or "severing" (as Ibn Ezra notes).[78] Others have noted that over the course of the

78. The HALOT dictionary favors this definition, while Ellen van Wolde argues that the verb *bara* in Genesis 1 also means "to differentiate, separate" rather than "to create"

chapter, the act of separation gradually moves from divine to human responsibility.[79] This is correct, but can be more precisely formulated thus: the expression "*havdala,*" "separation," does not feature at all on the third, fifth, and sixth days. While God makes separations again and again in the creation of heaven and earth, tracing the pattern of when these separations occur reveals the complexity of this picture. The act of separation is explicitly mentioned in the creation of light and darkness, when "God separated the light from the darkness" (v. 4), and this leads to the naming of each separate entity, "God called the light Day, and the darkness He called Night" (v. 5). On the second day, during the creation of the sky, the act of separation features repeatedly. In fact, the second day barely involves actual creation, so much as rearrangement of preexisting entities to form new ones. The waters are distilled into two layers, forming the sky and the sea, and again, the act of separation is followed by the act of naming: "God said, 'Let there be an expanse in the midst of the water, that it may separate water from water.' God made the expanse, and it separated the water which was below the expanse from the water which was above the expanse. And it was so. God called the expanse Sky" (vv. 6–8).

The exposure of dry land on the third day is not described with the verb "separate" (although this would certainly be appropriate). On the fourth day, the act of separation appears once again, referring not to God's actions but to the lights' function: "God said, 'Let there be lights

---

(Ellen van Wolde, *Words Become Worlds: Semantic Studies of Genesis 1–11* [Leiden, 1994], 184–200). Indeed, one meaning of *bara* is "to cut," as used in several verses of the Bible, such as, "Go up to the forest and cut it down (*uvereta*) for yourselves there.... It may be forest, but you may cut it down (*uvereto*) to its very ends" (Josh. 17:15,18), and, "Let the assembly pelt them with stones and cut them down (*uvare*) with their swords" (Ezek. 23:47, and possibly 21:24). Some reject this identification, as B-R-A in the sense of "creation" only appears in *qal* and *niphal,* whereas B-R-A in the sense of "cut" appears only in *piel* (Raymond C. Van Leeuwen, "*Bara,*" *NIDOTTE* 1: 728–735). See also Bob Becking and Marjo C. A. Korpel, "To Create, to Separate or to Construct: An Alternative for a Recent Proposal as to the Interpretation of *Bara* in Genesis 1.1–2.4a," *JHS* 10 (2010): article 3, who criticize van Wolde, as well as the discussion in Day, *From Creation to Babel,* 5–6.

79. Tikvah Frymer-Kensky, "Biblical Cosmology," in *Backgrounds for the Bible,* ed. M. O. O'Connor and D. N. Freedman (Winona Lake, 1987), 231–240.

in the expanse of the sky to separate day from night... to separate light from darkness' (vv. 14, 18). In parallel to the absence of the verb on the third day, the verb is absent on the fifth and six days of creation.[80]

The idea of separation functions as a key verb in this narrative, and its significance in Genesis anticipates the themes of Leviticus. There, certain kinds of separation are posed as ritual challenges for the Israelites. Leviticus commands "to separate between the sacred and the profane" (10:10), and "to separate between the impure and the pure, and between the animal that may be eaten and the animal which may not be eaten" (11:47), among other examples. There, too, the notion of separation is posed to Israel as the challenge of imitating God. God began the task of separating "light from darkness," and Israel is laden with the task of following in His footsteps through the act of separation. There, too, another act of separation is introduced, one that is central to biblical thought: the separation between Israel and the nations:

> I, the Lord, am your God who has *separated* you from other peoples. So you shall *separate* the clean beast from the unclean, the unclean bird from the clean. You shall not draw abomination upon yourselves through beast or bird or anything with which the ground is alive, which I have *separated* for you to treat as unclean. You shall be holy to Me, for I the Lord am holy, and I have *separated* you from other peoples to be Mine. (Lev. 20:24–26)

The roots of the concept of separation can be traced to the story of creation, which also influences various aspects of the book of Leviticus' attitude towards animals. God introduces this concept, which then emanates outwards. Both sets of three days begin with an act of separation, but whereas in the first half God is the sole agent of this separation (during the first two days), in the second half the lights are assigned with a task of separation, and from the fifth day, separation is not mentioned at all.

---

80. Cotter makes the interesting observation that during the first three days, separation and naming is central, while in the last three days, creation (*bara*) and blessing is more central, and Sabbath is concluded with the verb "*kidesh*." Cotter, *Genesis*, 19.

This transition, of course, is related to the nature of the creations as the week progresses; the first elements of creation are inherently formed from acts of separation, while the later creations are not elements but "inhabitants" that populate these spaces.

The pattern of these acts of separation thus casts a special light on the celestial bodies:

- Whether creation is divided according to days or divine acts of speech, they are the first creations of the second half of creation, and mark the beginning of creations with "souls," of living beings that move and populate the environments created during the first three days. Even if they are not actually alive, they are presented as "*moshlim,*" "rulers."
- The narrative space and concentric structure of the verses that depict their creation lend them weight and importance within the scheme of creation.
- The task of separation, performed by God Himself in the first half of creation, is then assigned to them, God's emissaries, at the beginning of the second half.

Once again, given the sun and moon's centrality in pagan worship, their elevation in the first chapter of the Bible is still somewhat surprising. This impression, however, is balanced out by a different division of the creation narrative.

THE THIRD DIVISION: THE ROOT B-R-A, "CREATION"

In addition to the narrative divisions according to divine acts of speech and days, another, more subtle division can be detected in the chapter: a division based on the occurrence of the root B-R-A, "to create." In the Bible, only God is described as "creating" in this sense. People do not "create," "*bara*"; they "form," "*yotzer,*" or "make," "*oseh,*" so that the root B-R-A can be defined as a miraculous, *ex nihilo* divine form of creation reserved for God.[81] This definition justifies the idea of a division based on the appearance of this root in the chapter.

81. Again, there is room to debate whether the meaning of the verb *bara* is to create or to separate/cut, as Ibn Ezra on Genesis 1:1 states: "And its meaning is 'to cut' and to

I will introduce this division with a discussion of the second occurrence of the root B-R-A in the chapter, on the fifth day of creation: "God *created* the great sea monsters, and all the living creatures of every kind that creep, which the waters brought forth in swarms, and all the winged birds of every kind. And God saw that this was good" (v. 21). This use of the verb has drawn much attention, given that this is the first occurrence of the verb since the opening verse of the Bible ("In the beginning, God *created*"). Why does it suddenly appear in this verse, when the verb has been absent from the descriptions of all previous creations until this point? There are three likely possibilities:

1. **The creation of the sea monsters**: Many associate this verb with the specific creation of the sea monsters. One example is the *Midrash Lekah Tov (Psikta Zutarta)* on Genesis 1, section 25 (during a discussion why the expression "and it was so" is missing from the creation of the water creatures):

> Another possibility: the three creations where the expression "and it was so" does not appear – heaven and earth, the sea monsters, and man, which are all important creations – all contain the root B-R-A. Because they contain "*bria*," "creation," the expression "and it was so" would be superfluous, as it says, "For He said, and it came to be; He commanded, and so it stood" (Ps. 33:9).

According to the midrash, the sea monsters were important creations that were described with the verb "*vayivra*." Nahmanides goes in a similar direction:

> Due to the sheer size of these creatures, which were many leagues long – the Greeks record that they were up to five hundred leagues long – our sages also spin tales of them (Bava Batra 73b) to explain why the verb *bara* is used in their creation, for God

place a distinct border." See further in Hayes, "Whose World?" This definition has no bearing on our discussion, however, as either way, the verb has a special meaning in our chapter.

> invented them from nothing, as I defined the meaning of the word "creation." The same applies to humanity, for its knowledge and intellect is also an exceptional creation that came out of nothing.[82]

Moreover, the very mention of the sea monsters is intriguing in itself, as they could easily have been included as part of the water creatures. Ibn Ezra takes note of this and explains, "God created the great sea monsters – He mentioned them because they are creations of such magnitude, as written in God's words to Job."

This approach was developed by Cassuto, and many have adopted his argument, that this conspicuous addition is a polemic against other Near Eastern creation stories. Cassuto makes special mention of Canaanite Ugaritic epics that describe the fierce battle between ferocious sea monsters and the Canaanite god Baal. Equally worthy of notice is the Babylonian creation epic *Enuma Elish,* which relates the god Marduk's triumph over the goddess Tiamat, who takes the form of a giant sea monster. The specific mention of sea monsters may well be a polemic subversion of these traditions (and see Is. 27:1 as well):

> It is as though the Torah said, in effect: Far be it from any one to suppose that the sea monsters were mythological beings opposed to God or in revolt against Him; they were as natural as the rest of the creatures, and were formed in their proper time and in their proper place by the word of the Creator, in order that they might fulfill His will like the other created beings.[83]

---

82. Nahmanides on Gen. 1:21. See also Yehuda Kiel, *Daat Mikra: Genesis* (Jerusalem, 1997), vol. 1, 21, who claims that *bara* refers specifically to the sea monsters, and should be read in parallel to the *bara* of humanity, as just as humanity is special given its creation in the image of God, sea monsters are also special, due to their monstrous size.

83. Cassuto, *From Adam to Noah,* 50–51, and see also Walter Vogels, "'And God Created the Great Tanninim' (Gn 1:21)," *Science et esprit* 63 (2011): 349–365. On theomachy in the Bible in general, see T. L. Penton, "Differing Approaches to the Theomachy Myth in Old Testament Writers," in *Studies in Bible and the Ancient Near East, Presented to Samuel E. Loewenstamm on His Seventieth Birthday,* ed. Y. Avishur and J. Blau (Jerusalem, 1978), 337–381.

Grintz does not read the mention of sea monsters as a polemic against pagan creation stories. Rather, he explains:

> The great sea monsters cannot be included as part of the fish in the sea, as most fish are small, and the text points this out. Moreover, their forms of reproduction are completely different from each other: sea monsters give birth, while fish come from eggs. Sea monsters, therefore, are a 'unique kind.'[84]

2. **An introduction to all the water creatures mentioned in the verse**: Some hold that the verb *vayivra*, "and He created," at the beginning of the verse refers to all the creations in that verse, and is not restricted to the sea monsters. Radak, for example, writes:

   > It says, "And God created," because there is no natural force in the water that could produce living creatures without God's help, so together with the nature that He granted them, the creatures were formed out of both of them. Therefore, it says, "And God created." It is a fact that in the watery depths far from land there are no fish, for water alone does not have the power to sustain living creatures, as they contain no food from the land, or plants or rocks close to the land, or any food that has fallen from fishermen or sailors who travel by ship. No fishermen will enter such places, for no boat can reach there – the fishermen who venture close to those places know that there are no fish there or anything moving, and the sea is very stormy there.[85]

3. **An indication of the beginnings of life**: Based on Radak's reading, the verb *vayivra* may serve to mark the beginning of life, beginning with the water creatures, whose creation was dependent upon special divine intervention. The verb *vayivra* signifies not only the beginning of the fifth day, but the beginning of a new degree of life.

84. See Yehoshua Grintz, *The Book of Genesis: Its Uniqueness and Antiquity* (Jerusalem, 1983), 49.
85. Radak on Gen. 1:21.

> From this point, all new creations are living beings, with water creatures and birds created on the fifth day, and land creatures created on the sixth. The Malbim may already have alluded to this reading in his commentary,[86] but Herbert Ryle states this explicitly: "Observe the use of the word 'create' (*bara*). It signalizes a new departure of the divine work, when the principle of animal life (*nefesh*) is first communicated on earth, and living animals are formed."[87]

This reading has wide implications for the structure and division of the chapter. In order to understand its full significance, let us turn to the first appearance of the verb "*bara*" in the story, the very first steps of this primordial journey: "In the beginning, God *created* the heavens and the earth" (v. 1). Given that the word "*bereshit*" is in a construct state – literally meaning, "in the beginning *of*" – various interpreters have sought to fill this gap. The beginning of what? Rashi suggests that the next word, "*bara*," should not be understood as a past tense verb ("created"), but as part of a dependent clause leading up to the main part of the sentence, "Let there be light." According to Rashi, the first verses reads, "At the beginning of God's creation of heaven and earth, when the earth was unformed and void … God said, 'Let there be light.'"[88] Nahmanides was one of the first to comment that this reading would imply that neither water nor land were actually created, as the land was not created on the third day, but only exposed.[89]

86. As Malbim writes on Gen. 1:21:

    > The questions: Why does it say, "And God created," if the term *bria* refers to *ex nihilo* creation, which is not stated about land animals…. We already explained that *bria* denotes *ex nihilo* creation, while animals were created from something, as it says, "Let the waters bring forth." However, water itself does not have the power to produce living creatures, for their living spirits are not from the actual water, so this creation had one aspect of *ex nihilo* creation by God alone…. Thus it states, "And God created," as the God of spirits created spirits out of nothing.

87. Herbert Edward Ryle, *Genesis* (Cambridge Bible for Schools and Colleges: Cambridge, 1921), 54.
88. See also Skinner, *Genesis*, 12–14; Ephraim A. Speiser, *Genesis*, AB 1 (New York, 1962), 12–13; Jon D. Levenson, *Creation and the Persistence of Evil: The Jewish Drama of Divine Omnipotence* (New Jersey, 1994), 121.
89. And indeed, some adopted this reading. For example, Menachem Haran claims that the narrative relates to three elements as if they had always existed, and God

Rashi's reading is not convincing, as this form of the root B-R-A is extremely rare, and indeed, not a single ancient translation understood the first verses in this sense. Unlike Rashi, most interpretations read *bereshit* as an independent phrase, although there are at least three variations of this interpretation:

1. Nahmanides sees the first verse as a statement that God first created heaven and earth *ex nihilo* as basic "primordial matter" (following Plato, as opposed to Aristotle, in this respect), whereas the rest of the chapter describe how God works with this matter to form the rest of creation.[90] The advantage of this reading is that it explains the source of the basic material God uses for creation (as opposed to Rashi, whose reading implies that water, earth, and darkness were never actually created), but its disadvantage lies in the subsequent understanding of the relationship between the first verse and the second day of creation. Heaven and earth are separated only on the second day, and this separation is crucial to their definition; indeed, they are named only on the second day. What is the meaning of their creation before the differentiation of the upper waters from the lower waters?
2. A bold new reading in recent years was proposed by Naftali Tur-Sinai (who also shows that he is not the first to make this suggestion). He holds that the first verse does not refer to "*shamayim*," "heaven," but rather to "*mayim*," "water." The actual creation of heaven on the second day is preceded by the creation of water, whose separation results in sky and water. This reading goes, "In the beginning, God created the waters and the land."[91] This reading is similar to that of

---

used them to create the world, the first being "the land" (which was unformed chaos prior to creation), the second being "darkness" (which is first mentioned as an actual substance rather than as a lack of light), and the third being "water" (primordial groundwater which covered everything). See Haran, "The Heavens and the Earth," *Olam HaTanakh: Genesis* (Tel Aviv, 1982), 16–17.

90. Rabbi Joseph Bekhor Shor also follows this reading. See also Brevard S. Childs, *Myth and Reality in the Old Testament* (London, 1962), 31–43; Wenham, *Genesis*, 11–13; Day, *From Creation to Babel*, 6–8.

91. Naftali Tur-Sinai, *Language and the Book* (Jerusalem, 1950), 197.

Nahmanides, as here too the first verse describes the creation of primordial matter – in this case, solid and liquid matter.[92] Yet this reading is difficult to accept. Not one ancient version of the text supports this omission, and "heaven and earth" is a classic biblical word pair, unlike "water and land" (with few exceptions, such as the first chapter of Jonah). Moreover, the expression "heaven and earth" at the beginning of the narrative forms an *inclusio* with the narrative conclusion, which makes this change even less likely. The first verse of Genesis 1 states, "In the beginning, God created the heavens and the earth," and is bracketed by the first verse of Genesis 2, "And the heaven and earth were finished, and all their hosts."

Nonetheless, we can adopt Tur-Sinai's reading without changing the text. The word *shamayim* may have a fluid meaning throughout the chapter.[93] The dialogue between the words *mayim* and *shamayim* is undeniable. *Shamayim* can even be broken up into "*sham-mayim*," "there, *sham*, is water." At first, *shamayim* contains water, as opposed to the land, but as God separates the upper waters from the lower waters, the word *shamayim* may take on the more specific meaning of "sky." As God introduces more precise order in creation, the meaning of the word *shamayim* is honed as well, reflecting the gradual arrangement of primordial matter.

3. I find Rabbi David Zvi Hoffmann's suggestion the most convincing (the roots of which can be found in Rashbam, and one many modern scholars have adopted as well). That is, the first verse is a general heading – a brief synopsis – of creation as a whole, which is then narrated in detail over the course of the chapter.[94] The creation story begins with a general introduction to "the creation

---

92. This reading was adopted by Itzik Peleg, although he claims that the addition of the letter *shin* was not an error but a deliberate attempt to downplay open polemics against Mesopotamian creation epics (Peleg, "In the Beginning, God Created Water and Earth," *Beit Mikra* 41 [1996]: 153–167).

93. As proposed by Itamar Eldar in a lecture given during Herzog College's annual week of Bible study lectures, Alon Shvut, summer of 2012.

94. For example, S. R. Driver, *The Book of Genesis* (Westminster Commentaries: London, 1916), 3; James Barr, "Was Everything That God Created Really Good? A Question in

> of heaven and earth," and then the story begins with the creation of light. This reading, however, like Rashi's, does not describe the actual creation of water and dry land.

How much narrative does this introduction span? Whether we adopt Nahmanides' or Tur-Sinai's reading, and especially if we adopt Hoffmann's, it remains to determine whether the creation story is one long narrative, under the title of, "In the beginning, God created heaven and earth," or whether there comes a point where the heaven and earth have already been established. The first new stage in the narrative seems to take place on the fifth day, with the creation of the celestial bodies. Rabbi Joseph Bekhor Shor describes this using vivid imagery:

> This is like a person who wishes to build a house and prepares all the necessary building materials, builds his house and sets everything in place, and then sees to its movable items. In this way, the Holy One, blessed be He, took care of all the necessary building materials on the first day and set the sky in place on the second day, providing it with some of the water to rain down upon the earth to make it grow. On the third day, He set the water to one side as a place for the fish and sea monsters, and from there He drew out rivers and springs into the dry land to moisten the earth and to provide water for all His creations. He set the dry land to one side, and He brought forth grass and trees from the dry land for the needs of His creations, for food and aesthetic enjoyment, like a person who plans out and shapes the area of his home so that it will be a pleasure to walk around and live there. On the fourth day, he hung lights in it so that His creations would be able to see, as one opens up windows in his home for light. *And after He finished constructing the house itself,* on the fifth and sixth days He created fish and birds and creeping things and domesticated

---

the First Verse of the Bible," in *God in the Fray: A Tribute to Walter Brueggemann*, ed. Tod Linafelt and Timothy K. Beal (Minneapolis, 1998), 55–65; Horst Seebass, *Genesis I: Urgeschichte (1,1–11,26)*, 3rd ed. (Neukirchen-Vluyn, 2009).

> and wild animals like the movable items inside a house, which can be moved back and forth.
>
> Note that from the first to the fifth day, you find neither the word "form," "*yetzira,*" nor "creation," "*bria,*" since on the second, third, and fourth days He dealt with and assigned places to what He had created on the first day. But on the fifth and sixth days He made movable items.... And because the world itself was completed on the fourth day, our sages said, "One should not complete something on the fourth day, as when the Holy One, blessed be He, finished His world on the fourth day, He did not begin again afterwards, so one who completes something on the fourth day has the custom of postponing the start of something else."[95]

Bekhor Shor compares the world's creation to building a house: the house itself was built during the first four days, while the "movable items," the inhabitants, were created on the fifth and sixth days. Days one to four can be seen as one unit, while the creation of water and land animals can be considered a separate unit. As Bekhor Shor himself notes, this division is based on the use of the verb "*bara*" in the narrative.[96] Heaven and earth are created in verses 1–19, while the next instance of the verb root B-R-A introduces a new unit. If so, however, then the second unit will conclude, and a new unit will begin, when the verb *bara* appears once more.

The verb *bara* appears a third time with the creation of humanity. The creation story can thus be divided into three parts: the creation of the world itself, the creation of animals, and the creation of people. Note that the root B-R-A appears three times in a single verse (v. 27), in bold

---

95. On the ecletic custom not to conclude something on Wednesday, see the Zohar on *Parashat Pinḥas*; *Shulḥan Arukh, Yoreh De'ah,* "Laws of Sorcery," 179:2; Responsa *Siaḥ Yitzḥak* (by Rabbi Yitzhak Weiss, who was murdered in the Holocaust), 414, which cites additional sources.

96. Behkor Shor himself includes the verb *yatzar* in his discussion, but this is not justified, as this verb does not appear at all in the first chapter of Genesis, but is first used to describe humanity's creation in chapter 2. It is problematic to draw any conclusions from its absence in the first chapter.

celebration of the birth of humanity: "And God *created* man in His image / in the image of God He *created* him / male and female He *created* them."

The centrality of humanity is highlighted through this intense, lyrical repetition, especially given the sparing use of the root in what is, after all, the *creation* narrative. The unique quality of humanity is also expressed in its designation as the ruler of all of creation (vv. 26, 28), and above all, in the description that man and woman were created in the image of God. Many interpretations tackle the meaning of this phrase, but all agree that it points to the special closeness between humanity and its Creator.

Excuse the comparison, but the description of man created in God's image recalls Bill Bryson's observation about Shakespeare in his biography of the celebrated playwright. He determines that the various famous portraits of Shakespeare are not authentic, and we therefore have no idea what he really looked like. Yet, because these portraits nevertheless became so famous, the "paradoxical consequence is that we all recognize a likeness of Shakespeare the instant we see one, and yet we don't really know what he looked like."[97]

Despite religious emphasis on God's formlessness, a spark of the divine image is reflected in the human figure. God's form and appearance – or lack thereof – remains a complete mystery, yet the reader is invited to recall God when he or she encounters the human form. Recognized by all, yet truly known to none, as Bryson writes, "He is at once the best known and least known of figures,"[98] albeit about the second, rather than the first, best-selling author in history.

Humanity's special status can also be recognized through the fact that in this chapter, God creates man and woman *ex nihilo*, not from any other secondary material. The water creatures are formed out of the water ("let the waters bring forth swarms of living creatures"), and land animals spring forth from the land ("let the earth bring forth…"), while God Himself creates the human by Himself, out of nothing.[99] Avraham Shammah points out that humanity's unique connection with God is

97. Bill Bryson, *Shakespeare: The World as a Stage* (London, 2007), 7.

98. Bryson, ibid.

99. Gunkel, *Genesis*, 112.

reflected in their blessing of fertility. While the water creatures are blessed by, "God blessed them, saying, 'Be fruitful..." (v. 22), the blessing to humanity opens with, "And God blessed them and said *to* them, 'Be fruitful..." (v. 28). The potential for dialogue between God and humanity, for conscious listening to God's word, glimmers in this blessing.[100] Another hint to humanity's special status lies in God's use of the plural form prior to its creation: "Let us make man in our image, after our likeness" (v. 26). Many a quill has splintered over the jarring use of the plural form in this verse, and there are far too many interpretations to summarize here, but the vast majority of readings fall under one of four categories:

1. Some claim that God is presented as holding counsel with His angels (Rashi, Rashbam, Ibn Ezra, and many modern scholars).[101] The idea of a "Heavenly Court" features in several biblical texts (II Kings 22; Job 1), so there is room to claim that this is alluded to without explicit mention. According to this approach, God takes counsel with His angels before the creation of humanity, a unique precursory act that anticipates the importance of this creation. Unanimous consent of all the heavenly hosts is required before the creation of a being that may challenge or compete with them.[102]
2. In contrast to my suggestion that there are no partners in the creation of humanity, and no use of any primordial matter in

100. Avraham Shammah, "*Parashot* of Revelation: Theological Studies and Reflections," in *People of Faith and Biblical Criticism*, ed. Y. Brandes, T. Ganzel and C. Deutsch (Jerusalem, 2015), 357. Rabbi Joseph B. Soloveitchik writes similarly: "Through the dialogue, God addresses Himself to man; God confronts man and speaks to him, and through this conversation it begins suddenly to dawn upon man who he is" (Soloveitchik, *Family Redeemed* [New York, 2000], 99).

101. Such as in A. Alt, "Gedanken über das Königtum Jahwes," in vol. 1 of *Kleine Schriften zur Geschichte des Volkes Israel* (Munich, 1953), 345–357; Gunkel, *Genesis*, 112. According to this reading, there is some similarity (even if only linguistic) between the description of the creation of humanity in Genesis and the description of the creation of humanity in *Enuma Elish*, where the gods seek counsel with each other prior to its creation. Ḥizkuni even claims that because only God creates and God first seeks counsel with the Heavenly Court, the verb *bara* is not yet used, as this verb does not even apply to angels.

102. Weinfeld, "God the Creator," 115–116.

this chapter, Nahmanides claims that the plural refers to God's cooperation with the earth – as described, of course, in chapter 2. Others suggest that this refers not only to earth but to all the elements, which all join together to create humanity (this was suggested by Radak, citing his father).

3. One prevalent reading is that God uses "the royal we" (compare this use of the *pluralis majestatis* to Ezra 4:18; I Maccabees 10:19). As the Tosafists express in this context: "Heretics claim that the use of the plural suggests multiple deities, but this is nonsense: *use of the plural is convention*, as it goes on to say, God created man in His image – he was the only one in creation."[103] Rabbi Samson Raphael Hirsch also supports this reading and adds that the use of the "royal we" is usually an indication that the ruler is speaking on behalf of, and for the sake of, the wider public, hinting that here the narrative tone of the chapter shifts to show that the whole world, and all of reality, willingly, necessarily comes together to bring humanity into existence, for it is humanity that will rule over the world and be responsible for universal harmony.[104]
4. Others have proposed that given that the form of the name "*elohim*" is used in both the singular or the plural (see, for example, Gen. 20:13; 35:7; Ps. 68:25), there is nothing unusual about the verb being in plural form, and it is purely an expression of the scene's festive tone.

These interpretations each have certain merit, yet I think that the use of the plural here serves a different purpose. The best way to explore the meaning of the plural verb is to consider it in its wider context, in

103. The *Tosafot* commentary *Hadar Zekenim* on Gen. 1:26. Saadia Gaon also proposes this, as Ibn Ezra cites. Some reject this possibility with the claim that the 'royal we' is not found elsewhere in the Bible, with the exception of the aforementioned source in Ezra (Westermann, *Genesis*, vol. 1, 145), as this custom only began in the Persian Era (Gunkel, *Genesis*, 112). Nonetheless, this unique style still invites more unusual readings.
104. Rabbi Samson Raphael Hirsch on Gen. 1:26.

comparison with other similar instances within this literary section (Genesis 1–11). God refers to Himself in the plural in two other places:

- And the Lord God said, "Now that the man has become like one of us, knowing good and evil, what if he should stretch out his hand and take also from the Tree of Life and eat, and live forever!" (3:22).
- "Let us, then, go down and confound their speech there, so that they shall not understand one another's speech" (11:7).

These verses may influence our understanding of the verse at hand in two ways. Firstly, there is no explicit mention of angels in either verse (although the Midrash adds them in both cases), and these episodes are certainly not references to the earth or to other elements. Secondly, while the use of majestic tone in the verse in chapter 1 is certainly self-evident, this is not the case in the two other instances. Why does God use the plural when expressing fear that mortal man may eat from the Tree of Life and become immortal, and why does He do so in the Tower of Babel story?

There is a theme common to the creation of humanity, the expulsion from Eden, and the Tower of Babel: all three verses describe an unusual encounter between the human and the Divine. In a description that is almost antithetical to biblical thought, the creation story has humanity described as being created in God's image. Likewise, just before Adam and Eve are banished from the Garden of Eden, God expresses concern that by eating from the Tree of Life, humans can become immortal like God. And, a similar fear rears its head in the story of the Tower of Babel, when humanity uses its creative powers to do as it pleases, and God descends to limit this power. In the words of Walther Eichrodt, the plural form of "our image, in our likeness" is a safety barrier that the singular form of "My image, in My likeness" fails to provide; the plural form serves to blur the "altogether too narrow" connection between the human and the Divine.[105]

---

105. Walther Eichrodt, *Theology of the Old Testament*, trans. J. A. Baker, vol. 1 (Philadelphia/London, 1961), 125.

The use of the plural in the two other narratives mentioned support this reading: the plural form distances the human from the Divine in these primordial narratives when the human hovers all too close to the Divine.[106] Humanity may be created in God's image, but for God to declare, "in My image, in My likeness," would be far too close for comfort. The plural form keeps God safely locked behind multiple doors; humans must still address the Creator using *vous*, not the familiar *tu*.

The other side of this coin is that this obscure, distancing use of the plural is an indication of the theological minefield that lurks beneath. Humans, hints the text, are unique creations indeed, so unique that it may be all too easy to forget who is in charge. "In our image, after our likeness" is definitely an expression of closeness to God, in the sense of, "You have made him little less than divine" (Ps. 8:6). The human proximity to the Divine is consistent with the portrait of humanity presented in these verses, whose creation is marked with threefold repetition of the root B-R-A to distinguish him from everything else. It is worth adding that this proximity is unique to chapter 1. A different portrait of the Divine-human relationship emerges from the story of Eden, where to "be like God" (3:5) is presented as a fatal sin. In the first chapter, it is God who wills this closeness, while in the following chapters, "being like God" is a deadly temptation that violates the divine will.[107]

Let us summarize the objective that emerges from this division. The first unit is devoted to the "creation" of heaven and earth, from light until the lights, while the second unit consists of the creation of living things, from water creatures to land animals, and the third unit focuses on the creation of humanity. This division has several implications, but I wish to point out two of them: one concerns the status of the lights, and the second, the status of humanity.

According to our previous divisions, the lights are the first creation of the second half of created things, which highlights their

106. Eichrodt (ibid., 121) claims that the special status of humanity is also expressed in chapter 2, especially given the phrase "the breath of life," which only describes humanity, as opposed to "living creature," which describes both people and animals.

107. Patrick D. Miller, *Genesis 1–11: Studies in Structure and Theme* (JSOTSup 8: Sheffield, 1978), 21.

important role. This final division, in contrast, challenges their importance. The key verb *bara is* mentioned for the second time only after the celestial bodies are hung in the sky. Only living creatures are included within this degree of creation, and unlike prevalent pagan beliefs, the sun and moon are not living beings with agency, will, or free movement. They are merely forms of lighting, hung in the house before the inhabitants move in. Moreover, their creation is postponed until the fourth day, as if lacking priority in the processes of creation.

The more crucial balance achieved by this division relates to the status of humanity. Here, too, this division serves as a foil to the effect of previous structures. Despite the humbling fact that humans and animals are created on the same day, this division groups water animals and land animals together under the same "*bara*," while humans are awarded their own unit, their own expression of "*bara*." In fact, the root is even repeated three times, elevating humanity to a far higher status than other creatures.

The first creation narrative, the first chapter of Genesis, encourages three parallel, overlapping structures. Different contours emerge simultaneously, forming different patterns from the same text all at once. These iridescent patterns may confuse the eye, yet there is no other way to express the complexity of reality. Are the celestial bodies creations like any other, or do they have a unique degree of importance, controlling time through their illumination of space? Are they to be eschewed as pagan deities, or honored as emissaries of God's glory?

More importantly, these different patterns reflect the ambivalence of humanity's place in the world, of its essence and meaning. Biologically, the human is a land mammal like any other, created on the same day as monkeys and lizards and cows, "For the fate of man is the fate of cattle, the same fate awaits them both.... The preeminence of man over beast is nothing" (Eccl. 3:9). Yet the biblical text is not calculated to reduce a person to this bleak perspective of human life, for this is not the only division prompted by the text. The text can be divided into days, but it can also be divided into units of "creation," based on the verb "*bara*." According to this division, humanity is awarded its own place, with the verses thrice emphasizing that humanity was "created," precisely in the image of God. While human cells appear no different from animal cells under the microscope, the text shouts out that man and woman were created with a spark of the Divine, in His image and after His likeness, that humanity is too unique to share this key verb with any other creation. Living between these two structures, balancing on the taut line between human dignity and human lowliness, a person must find equilibrium between humble recognition of his or her biological, physical, and animal needs, and celebration as the only creation created in the image of God. The human's superiority over the animal is an essential component of biblical thought, and it begins with the basic, bold idea that humanity was created in the image of God. This is true for every human, not just kings[108] or just select individuals on a higher spiritual plane. Common to every human, unique to humanity, the verb "*bara*" is humanity's burden and humanity's gift.

108. In the ancient Near East, and especially in Egypt, kings were often considered deities, based on their power and their personal status. The definition of every person as being created in God's image serves to equalize all ranks of humanity, and some justifiably saw this as a humanistic revolution, such as Annette Schellenberg, "Humankind as the 'Image of God'," *TZ* 65 (2009): 97–115. She rightly comments that the idea that humans are created in God's image grants them superiority, not over other humans – as is presented in ancient literature – but over animals. See further discussion in Joshua Berman, "'Who in His Goodness Renews the Act of Creation' – Parallels and Differences Between Bereshit Chapters 1 and 8," *Megadim* 9 (1989): 9–14.

Growing Up in Eden (Chs. 2–3)

How can we reconcile the first two chapters of Genesis? After six days of creation and a seventh day of rest, after the lights have been hung in the sky, trees and greenery carpet the land, and humanity has been created in God's image, the reader is suddenly told that man does not yet walk the earth and the grass of the field has not yet sprouted (2:5). Commentators and scholars have grappled with this question for thousands of years, and their explanations can be divided into two main approaches:

1. **General and specific:** According to this view, the first creation account is a general overview of creation as a whole, while chapter 2 focuses on the detailed process of certain creations.

    - Rashi, for example, argues that the second chapter describes the sixth day of creation in detail, with special focus on the creation of humanity. This entails the explanation that on the third day, as described in chapter 1, vegetation was created but it had yet to sprout and push its way up through the earth as "there was no man to work the soil" (2:5).

- Nahmanides holds that the "grasses of the field" do not refer to the vegetation created on the third day but to the crops that humans grow. The vegetation of chapter 1 grows wild, while chapter 2 refers to agriculture.
- Rabbi Tuvia ben Elazar (of the eleventh century), author of *Midrash Lekah Tov*, considers chapter 2 a detailed account of the third and sixth days, which focuses on vegetation and humanity.[1]
- Rabbi David Zvi Hoffmann makes a similar claim: "After the creation of humanity has been related in general, now the text focuses in detail on how the first couple was created, where they lived, what they ate, and what happened to them."[2] This reframes chapter 2 in a different light; it is not a creation account but the story of the first human couple. For example, he reads the biblical statement "when no shrub of the field was yet on earth and no grasses of the field had yet sprouted, because the Lord God had not sent rain upon the earth and there was no man to work the soil" as a description of the specific patch of earth that God uses to create humanity. The world is already blooming with trees and grass, as it has been from the third day of creation, but the first human is created from virgin soil that seed or sprout has never broken.[3]

2. **Two parallel accounts:** According to this approach, the first two chapters of Genesis present two separate accounts of creation, and the second narrative does not refer back to the first. Therefore, not only is there no need to reconcile the two descriptions, but the reader is faced with the challenge of reading each narrative in its own right in order to determine the objective of each separate account. There are also different formulations of this approach:

---

1. This is apparent from his comment on the verse: "No shrub of the field was yet on earth – this was on the third day" (*Midrash Lekah Tov*).
2. Hoffmann, *Genesis* (Bnei Brak, 1969), vol. 1, 52.
3. Ibid., 59–62.

- The prevalent view in modern biblical research sees chapters 1 and 2 as two separate accounts from two different sources, which present two different theological views.
- Rabbi Soloveitchik, Rabbi Breuer, Robert Alter, and others all express a variation of the opinion that these are two separate creation stories that reflect two parallel, necessary perspectives of creation.[4] In the words of Leon Kass, "The two stories in fact complement each other and form part of a coherent whole."[5] The complexity of creation cannot be conveyed through a single story; man experiences the world around him in two different ways. The first creation story focuses on the perfect, natural world, on heaven and earth, on the harmony of the cosmos, while the second story portrays human fragility, the agony of birth, the struggle of earning one's bread, and the imminence of death.
- Pamela Reis proposes reading the parallel accounts as a kind of *Rashomon* – a tale told from different perspectives. The first account is told from the perspective of God, while the second account is told from the human perspective.[6]

The following discussion is based on the premise that the first two chapters of Genesis are parallel accounts, in which the first describes the creation of the cosmos, and the second documents the birth of humanity, the birth of history, the birth of the "story" of heaven and earth, but not its technical creation. Each story also contains traces of the other perspective, but the central axis – the paradigm – of each story is completely different. This is reflected in the first two of the seven special blessings that celebrate marriage: the first blessing praises God for "creating" the world, "Who has created *all* for His glory," while the second thanks God for "forming *mankind*."

Based on this premise, the information related in one account cannot be used to interpret the other. For example, the relationship

4. See Robert Alter, *The Art of Biblical Narrative* (New York, 1981), 141–147.
5. Leon Kass, *The Beginning of Wisdom: Reading Genesis* (New York, 2003), 56.
6. Pamela Tamarkin Reis, "Genesis as *Rashomon*: The Creation as Told by God and by Man," *Bible Review* 17 (2001): 26–33.

between the "male and female" created in chapter 1 has no bearing on their relationship in chapter 2, because each narrative is set in a different context and presents a different facet of reality. The double narratives present two different, parallel aspects of reality, and being parallel, they never meet. In one account, the Creator is referred to as "God," while the second uses His unique name, the Tetragrammaton. To be precise, the stories never meet on a philosophical-literal plane, but in everyday life, we experience both worlds simultaneously. Rain falls because water from the ocean evaporates and forms clouds, but rain also falls because God sends rain to moisten the earth when His people obey His word.

There is, however, a certain textual link between chapter 1 and chapter 2: "These are the *toledot* of heaven and earth when they were created" (2:4). Does this verse conclude the first account, or introduce the second? This debate can be traced back to the medieval commentators. Rashi writes, "[This refers to] the events mentioned above," concluding the first account.[7] As this verse refers to "heaven and earth" in general, then Rashi's reading is consistent with his claim that the second account focuses on the sixth day of creation.[8] Many modern scholars favor this approach, and claim that the second creation narrative begins in the middle of verse 4, "When the Lord God made earth and heaven, when no shrub of the field was yet on earth..." Indeed, the word "*toledot*," which is derived from the root Y-L-D, to bear or give birth, is consistent with the themes of the first account, where heaven and earth themselves "give birth" to the rest of creation, in such verses as, "The earth brought forth vegetation: seed-bearing plants of every kind" (1:12), "Let the waters bring forth swarms of living creatures" (1:20), "Let the earth bring forth every kind of living creature" (1:24). The verb root Y-TZ-A, to bring forth, hints to fertility, but the verb *yishretzu* (which can also be translated as "bring forth") is even more profoundly linked to the semantic field of birth. Plants, fish, birds, and animals all spring forth from water and soil, as if they have the power to bear and give life. In this way, the verse is a fitting conclusion for the first narrative.

7. Rashi can be also understood differently, but this is the most obvious way of understanding his words.
8. Compare to Day, *From Creation to Babel*, 18.

Another convincing argument to this end is that the verb root B-R-A, which features in the word "*behibaram*," "when they were created," is mentioned six times in the first narrative, and not once in the second. There, the verb "*yatzar*," "formed," is used instead of *bara* (2:7, 8, 19). As the conclusion of the first narrative, the word *behibaram* becomes the symbolic seventh occurrence of the root B-R-A in the first creation story.[9]

On the other hand, one substantial argument that the verse in fact introduces the second creation story is that the expression "*eleh toledot*" appears eleven other times in the book of Genesis,[10] each time introducing a new literary unit,[11] which strongly implies that its appearance in 2:4 marks the beginning, rather than the end, of a unit.[12]

This verse is formulated similarly to the next instance of this phrase in the book of Genesis: the *toledot* of mankind. Compare "*These are the* toledot *of heaven and earth* when they were created, on the day that the Lord God made heaven and earth" (2:4) to "*This is the book of the* toledot *of man* on the day that God created man" (5:1).

This also implies that the verse serves as the introduction to the Eden narrative, just as the latter verse opens Adam's genealogical list. John Skinner adds that the biblical formula "*eleh toledot*" introduces a narrative not about the subject mentioned in the formula, but

---

9. As mentioned, this is the prevalent approach in modern research. See, for example, Odil Hannes Steck, *Der Schöpfungsbericht der Priesterschrift* (FRLANT 115: Göttingen, 1975), 241–243.

10. These are (including our verse under discussion): 2:4, 5:1, 6:9, 10:1, 11:10, 11:27, 25:12, 25:19, 36:1, 36:4, 36:9, and 37:2. On its use as a structural marker, see the discussion and references in Mathews, *Genesis*, vol. 1, 31–41.

11. This is also true of post-biblical books which imitated the biblical style, such as the beginning of the *Book of Adam and Eve:* "This is the book of the *toledot* of Adam and Eve. After they left the Garden of Eden…" in M. Hack, *The Book of Adam and Eve*, in vol. 1 of *The Apocrypha*, ed. Abraham Kahana (Jerusalem, 1940), 4.

12. As claimed, for example, by Frank Moore Cross, *Canaanite Myth and Hebrew Epic* (Cambridge, 1973), 302; Sven Tengstrom, *Die Toledotformel und die literarische Struktur der priesterlichen Erweiterungsschicht im Pentateuch* (ConBot 17: Lund, 1982), 54–59; Matthew A. Thomas, *These are the Generations: Identity, Covenant and the 'Toledot' Formula* (LHBOTS 551: New York, 2011), 127. Some, however, do claim that this formula functions as a concluding sentence of the previous unit; see Paul J. Wiseman, *New Discoveries in Babylonia about Genesis* (London, 1936); this theory was also defended by Dale S. DeWitt, "The Generation of Genesis," *EvQ* 48 (1976): 196–211.

rather about his sons. For example, "These are the *toledot* of Jacob," in 37:2, introduces the story of Joseph, not Jacob. Following this logic, the *toledot* of heaven and earth does not describe the actual creation of heaven and earth, but the story of what came from them.[13]

With convincing arguments for either case, a third option is that this verse is a Janus verse, looking both behind and ahead, connecting the two creation accounts together. Its semantic content clearly links it to the first creation story, while its form and structure imply that it introduces the second chapter. Why is this connection so important? The disparity between these accounts is so wide that the reader might mistakenly conclude that these chapters cannot be reconciled with one another, that they were penned by two different hands that had nothing to do with each other. Verse 4 of chapter 2 serves as a bridge between the first two chapters of Genesis. Even if they each paint a completely different picture of reality, between God and humanity, their root is one; they represent two different, complementary facets of creation, two theological portraits that hang side by side on a single wall.

The Structure of the Eden Story

Where does the story of Eden begin, and where does it end? Some argue that chapter 2 is an independent unit, the story of humanity's creation, while chapter 3 also stands alone as the story of the first sin and the expulsion from Eden. Certain elements planted in chapter 2 clearly anticipate the next chapter, especially the prohibition concerning the Tree of Knowledge of Good and Evil, but readers who favor the latter approach of chapter 3 as a separate story hold that these are merely hints which are not developed in chapter 2.[14]

---

13. Skinner, *Genesis*, 40–41, although eventually he favors the reading that this clause is the conclusion of the first creation. Some of the scholars who ascribe this clause to the first creation story acknowledge that this formula usually introduces a unit, and most of their solutions concern the formation of the text and various redactive issues (see, for example: Gunkel, *Genesis*, 103; Levenson, *Creation*, 67; Day, *From Creation to Babel*, 19), but they do not provide a cogent solution to the final form of the text.
14. Some respond by interpreting from a diachronic perspective (David M. Carr, "The Politics of Textual Subversion: A Diachronic Perspective on the Garden of Eden Story," *JBL* 112 [1993]: 577–595). One striking example of a reading which separates

Even if chapter 2 can be read on its own, it still functions as part of a narrative unit spanning 2:4–3:24:[15] "Rather, the two elements stand together as one unit, the one a reflect to the other."[16] These textual boundaries are prompted by the plot itself, which stretches cohesively and continuously over chapters 2 and 3.[17] The prohibition of eating from the Tree of Knowledge of Good and Evil is not the only narrative link between the two chapters; another example is the connection between "there was no man to work the soil" (2:5) and "to work the soil from which he was taken" (3:23). Based on the connection between the two chapters, George Coats proposes several symbolic connections between the narrative stages, such as the plight of the untended vegetation at the beginning of chapter 2 being a reflection of the human plight at the end of the story, when humans are banished from the blooming garden.[18]

---

chapters 2 and 3 into two units can be found in Gunkel, *Genesis*, 25–28, who defines chapter 2 as a "creation narrative" and chapter 3 as a separate account of sin and the expulsion from Eden, although he also holds that there are close connections between the two chapters. A good example of a reading of chapter 2 as an independent unit can be found in the structure proposed by Doukhan in *The Genesis Creation Story*, who claims that there is a parallel between chapter 1 and chapters 2: both creation narrative consist of three pairs. Chapter 1 is divided into the aforementioned structure of three pairs of days, and chapter 2 can be arranged similarly:

A. Creation from dust (2:7)	A'. The threat of death – return to dust (2:17)
B. God plants a garden for humanity (2:8)	B'. God creates companionship for humanity (2:18)
C. Humanity is in charge of the garden (2:15)	C'. Humanity is in charge of the animals (2:20)

I am skeptical as to whether this structure is intentional, but in any case, the premise of this structure is that chapter 2 functions as an independent literary unit with a cohesive structure.

15. Or, for example, see the discussion of Stordalen, *Echoes of Eden*, 214–216.
16. George W. Coats, *Genesis* (FOTL: Grand Rapids, 1983), 51. Stordalen notes intensive wordplay in these two chapters and certain repeated sounds, repetitions, and etymologies. He argues that this shows that the two chapters form a single story (Stordalen, *Echoes of Eden*, 198–201).
17. Gunkel (*Genesis*, 25) points out the following connections: 2:19–3:1; 1:15–16 and 3:1–5, 17; 2:25–3:7; 2:21–22 and 3:12; 2:7–3:19, 23.
18. Coats, *Genesis*, 51–52. Stordalen notes intensive wordplay in these two chapters and certain repeated sounds, repetitions, and etymologies. He argues that this shows that the two chapters form a single story (Stordalen, *Echoes of Eden*, 198–201).

Reading the two chapters as a single narrative results in an extraordinary literary structure:

A. The plight of the earth, when there is "no man to work the soil"; a garden is planted in the "east" of Eden; Adam is formed from the earth and placed beside the Tree of Life (2:4–17)

B. The search for a "fitting helper"; the creation of animals, woman, and naming; man and woman are "*arumim,*" naked (2:18–25)

C. The characters sin: the serpent convinces the woman to eat from the tree; man then eats from the tree (3:1–7)

D. Man and woman hide from God; dialogue between God and the sinners (3: 8–13)

C'. The sinners are punished: the serpent is punished, woman is punished, man is punished (3:14–19)[19]

B'. Woman receives a new name, Eve; Adam and Eve are clothed in "garments of skin" (3:20–21)

A'. Adam and Eve are banished from the garden and distanced from the Tree of Life "to work the soil from which he was taken"; the cherubim are stationed "east of the Garden of Eden" (3:22–24)

Above all, this structure draws a connection between crime and punishment (C-C').[20] Through this structure, the narrative emerges as multifaceted and sophisticated, crafted with artful ambiguity that reveals the complex nature of the story and its objective.

The Narrative Framework (A-A')

The story's framework monitors the characters' movement, opening with Adam's entrance to Eden and ending with his expulsion. There is emphasis on the "east" at both beginning and end: God plants a garden "in the

---

19. Bekhor Shor already commented here: "The Holy One, blessed be He, began to punish them in the order that they sinned: the serpent, who began, was cursed first, followed by Eve, and then Adam" (Bekhor Shor on Gen. 3:13).

20. Jonathan Grossman, "More on the Literary Structure of the Paradise Narrative (Gen. 2:4–3:24)," *Beit Mikra* 56 (2011): 5–39.

east" (2:8), and there He eventually stations the cherubim (3:24). The "Tree of Life," too, is mentioned only at the beginning (2:9) and the end (3:22) of the story, which strengthens the connection between the two chapters. This framework highlights the tragedy of human sin; instead of dwelling in the east, eating of the Tree of Life forever, man is cast away, his reentrance prevented by the ever-turning sword of the cherubim.[21]

Alongside these mirrored expressions, however, another, more surprising connection is revealed. As mentioned, the narrative opens with the plight of vegetation: "When no shrub of the field was yet on earth and no grasses of the field had yet sprouted, because the Lord God had not sent rain upon the earth and there was no man to work the soil" (2:5). This opening invites anticipation that this plight will be resolved: When does rain fall down and water the earth, and when will man begin to till the soil? Some propose that this is already solved in verse 15, when man is placed in the garden "to work it and keep it."[22] This reading, though, is problematic: despite the feminine tense, the simple reading is that man is placed in the garden to work the garden, not the "soil" and its vegetation in general.[23] The plight mentioned at the beginning of the story, therefore, is not solved when God plants Himself a garden; at that point, only a choice patch of soil is tended, while the rest of the world remains bare for lack of human labor (while God, not man, plants the garden).[24] The soil is tended only when Adam and Eve are banished from the garden: "So the Lord God sent him away from the Garden of Eden, to work the soil from which he was taken" (3:23). For

21. Despite the fact that the Tree of Life only features in the framework, it unifies the entire narrative. See Barr, *The Garden of Eden*, 59.
22. See a discussion of this complicated issue in Greenstein, "God's Golem" (233 in particular).
23. Ibn Ezra, and Radak's second suggestion. Radak initially proposes that the verse refers to "the earth." Even if the feminine language refers to the earth, it can be read as a hint to the soil of the garden (see also *Midrash Lekah Tov* on this verse).
24. Rabbi Yoel Bin-Nun and his son Eliad propose that the command, "to work it and keep it," refers to the land outside the boundaries of Eden. The person's place is indeed inside the garden that God planted, and the rivers there water the garden and the trees that God planted there, but man's role is to extend the borders of the garden – to work outside its borders and work the soil (Yoel and Eliad Bin-Nun, "The Garden of Eden and the Earth – Adam's Sin," *Megadim* 54 [2013]: 9–31).

two chapters, the soil waits patiently for man to come back and till the earth from which he sprung forth. There is tension between the choice patch of garden that God planted and the rest of the soil; as Adam makes his way among the lush trees and bushes of God's garden, the bare soil outside longs for human touch. This tension is the silver lining of the tragedy of human sin: while Adam and Eve's fall results in human mortality, curse, and expulsion, the soil outside awaits them; their return is anticipated from the beginning of the narrative.[25]

Both aspects, woven throughout the narrative, are given expression at the end of the story, when Adam is expelled from Eden:

- "So the Lord God sent him away from the Garden of Eden, to work the soil from which he was taken" (3:23).
- "He drove the man out, and stationed east of the Garden of Eden the cherubim and the fiery ever-turning sword, to guard the way to the Tree of Life" (3:24).

The combination of both verses reflects man's double role in the Garden of Eden, "to work and keep it (*lishamrah*)."[26] Each role is addressed in a different verse at the end of the story. Verse 23 relates to working the soil, a task which man retains after he leaves Eden, while verse 24 describes how man's second task, keeping the Garden of Eden, is transferred to the cherubim instead, who "guard (*lishmor*) the way to the Tree of Life."[27]

---

25. Carr places such importance on this tension that he concludes that chapter 2 is a positive story about the creation of man and the planting of Eden. This story presents working the soil as man's ideal state, and the animals and woman were created to help him. He therefore holds that some details in chapter 2 were added at a later stage in order to lead up to the narrative in chapter 3 – the story of sin and man's downfall. This explains why there is unsolvable tension between the beginning of the story, which presents working the land as an ideal state, and the end of chapter 3, where this work is presented as a punishment. See Carr, "Textual Subversion."
26. Therefore, one cannot accept the claim that the repetition in these verses serves as proof that the narrative was formed from two separate sources.
27. See Amos Frisch, *The Toil of Your Hands: The Bible's View of Labor* (Tel Aviv, 1999), 33. Intriguingly, the same is true in the next story, even if the root SH-M-R, "keep," relates to something completely different: Cain "was a worker of the soil" (4:2), and after the murder he answers God, "I do not know – am I my brother's *keeper*?" (4:9).

Indeed, these descriptions reflect two different aspects of the expulsion from Eden. Verse 23 focuses on man's new purpose: he is sent out of Eden to "work the soil from which he was taken." In contrast, verse 24 focuses on his expulsion from Eden, on his forced removal from God's garden; he must be distanced from the Tree of Life and kept away by cherubim with fiery swords. This contrast illuminates the difference between the verb roots SH-L-Ḥ, "sent," and G-R-SH, "drive out" or "expel." Someone is "sent" away with a purpose, with focus on his or her destination, while G-R-SH emphasizes the expulsion itself, with focus on leaving one's place of origin.[28] Adam and Eve are expelled *from* the Tree of Life and the Garden of Eden, but they are sent *to* work the land, which has been waiting for them since the beginning of chapter 2.

This ambiguity is so vital to the narrative objective that Adam's expulsion from the garden is not mentioned together with the rest of humanity's punishments. Had this punishment been mentioned in verses 17–19, when God expresses His rage at Adam's transgression, the human expulsion from Eden would have been an unequivocal punishment. By postponing their expulsion to the end of the story, however, only after man and his wife are clothed and Adam renames his wife Eve, their departure from Eden is also colored as a more ambiguous narrative conclusion that resolves the plight presented at the very beginning of the story. These two threads of purpose and punishment are interlaced throughout the story, until it cannot be determined whether humanity must leave Eden because of their sin, or in order to fulfill the destiny hinted to at the beginning of the narrative.[29] This ambivalence holds the key to the story of Eden – is it a straightforward story of sin, or does

28. See further in Aron Pinker, "The Expulsion of Hagar and Ishmael (Gen 21:9–21)," *Women in Judaism* 6 (2009): 16; Jonathan Grossman, "The Expulsion of Ishmael Narrative – Boundaries, Structure, and Meaning," in *Doubling and Duplicating in the Book of Genesis: Literary and Stylistic Approaches to the Text*, ed. E. R. Hayes and K. Vermeulen (Winona Lake, 2016), 32–35.

29. This is consistent with Frisch's claim that man is not sent to work the soil as a punishment, but as fulfillment of his destiny (Frisch, *Labor*, 27–33). On the various biblical perspectives of working the soil and work ethics, see also Jan Christian Gertz, "'Im Schweisse deines Angesichts': Alttestamentliche Perspektiven zum Thema 'Sinn der Arbeit – Ethos der Arbeit,'" in *Alttestamentliche Wissenschaft und kirchliche Praxis*, ed. M. Oeming and W. Boës (Münster, 2009), 267–283.

eating from the Tree of Knowledge represent a more complex course of events? To this end, I will first address another surprise that emerges through our narrative structure.

The Central Axis

The moment Adam and Eve sink their teeth into the forbidden fruit, their world comes crashing down – harmony and immortality give way to sin and death, they are cursed with pain and toil, and they are banished from God's garden. Or, rather, that is how the story resonates with generations of readers and listeners. Yet our narrative structure reveals – to great surprise – that the central axis is *not* the eating of the forbidden fruit. Though the central axis of chiastic and concentric structures is often assumed to be the narrative climax or turning point of its literary unit,[30] the central axis of the story of Eden takes place, in fact, *after* man and woman's first sin.

This is astounding largely due to the religious and historical emphasis on the place of sin within the story. From ancient exegesis to modern scholarship, many see the story of Eden as the story of Sin, of the first wrong step of humanity's history. This reading is sometimes rejected with the claim that the word "sin" or the like does not actually appear in the text, rendering it unlikely that "sin" is the main theme of this story,[31] but this argument has failed to quash this prevalent opinion. Sin is undoubtedly a significant component in the story, even if it is not explicitly defined as such. Some scholars have proposed alternative structures to my own, structures in which eating of the forbidden fruit is the central component of the story. Walsh, for example, traces the protagonists' movement through space, and sketches out a concentric structure arranged in two parallel, inverse halves. Situating the Tree of Knowledge in the center of the garden and the center of his structure,

30. Yehuda Thomas Radday, "Chiasmus in Hebrew Biblical Narrative," in *Chiasmus in Antiquity*, ed. J. Welch (Utah, 1981), 51. See further in Nils Wilhelm Lund, *Chiasmus in the New Testament: A Study in the Form and Function of Chiastic* (Chapel Hill, 1942), and Grossman, *Text and Subtext*, 248–256.

31. Carol Meyers, *Discovering Eve: Ancient Israelite Women in Context* (Oxford, 1988), 87; Barr, *The Garden of Eden*, 6. Jerome T. Walsh, "Genesis 2:4b–3:24: A Synchronic Approach," *JBL* 96 (1977): 161–177.

he claims that for the first half of the story, the characters move closer and closer to the center of the garden, while in the second half, their movement takes them farther and farther away, until they are eventually banished.[32]

A literary structure based on spatial movement can certainly be justified, especially in stories that touch upon the tension between inside and out, between the center and the periphery.[33] However, while this structure is intriguing, there is no evidence that the Tree of Knowledge is in fact in the center of the garden, as Walsh assumes. In fact, from ancient times, exegetes have argued that in contrast to the Tree of Life, the Tree of Knowledge was not in the center of the garden:

> Moses expressly states that [the Tree of Life] is placed "within the garden." But as to the other tree, the Tree of Knowledge of Good and Evil, he does not specify whether it is inside or outside the garden. Rather, he states, "and of the Tree of the Knowledge of Good and Evil," and says no more, revealing not where it is located.... What then must we say? That this tree is both within the garden, and also outside of it. In terms of its existence, it is within, but as to its power, it is out of it.[34]

---

32. See the structure of Walsh, which places the sin at the center of the narrative, in Walsh, "Genesis 2:4b–3:24":
    A. 2:4–17: The man is placed in Eden/Movement from outside the garden to inside the garden
    B. 2:18- 25: The creation of animals and woman/Takes place within the garden
    C. 3:1–5: Dialogue between the serpent and the woman/Takes place within the garden
    D. 3:6–7: The sin of eating from the Tree of Knowledge/Takes place at the center of the garden
    C'. 3:8–13: Dialogue between God and the sinners/Takes place within the garden
    B'. 3:14–21: Estrangement between man and woman, animal and human/Within the garden
    A'. 3:22–24: Adam and Eve are banished from Eden/Movement from inside the garden to outside
33. A good example of this kind of structure is the concentric structure of the Flood narrative, which I will discuss in context.
34. Philo, *Writings*, vol. 4, 49.

Basing an entire literary structure on information that is not provided in the text is problematic, even if we adopt the reading that the description of the Tree of Life's placement – "within the garden" (2:10) – also applies to the Tree of Knowledge (as Nahmanides claims, for example).

Even so, the motivation of Walsh, and of others who place the actual sin at the center of the narrative structure, is clear.[35] The sin is the moment of crisis, the first footstep that muddies the freshly fallen snow of humanity's existence. Yet the temptation to focus on the sin itself leads the reader away from the actual text.

The true center of gravity, the true turning point, in fact lies in the dialogue between God and the characters following their sin. Though surprising, the importance of this revelation cannot be overestimated. Despite the traditional focus on the sin itself, within the text the sin is presented as practically inevitable, as is the punishment that follows the sin. The jarring surprise in the plot, the narrative element that shatters expectations, is the sinners' reaction and the attitude that they display to God after their sin. At this point, man must confess his sin, and his evasion of responsibility marks the gravitational center of the whole narrative. The turning point, the *peripeteia* of the story, is not humanity's sin, but humanity's failure to take responsibility for its sin.

What, then, are the implications of a story arranged around this failure? It is worth noting that other attempts to trace an alternative structure are generally forced to admit that at least two narrative strands present themselves, strands interwoven yet difficult to reconcile: one plot line that is related to crime and punishment, and another plot, parallel to it, concerned with how the woman manages to obtain the

35. Similar to Walsh, Dorsey proposes the following structure (*Literary Structure*, 50):
A: The creation of man: joyful harmony with the earth and the garden (2:1–17)
B. The creation of woman: joyful harmony between man and woman (2:18–25)
C: The serpent – temptation of the woman (3:1–5)
D: Sin and God's discovery of their sin (3:6–13)
C'. The serpent's punishment – tension between serpent and woman (3:14–15)
B': The woman's punishment – tension between man and woman (3:16)
A': The man's punishment – tension between man, the earth, and the garden (3:17–24)

hidden powers of the forbidden fruit.[36] With this in mind, let us return to our main discussion, and to the meaning of the sin within the story.

The Tree of Knowledge of Good and Evil

What kind of tree is the Tree of Knowledge, and why are its fruits forbidden? At first glance, the species of tree does not seem particularly important; the narrator casually refers to it as "the Tree of Knowledge of Good and Evil," without any hint to its botanical identity. Various midrashim have attempted to fill this gap,[37] deeming it a citron tree,[38] a fig tree,[39] wheat,[40] a grapevine,[41] and more. However, as I already mentioned in the introduction, Ibn Ezra seems to be correct in defining it as a unique, mythical tree with wondrous qualities. What, then, are these qualities, and why were its fruits off-limits to humanity?

Out of generations of biblical interpretation, two main approaches can be pointed out. Most traditional exegetes associate the Tree of Knowledge with human cognitive ability and capacity. In this sense, "good and evil" can be read as a merismus that represents "everything." Some explain that upon eating the fruit, man gained a new level of consciousness of his surroundings.[42] Another variation of this reading is that

---

36. A striking example of this is Robert Culley's attempt to present the story of Eden as what he refers to as "a sequence of actions." See Zvi Shimon's opinion and criticism on this approach in Shimon, *Human Choice Biblical Narrative and the Drama of Choice* (Jerusalem, 2015), 41–42.
37. See Louis Ginzberg, *The Legends of the Jews*, vol. 1 (Ramat Gan, 1966), 188; Iris Yaniv, "From What Kind of Tree Did Adam Eat?" *Al HaPerek* 14 (1998): 8–15. Compare to scholars' debates whether the tree is a unique, miraculous tree (von Rad, *Genesis*, 90) or an actual, real-life tree (Sarna, *Understanding Genesis*, 25–26). I bring Ibn Ezra's opinion below (who favors the former opinion).
38. Genesis Rabba 20:8
39. Ibid., 15:7, *Yalkut* for Psalms 36:12.
40. Sanhedrin 70a, Genesis Rabba 15:8, and elsewhere.
41. Sanhedrin 70a, Genesis Rabba 15:8, and 19:5.
42. Cassuto, *From Adam to Noah*, 113–114; von Rad, *Genesis*, 79; Westermann, *Genesis*, vol. 1, 243; Oden, "Divine Aspirations." He claims that according to biblical theology, it is difficult to believe that God created man without the capacity for moral distinction, and that man only achieved this through sin (ibid., 212). A similar claim is made by Skinner, *Genesis*, 96; Robert Gordis, "The Knowledge of Good and Evil

by eating the fruit, humanity gained a new moral awareness, such that "good and evil" should be interpreted in a moral sense.[43]

A second approach holds that this "knowledge" refers to carnal knowledge. This reading is acutely reflected in some midrashim, as well as early Christian exegesis. Ibn Ezra is one medieval proponent of this approach:

> I believe that the two trees within the garden cannot be found anywhere else on Earth. One, the "Tree of Knowledge," awakens sexual lust, and that is why man and his wife covered their nakedness.... When Adam ate from the Tree of Knowledge, he "knew his wife," and this means carnal knowledge, and that is why the Tree of Knowledge was called so. When a boy, too, knows about good and evil, that is when sexual lust begins.[44]

This reading is the source of the expression "carnal knowledge," as in such verses as, "And Adam *knew* his wife" (4:1), "And he did not know her ever again" (Gen. 38:26), and many more.[45] This reading is famously held by the Catholic Church, as well as many modern scholars.[46] A surprising midrash extends this metaphor by stating that the serpent's motivation for causing them to sin was sexual: "He saw them involved

---

in the Old Testament and the Qumran Scrolls," *JBL* 76 (1957): 125. A discussion of the various versions of this reading can be found in Howard N. Wallace, *The Eden Narrative* (Atlanta, 1985), 115–130.

43. August Dillmann, *Genesis: Critical and Exegetically Expounded*, trans. B. Stevenson (Edinburgh, 1897), vol. 1, 137–140; Driver, *Genesis*, 41; Barr, *The Garden of Eden*, 62; Kiel, *Genesis*, 53–55.

44. Ibn Ezra on Gen. 3:6–7.

45. Brown-Driver-Briggs, *A Hebrew and English Lexicon of the Old Testament* (Oxford, 1906), 395.

46. An extensive discussion of this reading can be found in Gordis, "The Knowledge of Good and Evil"; Ivan Engnell, "'Knowledge' and 'Life' in the Creation Story," in *Wisdom in Israel and the Ancient Near East Wisdom in Israel*, ed. M. Noth and D. Winton Thomas (VTSup 3; Leiden: Brill, 1955), 103–119; Edmund Leach, *Genesis as Myth and Other Essays* (London, 1969), 14–15; Lisbeth Mikaelsson, "Sexual Polarity: An Aspect of the Ideological Structure in the Paradise Narrative, Gen 2:4–3:24," *Temenos* 16 (1980): 84–91; Sam Dragga, "Genesis 2–3: A Story of Liberation," *JSOT* 55 (1992): 3–13.

with the way of the land [i.e., having sexual relations] and was struck by desire for her."[47] Sexual allusions can be found throughout the narrative, as I will discuss below, but is there a basis for this idea of the serpent's desire for the woman? Even this midrash, as surprising as it sounds, is actually grounded in the text.

The Role of the Serpent

Some modern scholars see the serpent as the symbol of some kind of Canaanite god, such as Baal[48] or El.[49] These readings suggest that the story is a primordial struggle between monotheism and paganism, wherein the serpent successfully persuades the first man and woman to turn their back on their Creator to follow other deities. The serpent indeed refers to God as "God" (3:1–5) rather than "the Lord God," which some interpret as a religious affront,[50] but this reading remains unconvincing. Firstly, the serpent is not associated with these deities in ancient pagan culture,[51] but more importantly, this theme is not consistent with the atmosphere, components, or sequence of the story.[52]

47. Genesis Rabba 18:6. Some modern scholars also perceive the serpent as tempter of the woman, such as Bruce Vawter, *On Genesis: A New Reading* (Garden City, 1977), 71. See also the references made by Stratton, *Out of Eden*, 43.
48. Flemming Hvidberg, "The Canaanitic Background of Gen i–iii," *VT* 10 (1960): 285–294; Arnold, *Genesis*, 62–63.
49. Nicolas Wyatt, "Interpreting the Creation and Fall Story in Genesis 2–3," *ZAW* 93 (1981): 18–20.
50. Many question why God is referred to as "the Lord God" throughout the narrative while the serpent says only "God." Cassuto proposes that "it was unfitting that the personal name of God, which is supremely holy, should be used by the creature that counsels evil, or by the woman holding converse with it" (Cassuto, *From Adam to Noah*, 88). Joseph Titus suggests that the serpent was keeping his distance from God (Titus, *The Second Story of Creation (Gen 2:4–3:24): A Prologue to the Concept of the Enneateuch?* [Frankfurt, 2011], 326). For the suggestion that none of the animals, including the serpent, knew God's name, which only takes place in 4:26 ("Then people began to call on the name of God"), see my discussion in context.
51. Day, *From Creation to Babel*, 36.
52. If the serpent is indeed related to pagan Canaanite symbolism, it would make more sense to adopt the claim that the serpent is related to Canaanite fertility rites (Joseph Coppens, *La connaissance du bien et du mal et le péché du Paradis: contribution*

The most prevalent reading, of course, perceives the serpent as an embodiment of the *yetzer hara*, the "evil inclination." Despite this widely accepted opinion, James Charlesworth claims that in the ancient world, the serpent was largely considered a positive symbol, and the same holds true in Genesis 3.[53] The serpent never actually tempts Eve, he argues, but merely asked her an innocent question; unlike God, it speaks the truth, and it is portrayed as wise and not necessarily sly.[54] Charlesworth's reading, of course, is inaccurate. At the very beginning of the chapter, the serpent is explicitly characterized as "the most cunning of all the wild animals," and this characterization has bearing on the rest of the story. At the end of the story, too, it is bitterly cursed by God, which proves that God does not view it as a positive or innocent figure by any means – and the reader, of course, identifies with God's evaluation.

The serpent is unquestionably a villain, but determining what *kind* of villain is nonetheless significant. Is it a symbol of evil for evil's sake, the first active agent of darkness in the story, or can other motivating forces be unearthed between the lines? Is it a substantial character in itself, or merely a symbol – the little devil who sits on Eve's shoulder, in serpentine form? In the apocryphal *Adam and Eve*, the devil stands behind the serpent and says to it, "Be a vessel for me, and I will speak words through your mouth to deceive him."[55]

However, there is another possibility. The serpent could be a character in its own right, with its own motives for leading the first man and woman astray. Dr. Yoshi Farjun recently suggested that the serpent's motivation can be understood in light of the previous scene,

---

à l'interprétation de Gen., II–III [Louvain, 1948]; J. Alberto Soggin, "The Fall of Man in the Third Chapter of Genesis," in *Old Testament and Oriental Studies* [Biblica et Orientalia 29: Rome, 1975], 94–100), but again, I am skeptical that this is the case.

53. James H. Charlesworth, *The Good and Evil Serpent: How a Universal Symbol Became Christianized* (Anchor Yale Bible Reference Library: New Haven, 2010), 275–324.

54. He also believes that the serpent had legs until they were removed with God's punishment. As the serpent as a speaker of truth in contrast to God, see R. Walter L. Moberly, "Did the Serpent Get It Right?" *Journal of Theological Studies* 39 (1988): 1–27.

55. *Adam and Eve* 16:1–7. See other ancient sources who also portray the serpent thus in Ephraim E. Urbach, *The Sages: Their Concepts and Beliefs*, 2nd ed. (Jerusalem, 1971), 146–148.

when Adam rejects the animals as his "helpmate." When God sought out a partner for man, He first created all the animals and brought them before him: "The Lord God had formed from the ground all the wild animals and all the birds of heaven, and He brought them to the human to see what he would call them" (2:19). Man's naming of each creature can be understood as a statement of its nature and its relationship with humanity. By the end of the process, every animal has a name, but "the human found no helper-counterpart" (v. 20). God therefore decides to split the human himself into two, creating his helpmate out of his own body.[56] Man is delighted to see woman, and continues his naming with their special compatibility in mind: "And the man said, '*This* time, bone of my bones and flesh of my flesh, *this one* shall be called Woman, for *this one* was taken from Man" (v. 23).[57]

Animals, then, can be considered man's rejected dates; only woman is good enough for him. The serpent, "the most cunning of all the wild animals" (3:1), is the representative of all these jilted lovers. The phrase "*kol ḥayat hasadeh,*" "all the wild animals," is a rare phrase in Genesis, associated only with man's naming of the animals and the serpent itself.[58] Stung by this rejection, the serpent plots its sweet revenge. The

---

56. Gary Rendsburg proposes that the term "*ezer kenegdo,*" "a helper-counterpart," was purposely chosen for its alliterative soundplay with "*etz hagan,*" "the tree of the garden," mentioned in God's command to man (Rendsburg, "Alliteration in the Book of Genesis," in *Doubling and Duplicating in the Book of Genesis: Literary and Stylistic Approaches to the Text,* ed. E. R. Hayes and K. Vermeulen [Winona Lake, 2016], 92–94). If this connection is intentional, then the fact that woman will turn against him and lead him to sin by eating from the forbidden tree is already anticipated during man's search for his helpmate.
57. This is the accepted reading, which sees the word "*paam*" in the sense of "time." Rabbi Yehuda Shaviv points out that the Tosafists present a reading of this word in the sense of "shape," as in, "this *shape* is like my own." With this in mind, Rabbi Shaviv proposes reading this verse in dialogue with the description of the Ark: "Cast four gold rings for it, to be attached to its four corners (*paamotav*), two rings on one of its sides (*tzalo*) and two on the other of its sides (*tzalo*)" (Ex. 25:12). The "*paamotav*" of the Ark are divided into two "*tzlaot,*" similar to the "*paam*" in our verse, with the woman's shape derived from man's rib, called a *tzela* (Rabbi Yehuda Shaviv, "*Zot HaPaam,*" *Beit Mikra* 33 [1988]: 129–130).
58. David Fohrman, *The Ancient History of Good and Evil: Study of Adam and Eve and Cain and Abel* (2011), 39.

bride that man *did* choose for his helpmate, the bride that man chose over every other creature, will be the one to bring about man's downfall. As man himself points out a few verses later, "And Man said, 'The Woman whom You gave to me – she gave me from the tree, and I ate'" (3:12).

Rabbi David Fohrman, who favors this theory, perceives the envious serpent as the embodiment of a fundamental question:

> The serpent's suggestion results from Adam's preference of Eve over the animals. As a result of this rejection, the living world, represented by the serpent, poses a challenge for Man and his partner: "What makes you so special? How are you so different from us that you remain by yourselves, needing only each other as partners? We could be your partners too."[59]

Rabbi Fohrman believes that this detail sheds crucial light on the narrative. Even those who believe that the serpent is merely a symbol of the evil inclination ought to consider why this symbol takes the form of an animal.[60]

The serpent is indeed presented as a jealous lover, motivated by envy and rejection. This idea is supported by the fact that Cain, too, in the very next chapter, also acts out of envy and rejection, and I will return to this connection.

Several narrative details support the reading of the serpent as a jilted lover:

- First of all, recalling Ibn Ezra's interpretation, the verb *yada*, "to know," sometimes functions as a euphemism for sexual relations. This meaning is used just a few verses later, at the beginning of the next chapter: "And the man knew Eve his wife, and she

---

59. Fohrman, *Good and Evil*, 40.

60. In several ancient Near Eastern traditions, the serpent represents renewed life and reincarnation because it sheds its skin as if beginning life anew. If this theme also accompanies our story, it makes sense that this creature is the one who tempts the woman, expert as he is in the secrets of life and death. While their sin indeed results in their mortality, it also admits them into the world of birth and renewal through their children. See below, where I discuss Paul Kübel's development of this idea.

conceived and gave birth to Cain" (4:1); "And Cain knew his wife, and she conceived and gave birth to Enoch" (4:17); "And again Adam knew his wife, and she gave birth to a son, and called his name Seth" (4:25). This certainly hints that the Tree of Knowledge is the Tree of Carnal Knowledge, which, in the words of Ibn Ezra, "awakens sexual lust," which encompasses both positive, "good" aspects, as well as threatening, "evil" aspects, making it truly the Tree of Knowledge of Good and Evil.

- The most sexually evocative component of the story is the emphasis on Adam and Eve's nakedness. Before they eat from the tree, "The two of them were naked, the man and his wife, and they were not ashamed" (2:25). As soon as they eat from the tree, however, "The eyes of both of them were opened, and they knew they were naked" (3:7). This is no casual observation; as soon as they become aware of their naked state, they hurriedly "sewed fig leaves together and made coverings for themselves" (3:7). Their nakedness is brought up once again at the end of the story, when God takes pity on the wretched sinners shivering in their fig leaves, and, "The Lord God made garments of skin for Adam and his wife and clothed them" (3:21). Now their bodies, not just their private parts, are covered, and although this gradual covering up may be a metaphor for humanity's gradual cultural awakening,[61] the repeated focus on their naked state colors the sin and its aftermath in sexual overtones.[62]

---

61. Clothing, as opposed to nakedness, is a symbol of culture and symbolization in general literature. This is salient, for example, in the *Epic of Gilgamesh*, where the wild man Enkidu gradually undergoes a process of civilization by the harlot Shamhat. One of the first things she does is dress him in proper clothing. Others argue that Enkidu's process is an inversion of Nebuchadnezzar's dream in Daniel 4, when he dreams that he is among the wild animals, symbolizing his return to a primary state of wildness (Peter W. Coxon, "Another Look at Nebuchadnezzar's Madness," in *The Book of Daniel in the Light of New Findings*, ed. A. S. van der Woude [BEThL 106: Leuven, 1993], 211–222. According to this reading, it is interesting that in this dream there is no focus on clothing, but rather on other aspects of wildness.

62. There is room to debate about the meaning of the shame and nakedness in the story. Westermann makes three suggestions. First, it is an expression of a sense of shame. Second, it is testimony to sexual awareness. Third, it reflects the transition from a

- In Mesopotamian and Canaanite cultures, the serpent was, among other roles, a sexual symbol for fertility, and there is room to claim that this symbolism is retained in its biblical context.[63] Even without adopting the reading that the serpent represents the rejected lover, it is a truth universally acknowledged that the sages also refer to the serpent as a symbol of sexuality, associations which are famously found in modern psychoanalysis as well.[64]
- There are two main interpretations of the name "Eden."[65] Some read it as related to the Akkadian word *edinu*, which means "plain," or "steppe," while others link it to the Western Semitic root E-D-N, meaning "abundance," "pleasure," and "ripe."[66] This second meaning links Eden to the semantic field of fertility and sexuality, similar to Sarah's exclamation, "After I am worn out, shall I have pleasure (*edna*)?" (Gen. 18:12), as if to say, could my shriveled body once again swell with fertility? The Ugaritic cognate also seems to support this reading.[67] The rivers that flow out of Eden

---

primitive to a cultured civilization (Westermann, *Genesis*, vol. 1, 250–251). On the sense of shame, see further in Reuven Kimelman, "The Seduction of Eve and Feminist Readings of the Garden of Eden," *Women in Judaism: A Multi-Disciplinary Journal* 1 (1998): 1–39. In many places in the Bible, nakedness is an expression of destitution, yet it is difficult to dismiss the sexual dimension that nakedness represents in our narrative, especially given the fact that man and woman attempt to cover their nakedness when they become aware of it. Nonetheless, their nakedness may symbolize other elements as well.

63. Yehoshua Klein, "Serpent in the Bible," in *Olam HaTanakh: Genesis* (Tel Aviv, 1993), 32.
64. Freud was the first to claim that the serpent was a universal subconscious phallic symbol (see, for example, Freud, *The Works of Sigmund Freud*, trans. H. Isaac, vol. 1, 103 [Tel Aviv, 1966]).
65. See A. R. Millard, "The Etymology of Eden," *VT* 34 (1984): 103–106; I. Cornelius, "*Eden*," *NIDOTTE* 3: 331–332; Howard N. Wallace, "Eden, Garden of," *ABD* 2: 281; Benjamin Kedar-Kopfstein, "*Eden*," *TDOT* 10: 482–483.
66. This is apparent in the Septuagint translation of "the Garden of Eden," which is "*paradeisos en edem*," "the Garden of Pleasure," and as Bekhor Shor writes on Gen. 2:8: "A luxurious, good, rich land, which is therefore called 'Eden.'"
67. Cassuto (*From Adam to Noah*, 107) proves this from the description of Baal in context of watering the earth, which uses the root E-D-N (*The Epic of Baal*, Tablet AB II, V, lines 67–68). See also Gunkel, *Genesis*, 7; Klein, *Genesis*, 27; A. Kahana, "Why Was Eve Punished with 'In Sorrow You Will Bear Children'?", *Al HaPerek* 14 (1998): 20–22.

are also an expression of Eden's fertility and abundance, especially if we accept the reading that the names Pishon and Gihon mean "to burst out."[68] The name Pishon can be seen as a derivation of "F-U-SH," as in, "You will go out and frolic (*ufishtem*) like stall-fatted calves" (Mal. 3:20);[69] while Gihon may be derived from the root G-Y-Ḥ, as in, "The Israelite ambush burst out (*megiyaḥ*) from its position at Maareh-Geba" (Judges 20:33).[70] While Eden is associated with fertile soil, not human fertility, the link between earth and womb is strong in biblical and extra-biblical literature;[71] in fact, the bubbling, life-giving rivers that snake around the edges of the lush green garden and water its soil may themselves be symbols of fertility and sexuality.[72]

- The woman's punishment hints that the sin itself is related to sexuality, as her punishment focuses on pregnancy and birth: "I will intensify your pain in pregnancy, in pain shall you give birth to children. Your longing (*teshukatekh*) will be for your husband, and he will rule over you" (3:16). If the punishment must fit the crime,[73] then the crime itself is presumably related to sexuality

68. As posited by, for example, Westermann, *Genesis*, vol. 1, 217; André LaCocque, *Trial of Innocence: Adam, Eve, and the Yahwist* (Eugene, 2006), 80.
69. For this sense of "F-U-SH," see John E. Hartley, "F-U-SH," *NIDOTTE* 3: 592.
70. For this sense of "G-Y-Ḥ," see R. A. Taylor, "G-Y-Ḥ," *NIDOTTE* 1: 853.
71. See, for example, Barbara Green, *A Study of Field and Seed Symbolism in the Biblical Story of Ruth* (PhD diss., Michigan and London, 1982).
72. Unlike other ancient Near Eastern narratives, where God's seed fertilizes the earth and makes it grow (see especially the myth of Enki and Ninhursag), in Genesis, the rivers that flow out of Eden water the earth. Of especially worthy mention is that in the foundation myth of the Sumerian city Eridu, the god Kush marries his sister and makes the ground abundantly fertile (see the translation of the myth in Patrick D. Miller, "Eridu, Dunnu, and Babel: A Study in Comparative Mythology," *Hebrew Annual Review* 9 [1985]: 248, lines 25–27). As mentioned, the second river that comes out of Eden, Gihon, "winds throughout the land of Kush" (2:13). It could be that this fertility is already manifest in the mist that waters the ground at the beginning of the story (2:6). This "mist" may be a jet of water that bursts out from below above the earth's surface, like the Akkadian word *edû*.
73. Jonathan Jacobs, *Measure for Measure in the Storytelling Bible* (Alon Shvut, 2006), 186–191. Unlike Miller (*Genesis*, 30–31), who claims that there is no connection between woman's sin and her punishment, and unlike Yael Shemesh's hint of the same

and procreation. Many also interpret the word *teshuka*, longing, as sexual longing, such as, "I am for my beloved, and his longing (*teshukato*) is for me" (Song. 7:11);[74] this, too, intensifies the narrative's sexual atmosphere.[75]

- It may be that the prohibition's accompanying warning – "For on the day you eat from it, it will be certain that you will die" (2:17) – can also be linked to the semantic field of sexuality and fertility, as death is the opposite of birth. God is warning humanity that if they eat of the tree and enter the realm of sex, birth, and reproduction, they will automatically enter the realm of death;[76] their sexuality will cost them their immortality.[77] The Tree of

---

when she mentions how this principle is fulfilled in relation to the serpent and man's punishments (Shemesh, "Measure for Measure in Biblical Narrative," *Beit Mikra* 44 (1999): 262n9).

74. "Desire, longing, craving (a) of man for woman, (b) of woman for man" (*Theological Wordbook of the Old Testament*, ed. R. L. Harris [Chicago, 1980], #2352a), and compare to Even-Shoshan, *Dictionary*, 1889: "The meaning is according to what is written in the text." On this reading and alternative readings from medieval times, and for the influence of these different readings on the status of women, see Avraham Grossman, *Pious and Rebellious: Jewish Women in Europe in the Middle Ages* (Jerusalem, 2001), 31–34. Song of Songs may well reflect a reversal of this curse, as many have noted, and the woman's desire for her beloved is not mentioned, but rather the opposite, "and his longing is for me." See, for example, Phyllis Trible, *God and the Rhetoric of Sexuality* (Philadelphia, 1978), 159–160; Yair Zakovitch, *The Song of Songs: Introduction and Commentary* (Mikra Leyisra'el: Jerusalem/Tel Aviv, 1992), 126. As Rabbi Yuval Cherlow has shown, some rabbinical sages did not accept this interpretation and saw the verse as an expression of the lover's longing for her beloved (Cherlow, *Song of Songs: 'Let Us Run After You'* [Tel Aviv, 2003], 289).

75. Nonetheless, it is worth noting that the term *teshuka* is more conveniently interpreted as a synonym for "dependence," "to be under the authority of." This seems to be the case in Genesis 4:7. See the discussion of this verse below, and in Susan Foh, "What Is Woman's Desire?" *WTJ* 37 (1974–5): 376–383; Karel A. Deurloo, "*Teshuka* – 'Dependency,' Gen 4:7," *ZAW* 99 (1987): 405–406.

76. This especially holds true for women, given that pregnancy and childbirth, up until the previous century, spelled death for countless women. For women, sex itself was liable to result in a nine-month countdown to death, which presents an even stronger, direct link between sex and death.

77. My opening comment that the chapter would be analyzed based on the premise that this is a parallel account to the first creation account, and therefore, the fact that humanity receives the blessing to "be fruitful and multiply" at the end of chapter 1,

Life represents immortality, and the Tree of Knowledge bears fruits of sex and death.[78]

- The story of humanity's sexual maturation can be compared to another Mesopotamian story of maturation – the story of Enkidu, companion of Gilgamesh.[79] In the story, Enkidu is created in the field and lives among the animals as one of them. In order to transform him into a cultured member of civilization and alienate him from his animal companions, the harlot Shamhat is sent to lure him. Once he succumbs to her temptations, he "forgot the field" where he was born (Tablet II, lines 1–3) and allows Shamhat to dress him (25–28), feed him bread and wine (40–56), and cut off his unruly hair (59). By the end of this process, Enkidu had "become a person, dressed in clothes, just like a man" (63–64). The underlying premise of this transformation is that sexual awakening leads to maturity; after living among

---

does not contradict the claim that birth was established only after the sin in chapter 2. Bekhor Shor (3:17) makes the intriguing suggestion that both accounts should be read as one long narrative, but birth was renewed only after the sin. He holds that the blessing of "Be fruitful and multiply" (1:28) was said only after their sin, but it is nonetheless presented immediately after their creation:

> And that blessing He gave them on the sixth day, that is, "Be fruitful and multiply," was after their transgression, when they needed to be fruitful and reproduce. The fact that it says, "Fill the earth and subdue it," shows that this is after the sin, for otherwise it should have said, Fill the garden," for they lived there before. But this blessing was said only after their transgression, only it was written there, following their creation.

78. See especially in Engnell, "'Knowledge' and 'Life.'" In this context, it is interesting to consider the suggestion of Matitiahu Tsevat, "The Two Trees that were in the Garden," *Eretz Yisrael* 12 (1975): 40–43, who compares our story to an Ugaritic text and claims that the Tree of Knowledge is in fact the Tree of Death, the opposite of the Tree of Life. Its name is changed because otherwise it would be unclear why the woman is tempted to eat from it. However, according to our reading, this "Tree of Death" is in fact a "Tree of Birth" which poses birth as the solution to death.

79. Gordis, "The Knowledge of Good and Evil"; John A. Bailey, "Initiation and the Primal Woman in Gilgamesh and Genesis 2–3," *JBL* 89 (1970): 137–150; Robert Davidson, *Genesis 1–11* (CBC: Cambridge, 1973), 34–35; Westermann, *Genesis*, vol. 1, 336–337; Joel Rosenberg, *King and Kin* (Bloomington, 1986), 54. Rosenberg also compares the conclusion of both stories, where in both, the hero (Gilgamesh, the woman) lose their immortality because of a serpent (ibid., 63).

> the animals, Enkidu begins to walk upright, dons clothing, and leaves the rural setting where he was born. The parallel elements between the texts are clear, even if not explicit: sexual awakening leads to human maturity, to covering up, to movement towards culture and away from nature.[80]

Nonetheless, despite the sexual overtones that permeate the narrative, this reading does not easily function on a literal level. While Westermann's claim that this interpretation is "quite untenable"[81] is grossly exaggerated, it does indeed present several difficulties. These can be summarized in three points:

1. The tree's name is not simply "the Tree of Knowledge" but "the Tree of Knowledge of Good and Evil." Even though the root of the word "knowledge" functions as a euphemism for sexual relations in the Bible, the phrase "good and evil" does not appear again in this sense. This part of the tree's name, then, cannot be automatically associated with sexuality.[82] Attempts to read the name this way (based on comparisons with II Sam 19:36, for example) only prove the problematic nature of this reading.
2. The description of the tree later on in the story connects the "knowledge of good and evil" with the phrase "*neḥmad… lehaskil*" (3:6). The word *sekhel* is associated with intellect, wisdom, and knowledge,[83] resulting in translations such as, "desirable for

---

80. Drewermann makes the (grossly exaggerated) claim that the story represents stages of sexual development. He interprets every element of the story in a sexual light. For example, he deliberates whether the two trees represent breastfeeding, or whether they are phallic symbols. See a discussion of his reading in Bernhard Lang, *Eugen Drewermann: interprète de la Bible* (Paris, 1994), 79–108. On sexual maturity in the story, see also Lyn M. Bechtel, "Genesis 2.4b–3.24: A Myth about Human Maturation," *JSOT* 67 (1995): 3–26.
81. Westermann, *Genesis*, vol. 1, 243. For a detailed rejection of a sexual reading, see, for example, Kimelman, "The Seduction of Eve."
82. As noted by Day, *From Creation to Babel*, 43.
83. Onkelos translates *lehaskil* as "to look at" (and see also Ibn Janah, *The Book of Roots*, 'S-KH-L'), but it is important to remember that Onkelos uses terms of "seeing" or

gaining wisdom,"[84] and, "to be desired to make one wise."[85] This certainly implies that the sin is related to cognitive knowledge rather than to carnal knowledge.[86]

3. At the end of the story, God states, "Man has now become like one of us, knowing good and evil" (3:22). Nahmanides already observed that this verse cannot be easily reconciled with the idea that Adam and Eve's sin was related to carnal knowledge.[87] Some argue that as sexuality is related to birth and reproduction in the story, humanity now has a godlike ability to create,[88] but as the text focuses on "knowledge" rather than its consequences, this reading is not easily adopted.[89]

The conclusion, if so, is complex. Neither reading can be fully embraced, but neither can be fully rejected. The Tree of Knowledge seems to be grafted from both elements – whose connection I will shortly clarify – and a bite from its fruit imbues cognitive ability as well as sexuality.[90]

Over the course of the story, both elements are manifest in different places. This oscillation is especially evident in the dialogue between the woman and the serpent. When the serpent attempts to persuade her to eat from the tree, it says, "For God knows that on the day you eat from it your eyes will be opened, and you will be like God, knowing good

---

"looking" in the deeper sense of "understanding," similar to how the sages often use those terms (see Rabbi Refael B. Posen, *Parshegen: Exegesis and Sources for Onkelos' Translation – Genesis* [Jerusalem, 2013], 112–113).

84. New International Version Bible (NIV).

85. New Revised Standard Version Bible (NRSV).

86. BDB, 968.

87. Nahmanides 2:9. See also Umberto Cassuto, *Encyclopedia Biblica,* s.v. "*Etz HaDaat,*" vol. 6 [Jerusalem, 1972], among many others who have interpreted this way.

88. Gordis, "The Knowledge of Good and Evil," 135.

89. The suggestion that the narrative premise is that God also has "sexual awareness" is not convincing (Knohl, *Biblical Beliefs,* 34). As I will explain, the intentional wordplay with the word *daat* in the story allows a sexual reading without its pertaining to God. Therefore, Kaufmann's conclusion (which Knohl opposes) that sexuality in the story applies to humanity but not to God stands (Kaufmann, *The Religion of Israel,* vol. 2, 410).

90. I do not necessarily mean to say that the story's premise is that there were no sexual relations between man and woman before the sin (see 2:24). Rather, following the sin, the nature of sexual desire changed and became part of reality, as Ibn Ezra claims.

and evil" (3:5). Given the comparison to God's knowledge of good and evil – and the root Y-D-A, indicating knowing, appears twice, both times associated with God – the sin seems to be related to cognitive awareness.

After the serpent's persuasion, however, the narrator describes the tree from the woman's perspective, a description which raises both intellectual and sexual connotations: "The woman saw that the tree was good for food, enticing for the eyes, and a pleasing source of wisdom" (3:6). As mentioned, the third description associates the tree with intellectual knowledge, but this phrase is preceded by the description of the tree as "good for food" (not "good and evil") and "enticing for the eyes." The word "*taava*," "enticing," appears in different biblical contexts, always as an expression of great longing – mostly physical craving, such as craving for meat,[91] a particular kind of drink,[92] certain valuable objects,[93] and so on – and is certainly consistent with a sexual reading.[94] Note the difference between the narrator's description of the tree in chapter 2 and the woman's perception of it just before her sin:

2:9	**3:6**
Every tree of pleasing appearance	That the tree was good for food
And good for food	That it was enticing for the eyes
	And a pleasing source of wisdom

The description focalized through the woman makes use of the same expressions in reverse order.[95] The description "good for food" is echoed in full, while the woman in Genesis 3:6 makes two observations in parallel to "pleasing appearance": "enticing (*taava*) for the eyes," and "a pleasing source (*neḥmad*) of wisdom." Though the roots

91. Num. 11:4; Deut. 12:20; I Sam. 2:16.

92. II Sam. 23:15.

93. Deut. 5:18.

94. See also W. C. Williams, "*Ava*," *NIDOTTE* 1: 304–306. I believe that there is deliberate wordplay in Proverbs that juxtaposes desire with the Tree of Life: "Hope deferred sickens the heart, / But desire realized is a tree of life" (Prov. 13:12).

95. Kiel, *Genesis*, 73.

Ḥ-M-D and T-A-V-H are frequently paired,[96] the first description in 2:9 seems to be purely aesthetic, while the woman's observation touches on a deeper point.[97]

This wordplay invites comparison between two instances of another acutely ambiguous word in the narrative, "*arum*." The description of the serpent as *arum*, where the word takes on the sense of "cunning," or "sly," can be associated with knowledge, intellect, and awareness,[98] whereas the man and woman's literal "nakedness," "*arumim*," raises sexual connotations.[99]

Both themes, in fact, accompany the reader until the end of the story. Verses 21–22 conclude the story on a note of sexuality and fertility, when Eve is given a name redolent with fertility and motherhood, and Adam and Eve are dressed in garments of skin.[100] In verse 23, however, God expresses concern that "Man has now become like one of us, knowing good and evil," which, again, implies that through their sin, humanity has gained knowledge and understanding.

---

96. See also Williams, "*Ava*."
97. Compare to Kimelman, "The Seduction of Eve."
98. Regarding the connection between the two terms, compare the verse that features a few verses after the aforementioned verse in Proverbs: "Every clever man (*arum*) acts knowledgeably (*bedaat*), but a dullard exposes his stupidity" (Prov. 13:16).
99. Paul Kübel makes the interesting observation that the wordplay between the two instances of the word "*arum*" in 2:25 and 3:1 shows that the serpent, like that in Gilgamesh, is able to shed his skin and renew himself. He claims that the serpent promises the woman that she will become like him if she eats from the tree, but instead of life, the fruit results in mortality (Kübel, "Ein Wortspiel in Genesis 3 und sein Hintergrund: Die 'kluge' Schlange und die 'nackten' Menschen," *Biblische Notizen* 93 [1998]: 11–22). This theory would have been more plausible if it revolved around the Tree of Life. As the Tree of Knowledge is the focus, there is room to debate whether the snake promises the woman renewal and immortality. John W. Rogerson suggests that the garments God dresses them in – *ketonet or* (3:21) – also play on the word *arum*, in the connection between "*or*" and "*arum*," which are spelled similarly in the Hebrew (Rogerson, "Genesis 1–11," *CR:BS* 5 [1997]: 79). Bernard Gosse suggests that the serpent's curse, in which it is declared "*arur*," also participates in this wordplay (Bernard Gosse, "L'écriture de Gn 3, le serpent dualité de la femme et de l'homme," *Biblische Notizen* 98 [1999]: 19–20.).
100. Hans Gottlieb, Knud Jeppessen, and Benedikt Otzen, *Myth in the Old Testament*, trans. F. Cryer (London, 1980), 49.

This fundamental dichotomy is also at play in verse 23. The serpent promises the woman that if she eats from the tree, she will become like God: "On the day you eat from it your eyes will be opened, and you will be like God, knowing good and evil" (3:5). Is this promise fulfilled? The serpent is certainly a nasty character, but is he also a liar? As soon as they eat from the fruit, "The eyes of both of them were opened, and they knew," not good and evil, as the serpent promised them, but that "they were naked" (3:7). Their illusions are shattered. They become aware not of divine knowledge, but of their own naked state.[101] Yet verse 23 is in clear dialogue with the serpent's promise: "And the Lord God said, 'Man has now become like one of us, knowing good and evil.'" The serpent promised divine knowledge; now God confirms that they have "become like one of us." Despite the immediate narrative focus on their sexuality, it emerges that they have indeed become like God, knowing what is good and what is evil.

The characters of Adam and Eve undergo a dual process over the course of the narrative. The particular powers of the wondrous tree are never explicated, but the characters' lives are suffused with both sexual and cognitive awareness as the forbidden fruit courses down their veins.

How can we explain this two-sided theme? How can sexual and cognitive awareness result from a single bite? In this context, I wish to return to my original question: Is the story of Eden a story of straightforward sin, or does the ancient text depict a more complex scenario? I believe that this double characterization of the Tree of Knowledge is related to the fundamental theme of maturity. The process Adam and Eve undergo is a reflection of every child's path to adulthood, where on the brink of maturity, the youth's mind is opened to the moral and intellectual expanses of the world at the same time that his or her body begins to erupt with physical changes. A small child is neither aware nor ashamed of his own nakedness, nor can he truly distinguish between good and evil. If he wants something he will scream and cry for it, regardless of whether it belongs to him. With maturity, and decent education, a child learns that other values take precedence over his own desires; he cannot

101. Unlike Stratton's claim that the serpent spoke the truth, and they indeed became like God, to a certain degree (Stratton, *Out of Eden*, 87).

simply take something that belongs to someone else, even if he wants it. As a child's moral and intellectual horizons expand, their bodies, too, change and mature, and they stumble on a new, sexual consciousness. This double consciousness is reflected in the story of Eden: man and woman acquire moral, intellectual awareness along with sexual awareness.

This reading challenges the notion that eating from the Tree of Knowledge is an actual sin in the usual sense. While human acquisition of knowledge is characterized as a rebellion against God, the situation can be compared to a teenager who rebels against authority in order to achieve autonomy. Adam and Eve, after all, have no parents besides God.[102] Therein lies the key to understanding of the story – God's role is that of parent who watches His children as they mature, that of parent who arranges for their livelihood. Upon maturity, they leave His home and make a home for themselves. Their so-called punishments can be read as reflections of their maturity. While children are fed and cared for, adults must work for their bread; children have little concept of pain or hardship or responsibility, the heavy burdens of adult life. And while children are blissfully unaware of their own mortality, the sobering knowledge of death hovers in the background of adult life, and each moment brings a person closer to death, understanding from dust you came, and to dust you will return. The Tree of Life was never off-limits to man and woman, who presumably ate freely of its fruits and took their immortality for granted. Once they ate of the Tree of Knowledge, however, the knowledge of death burst into their lives and shattered their perception of their existence.[103] Adam and Eve choose to eat from the Tree of Knowledge – sacrificing the blissful ignorance of childhood – and must leave the Garden of Eden to begin their adult lives, lives full of responsibility, toil, and pain.

One piercing contradiction, however, threatens to undermine the reading of the Eden narrative as a story of maturation. As Rimon Kasher asks, how could it be that God leads the characters to sin and

102. See especially Avivah Gottlieb Zornberg, *The Murmuring Deep: Reflections on the Biblical Unconscious* (New York, 2009), 3–35.

103. A similar formulation can be found in Herbert C. Brichto, *The Names of God: Poetic Readings in Biblical Beginnings* (New York, 1998), 95.

then punishes them for it?[104] The act of eating from the Tree of Knowledge is presented as a sin; man and woman are commanded not to eat from the tree and God is furious when they do. There is no sense of a "happy ending," where the characters eventually regain what is taken away. Instead, the story concludes with a sense of despair, of paradise lost.[105] If God is interested in Adam and Eve's intellectual and moral development, then why is this process characterized as a sin?

This question spurs the complex conclusion of this unique narrative. Like Immanuel Kant, and others, I believe that the story of Eden is indeed a story of human development, of coming of age.[106] At the beginning of the story, Adam and Eve are naked, carefree children running through God's garden, and by its end they have acquired the moral, intellectual, and bodily awareness of mature adults. The ability to distinguish between good and evil is a marker of adulthood in several places in the Bible, such as, "Your children *who do not yet know good from bad,* they shall enter it" (Deut. 1:39), or, "Look, the young woman is with child and about to give birth to a son. Let her name him Immanuel. *By the time he learns to reject the bad and choose the good,* people will be feeding on butter and honey. *For before the lad knows to reject the bad and choose the good,* the ground whose two kings you dread shall be abandoned" (Is. 7:14–16).

However, the characters' development is presented through an act of rebellion. But is this rebellion positive or negative? Every parent dreads the moment when their teenage child disobeys their word – when they ignore their curfew, go out drinking, neglect their studies – and this moment is always met with disappointment, but not surprise. The

104. Kasher, "Beliefs and Exegesis: Review of Israel Knohl, *Biblical Beliefs*." *Katharsis* 8 (2008): 88.

105. Shammai Gelander suggests that God is not presented as angry in the story; rather, His words can be understood as words of counsel and guidance (Gelander, "The Story of Paradise: A Different Trial," *Beit Mikra* 39 [1994]: 350). However, the dominant atmosphere is one of punishment, not guidance. The repetition of "*etzev*" in the punishments of both man and woman leaves no room for doubt that life in the Garden of Eden is preferable to life outside of Eden.

106. Kant repeats this in several places, such as in Kant, *Religion and Rational Theology,* trans. and ed. A. W. Wood and G. Di Giovanni (Cambridge, 1996), 411.

parents' anger is justified, even though they have expected this rebellion from the moment of their child's birth. The teenager establishes his or her autonomy through disobedience, by breaking away from his or her parents, and the fact that they made the same mistakes in their own youth, rebelled against their own parents to establish their own autonomy, does not lessen the anger or ease the growing pains that they feel when their own children break away.

The story of Eden is the story of autonomy achieved by rebellion.[107] Though this rebellion results in punishment, only through it can a person gain independence, stake his or her own path, and become aware of his or her own body and its mortality. Sigmund Freud writes:

> The freeing of an individual, as he grows up, from the authority of his parents is one of the most necessary *though one of the most painful results* brought about by the course of his development. It is quite essential that this liberation should occur and it may be presumed that it has been to some extent achieved by everyone who has reached a normal state.[108]

People have free choice; their choices, therefore, will not always be wise, or good, or correct. If they were, they would not have been free to make. As Leon Kass points out, "In the first story, human freedom appears to be our badge of distinction; in the second story, human freedom is the source of our troubles."[109]

Knohl argues that this freedom is so necessary to the state of the human condition that God Himself places the serpent at the Tree of Knowledge, "to help them become mature and become like God, Knower of good and evil."[110] Suspended in their innocent state of

---

107. In addition to Kant, Buchanan already emphasized the motif of maturation in the story (George W. Buchanan, "The Old Testament Meaning of Good and Evil," *JBL* 75 [1956]: 114–120, and a similar approach is taken by Gelander, "A Different Trial," especially 347–348); Knohl, *Biblical Beliefs*, 28–34.

108. Sigmund Freud, "Family Romances," in *Collected Papers*, vol. 5, ed. C. J. Strachey (New York, 1959), 74–78.

109. Kass, *The Beginning of Wisdom*, 56.

110. Knohl, *Biblical Beliefs*, 31.

childhood, devoid of rebellious spirit and curiosity, neither man nor woman would have ever taken interest in the tree on their own. The serpent, created by God and placed at the Tree of Knowledge, convinces Eve to look at the tree through its own eyes, the eyes of the "most cunning of all the wild animals." For a moment, she sees the bold, bright colors of the tree and its fruit, and succumbs to temptation, temptation she would never have reached on her own. This reading presents Eve's sin as an inevitable, unavoidable rite of passage. Again, the sin is not the narrative's turning point, but an integral part of humanity's story.

From this perspective, God's decree of man and woman's punishment is an especially tragic scene. The "adolescent" characters believe that eating the forbidden fruit will bring them independence, autonomy, and control over their own lives, but their punishments reveal the truth: rebellion leads to enslavement, not freedom. Woman will long for man, and he will rule over her; man will toil away at the earth, and reap in sorrow for the rest of his life. Woman's freedom is handed over to others; man no longer controls the ground that he must work and keep, and it will bring forth thorns and thistles along with man's hard-earned bread. The serpent's promise of godlike power and freedom is eclipsed by the daily struggle of survival this freedom exacts.

This brings us back to our initial question: Is man's reassignment to the earth a solution for the earth's plight or a punishment for humanity? Is his transition from God's private garden to the rest of the world's soil colored in a positive light, or in the bleak tones of punishment and failure? The answer is that both readings are justified. In this narrative, maturity is presented as a painful process, not a joyful celebration. Knowledge comes at a heavy price, shattering the child's world of blissful ignorance. The rebellious teenager leads himself to a world tainted with sin and burdened with toil, but the ground is waiting for him, waiting for him to break the crust of the soil and tease out its fruits.

The narrative's conclusion holds the rope at both ends. Adam's expulsion from the garden is a punishment for rebelling against God, and he is not just banished, but *sent,* back to the earth from whence he came, to heal its plight. The plight of the earth at the beginning of the story hints to its etiological nature, explaining why man must toil away at the earth and earn his bread with the sweat of his brow, why children are born in pain and suffering, why humans, unlike animals, wear clothing, why women and men instinctively shy away from serpents and other creatures who creep, why there is death in the world, and why we no longer live in God's lush, richly watered garden.

In this way, the Garden of Eden plays a dual role in the narrative: it is a physical site, the source of four mighty rivers and the setting of humanity's first drama, but it also functions as a symbolic site that every person passes through over the course of his or her development.[111]

How, then, is human adolescence depicted? Moved by the serpent's words, the woman sees the tree through new eyes. It is now seen as a source of temptation, hiding a promise within. This promise is the promise of "becoming like God." Each and every teenager effectively aspires to be like God, to be unlimited, all powerful, unstoppable, and, at the same time, perfect, magnanimous, idealistic:

> There is an evil inclination hidden deep in the depths of the soul, a bone-rotting envy that drenches any hint of light in dismal darkness. It is an unfamiliar envy – many will never know it, for different factors prevent it from being expressed. But it sleeps – it is dormant in the recesses of the mortal soul, and it sometimes flares out in forms other than its real form, as all products of envy do; they don alien guise and always bear a foreign name. This unfamiliar envy is *envy of God*; humanity envies God for His infinite joy, His absolute perfection. This envy distorts reason and plunges sense into darkness, dulls intellect and riles the spirit. And when its fury can no longer be contained, it results in utter heresy, in order to relieve the aching, decayed spirit of the piercing sting of envy. There is no cure for this ailment, besides divine illumination.[112]

111. See a similar formulation in Stordalen, *Echoes of Eden*, 299–301.

112. Rabbi Abraham Isaac Kook, *Shemona Kevatzim*, 1:129; it was also published in a slightly different form in *Orot HaKodesh*, vol. 2. The covert reference to Nietzsche (envy that leads to heresy) is clear in this excerpt.

The transition from the innocence of childhood to adolescence is explored from different perspectives, including between the human and God, between the human and his or her surroundings (especially their significant other), and between the human and his or her self.

The Adolescent and God

Once again, the narrative's turning point is not the sin itself. The sin, of course, propels the plot forward, but the ensuing dialogue between the sinners and God is the central axis of the story, and this has broad implications. Maturation is a necessary process; rebelling against authority to achieve autonomy is a necessary stage that every parent anticipates and dreads as one. The teenager, heady with his or her own newfound freedom, will make mistakes. It is their reaction to their own mistakes, and their ability to interpret the nature of their actions, which will determine whether the parents will sigh with relief or reel with dread at the inarguable fact of their child's autonomy.

The tragedy of the Eden story is not human sin; it is the sinners' reaction to their sin in the face of God.

"Did you eat from the tree?"

"The woman made me do it!"

"Did you eat from the tree?"

"The serpent made me do it!"

This dialogue reflects a crucial element of human development. Children cannot be held accountable for their actions; true sin is an adult accomplishment, reserved for those who dress to hide their nakedness. Yet adulthood is defined not only by sin, but by the ability to face God and admit these sins. Children are not plagued by profound religious guilt; guilt, too, is an adult burden. Despite the New Age vilification of guilt, the recognition and acceptance of guilt is the key to repentance in the Bible, and this is what makes Adam and Eve's response to God's questions so disappointing. Denial is a tempting path, but a person's religious world is formed through taking responsibility for one's actions.

Through sin, the religious teenager is able to form a dialogue with God; through sin, he or she learns how painful and difficult it is to take responsibility and admit guilt.

The Adolescent and Society: Intimacy

The narrative focuses intensely on the relationship between man and woman. The story opens with an idyllic picture of marital harmony: "That is why a man leaves his father and mother and clings to his wife and they become one flesh" (2:24). The man chooses the woman who was formed from his side, after rejecting the animals that were, like him, created from the earth itself. According to a straightforward reading of the text, God removed one "*tzela*," "side," from the man, "built" it up into the form of a woman, and sealed off the man's flesh. *Tzela* is usually an architectural term,[113] such that the verb "*vayiven*," "and He built," is apt in this context, and this language reflects the almost technical division of man into two separate entities, man and woman. Technically separated like puzzle pieces that fit together to form a whole, the question becomes if man and woman are two distinct entities, or two halves, waiting to be reunited to form "one flesh"? This harmonious imagery reflects a union – or reunion – both physical and spiritual.

This is how the story begins, but its ending is vastly different. The temptation that stirs the Garden of Eden shatters this idyllic harmony. The woman who turned her back on the divine command her husband taught her is now subjected to his authority; the woman who led her husband to sin will now be under his dominion. As Nahmanides comments: "This is measure-for-measure, for she gave to her husband and he ate at her command, and her punishment is that she will no longer command him, while he will command her with his every desire."[114] Their union began with the promise of steadfast, mutual devotion (2:24), but ends as a hierarchic, authoritative relationship (3:16). Woman's name is first derived from her relationship with her husband: "This shall be called Woman (*isha*) because from Man (*ish*) was taken this" (2:23), while her name at the end of the story is derived from her status as the "mother of all living things" (3:20). Now her name is defined not by her

113. Kiel, *Genesis*, 66.

114. Nahmanides, Gen. 3:16. See also Frisch, *Labor*, 30–31; Jacobs, *Measure for Measure*, 145–150; Shemesh, *Measure for Measure*, 262.

relationship with her husband, but from her role as the mother, the bearer, of the next generation.[115]

The change in man and woman's relationship is expressed not only in the new name of "Eve," but in the text's renewed reference to the man as "Adam." The man is usually referred to as "Adam" (either as an actual name or with a definite article as a noun, "*ha'adam*," "the man"), but at the moment of woman's creation, the word "*ish*" is used for the first time: "This shall be called Woman (*isha*) because from Man (*ish*) was taken this" (2:23). Given the similarity between the words "woman" and "man" (*isha* and *ish*), from the moment of her creation the text is attuned to this connection: "That is why a man (*ish*) leaves his father and mother and clings to his wife (*isha*) and they become one flesh" (2:24). Though the word "*adam*" is still the default word for "man" in the text, the word "*ish*" is used in thematic conjunction with the woman, such as, "She took of its fruit and ate it, and she gave some also to her husband (*ish*) who was with her, and he ate" (3:6), or, "Your longing will be for your husband (*ishekh*), and he will rule over you" (3:16). This is not the case, however, in the verse where Adam changes the woman's name; while we might expect him to be referred to as "*ish*" because he is relating to his wife, the verse states: "And *the man* (*ha'adam*) named his wife Eve, because she was the mother of all life" (3:20). This expresses the change in their relationship. Though they appear together, Adam is

115. The name *Ḥava*, Eve, may also echo the Aramaic word for "serpent," *ḥivya* (this wordplay is already hinted to in Genesis Rabba 20:11); Stade already noted that this may be intentional wordplay (Bernhard Stade, *Geschichte des Volkes Israel* [Berlin, 1887–1889], vol. 1, 633). See, in his wake, Julius Wellhausen, *Reste arabischen Heidentums* (Berlin, 1897), 154; Jan Heller, "Der Name Eva," *ArOr* 26 (1958): 636–656; Skinner, *Genesis*, 85; Moshe Garsiel, *Midrashic Name Derivations in the Bible* (Ramat Gan, 1987), 49–50. Cassuto even claims that this is the *primary* meaning of the name in the biblical context, while the explicit etymology is only secondary (Umberto Cassuto, *Encyclopedia Biblica*, s.v. "*Ḥava*," vol. 3 [Jerusalem, 1958]). After their expulsion from Eden, therefore, every mention of Eve's name evoked the memory of the serpent. Talia Sutskover suggests that the name *Ḥava* recalls the verb *hishtaḥavaya*, "bowing down," which is related to the new hierarchy between man and woman (Sutskover, "Name Giving in Genesis and Establishing Authority," *Beit Mikra* 57 [2012]: 38–40).

associated with the earth (*adama*) once more, while Eve is defined by her impending motherhood. No longer "man" and "woman," they are now Adam and Eve, covering their shame and nakedness from each other with garments.

My point is not that romantic intimacy is experienced only by the young and innocent, to be replaced with a strictly pragmatic relationship once adult life and responsibilities set in, but rather that the story presents two models of a marital relationship, one of which develops only after rebellion against God. This rebellion, it emerges, has ramifications for intimacy as well as other relationships with society.

As part of the new world order "after the fall," the relationship between humanity and animals also undergoes changes. Though Adam rejected the animals as his life partner and personal, intimate "helpmate," he nonetheless named them, defining their role in the world according to their nature as an expression of his relationship with the living world. And indeed, humanity maintains a certain connection with the animal world. Man plows the earth with oxen, uses dogs to herd his flock, consumes their milk for food, and their wool for clothing. The serpent exploits humanity's connection with the animal world to lead the woman to temptation and rebellion against God, and this results in tension and enmity between the human and certain animals. Could it be that this story seeks to explain why very young children do not seem to have the natural, almost universal, fear of snakes and creepy-crawlies? Perhaps this fear, too, is acquired with maturity, with the developing understanding of the dangers of the natural world. However, it may be that like the new model of human intimacy that emerges as a result of sin, the narrative is presenting a new model of the human's relationship with the natural world. While positive human-animal relationships are maintained with certain animals, other creatures become sources of fear and danger. Most people have an innate fear of serpents, insects, spiders, those creatures that creep and scuttle across the ground.[116]

---

116. There is, of course, the possibility that the serpent does not represent the animal kingdom in general, but is its own character, in which case the narrative illuminates the relationship between humanity and the serpent. Indeed, the snake is not a domestic animal, and is perceived as a danger by many cultures.

The Adolescent and the Self

The most profound change every adolescent experiences is their relationship with their own self. An innocent child has no concept of death, or responsibility, or the burden of earning one's bread. With God's decree, the lives of man and woman are suddenly plunged into pain and sorrow: "I will intensify your *pain* in pregnancy; in *pain* shall you give birth to children" (3:16), and, "Cursed is the ground because of you; through *painful* toil will you eat of it all the days of your life" (3:17). Both fruit of the womb and fruit of the earth will only be yielded through pain and toil. This key word, "*itzavon*," "pain" or "sorrow," which crops up again over the following chapters (5:29; 6:6), reveals the most crucial change mentioned in the story.[117] In their innocent, childlike state, man and woman walk naked through the garden, with no awareness of their vulnerability. They eat freely of the fruits of the garden, with no concept of lack or need. They have no idea of mortality or the need for continuity. All of this changes when they are expelled from the Garden of Eden, which is to say, when they reach maturity.

Woman's curse is not that childbirth causes pain; the need for birth itself, a long and painful process, is the new concept that shatters her world. According to this creation story, man and woman wander through the garden, eating freely from the Tree of Life (which, again, is not forbidden to them). Within the garden, they are immortal; within the garden, there is no place for birth, as there is no idea of death. Birth is the immanent result of death, which is only introduced once woman and man eat from the Tree of Knowledge. Once humanity becomes mortal, man and woman are introduced to the idea of birth, which means they must produce the next generation to replace them. This process is a punishment in itself – the once little girl who had roamed free and naked in the garden suddenly learns that her body is a temporary vessel, a vessel for birth and propagation,

117. Stordalen, in *Echoes of Eden*, 209, sees the incorporation of the word *etzev* in the story as a characteristic of "wisdom literature" (see Ps. 127:2; Prov. 5:10; 10:22; 14:23; 15:1). This is indeed in sync with the narrative atmosphere: a piercing, painful look at the suffering of human life, and the interpretation of this phenomenon as the result of human sin.

and she must begin a process fraught with physical and emotional pain. Her physical pain culminates with birth itself; her emotional toil lasts for a lifetime. The man's life is not colored in a more optimistic light. He receives the burden of keeping himself and his family alive, of feeding and sustaining them. The life that awaits him outside of Eden is a life of pain and toil. Every morning he must venture out into the field to tame the cursed soil and extract its fruits from among the thorns and thistles; every evening he returns home to renew his strength for the next day's toil. Man and woman's knowledge of death costs them dearly, and now their lives are spent in a struggle against death. Woman's task is to produce the next generation so that humanity will endure after they themselves succumb to death; man's task is to defy death each day by producing bread to sustain them on a daily basis.

The triangle of earth-man-woman (*adama-adam/ish-isha*) forms an inextricable, interdependent triangle. Man, *adam,* is formed from the earth, *adama,* just as woman, *isha,* is formed from man, *ish*. Man must struggle to produce the fruits of the earth, and woman must struggle to produce the fruits of her womb. Man is dependent upon the earth for his sustenance and upon woman for the next generation, but woman, too, is dependent on man, and he rules over her. In a certain sense, the earth is also dependent on man to cultivate and bring forth its fruits – this is, of course, the narrative framework, which concludes with God sending man "to work the earth from which he had been taken" (3:23). Earth needs man, but it is the source of man's sorrow and pain. Woman needs man's protection and sustenance, but he rules over her. Man needs woman and earth for their fruits, which he cultivates with painful toil.[118]

Man and woman once walked through God's garden with no burdens, no responsibilities. There, they picked fruit from its trees, and were naked without shame. Their knowledge of sex and death costs them dearly, and they are sent away to raise their own fruits through painful toil. This pain is the result of sin, of rebellion against God; this pain is the burden of adulthood and responsibility.

118. Compare to van Wolde, *Words Become Worlds*, 28.

Cain and Abel: Seeds of Hatred, Seeds of Exile (Ch. 4)

The story of Cain and Abel consists of three acts: Cain and Abel's birth and the rejection of Cain's sacrifice, murder and punishment, and Cain's dynasty. Each act can be read on its own, but they form a sequence: Cain's rejection in Act One leads to Abel's murder in Act Two, and, as I will discuss, Cain's dynasty in Act Three can be read in light of the figure of Cain, the founder of the dynasty. The three acts of Cain's life read easily as a single narrative spanning chapter 4, which opens with the birth of Cain and Abel and ends with the birth of Seth, Abel's "replacement."[1] The use of the expression, "Adam *again* knew his wife," refers back to the beginning of the

1. Practically, the chapter concludes with verse 26: "And Seth too had a son, and he named him Enosh. Then people began to call on the name of the Lord." This is a key verse when tracing the relationship between the God of Israel and humanity, and I will discuss it in context. This has no implications for the narrative framework, however.

chapter and recalls Cain and Abel once more, implying that what has transpired since the first time Adam "knew" his wife is the story of their descendants. I will focus on each individual act, and on the drama as a cohesive whole.

In general, the biblical text implies that there is definite order within reality, definite logic, divine reward and punishment. With few exceptions, such as Ecclesiastes, which challenges the notion of "world order" (a notion ancient Egyptian wisdom literature refers to as *maat*), the Bible generally presents a view that there is definite world order.[2] Even those who challenge this view do so on the premise that order is ideal. The concept of "measure for measure" is a principle which highlights the idea of justice and logic within reality. Moreover, this balance does not only apply to human reality, but is extended to animals and even objects.[3]

Can this idea be traced in the story of Cain and Abel? Zvi Adar believes that this is the moral premise of the narrative:

> God is the punisher, who deals with the wicked according to their wickedness. Cain, who cut Abel off from the world, is cut off from the earth that gave him its produce, from the world of order, and from divine providence.[4]

The motivation for this approach is clear: this is the first instance of murder in the world, and it should serve as a moral precedent, as a logical, "fair" case study that draws on the principles of *midda keneged midda* in order to execute justice. Yet there are two surprising scenes in this case study; both the sacrifice scene and the murder scene generate expectations of logic and order, but both shatter these expectations.

2. See Michael Fox, "The Conception of Divinity in Didactic Wisdom Literature," *Beer Sheva* 1 (1973): 162–170.
3. See especially Jacobs, *Measure for Measure*; Shemesh, *Measure for Measure.*
4. Zvi Adar, *The Book of Genesis: An Introduction to the Biblical World* (Tel Aviv, 1967), 25. Others disagree, such as Jacobs: "There is no linguistic-stylistic connection between the act and its proposed result, and the relevant connection is not convincing" (*Measure for Measure*, 11n4, 143).

ACT ONE: BIRTH AND SACRIFICE

From ancient exegesis, through medieval commentary, and in modern scholarship, Cain is generally read as a negative figure from the beginning of the story, not only during the murder scene.[5] At least three readings express this view:

1. Cain is the Son of the Devil

Pirkei DeRabbi Eliezer states:

> The Serpent-Rider had intercourse with her, and she conceived Cain. Afterwards, Adam had intercourse with her, and she conceived Abel, as it says, "And Adam knew Eve his wife." What did he know? He knew that she was pregnant, and perceived that it was not from the lower world but from the upper world.[6]

This midrash draws a distinction between Cain and Abel from the moment of their conception, claiming that Cain is not the son of Adam, but of the "Serpent-Rider." This view may already be evident in the Peshitta, the Syriac-Aramaic translation of the Torah, which translates, "Cain's face fell," as "*ve'itkamrei apohei,*" that "his face blackened" (from the root of K-M-R), which some interpret as a reflection of his satanic nature.[7] Though this reading was not unanimously accepted,[8] it nonetheless

5. For a survey of early exegesis in this direction (especially that which is reflected in the Septuagint, Philo, and the Wisdom of Solomon), see Robert Hayward, "What Did Cain Do Wrong? Jewish and Christian Exegesis of Genesis 4:3–6," in *The Exegetical Encounter between Jews and Christians in Late Antiquity*, ed. E. Grypeou and H. Spurling (JCPS 18: Leiden, 2009), 101–123.
6. *Pirkei DeRabbi Eliezer*, ch. 21
7. As held by Etan Levine, "The Syriac Version of Genesis IV 1–16," *VT* 26 (1976): 70–78. Compare also to Genesis Rabba, where it says that Cain's face "became like charred wood." This is generally interpreted as blackened, like the Syriac. Even the interpretation "grew red" is suitable for the figure of the devil.
8. Yeshayahu Maori disagrees with this reading. He believes that the root K-M-R can mean "became sad," and that this is the meaning of the verb here (Maori, *The Peshitta Version of the Pentateuch and Early Jewish Exegesis* [Jerusalem, 1995], 238–239n63).

had a strong influence on exegetical Jewish and non-Jewish traditions.[9] Targum Pseudo-Jonathan, for example, interprets: "And Adam knew that Eve his wife had become pregnant from Samael, the angel of the Lord."[10]

2. Worker of the Cursed Earth

In the eyes of Rashi, Cain represents evil, while Abel is good.[11] Abel is already favored from birth: "The word "*et*" appears three times, indicating that a twin sister was born with Cain, while two were born with Abel; it therefore states, 'she *also* gave birth.'"[12]

Rashi's preference is more marked in the next scene, when Cain and Abel choose their professions. On Genesis 4:2, Rashi states, "Shepherd – because the earth was cursed, he ceased to work it." While Abel chooses not to work the cursed land, Cain is drawn to it. Rashi

9. James Kugel shows how early Christian exegesis depicts Cain as the son of the devil: "This is what distinguishes between the sons of God and the sons of the devil: Anyone who does not act charitably is not from God, as well as anyone who does not love his brothers. For this is the order which you heard before, for each to love his brother. Not like Cain, who came from an evil source, and murdered his brother. Why did he kill him? For all his deeds were evil, and his brother's deeds were true" (John, First Letter, 3:9–12). Beyond the contrast between Cain, whose "deeds were evil," and Abel, whose "deeds were true," note that Cain "came from an evil source," which clearly implies that he was the son of the devil. Kugel adds that the textual source of this argument may have come from the curious expression, "I have acquired a *man* through God" – why refer to a newborn baby as a "man"? He proposes that the word "man" often means "angel" in the Bible, and the verse can be read as, "I have made a pact with the *man* – i.e., the angel Satan – as the father of her child (Kugel, *How to Read the Bible: A Guide to Scripture, Then and Now* [New York, 2007], 60).
10. See the discussion in Mark W. Scarlata, *Outside of Eden: Cain in the Ancient Versions of Genesis 4.1–16* (LHB/OTS 573: New York and London, 2012), 39–41.
11. Compare to the words of Meir Rafeld, in "The Figure of Cain in the Eyes of Rashi and Nahmanides," *Tallelei Orot* 9 (2000): 23, where it says: "The conceptual-educational idea of Rashi in this tractate is to portray the epitome of evil and destruction. To embody this, Cain is elected from the beginning of his despicable behavior following his offering, through his cruelty as the spiller of blood without reason, his rebellion against divine providence, and his refusal to admit his sin."
12. His commentary on Gen. 4:1–2. This is based on Genesis Rabba 22:3, which predicates its argument not on the verb alone but on "she also *gave birth*" – not an extra pregnancy but an extra birth, as it refers to a twin.

seems to base his words on the *Midrash HaGadol*,[13] which is more caustic: "Abel was a shepherd – he feared God's curse of the land, as it says, 'In sorrow shall you eat of it,' and he was involved with shepherding livestock. But Cain did not fear God, and stubbornly said, 'I will work the earth.'" The author of this midrash connects their choices with the previous episode, where God curses the ground, and goes so far as to accuse Cain of stubbornly refusing to fear God.

3. A Pathetic Offering

A third exegetical bias against Cain focuses on the quality of the offering he presents. As Rashi famously claims, "From the fruit of the earth – of the most inferior," while Genesis Rabba accuses Cain of offering "from the waste; this can be compared to an evil peasant who would eat the first, finest fruits and leave the worst, latest produce for the king."[14] At its mildest, this reading characterizes Cain as someone who does not maintain a close, meaningful relationship with God, and therefore does the very least required of him. A harsher interpretation of this midrash sees Cain as a haughty, arrogant figure who believes that he deserves to eat the best of his produce, for all his own hard work. The midrash's use of "the first fruits" and "the last of the fruits" hints to a connection between Cain's attitude and the mitzva of bringing *bikkurim*, the first of the crop. The sages decreed that this mitzva applies only to the seven species of grains indigenous to Israel, and a person must take care to choose only the finest of his produce. In contrast to these guidelines, Rashi and the Midrash hold that Cain brings inferior, leftover produce as an offering to God.

Rabbenu Baḥya also casts Cain in this negative light:

> "And Abel was (*vayehi*) a shepherd, and Cain was (*haya*) a tiller of the soil." It should have said, *vayehi* for Cain, just as it says *vayehi* for Abel. But the two of them were not equal, but opposites; one was

13. As suggested by Rabbi Menchem Mendel Kasher, *Torah Shelema* (Jerusalem, 1992), Genesis 4, notes on no. 24.
14. Rashi on Gen. 4:3; Genesis Rabba 22. On "the latest produce," see, for example, Mishna Terumot 4:6.

> righteous, and the other was evil. And from here we learn that good and evil share a single root; both come from good, for the first man was entirely good, yet both evil and good issued forth from him....
>
> [Cain] should have brought the first fruits of one of the seven species, but the text reveals his inferiority and the narrowness of his eye *for he was a man of evil eye*. The fact that it does not say "from *the first* of the fruits of the land," but rather, just "from the fruits of the land" implies that they were of the most inferior – flax seed, as the sages say. The text teaches that for this reason, He rejected his offering, which was not worthy, and accepted Abel's worthy offering. It says, "from the first of his flock and from their fat portions," because Abel brought from the first of his flock, worthy as an offering, while Cain brought fruits that were unworthy as an offering, not the first of the fruits but the least of the fruits.[15]

This bitter characterization of Cain seems to be an attempt to foreshadow later events in the narrative, God's rejection of Cain's offering, and, of course, Cain's murder of Abel. Why do these events unfold? The sages sought an answer. His offering was unworthy, they said; his father was the devil, they said. There must be an explanation for his downfall; the seeds of his destruction must have been planted at the start.

With Rashi in tow, then, the reader is not surprised when Cain's offering is rejected. Why, he chose to work the soil, even though it was cursed, and he brought an inferior offering! It would have been more surprising if his offering *would* have been accepted!

Yet there is danger in projecting a story's end on its beginning. Though the story is so familiar, a careful, unbiased first reading is crucial to the understanding of the narrative's meaning. In the words of Menachem Perry, "The dynamics of the literary text give birth to the meaning of the story."[16]

---

15. Rabbenu Baḥya on Gen. 4:2.
16. Menachem Perry, "Literary Dynamics: How the Order of a Text Creates Its Meaning," *Literature* 28 (1979): 6–46. I develop this basic theory in Grossman, *Text and Subtext*, 281–337.

A close reading of our text reveals not only that Cain is *not* characterized as a villain at the beginning of the story, and instead, the text is actually designed to generate identification with him.

The story opens with the birth of the two brothers: "And the man knew Eve his wife and she conceived and gave birth to Cain, saying, 'I have produced a man through God'" (4:1). The verb "*yada*," "knew," is not commonly used in this sense (compared to other verbs for intercourse, such as "*shakhav*," "lie [with]," or "*ba*," "come toward"), but this verb appears at the beginning (4:1) and end (4:25) of this narrative, and even in relation to Cain and his wife after he is banished ("And Cain knew his wife" – 4:17). This particular verb generates a connection with the previous episode, when Adam and Eve eat from the Tree of *Knowledge* of Good and Evil, a connection I will return to at the end of my analysis of this chapter. Moreover, though, the use of this particular verb reflects an emotional aspect that is not conveyed through other biblical synonyms for intercourse. To "know" someone is to have an emotional connection with him or her; in the words of Franz Delitzsch: "The work of procreation is common both to man and to animals, but *yada* never occurs in this sense of the animals."[17] The animal drive to procreate is purely biological, while human fertility and sexuality are inextricable from their emotional, moral world.

The reader's first encounter with Cain and Abel is through their name. Eve connects Cain's name to creation, to formation: "And she said, 'I have produced (*kaniti*) a man through God'" (1:4).[18]

Through this naming, the reader is introduced to Cain as an expression of human creation, of the first time a human being is born

---

17. Franz Delitzsch, *A New Commentary on Genesis*, vol. 1, trans. S. Taylor (Edinburgh, 1888), 177.
18. Albright bases this on the Ugaritic root K-N-Y, while others (such as Skinner, Hamilton, and Kiel) based this on the use of the root K-N-H in biblical Hebrew. Cain's name (the root K-Y-N), occurs in late Aramaic and Arabic with the meaning of "smith" or "ironworker" (Richard S. Hess, "Cain," *ABD* 1: 806), but the primary meaning associated with it is of course Eve's etymology in the text. Interestingly, one of Cain's descendants is the "father of those who live in tents and raise livestock (*mikne*)," and one might think that there is a connection between *Kayin* and *mikne* (Hess, "Cain," 806). Note, however, that Abel, not Cain, is the shepherd of the two.

from another human being.[19] Though some accuse Eve of arrogance, of comparing herself to God,[20] her exclamation seems to express the opposite: she is expressing faith in God, and delight in their cooperation,[21] as if to say, I have created a human being, together with God.[22] Cain's name reveals much about his mother's mind-set, but it also hints to the nature of the name bearer himself. Cain's name is a celebration of cooperation between the human and the Divine,[23] and all that remains is to wait and see whether Cain will fulfill the destiny imprinted in his name, to develop a meaningful, productive relationship with God.

Although the reader might have expected Eve to declare that she has produced a man with *Adam*, the husband who "knows" his wife at the beginning of the verse, I do not interpret this as a sign of her rejection of Adam's role. On the contrary, the verse in its entirety imparts a sense of inclusion, of expanding the partners of a person's creation to three instead of two: man, woman, and God, "with (*et*) the Lord." It was as if to say, when He created my husband and me, He alone created us, but with this one, we are partners with him.[24]

19. "The first woman, in her joy at the birth of her first son, is proud of the creative power within her, which seems, in her eyes, close to the creative power of the Creator" (Cassuto, *From Adam to Noah*, 135).

20. Borger claims that based on the Akkadian, the "*et*" should be understood as "from," as in, I have acquired a man *from* God (Rykle Borger, "Gen iv 1," *VT* 9 [1959]: 85–86). For the possibility that this verse hints to divine intervention in Cain's birth, see Cyrus Gordon, "Notes on Proper Names in the Ebla Tablets," in *Archivi Reali di Ebla-Studi*, ed. A. Archi, vol. 1 (Rome, 1988), 153–158.

21. Similar to Westermann, *Genesis*, vol. 1, 289–299.

22. How much can God be considered a participant in Cain's birth? See, for example, the discussion of David Bokovoy, "Did Eve Acquire, Create, or Procreate with Yahweh? A Grammatical and Contextual Reassessment of K-N-H in Genesis 4:1," *VT* 63 (2013): 19–35, where he compares this to the description of Sarah giving birth in 21:1 – "And the Lord took note of Sarah, as He had promised."

23. This positive reading is even more salient if we adopt the Peshitta's interpretation of "*et* YHWH" as, "I have produced a man *for* God." That is, Eve devotes Cain to service to God, similar to Hannah. See a relevant discussion in Scarlata, *Outside of Eden*, 36. Nahmanides' commentary on Gen. 4:1 is similar: "I believe that she said: This son shall be my acquisition for God, for when we die, he will serve the Creator in our place."

24. See Gunkel, *Genesis*, 42, for a similar comment. On the possibility that this presentation of partnership with God is problematic, see below.

After Cain is born, the birth of Abel is then described: "And she also gave birth to his brother, Abel" (4:2). Despite its brevity, the text manages to convey the sense that Abel is secondary to Cain. Firstly, Abel's birth is described with the verb "*vatosef*," which is an expression of addition: "And she *also* gave birth." Thus, Abel is initially characterized as an addition, as an appendix, to Cain. As the text itself states, Abel is "Cain's brother,"[25] which reinforces the connotations of the verb "*vatosef*." The fact that there is no etymology for Abel's name is only salient given the fact that Cain's name is explained by his mother. Rather than the result of an omission in the text, as some have posited, this seems to be an intentional move designed to generate asymmetry between the brothers. Cain is the protagonist; Abel is merely a supporting character.[26]

This asymmetry, of course, is only background to the most obvious hint to Abel's secondary nature: the meaning of his name. In the words of Gerhard von Rad: "An explanation of the name is not given, but everyone who hears it thinks of the other Hebrew word, *hevel* ("breath," "futility"), and takes this connotation as a somber allusion to what follows."[27] In a sense, the absence of an etymology for Abel's name is an etymology in itself: "*hevel*" is related to futility, to transience, to instability,[28] to the extent that there is no point in clarifying the meaning of his name. Whether Abel's name foreshadows his end, or is a universal symbol of human mortality, the contrast between the

25. On breaking symmetry by adding or omitting words as an intentional literary device, see Zvi Shimon, *Contrast in Biblical Narrative* (PhD diss., Bar-Ilan University, 2008), 109–112.

26. von Rad, *Genesis*, 100.

27. Like the meaning of "*hevel*," "vanity," in the book of Ecclesiastes. For the resonance of this meaning in our story, see Hillel Barzel, *New Interpretations of Literary Texts: From Theory to Method* (Ramat Gan, 1990); Russell Meek, "The Meaning of *Hevel* in Qohelet: An Intertextual Suggestion," in *The Words of the Wise Are Like Goads: Engaging Qohelet in the 21st Century*, ed. M. J. Boda et al. (Winona Lake, 2013), 241–256.

28. It may be proposed that whoever favors Rashi's interpretation that Cain's birth took place when they were still living in the Garden of Eden, before death became decreed for humans, might reason that Cain's birth took place before their sin and punishment, while Abel's birth took place after. This, however, is not likely, as I have discussed, given that this would imply that the concept of birth existed before the introduction of death, which is problematic.

brothers' names is stark. And it is through their names that the reader first becomes acquainted with the brothers: one represents partnership with God, his name resonant with strength and endurance, while the younger brother is presented as an afterthought, his name testimony to his transience and lack of importance.

Based on this introduction, the reader then learns of each brother's chosen profession: "Abel was a shepherd / while Cain was a worker of the ground" (4:2). As mentioned, Rashi sees this exposition as a positive characterization of Abel, who is duly reverent of God's curse. In the words of Abrabanel: "But Cain was a worker of the ground, his nature inclined towards the material, which God had cursed." Elchanan Samet also writes to this effect:

> Cain is a representative and founder of agriculture, before the ground was sweetened and healed by the laws of the Torah. His choice of this negative lifestyle and the influence of this lifestyle on his character led to God's rejection of his offering; this is what essentially led to the murder of his brother.[29]

This premise, which gave birth to the notion that there is fundamental tension between shepherds and farmers, is challenged by Amos Frisch:

> It is difficult to accept that Cain's actual profession is problematic. Working the land has the power to lead one to "lifting your eyes up to the heights" (Is. 40:26), and to a sense of dependence on the Creator. Conversely, shepherds are not necessarily good-hearted types (for example, the shepherds in Ezek. 34). It is difficult to find inherent criticism of working the land in this story.[30]

Frisch seems to be correct, at least in relation to the narrative's starting point. If anything, the text seems to *praise* Cain, rather than condemn him for his choice. His profession is described with precisely the same language that is used to describe man's role following his expulsion from

29. Elchanan Samet, *Studies in the Weekly Parasha*, Series 1, (Jerusalem, 2002), 17.
30. See Frisch, *Labor*, 38.

Eden, as an archetype of the future working man: "So the Lord God sent him away from the Garden of Eden, *to work the soil* from which he was taken" (3:22). As I have already noted, this verse closes a narrative circle by providing relief for the earth's plight, which is introduced at the beginning of chapter 2: "No shrub of the field was yet on earth, nor had any plant yet sprouted, for the Lord God had not brought rain upon the earth, nor was there a human to work the ground" (2:5). Cain is prepared to fill the role God intended for humanity: "And Cain was a worker of the ground." Cain is the one who fulfills God's will, who steps forward to bear humanity's burden after man is banished from Eden. Once again, the phrase, "and the man knew," at the beginning of the story harks back to the previous episode, the story of the expulsion from Eden, of eating of the Tree of Knowledge. Cain continues where the story left off.

This does not imply that Cain's profession casts criticism on Abel for failing to meet expectations; this reading is not grounded in the text either. But the fact that Cain's profession *can* be read as the nobler of the two vocations shows that there is room for both professions, and no real preference for either of them; so far, there is no criticism cast against either brother in the text.[31]

This brings us to the painful scene of Cain's rejection: "And in the course of time, it happened that Cain brought from the fruit of the ground an offering to the Lord, and Abel also brought from the firstborn of his flock and from their fat portions" (4:3–4). As mentioned, the prevalent approach sees a design of contrast, of opposition, between the brothers: Abel brings a worthy, impressive offering, "from the firstborn of his flock and from their fat portions," while Cain's offering, in contrast, can be read as inferior, only brought "from the fruit of the ground." Even if the lack of adjectives used to describe Cain's offering does not necessarily mean that Cain brought "the least of the fruits," as Rashi accuses,[32] this silence at least hints to a contrast between his

31. Another view will emerge from the story of the scattering of the nations and the Tower of Babel, that the text favors wanderers to permanent settlers, but this is not relevant at this stage of Genesis.
32. Rashi on Gen. 4:3.

offering and his brother's offering; unlike his brother, Cain did not take any pains to choose the best of his fruits. As Ibn Ezra points out, "Since it is written, 'from the firstborn of his flock' [in regard to Abel], this implies that Cain did not bring from the first of his fruits."[33] Or, as Radak notes:

> It seems that they were of inferior quality. Or, he brought from what was left over after he had eaten. This is all a display of contempt, and therefore his offering was not accepted. And he did not bring from the first of the fruits either, for if he had, it would have said so, as it did in regard to Abel. Therefore his offering was not accepted.[34]

Is this reading binding? A comparison between characters certainly contributes to evaluation in biblical narrative,[35] but is this analogy necessarily encouraged by the narrator in this specific case? While there is contrast between the brothers, Cassuto claims, this contrast is not sharp:

> On the one hand, it is clear that since in regard to Cain it is stated simply that his offering was *of the fruit of the ground,* and in Abel's case the Bible uses two expressions to emphasize that the oblation was the best of its kind (*of the firstlings ... and of* their fat portions), this distinction is not made pointlessly. On the other hand, it must be noted that although there is a *distinction,* there is no *contrast*.... In other words: Abel endeavored to perform his religious duty ideally, whereas Cain was content merely to discharge this duty.[36]

Might we challenge the premise that the text presents contrast – to whatever degree[37] – between the brothers, by looking more closely at verse 4? If the text indeed attempts to create a contrast between the brothers,

---

33. Ibn Ezra on Gen. 4:3.
34. Radak on Gen 4:3. Similarly in Bekhor Shor and many others.
35. See many examples in Shimon, *Contrast.*
36. Cassuto, *From Adam to Noah,* 205. Emphasis in the original.
37. Some argue that there is no contrast here at all, such as Westermann, *Genesis,* vol. 1, 296–297.

then the description that "Abel *also* brought an offering" is very curious. This language implies that Abel was imitating Cain by bringing an offering as well, and that *he too* brought the finest of his sheep, which infers that Cain also – or, to be precise, was the first – to bring the finest of his fruits.[38] Intriguingly, Pseudo-Jonathan characterizes Cain's offering as an offering of his first fruits: "And it was at the end of days, on the fourteenth of Nisan, that Cain brought of the produce of the earth, cottonseed, *the first of his fruits* as an offering before the Lord." This, of course, is a midrashic addition to the verse itself,[39] but this adaptation testifies to the possibility of reading that Cain, like Abel, brought the finest of his crops, as the phrase "also" implies. As Hermann Gunkel writes: "'*From* the fruit' – part of the fruits, and from the context, the plain meaning is that he brought the finest part."[40] I do not wish to claim that Cain brought the first or finest of his fruits; rather, I wish to point out that had the narrative intention been to generate a sense of contrast between the brothers, there would not have been use of the word "*vegam*," "and also," which suggests similarity and continuity. The text easily could have read: "And in the course of time, it happened that Cain brought from the fruit of the ground an offering to the Lord / and Abel brought from the firstborn of his flock and from their fat portions." In its actual form, however, the expression "also" tempers any sense of contrast implied in the verse.

Moreover, what is the significance of the temporal description that introduces this scene: "And in the course of time (*miketz yamim*)" (4:3)? Its role may merely be introductory, but various commentators suggest that it can be understood in the sense of "once a year," as in the description of Absalom's annual haircut: "When he cut his hair, which he would have cut once a year (*miketz yamim leyamim*), when it grew too heavy for him" (II Samuel 14:26).[41] The expression "*miketz*," "at the end," is usually used

38. Compare to Benjamin Oppenheimer, "Cain and Abel: The Evolution of the Motif from the Ancient Near East, by Way of the Bible and on the Aggadic Literature and the Books of the Church Fathers," in *Gedaiyahu Alon Memorial Volume*, ed. S. Safrai and M. Stern (Tel Aviv, 1970), 27–68.

39. For a discussion of this addition, see Scarlata, *Outside of Eden*, 69–71.

40. Gunkel, *Genesis*, 43.

41. Indeed, *Ḥazal* derive from this that a Nazirite can cut his hair once a year. See Radak (on II Samuel 14:26), who writes: "And from this, they learn that whoever takes a

as a specific temporal expression,[42] making it likely that the expression in this context also refers to the end of a specific period of time. Given Cain's profession, it is likely that it refers to the end of the agricultural year.[43] At the end of a year of plowing, planting, watering, and reaping, Cain offers up the fruits of his toil to God, as Radak, for example, expresses:

> "And in the course of time…" From the time he began to work the soil, after a certain amount of time he brought an offering to the Lord, but it does not state how many days. "Days" should be read as "a year," as in, "Days will be his redemption" (Lev. 25:29). That is, after a year of working the soil, he brought an offering out of what the soil had brought forth.[44]

In other words, Cain brought his offering at the end of the agricultural year, as soon as his crop ripened, which implies that he offered up the first of his fruits. While some argue that the expression "fruit of the ground" suggests an inferior offering (as opposed to "fruits of the tree," perhaps),[45] this claim can easily be dispelled by the fact that the mitzva of *bikkurim* uses the same expression: "You shall take the first of all the *fruit of the ground* which you will bring from the land that the Lord your God has given you, and you shall place it in a basket" (Deut. 26:2).

Once again, it does not explicitly state that Cain brought the first of his fruits, as Abel did, but it is problematic to assert that the text unequivocally implies that Cain, unlike Abel, brought an inferior offering.

---

vow to be a Nazirite forever can use a razor when it grows too heavy for him every twelve months, as it says, 'He would have it cut "*miketz yamim leyamim.*"' This is from year to year, as 'days' means a year, as in, 'Days shall be his redemption.'"

42. See Gen. 8:6; 16:3; 41:1; Ex. 12:41; Num. 13:25; Deut. 9:11; 15:1.

43. See the discussion in Scarlata, *Outside of Eden*, 49–50, though he eventually states that this reading is not absolute, but definitely possible.

44. Radak on Gen. 4:3.

45. This was proposed by Rabbi Avraham Shmuel Binyamin Sofer, the son of the Ḥatam Sofer, in his commentary *Ktav Sofer* on Genesis 4:3: "The commentators sought to determine what was offensive about his offering. They write that he brought inferior flax, as it states in the Midrash, but it is not explicit in the text. It seems to me that there is 'fruit of the tree' and 'fruit of the ground,' and Cain brought from the 'fruit of the ground' and not from the fruit of the tree, and he chose the worst."

On the contrary, the case that Cain brought a worthy offering – as Abel "also" did – is so strong that it challenges the reading that Cain's rejection is related to the quality of his offering.

The fact that Abel "also" brings an offering has an additional effect, which is that it reinforces Abel's characterization as an appendix to his brother; he imitates, but does not initiate, the process of bringing an offering. Like a typical younger brother, Abel imitates Cain's actions; he is, after all, introduced as "Cain's brother" even before we know his name.

Up until this stage, then, there is no reason to assume that Cain's offering will be rejected. On the contrary, from the story's start, Cain is presented as the chosen firstborn, while Abel is characterized as an afterthought. Cain's name is a celebration of God's co-creation with humanity. Cain is the one who initiates the idea of humans bringing offerings to God; just as his mother celebrates the gift of fruit of the womb, Cain celebrates the gift of fruit of the earth.

This anticipation is therefore shattered with the rejection of Cain's offering: "And God had regard for Abel and his gift offering. But for Cain and his gift offering, He did not have regard" (4:4–5). Without any prior warning, without any obvious rhyme or reason, despite his connection with God and his efforts and initiation, Cain is left out in the cold, the door slammed shut in his face.

Why is the reader led thus astray? Is there a purpose in generating expectations, only to have them shattered, beyond the inherent advantages of narrative surprise and suspense?

In this context, two perspectives should be taken into account: literary and theological. From a literary perspective, Cain is the narrative protagonist. It is Cain we follow throughout the story. Cain's name is given an explanation, while Abel's is not. Cain initiates, while Abel imitates. This is even more salient after God accepts Abel's offering. The focus is on Cain's reaction, "Cain became furious and his face fell" (4:5), while there is no mention of Abel's response. This silence is striking in light of the chiastic structure of the brother's appearance throughout the narrative:

"She conceived and gave birth to **Cain** / She also gave birth to his brother **Abel**."

"**Abel** was a shepherd / while **Cain** was a worker of the ground."

"**Cain** brought an offering to the Lord / **Abel** also brought."

"God had regard for **Abel** / But for **Cain** ... He did not have regard."

"**Cain** became furious and his face fell..." / [no reaction from Abel]

This lack of response, this vacuum, more than anything else, reveals that Cain is the protagonist while Abel is a mere supporting actor. The plot has reached boiling point and Cain burns with rage, but Abel's reaction is irrelevant. In fact, God's subsequent appearance to Cain only proves that Cain is the focal character of the narrative; Abel's offering may have been accepted, but he remains silent and voiceless throughout his brief appearance onstage.

Cain, then, has the starring role; along with him, the audience experiences the shattering of expectations and the pain of rejection. If Cain is read in a negative light from the outset, however, the reader is not able to identify with his pain. If one assumes that Cain was merely getting what he deserved, it is not clear why he is so angry. Had Cain brought an inferior offering, would he really be angry and disappointed that God rejected his gift and accepted his brother's prime sacrifice? If Cain was angry even so, he would emerge not only as irreverent, but foolish as well. A less accusative, prejudiced reading, however, leads the reader to identify with Cain as he awaits his offering's acceptance, and to suffer along with him at its rejection.

To this end, I believe, the text refrains from offering any explanation for the rejection of Cain's offering. From a literary perspective, this vacuum leads to greater sympathy with Cain – his anger and disappointment is more acute if there is no explanation, no justification, of his rejection. God's decision seems arbitrary to both Cain and the reader, arousing greater indignation than if the rejection was given an explanation.[46] This brings another subject to the surface – the human's utter vulnerability in the face of divine decisions which are seemingly arbitrary to the human subject – which leads us to the theological sphere.

Beyond the literary perspective, the shattering of Cain's expectations also has theological value. Cain's offering is rejected for no apparent

46. Gali Dinnur's formulation is similar; see "The Story of Cain and Abel (Gen. 4:1–16): The Supreme Value of Human Life," *Mo'ed* 18 (2008): 4–5.

reason, and this seeming arbitrariness is unsettling. The human cannot determine who is worthy of God's acceptance. God's rejection of Cain comes as a rude shock to the human characters and their human readers in its disturbing deviation from the logical sequence of events that leads up to it. I do not believe that the narrative objective of this scene is that divine decisions are irrational or meaningless, but rather that their meaning is not always accessible to us. Stripped of judgmental preconceptions of Cain's character, the reader can deeply identify with his raw cry of indignation.

God's Words to Cain: Transition Verses

Between the offering scene and the murder scene, God responds to the wounded Cain, hinting to the fraternal struggle about to unfold. In this sense, God's words to Cain can be seen as verses of transition from a scene of deep religious significance – of sacrifice to God and the question of divine acceptance – to a scene of deep moral significance – fratricide. God's revelation to Cain offers certain consolation; his offering was not accepted, but he has not been rejected from God's presence. Although Abel's offering was accepted, he is not granted the privilege of being addressed by God. In the apt words of Elchanan Nir: "Abel received a very good grade, but Cain is the child who receives the most attention from the teacher. He is the student who threatens the flow of the orderly lesson by challenging it relentlessly."[47]

It is worth asking exactly why Cain's face falls. God Himself asks this question in verse 6: "Why are you furious, and why has your face fallen?" The narrative relates Cain's (unusual) reaction without any explanation, presumably because it is clear that Cain is responding to his rejection. However, there may be other reasons for Cain's disappointment. First and foremost, of course, Cain is angry that God did not accept his offering, an anger all the more intense because *he* was the one who initiated the concept of sacrifice to God, while his younger brother merely copied him. This is the most common of religious frustrations: a person attempts to connect with God, to no avail. His or her prayers, good deeds, religious efforts, are all to no avail, leading to desperation, despair, a "fallen face."

47. Elchanan Nir, "The Mark of Cain: Derash," *Makor Rishon*, Motzash Supplement, 19 Tishrei 2017, 24.

But Cain is not only angry at God. Some of his frustration may well be directed towards his younger brother. His younger brother copied him and stole his place, winning God's attention at Cain's expense. Regardless of whether more than one brother can theoretically win God's favor, the rejected brother certainly blames his brother's success for his own failure. Emmanuel Levinas would claim that Cain's face falls because he cannot bear to show his face to his brother, cannot bear to look at him; according to Levinas, a person can only turn to face his brother through a shared being in God's presence, by "the monotheistic capacity to make a person tolerable unto his surroundings and to bring the other to respond."[48] Without divine acceptance, Cain cannot tolerate his brother's presence.

These, however, are not the only possible reasons for Cain's anguish. Could Cain possibly be angry at himself? Is he not obsessing over where he went wrong, what aspect of his offering might have offended God? Cain, presumably, believes that he and his offering were truly worthy, and he cannot put his finger on his mistake. Such inner torment can also make a person's face fall, can puncture his sense of self-worth, make him lose his sense of dignity, drive, and meaning. As R. Ḥayim ben Attar writes:

> And Cain became furious and his face fell – fury due to elevation, and his fallen face due to humiliation. His fury is against his brother, whose position was elevated while he was brought down low, for he thought that through his superior, worthier offering the inferiority of his own offering became evident; and humiliation when he became aware of his inferiority in the eyes of God.[49]

All three possibilities may be flashing through Cain's mind, but God's answer brings one main focus to the forefront: his relationship with his brother.

God's words to Cain have been interpreted – and can be interpreted – in a broad spectrum of ways, in regard to language, syntax, and content. Due to the plethora of readings, I will not list them here.[50] Rather,

48. Emmanuel Levinas, *Difficile Liberté – Essais sur le judaisme*, trans. Ido Bassok and S. Wygoda (Tel Aviv, 2007), 252.

49. *Or HaḤayim* on Gen. 4:5.

50. For a survey of ancient translations, see Scarlata, *Outside of Eden*, 74–110.

I wish to propose a reading which may be less widely accepted, but one that most simply, straightforwardly, reflects the plain meaning of the text.

Some proposed reading verses 6 and 7 thus:

> "Why are you angry and why is your face fallen?
> Whether (*im*) you do well and find favor, or (*ve'im*) not – sin is crouching at the door. It longs to have you, but you must rule over it."

That is, regardless of your behavior, sin is lying in wait for you.[51] This cannot be ruled out, but biblical (and general) use of the expression, "*im… ve'im,*" is usually an indication of two different possibilities. This is how it is used, for example, in Genesis 13:9, "If (*im*) you go left, then I will go right, and if (*ve'im*) you go right, I will go left."[52] Therefore, the more prevalent reading is more logical – that this verse relates a condition and an outcome:

> "If you do well, [then] *se'et.*
> But if you do not, [then] sin crouches at the door."

What, however, is the outcome of "if you do well"? What does the object *se'et* mean? The root signifies "to carry" or "raise up," but regarding what? Ibn Ezra, for example, suggests, "You will raise up your face," in contrast to his fallen face, while Radak, based on the following verse, fills the gap with "sin."[53] The second verse is far more problematic, even on a simple grammatical level. If sin, which is in the feminine, "*ḥatat,*" is the subject of the second verse, then why is the accompanying word

51. Malbim on 4:5. Alter's translation is similar: "For whether you offer well, or whether you do not…" (Robert Alter, *Genesis: Translation and Commentary* [New York, 1996], 17). Cotter (*Genesis*, 42) adopts this reading. Both understand the continuation of the verse as sin trying to lure Cain, unlike the aforementioned suggestion.
52. This is Cassuto's criticism of the Malbim (Cassuto, *From Adam to Noah*, 209). See also Nechama Leibowitz, *Studies in Bereshit – Genesis*, trans. A. Newman (Jerusalem, 1983), 41–42.
53. Castellino proposes a textual emendation to deal with the issue (G. R. Castellino, "Genesis IV: 7," *VT* 10 [1960]: 442–445).

in the masculine form of "*rovetz*," "crouches"? The use of the masculine tense continues in the second part of the verse: "It (masculine) longs to have you, and you will rule over it (masculine)," and presumably the "it" refers back to the subject of the first part of the sentence.[54] Some commentators explain that the masculine form refers to other terms in the same semantic field as "sin." Radak, for example, writes: "The masculine form refers to the evil inclination, which causes sin – the serpent, the devil."[55] However, beyond this grammatical issue, which can be glossed over by ascribing to it the use of poetic license, it is somewhat bizarre to present the evil inclination as an entity that yearns for man and longs to snare him in the net of sin, as Rashi, for example, writes: "It longs to have you – sin, that is, the Evil Inclination, perpetually yearns and craves to trip you up."[56] This kind of theory may be acceptable in later thought regarding the evil inclination, but in the Bible, people are the ones who long to sin, rather than the evil inclination yearning for people to sin. This kind of personification has no counterpart in the Bible, and it is problematic to assume that God is describing how Cain's evil inclination yearns for him.

My own reading of God's words begins with Nahmanides' (and others') interpretation of *se'et* in the sense of dominion and leadership. *Nasi*, for example, means "prince" or "leader," as in Jacob's words to Reuben: "Reuben, you are my firstborn, my strength, and the

54. Deurloo proposes that Cain himself is the subject of "crouches," for he is the one crouching at the brink of sin (Deurloo, "*Teshuka*," 405). This approach is already raised by Ibn Ezra. Robert Gordon proposes that the serpent in chapter 3 is the subject alluded to in this verse (Gordon, "'Couch' or 'Crouch'? Genesis 4:7 and the Temptation of Cain," in *On Stone and Scroll*, ed. J. K. Aitken, K. J. Dell, and B. A. Mastin [BZAW 420: Berlin, 2011], 195–209). This baffling verse has been the subject of many emendations. The most extreme, perhaps, is that of Driver – "If you do well – your face will be raised up, but if you do not do well – you will crouch at the brink of sin and it will long for you and you will be ruled by it" (G. R. Driver, "Theological and Philological Problems in the OT," *JTS* 47 [1946]: 157–160). Not surprisingly, some see the word "sin" as a later addition, an explanation which settles the gender discrepancies in the verse (Carly L. Crouch, "*Ḥatat* as Interpolative Gloss: A Solution to Gen 4,7," *ZAW* 123 [2011]: 250–258).

55. Radak on Gen. 4:7.

56. Rashi on Gen. 4:7.

first of my manhood, excelling in rank (*se'et*) and excelling in power" (Gen. 49:3). According to Ibn Ezra, this literally means, "You would have been worthy of the advantage of leadership, and the advantage of power and rule over your brothers."[57] God is saying to Cain that if he does well, he will have "leadership," in that he will become the leader of the family.

This meaning can also be expanded in light of Moses' words: "And I said to you at that time, 'I cannot bear (*se'et*) you myself.... How can I bear (*esa*) your toil and burden and quarrels myself?" (Deut. 1:9, 12). Here, leadership refers to not merely the privilege of ruling, but to the responsibility, to the burdens, which come with it; the leader must work the hardest of all, dealing with the conflicts of his subjects. God is telling Cain that if he does well, if he improves his relationship with his surroundings, he will be granted the privileges and burdens of leadership, the responsibility over his family, as is expected of the firstborn. God is redirecting Cain's attention to his behavior, to his dominion over his brothers.[58]

God's next words can also be interpreted through focus on fraternal relationship: "It (masculine) longs for you, and you will rule over it (masculine)." Once again, the gender discrepancy challenges the idea that sin is the subject of this clause. Could these words refer to another, unmentioned subject? Who longs for Cain? Over whom will he rule?

In Modern Hebrew, the word for longing, *teshuka,* is associated with lust or strong desire, and though many tend to ascribe the same meaning to its biblical occurrence, this may not be the case. The word *teshuka* appears in the Song of Songs, where it certainly functions in this sense: "I am my beloved's, and he longs (*teshukato*) for me" (7:11). However, the same word appears in a more similar context in the previous chapter, when God punishes the woman. The parallels between the two verses are clear: "Your *longing* shall be for your husband, and he shall *rule over* you" (3:16). Longing and dominion are juxtaposed, just as they are in God's words to Cain.

---

57. See further in Kiel, *Genesis*, 109.

58. A further proposal is Kiel's, that "*lapetaḥ*," "at the door," means the *potḥei hareḥem*, "openers of the womb," that is, the "firstborn" (Kiel, *Genesis*, 109). It is difficult to accept this theory, although it works well with the continuation of the verse.

What does "longing" mean in that context? I have already suggested that in addition to sexual longing, some scholars interpreted *teshuka* in the sense of being in need of dominion, of accepting authority – that is, that the first half of the verse is fully parallel to the second.[59] This reading seems to apply equally to the story of Cain, and Ibn Ezra interprets *teshuka* in this sense: "It longs to have you – for the Inclination will submit to *your discipline* at your will. You, too, have the power to rule over it." Yehuda Kiel also favors this reading and takes note of the phrase "the one in charge (*ben meshek*) of my household" (Gen. 15:2), referring to Abraham's chief servant. He also points out that Pharaoh says to Joseph, "You shall be in charge of my household, and by your word all my people will be ruled (*yishak*)" (Gen. 41:40). In both places the root M-SH-K, from which he proposes that *teshuka* is also derived, are related to accepting the authority of a leader (especially over a household, from an economic point of view). This could even be the meaning of the phrase in the Song of Songs, as the *teshuka* in question can be read as mutual dependency rather than mutual desire. Several verses employ this meaning to generate wordplay, such as: "A roaring lion and a *charging* bear (*shokek*) is a wicked man ruling meek people" (Prov. 28: 15).

In light of this sense of *teshuka*, God's words to Cain can be read in reference to Abel, who, as younger brother, will submit to Cain's authority, and be dependent on his leadership.[60] These words, then, are not only a warning, but encouragement and consolation: God is restoring Cain's dignity and authority to him, promising him leadership. Abel "longs" for his guidance, and he – Cain – will lead the family. From beginning to end, God's words refer to fraternal relationships and family dynamics: "If you do well, you will once again become the family leader; but if not, you will crouch at the brink of sin. But know that Abel is devoted to you, and you must rule over him with responsibility and wisdom." The verse is concerned with any leader's abuse of his power. God reassures Cain that despite the rejection of his offering, he is still the leader of the family, but warns him not to exploit his authority. Similarly, Ibn Ezra

59. Foh, "Woman's Desire"; Deurloo, "*Teshuka*."

60. See further about this possibility in Theodore Anthony Perry, "Cain's Sin in Genesis 4:1–7: Oracular Ambiguity and How to Avoid It," *Prooftexts* 25 (2005): 258–275.

cites nameless commentators toward the effect: "*Teshukato* – over Abel. Meaning, 'why are you furious' that I accepted Abel's offering? He is subject to your authority, and it is as if you rule over him."[61]

God, then, focuses on sibling rivalry as the main reason that Cain's face fell, and this subject becomes the central axis of the narrative. When his younger brother's offering is accepted, Cain feels as if his firstborn status has been stripped from him (just as it will be stripped from the aforementioned Reuben). God reassures Cain that this is not the case; that it is his attitude towards his brother and family that will dictate the future of his status. He also warns him that his firstborn privileges – like those of any other leader – are liable to lead to arrogance and the exploitation of his subjects.

This interpretation of the verse and its main theme of sibling rivalry enables comparison between this narrative and the story of Joseph and his brothers.[62] The envious brothers mockingly ask Joseph: "Will you indeed reign over us? Will you indeed rule (*mashol timshol*) over us?" (Gen. 37:8). In both narratives, the elder brothers' fierce envy of their younger brother leads to an act of violence against him. In each story, the father figure attempts to diffuse this envy: God

61. Ibn Ezra on Gen. 4:7. Compare also to Rabbi Naftali Zvi Yehuda Berlin, the Netziv, in his *HaEmek Davar*. Also see the reading of Rabbi Isaac Karo (1458–1535), who experienced the Spanish Inquisition and was the uncle of Rabbi Joseph Karo. Rabbi Isaac, in his *Toledot Yitzchak*, writes: "It may be that He would say, Even if I did not accept your offering, your brother's was not better, and if you thought that Abel did so to shame you, it is not so, for your brother Abel's desire is to do as you wish, and that is the meaning of 'and his longing is for you,' and moreover, he wishes to serve you and that you will rule over him as the firstborn rules over his brothers, and you are the firstborn, and he is aware of your status and your dominion over him."

62. "As Rabbi Menachem Azariah wrote in his book *Ten Discourses*, in his discourse "The Mother of All Living," section 22, that Joseph's brothers were stirred with the envy of Cain" (Rabbi Naftali Hertz Bacharach, *Emek HaMelech*, 5:69). Rabbi Meir ben Eliezer Horovitz of Dzhikov, *Imrei Noam* on the Festivals, *Teshuva* 3, writes: "And as explained in the books, Joseph's brothers caused harm with the sale of Joseph, similar to how Cain caused harm by killing Abel (see *Megaleh Amukot, Parashat Miketz* 60b, and *Bnei Yissaschar*, Discourse 4 of the discourses of *Kislev-Tevet*, no. 34), and Joseph was, of course, the reincarnation of Abel (see *Sefer HaLikutim, Parashat Vayeshev* 48), and the same is written in the book of *Yaarot Devash*, vol. 2, in Sermon 12 for the Tenth of Tevet."

reassures Cain that he still has all the authority of the firstborn, while Jacob chides Joseph for speaking of his dreams. Both attempts, however, fail to prevent the violence that erupts against the favored son in the following scene.

The similar language reinforces this analogy:

Cain and Abel (Gen. 4)	**Joseph and His Brothers (Gen. 37)**
(7) It longs to have you, but *you must rule over it."*	(8) Then his brothers said to him, "Do you really mean to be our king, *do you really intend to rule over us?"* And they hated him all the more because of his dreams and because of his words.
(9) And the Lord said to Cain, "*Where* is Abel your brother?"	(16) Please tell me *where* they are pasturing."
(9) And he replied, "I do not know. Am *I my brother's* (*aḥi anokhi*) keeper?"	(16) And he said, "*My brothers I* (*aḥai anokhi*) seek."
(8) And it came to pass when they were *in the field.*	(15) And a man found him, and look, he was wandering about *in the field.*[63]
(8) *that Cain rose up against Abel his brother and killed him.*	(20) Come now, let us *kill him.*
(11) And now, cursed will you be from the ground that opened its mouth to receive *your brother's blood from your hand.*	(26) Then Judah said to his brothers, "What do we gain if we kill our *brother and cover his blood*? (27) Come, let us sell him to the Ishmaelites, and *not harm him with our own hands, for he is our brother,* our own flesh."

This analogy largely serves to illuminate the Joseph narrative. As the Joseph narrative comes later, it takes into account that the reader is aware of the story of Cain and Abel, and plays on its parallels to focus

63. Philo focuses on the meaning of the field in both stories at length in his allegorical interpretations (Philo, *Writings*, vol. 4, 231–239).

on the perils that lay in store for Joseph. Will he, too, fall victim to his brother's envy? However, beyond the analogy's contribution to the reading of the later story, it has significance for the overall pattern of the book of Genesis as a whole, and therefore also serves to shed light on the story of Cain.

Some have proposed reading the Cain and Joseph narratives as an intentional literary framework for the entire book of Genesis, pointing to human anger and envy as the motivating forces that shape the book as a whole. However, this framework is not merely symmetrical; it reflects a certain inner process that takes place over the course of the book. In the story of Cain, which marks the beginning of humanity's history outside of Eden, human envy and anger flare up uncontrollably and lead to fratricide. By the time Joseph's brothers plot against their father's favorite, their envy and anger is tempered by human compassion.[64] While Joseph's ensuing enslavement can hardly be considered a corrective act for Abel's murder, the twelve tribes of Israel are founded by twelve brothers whose positive emotions ultimately eclipse their negative emotions, and their story ends in reconciliation and coexistence rather than murder and discontinuity.

ACT TWO: MURDER

Needless to say, the murder scene also leaves its readers in shock – the brother whose offering is accepted by God is murdered by his elder brother. There is no happy end to this story, and the jarring sense of chaos and disorder generated by Abel's murder is yet more acute when this narrative is compared to the stream of similar narratives that comprise the book of Genesis. In each narrative, the elder brother is rejected and the chosen younger brother is the one who continues the family line. Here, however, the envious, spurned elder brother murders the chosen younger brother; Cain actually executes what Esau schemes to do to Jacob.[65]

---

64. Matthew Richard Schlimm, *From Fratricide to Forgiveness: The Language and Ethics of Anger in Genesis* (Winona Lake, 2011).

65. Knohl, *Biblical Beliefs*, 146.

Abel's death, I believe, is all the more jarring given that he is favored by God. If God accepts his offering, why does He fail to protect him from his brother's murderous wrath? This archetypal act of murder illuminates every act of murder that has taken place ever since: it is humans who choose to murder, and even this grave violation is an act of free will.

This is alluded to in a bold midrash from R. Shimon bar Yohai:

> R. Shimon bar Yohai said: This is difficult to say, and the mouth cannot state it plainly. Imagine two athletes wrestling before the king. The king could separate them, if he so wished. He does not wish so, and one overcomes the other and kills him. [The victim] screams out and says, "Let my case be pleaded before the king." Hence, "The voice of your brother's blood is crying out to me from the ground."[66]

R. Shimon bar Yohai likens Cain and Abel to two athletes in the Roman circus. The emperor would sit and watch athletes struggle to their death, though it was fully in his power to bring the game to a halt at any given moment. This same sense lingers in Genesis 4, especially given that God speaks to Cain immediately before and after the murder. Why did God not intervene during the murder itself? The image of Abel's blood crying out from the earth is poignant, moving. So why is his blood allowed to spill in the first place, if God is watching as Cain launches his deadly attack?

This sense of surprise is only exacerbated in comparison with other ancient Near Eastern literature. In Sumerian literature, there is a certain genre that can be referred to as the "contest parable" (the ox versus the donkey, or the date palm versus the tamarisk). Among them are stories of conflict between the farmer and the shepherd. Samuel Kramer deciphered one relevant myth he refers to as, "Dumuzi and Enkimdu: The Dispute between the Shepherds and the Farmers."[67] Dumuzi, the

66. Genesis Rabba 22:9

67. Samuel Noah Kramer, "Dumuzi and Enkimdu: The Dispute between the Shepherd God and the Farmer-God," *ANET* 2 (1955): 41.

shepherd god, and Enkimdu, the farmer god, fight for the hand of Inana, the goddess of love. Their dispute is structured as a series of monologues in which each god attempts to prove his superiority, and eventually Dumuzi, the farmer god, emerges triumphant. Its parallel with the story of Cain and Abel is so obvious that Kramer defines it as the "Cain and Abel motif."[68] This story, along with similar Sumerian myths, concludes in victory for one party, and conciliation, as the loser accepts the victor's authority.[69] In sharp contrast, however, the archetypal biblical conflict between farmer and shepherd ends with the death of the one favored by God. In this sense, Benjamin Oppenheimer is correct in defining the Sumerian myth as narrative concerned with social issues, while the story of Cain and Abel is associated with moral and religious issues.[70]

The sheer shock of Abel's murder, it seems, is calculated to generate a certain reading experience. The first murder in history reflects the essence of the act of murder: the disruption of order, chaos, disarray. Every murder is supposed to be a rude shock, an unexpected disruption. The story of Abel's murder imparts a message which is yet more acute: not every victim is guilty. Abel's offering was accepted by God right before his death, but this did nothing to protect him from his brother's murderous rage. Moreover, Abel's death is not the result of divine providence. In fact, the opposite holds true: Abel's death marks a deviation from the divine order. God is angry with Cain for his act of murder because God had no interest in Abel's murder. The intense incorporation of surprise in the story of the first murder is meant to reflect the disruptive, violent nature of murder.

This sense of surprise and disorder is further provoked by God's treatment of the world's first murderer. Rather than being sentenced to death, which is the *midda keneged midda*, rational penalty for murder (the words of Numbers 35:33 should suffice: "The land can have no expiation for blood that is shed on it, except by the blood of him who shed

68. Kramer, ibid. On the relationship between our story and other stories from the ancient Near East, see Westermann, *Genesis*, vol. 1, 315–317; Chaim Gilad, "Cain and Abel," *Beit Mikra* 29 (1983): 14–28; Oppenheimer, "Cain and Abel."

69. As emphasized by Kramer, Oppenheimer, and Sarna.

70. Oppenheimer, "Cain and Abel."

it"), the reader is once again thrown into confusion. For some reason, contrary to broader biblical thought, Cain's blood is not shed; rather, he is punished with exile and displacement.[71] This punishment is so unsettling that some have proposed that this surprising end conveys a narrative objective that challenges the notion of the death penalty for murders and the concept of blood vengeance.[72] This is an intriguing theory, especially in relation to blood vengeance, but objection to the death penalty is inconsistent with general biblical thought, and it is difficult to apply this narrative's conclusions to other cases.

Various commentators have attempted to explain Cain's punishment, and most characterize him as an accidental killer, reading Abel's death as a case of manslaughter, not murder. One prevalent version explains that Cain did not know that murder was forbidden, as the following midrash explains: "Cain's punishment was not that of murderers. Cain killed and he did not have anyone to teach him; from this point on, anyone who killed will be killed."[73] A variation of this approach is that Cain, being one of the first people in the world, had no concept of death or murder, as Radak writes: "It can be considered an accident, as he did not think that the stone, or whatever it was, would actually kill him, as he had never before seen a killed man, and did not realize it would kill. Therefore, his fate is that of the accidental killer, which is exile."[74]

71. Westermann claims that in the ancient Near East, murder within the family had a lesser punishment than the murder of an outsider, and it was customary to exile the murderer of the family member rather than to kill him. He holds that in the ancient world, murder and exile were closely related: a person who killed a family member was exiled, but this exile was considered tantamount to death (Westermann, *Genesis*, vol. 1, 315–317, and also see 307). Westermann's claim does not fully justify why Cain is not punished with death. The Bible's attitude towards murder is uniquely severe (see for example, Moshe Greenberg, "Some Postulates of Biblical Criminal Law," in *Torah Nidreshet: Three Interpretative Essays on the Bible*, ed. A. Shapira [Tel Aviv, 1984], 13–37), and there is no such distinction in biblical law, and as God, rather than a human authority, is the executor of punishment, it would be appropriate for the broader biblical view to be implemented here. Similar criticism can be found in Oppenheimer, "Cain and Abel."

72. Cassuto already proposes this idea (*From Adam to Noah*, 184–185), but see a wider discussion in Dinnur, "Cain and Abel."

73. Genesis Rabba 22:4.

74. In Radak's second explanation on Gen. 4:12.

The advantage of this approach is that Cain's fate indeed resembles that of the accidental killer who is sent to the city of refuge. Its disadvantage, however, is that, "Not only does the text lack evidence that the murder was accidental, but the text explicitly states that he murdered him on purpose."[75] The formulation "Cain rose up against Abel his brother and killed him" conveys a clear sense of intent; the phrase "rose up against him" suggests calculated, deliberate actions. This is certainly the case if we adopt the reading that the verb "*vayomer*," which is mentioned before they head for the field, can be understood in the sense of "looking," or "searching,"[76] meaning that Cain watched Abel to determine the perfect time to take action, as Philo imagines: "What Cain wanted was to provoke Abel and call him to settle matters in order to overcome him with wiles."[77] Rashi's interpretation of Lamech's words seems consistent with the textual atmosphere: "Cain, *who killed on purpose*, was pardoned for seven generations; I, who killed by mistake, should therefore be pardoned for seven times that."[78]

I wish to take a different direction, one that can be traced back to the words of Radak:

> He was not put to death, as one who kills someone on purpose, so that the world would not remain devoid of people. For Cain had not yet produced children, and Adam did not beget more children until he was 130 years old. Therefore, he was not put to death, but besides for the ground being cursed to him, he received another punishment for murderers, and that is exile, as He said to him, "You will be a restless wanderer upon the earth."[79]

Radak explains that were Cain to receive the death penalty, humanity would be in grave danger of extinction, for at this point Adam, Eve, Cain,

75. Dinnur, "Cain and Abel," 10.
76. Following the Akkadian and the Ugaritic. Hamilton adopts this position and translates: "Cain was looking for Abel his brother" (Hamilton, *Genesis*, 228). See his discussion and relevant references on p. 230.
77. Philo, *Writings*, vol. 4, 231.
78. Rashi on Gen. 4:24, following the Midrash. Ibn Ezra writes similarly: "Anger was withheld from Cain, who killed on purpose, for seven generations."
79. Radak on Gen. 4:12.

and Abel were the only humans in the world. This reading retains the allusion to the punishment for accidental killers, not because Abel's murder was accidental, but because the alternative punishment for murder – in cases of accidental murder, or cases when the murdered cannot be punished with death – is exile, estrangement from society. In biblical thought, an exile is not "dwelling on his land," and only thus can land that was tainted with innocent blood come to rest.

This reading generates a comparison between the story of Cain and Abel and the tale that the woman of Tekoa spins to King David. After Absalom murders Amnon, he escapes to Geshur and settles there for three years. Joab senses that David misses his son and takes action to move the king to bring back his son. He asks a gifted actress from Tekoa to describe her fictitious dilemma to the king and ask for his verdict:

> "I am but a widow-woman," she said. "My husband died. Your servant had two sons, but they brawled in the field, with no one to come between them, and one struck the other and killed him. And now, the whole family has risen against your servant, saying, 'Give over the one who struck his brother, so we can put him to death for snuffing out his brother's life – we will destroy the heir as well.' They would extinguish my last remaining ember, leaving my husband without name or remnant on the face of the earth." (II Sam 14:5–7)

The woman's – Joab's – purpose is to stage a situation in which the king inadvertently decrees a verdict about his own situation, which will then move him to bring Absalom back from his state of exile.

The fictitious story described by the woman of Tekoa is uncannily like the story of Cain and Abel.[80] Two brothers quarrel, alone in the field, and the fate of the murderer hangs in the balance. If he receives the usual death penalty, an entire line will be cut off, as the woman is a widow with no other children. Her son's only chance lies in the hope

---

80. On this comparison see Gilad Strauss, "Three Wise Women in the Book of Samuel," *Megadim* 21 (1994): 57–58; Rabbi Amnon Bazak, *Parallels Meet: Literary Parallels in the Book of Samuel* (Alon Shvut, 2006), 166–170.

that the king will look beyond the boundaries of formal law and make an exception in this tragic case. Beyond the parallel plotlines, note the woman's surprising emphasis on the fact that her sons were "in the field" when the murder took place, a detail whose legal relevance is not initially clear.[81] Perhaps the woman, who hopes that David will pardon her fictitious son, is intentionally echoing the story of Cain, who also killed his brother in a field, in order to assert his case as precedence to her own.[82] The woman hopes that the king will take his cue from God and pardon her son from death as Cain was pardoned. The phrase "name or remnant on the face of the earth" may also be calculated to recall Cain's punishment: "You have driven me today from the face of the earth" (4:14).[83] The wise woman's words hit their mark, and David indeed pardons "her" son from the death penalty, paving the way for Absalom's return.

This analogy serves to illuminate the narrative in II Samuel and its role in convincing David, but the light it sheds also contributes to the understanding of Cain's fate. The woman (or Joab, or the narrator) seems to believe that God did not punish Cain with death because the death of Cain, like the death of her son, would result in the end of the family line.

This reading has important implications for the understanding of the next stage of Cain's story. If this is indeed so, then the birth of Seth will result in the reopening of Cain's case. Cain is punished with exile not because he is innocent; rather, he is exempt from murder because his death would mean the death of all humanity. Once there is alternate hope for the family, however, his fate is reexamined. The roots of this reading can be found in Ibn Ezra's interpretation of the song of Lamech: "He mentions killing Cain to show God's justice. Though He is slow to

81. Unless the site of the murder conveys that death resulted from an accidental argument rather than a premeditated act.

82. Diana Lipton comments that besides these two instances of murder, the "field" appears in a similar context in the law of the rapist in Deut. 22:25–27, where the site of the rape dictates the law (Lipton, "Legal Analogy in Deuteronomy and Fratricide in the Field," in *Studies on the Text and Versions of the Hebrew Bible in Honour of Robert Gordon*, ed. G. Khan and D. Lipton [Leiden and Boston, 2012], 21–38).

83. Bazak, *Parallels*, 168.

anger, He eventually punished him, in the same fashion as, 'He will not clear the guilty' (Ex. 34:7)."[84]

Even if we do not accept that Lamech killed Cain, I believe that this is still the function of the description of Cain's line, as we will shortly see. Eventually, Cain's line is wiped out, and humanity only continues through Seth. We will continue exploring this idea in the context of Cain's line and its relationship with the line of Seth.

ADAM'S SIN AND CAIN'S SIN

We cannot move on from Cain's story without pointing out the profound connection between his sin and the previous episode – the story of Eden. There are parallels between Cain and all three sinners of that story – the man, the woman, and the serpent:[85]

1. In both stories, God approaches the sinner with a rhetorical question: "He knew where he was, but he wished to initiate conversation with him."[86] Both questions inquire after a person's whereabouts. God asks the man in Eden: "Where are you?" (3:9), and asks Cain, "Where is Abel, your brother?" (4:9).
2. Both sinners' responses are evasive, using the expression "*anokhi*." The man says, "I heard You in the garden, and I was afraid because I (*anokhi*) was naked, so I hid" (3:10), and Cain responds, "I do not know. Am I (*anokhi*) my brother's keeper?" (4:9).[87]
3. In both stories, the sinners hide from God, even if in different contexts. After eating from the forbidden fruit, the man and woman hear God's voice and hide "from the Lord God among

84. Ibn Ezra on Gen. 5:1–3.
85. For the possibility of a dynamic analogy in which one figure is compared to more than one figure in a parallel narrative, and the possible contribution of such an analogy, see Grossman, *Text and Subtext*, 364–368.
86. Rashi on Gen. 3:9. On the differences between Rashi's interpretation of God's question to Adam and God's question to Cain, see Leibowitz, *Genesis*, 47–48.
87. The term "*kol*," "voice," "noise," is also common to both narratives, but it is used in other contexts as well. The "*kol*" of God walking in the garden is heard by the man and woman, and God hears the "*kol*" of Abel's blood crying out from the ground.

the trees of the garden" (3:8). Cain tells God that now, after his crime and punishment, from "Your face I will be hidden" (4:14).[88]

4. After God hears their answers, He reproaches them similarly: He asks the woman, "What is this that you have done?" (3:12), and He asks Cain, "What have you done?" (4:10).
5. The sinners' punishments are related to the earth's fertility and yield. Regarding man's punishment: "Cursed is the ground because of you; through painful toil will you eat of it all the days of your life. Thorns and thistles it will sprout for you, and you will eat the grass of the field" (3:17–18). And regarding Cain's punishment: "When you work the ground, it will no longer yield its strength to you" (4:12).
6. Beyond the punishment related to the fertility of the earth, the ground (*adama*) has a still more dramatic role in both narratives. As stated above, working the land is the framework for the Garden of Eden narrative. Adam was placed in the garden, but his more natural place is upon the ground. From the earth he was taken and to the earth he will return, and from birth to death he works the land to which he is sent at the end of the Eden story. In the story of Cain, *adama* plays a crucial role; it is mentioned six times and serves as a key word in that passage.[89] Verse 11 is especially significant: "Therefore, you shall be more cursed than the ground (*adama*), which opened its mouth to receive your brother's blood from your hand." The ground is presented as a kind of accomplice to the murder: it conceals the evidence by receiving the blood of the victim from the murderer's hand.

88. It is not entirely clear whether there is a difference between the verbs "*lehitkhabe*" in chapter 3, and "*lehistater*" in chapter 4, both meaning "to hide." In any case, both characters "hide" from before God. For a discussion of "hiding" verbs in the Bible, see Samuel E. Balentine, "A Description of the Semantic Field of Hebrew Words for 'Hide,'" *VT* 30 (1980): 137–153. He notes the common juxtaposition of "hide" and "face," including when God hides His face from His creations. He also discusses the roots TZ-F-N, K-Ḥ-D, T-M-N, and A-L-M.

89. It should be noted that the ground accompanies the reader (and Cain) throughout various episodes in the narrative: In the description of his service (v. 2), the description of his offering (v. 3), God's response to the murder (v. 10), and Cain's punishment and his request for leniency (vv. 11–12, 14).

In this context, the connection between the role of the earth in both narratives is highlighted in Cain's punishment, mentioned earlier: "When you work the ground (*adama*), it will no longer yield its strength to you; you will be a restless wanderer upon the earth" (4:12). At the conclusion of the Eden narrative Adam is sent "to work the soil (*adama*) from which he was taken" (3:23). The next stage, alluded to in Cain's punishment, is clear: From now on, this ground that Adam was sent to work will no longer yield its strength to you. At the end of the Eden narrative, Adam and his wife found themselves sitting on the ground outside the garden; now, even the ground is no place for Cain, and he must detach himself from it: "You will be a restless wanderer." The punishment of expulsion will be discussed in greater depth later.

7. Beyond their specific punishments, God curses each of the sinners. Such a specific curse is a rare biblical occurrence, yet this takes place in two consecutive narratives. In the Eden narrative, God curses the serpent, "Cursed are you more than any animal or beast of the field" (3:14), and curses Cain with similar language, "And now, cursed will you be from the ground" (4:11). Intriguingly, both punishments also describe how each cursed party will continue to make his way around the world. For the serpent, "On your belly you will crawl" (3:14), and for Cain, "You will be a restless wanderer upon the earth" (4:12). Both curses put the sinner at odds with his environment. For the serpent, "Enmity will I set between you and the woman, and between your offspring and hers; he will strike your head, and you will strike his heel" (3:15), and for Cain, "I will be a restless wanderer on earth, and whoever finds me will kill me" (4:14).

   Besides for the similarities between the curses, it is worth noting the difference between them. In the story of Eden, it is not the sinning man who is cursed, but the snake. It is even salient that the ground – not man himself – is cursed when God decrees the man's punishment. In contrast, Cain himself is cursed in the wake of his sin. This can be considered from different perspectives (for example, the first man represents all of humanity, and God thus refrains from cursing him), but above all, this disparity is the result of the nature of each sin: the transgression of God's word does not result in a curse on the sinner, but the murder of one's own brother does.[90] I will discuss this further below.

8. The threat of death hovers over the head of each sinner. Man's punishment focuses on his mortality: "For dust you are, and to dust you will return" (3:19). After all, this is the sole consequence of eating from the tree that God mentions in 2:17. Cain also complains that his punishment will result in certain death: "Whoever finds me will kill me" (4:14).
9. In each narrative, God's severe punishments are nonetheless accompanied by a sense of compassion, by the readiness to protect the vulnerable sinner from his newly wretched state. God makes garments for the naked man and woman, whose new need for clothing is a direct result of their eating from the Tree of Knowledge. "And He dressed them" creates a new sense of closeness between God and the sinners, like a parent dressing his or her child. Similarly, God provides Cain with a mark of protection: "'Therefore, whoever kills Cain will suffer sevenfold vengeance,' and the Lord placed on Cain a mark so that no one who found him would kill him" (4:15). The precise nature of this mark is not clear. Is it a wondrous act that renews Cain's confidence and strength (like the signs Moses receives at the Burning Bush),[91] or a physical mark on Cain's body? The verb "and He placed" (rather than "and He did") seems to suggest the second reading. God may have marked His name on Cain's forehead,[92] like tefillin on the head, or the sign of protection marked on the heads of the Jerusalem residents who are to be saved from destruction in Ezekiel: "Pass through the city, through Jerusalem, and put a mark on the foreheads of the men who moan and groan because of all the abominations that are committed in it" (Ezek. 9:4).

90. Westermann writes similarly in *Genesis,* vol. 1, 306–307.

91. Genesis Rabba 22:4 suggests different signs, such as, "He caused the orb of the sun to shine for him." Another possibility is that he was struck with leprosy, and therefore the connection between this and Moses' sign at the Burning Bush is clear.

92. As suggested by Pseudo-Jonathan and Rashi, and others.

Or, perhaps, "He made a horn grow on his head," as Abba Yosi suggests in Genesis Rabba 22:4. In any case, God provides Cain with this mark in response to Cain's fear for his life following his punishment.

10. Immediately after the sinners are granted certain protection, they are sent away. The man and his wife must leave the Garden of Eden, while Cain must leave the place where he grew up and grew crops, leaving the region of Eden entirely: "And Cain went out from the presence of the Lord and dwelled in the land of Nod to the east of Eden" (4:16). That both Cain and his parents before him must make their way eastward leaves no room for doubt that this connection is significant; Adam and Eve leave God's garden for the surrounding region, and Cain leaves Eden entirely and wanders outside of God's territory, to the land of Nod. This pattern of movement may lie at the heart of this comparison, as I will soon discuss.
11. Even the next stages of each plot are similar. Immediately after their expulsion, the sinners take comfort in their wives, and produce the next generation: "The man knew Eve his wife, and she conceived and gave birth to Cain" (4:1). Similarly, as soon as Cain settles in the land of Nod, "Cain knew his wife, and she conceived and gave birth to Enoch" (4:17). The response of intimacy and birth is the nexus between these narratives, the story of Adam and Eve giving birth to the story of Cain himself.
12. From a linguistic perspective, we have already mentioned the striking connection between the two narratives, which alone suffices to draw an analogy between them. God tells the woman in Eden, "Your longing will be for your husband, and he will rule over you" (4:7), and God similarly warns Cain, "It longs to have you, but you must rule over it." In both stories, we determined, God is submitting one person to another's rule. In both cases, the new hierarchy transpires within the family, but in two distinct contexts: the husband and wife's new hierarchy affects the marital relationship, whereas Cain and Abel's relationship is fraternal. These strikingly similar expressions highlight the similar development of each narrative, as mentioned above.

If so, what is the narrative objective of this obvious analogy between the sin of the first humans and the sin of the second generation? First and foremost, this connection may be traced to the field of psychology: the sinners' initial reactions point to the predictability of human nature, the nature of human sin, and especially the tendency to shy away from responsibility.[93]

It seems, however, that this analogy has much wider significance. Their shared threads can be teased into two different patterns, simultaneously forming an analogy between two parallel stories, and one long tragedy divided into two acts.

The objective of the analogy between two separate stories is related to the different character of each sin: one is a religious sin, the other is moral. As I already mentioned, it is difficult to define the prohibition against eating the forbidden fruit as logical. As Beverly Stratton points out|

> The narrator provides no explanation for this unexpected prohibition, no comment on why this tree or its knowledge should be dangerous, no hints of God's aims or motives in proscribing it, not even a clue about whether the man understood God's command or the warning of death.[94]

Whether certain logic is hinted to in the text or not, the focus is on the actual prohibition. It is forbidden because God forbade it; the man is punished "because you listened to the voice of your wife and ate fruit from the tree *about which I commanded you*, 'You must not eat from it'" (3:17). "Which I commanded you" is the focal point of the sin. The man obeys his wife instead of God, and for this he is punished. This, if so, is the archetype of the "religious sin" – the human must obey the Divine because he is commanded to obey, as an expression of his loyalty to God.

Unlike the sin of Eden, Cain's sin is of an entirely different nature. Why doesn't Cain defend his actions by arguing that God never forbade him to murder? This would not only defend Cain, but cast an

93. See especially Nissan Ararat, "The Story of Cain and Abel," *Beit Mikra* 30 (1985): 312–321.

94. Stratton, *Out of Eden*, 35.

accusation back against God: How can God punish Cain without prior warning, without explaining to him that murder is forbidden and results in dire punishment?[95] The answer to both questions is clear: there is no need for God to prohibit murder, and Cain cannot be excused with this claim. The taboo of murder is inherently, innately clear to any sane being. Even if a relativistic grasp of morality dictates that murder cannot be defined as an absolute moral violation, this is nonetheless a clear violation within the biblical context. As David Hume might define it, this innate understanding is a "natural virtue" humans grasp intuitively. According to biblical thought, the prohibition of taking another human life is a cornerstone of morality, and there is no need for an explicit prohibition to this effect.[96]

If the story of Eden represents the archetype of religious sin, and the story of Cain is the archetype of moral sin, then drawing an analogy between the two reveals a profound aspect of biblical theology: moral sin is tantamount to religious sin! A person's relationship with God is not only harmed by religious transgression; he or she will become estranged from God by moral transgressions against his or her surroundings. While there is no need for divine command in regard to innate moral values, a person's moral world is an integral part of his or her religious world. In this context, George Smith writes eloquently about the unique "genius" of ancient Israel:

> The tribal character of the gods of the Semites (to use a convenient if not wholly accurate name for the people to whom the Hebrews were most akin) ensured the association of religion with the practical life of the tribe, the discharge of justice and government and the waging of war.... But in these effects the ethical force of the Semitic religions appears to have spent itself....

---

95. As mentioned, some commentators believe that for this reason Cain could not be punished as an intentional murderer. I already wrote that it is difficult to find textual proof for this position, and on the contrary, a significant part of the narrative objective is to punish Cain as a murderer without prior warning.

96. The formal prohibition integrated later on in the Torah transforms this intuitive moral world into part of the covenant with God. In Genesis, moral behavior is presented as a precondition for a covenant with God.

> There can have been little feeling for humanity as a whole and no profound sense of the spiritual value of the individual. Of this system the Hebrews inherited both the practical advantages and the limitations, but, by whatever inspiration, they gradually grew away from the latter, developing not only higher standards of public justice and ideal of social purity, but an ethic which embraced at once more penetrating and articulate claims on the inner life of the individual and a sympathetic and generous attitude to other races.... This ethical development was concurrent with as advance to higher conceptions of the character of the Deity.... The Hebrews – admittedly from the time of Moses onwards – came to see in Him attributes of righteousness, faithfulness, holiness, and mercy far above what other people of their world have told us of the Deity.[97]

Up until now, the discussion assumed that the analogy between the narratives sought to draw a parallel between them. As stated, because the narratives in question are consecutive, it is also possible that the connection between the chapters is calculated to bring the reader through a certain process, based on the repetitive pattern within the text. If so, this process is even more important than the actual comparison between them. The curse of the soil reflects such a process. The man is told that as a punishment for his sin, the earth will only yield its fruit through painful toil, while Cain's punishment is yet harsher: "When you work the ground, it will no longer yield its strength to you" (4:12).[98]

This sequence is a bleak introduction to the history of humanity, which begins its journey with two acts of sin and violation. Envy of the Divine, which resulted in expulsion from the Garden of Eden, developed into fraternal envy in the story of Cain and Abel.[99] With such a grim

---

97. George Adam Smith, "The Hebrew Genius as Exhibited in the Old Testament," in *The Legacy of Israel*, ed. E. R. Bevan and C. Singer (Oxford, 1927), 6–8.
98. However, see also Nahmanides on 4:11–12, who proposes drawing a distinction between the curse of the soil itself in chapter 3 and Cain's curse.
99. See especially Wénin, "Adam et Eve: la jalousie de Cain, 'semence' du serpent: Un aspect du récit mythique de Genèse 1–4," *Revue des sciences religieuses* 73 (1999): 3–16.

beginning, what kind of future could possibly lie in store? Does this already anticipate that the world will be washed away, to begin anew?

Nonetheless, these acts of sin lead to human progress. As we discussed in depth, the "sin" of Eden can be read as an act that leads to maturity, casting humanity out of its idyllic childhood and leading it to its calling – to work the soil that awaits man's touch. Similarly, Cain's expulsion from the Eden area forces him to deal with a new life, one in which he is cut off from the soil, and he indeed builds a city (4:17).[100] It is no coincidence that it is Cain's descendants who make breathtaking strides in culture and technology: Jabal develops shepherding, Jubal invents musical instruments, and Tubal-cain is the first to work with metal (4:20–22).[101] All three sons of Lamech, descended from Cain, develop the world that their ancestor was plunged into against his will. This complicates the attitude towards sin: the guilty character is punished with the loss of everything good in their life, yet this state of loss leads to resourcefulness, development, and progress.[102]

Nahmanides hints to this process in the introduction to his commentary on Genesis. Rabbi Isaac's position brought in Genesis Rabba, which Rashi's first comment on Genesis also cites, suggests that the stories of Genesis are an important introduction to the Torah because they serve as moral justification for giving the land of Canaan to Abraham's descendants. There is room to debate how the creation narrative justifies the conquest of the land and the expulsion of its Canaanite inhabitants, but Nahmanides explains Rabbi Isaac's answer thus:

> And Rabbi Isaac gave the following reason why the Torah began with, "In the beginning, God created," and records all the works of creation until the creation of man, and appointed

100. Assuming the narrative sees the building of the city in a positive light. Some claim that the biblical attitude towards cities is negative. See Yitzchak Meitlis, *Parashat Derakhim: Archaeology and Geography in the Weekly Torah Reading* (Jerusalem, 2014), 14–20.

101. Some also perceive this with criticism (Charles Hauret, "Réflexions pessimistes et optimistes sur Gen. IV, 17–24," in *Sacra Pagina Miscellanea Biblica Congressus Internationalis Cathohci de Re Biblica*, ed. J. Coppens et al. [Paris, 1959], vol. 1, 358–365). See my discussion of these verses below.

102. Compare to Brichto, *The Names of God*, 94–96; Knohl, *Biblical Beliefs*, 146–147.

> him in charge of all that was beneath him, and established his abode in Eden, until his sin drove him out of there. And in their sin, the generation of the Flood was driven out from the world itself, and only the righteous one among them and his sons escaped. As for their descendants, their sin resulted in dispersion from their place and estrangement from their land. If so, it is fitting that when a nation sins, it will be lost from its place and another will come to inherit its land, for that has always been God's practice forever.[103]

Nahmanides reads the first stories of Genesis as a blueprint for a natural law – sinners are displaced. This takes place for the first time in the Garden of Eden, and will take place in the land of Canaan – Israel in the future. He holds that the conquest of the land is justified not because God created and owns the world, but because of the Canaanites' sins, which strip them of the right to dwell upon this special land.

The story of Eden and the story of Cain both reflect this pattern: both tell the story of a figure dwelling in Eden, close to God, who is then displaced and sent away because of their sin. This is a tragedy in two acts: first the man and his wife are sent away from the Garden of Eden itself, and then their son is sent away from the land of Eden and exposed to the raw, godless expanses of reality, where he builds the first city. Holy soil cannot tolerate sin; it spews sinners away from it.

In this way, the land of Israel functions like the Garden of Eden, and acts according to its criteria. Two particular sins defile the ground itself and lead to the sinner's expulsion from the defiled area. One is forbidden sexual relations (and as noted, the sin of Eden has certain sexual overtones):

> Do not defile yourselves in any of those ways, for it is by such that the nations that I am casting out before you defiled themselves. Thus the land became defiled; and I called it to account for its iniquity, and the land spewed out its inhabitants…for all those abhorrent things were done by the people who were in

103. Nahmanides on Gen. 1:1.

> the land before you, and the land became defiled. So let not the land spew you out for defiling it, as it spewed out the nation that came before you. (Lev. 18:24–28)

Murder, as committed by Cain, also defiles the land itself, as it offends the Divine Presence that dwells in the land:

> You shall not pollute the land in which you live; for blood pollutes the land, and the land can have no expiation for blood that is shed on it, except by the blood of him who shed it. You shall not defile the land in which you live, in which I Myself abide, for I the Lord abide among the Israelite people. (Num. 35:33–34)

The parallels between the first two sins in Genesis hint to the pattern they establish, and that is that sin leads to displacement. When God dwells upon the land, there are certain requirements which must be fulfilled – conventions both religious and moral. This process is established at the very beginning of the Torah, and as Nahmanides writes, it serves as a precedent that accompanies the reader throughout the entire Bible. Both the first man and woman are sent to the east of Eden, and Cain is also sent eastward, to the land of Nod, a geographical pattern which anticipates Israel's future exile from the west, from the Holy Land, to the east, to Babylon.[104]

EDEN, ISRAEL, AND THE BIBLE

If the first two sins and their punishment indeed establish a pattern that will resonate throughout the Bible, then Eden and its heart – the Garden of Eden – can be compared to the land of Israel and its heart – the Temple. Early midrashim already draw a connection between Eden and Israel, Jerusalem, and the Temple. This has also been pointed out

---

104. See especially in Cynthia Edenburg, "From Eden to Babylon: Reading Genesis 2–4 as a Paradigmatic Narrative," in *Pentateuch, Hexateuch, or Enneateuch: Identifying Literary Works in Genesis through Kings*, ed. T. Dozeman, T. Römer, and K. Schmid (Atlanta, 2011), 155–167. She sees the two stories as two models of sin and human failure that leads to exile, all background to the Babylonian exile as described in II Kings 24–25.

by modern scholars, who believe that this link is intentional.[105] I will mention the most striking parallels:

1. The rivers that flow from Eden hint to the geographical region of the land of Israel.[106] The Euphrates and Tigris run to its northeast; Pishon and Gihon (which are the Nile and the Besor stream south of Gaza), flow to its southwest. I hesitate to present this theory, but if it is justified, then the congruence between Eden and Israel surpasses the figurative and reaches the realm of the literal-geographical.
2. Others have argued that from a geographical point of view, the Garden of Eden does not reflect the land of Israel as a whole, but only Jerusalem, as the Gihon River, which flows out of Eden, is one of the rivers that marks the borders of Jerusalem (I Kings 1:33, 38, 45; II Chr. 32:30; 33:14).[107]
3. Several textual hints generate a connection between the Garden and the Temple:[108]

---

105. Effectively, reading the story of Eden against other Near Eastern creation stories is almost obvious. The Babylonian creation myth *Enuma Elish* also emphasizes dedicating a special site for a holy temple on earth as part of creation. I will develop this in my discussion of the Tower of Babel.
106. Magnus Ottosson, "Eden and the Land of Promise," in *Congress Volume: Jerusalem 1986*, ed. J. A. Emerton et al. (VTSup 40: Leiden, 1986), 177–188. For other attempts at identifying the specific geographic location of Eden, see Day, *From Creation to Babel*, 27–32.
107. Lawrence E. Stager, "Jerusalem and the Garden of Eden," *Eretz-Israel* 26 (1999): 183–194. For reservations about Stager's position, see Ron Hendel, "Other Edens," in *Exploring the Longue Durée: Essays in Honor of Lawrence E. Stager*, ed. D. Schloen (Winona Lake, IN: Eisenbrauns, 2008), 185–189.
108. On the connection between the garden and the Temple, see especially Gordon J. Wenham, "Sanctuary Symbolism in the Garden of Eden Story," in *Proceedings of the Ninth World Congress of Jewish Studies, Division A* (Jerusalem: World Union of Jewish Studies, 1986), 19–25; Peter Thacher Lanfer, *Remembering Eden: The Reception History of Genesis 3:22–24* (New York, 2012), 127–157; Yehuda Kiel, "The Tabernacle, the Temple, and the Garden of Eden," *Shana Be-shanah* (1966): 225–255; Lea Mazor, "The Correlation between the Garden of Eden and the Temple," *Shnaton* 13 (2002): 5–42; Arieli, "The Temple as Eden."

- **The cherubim:** The most striking connection between the Garden of Eden and the semantic field of the Tabernacle-Temple is the cherubim mentioned at the end of the story: "He drove out the human, and placed east of the Garden of Eden cherubim and the flaming, ever-turning sword to guard the way to the Tree of Life" (3:24). The "cherubim" feature so rarely in the Bible that this particular detail can hardly be a coincidence; they presumably hint to the cherubim which will be placed in the Tabernacle and the Temple, both those that shade the Ark with their wings (Ex. 25:2; I Kings 6:23), and those that adorn the Tabernacle hangings and the Temple doors (Ex. 26:1, 31; I Kings 6:32–35). This connection is reinforced by the verb used to describe God's assignment of the cherubim at the Garden of Eden: "He placed (*vayashken*) east of the Garden of Eden cherubim" (3:24). The more common verb referring to placement, "*vayasem*" (as in Gen. 2:8), or "*vayanaḥ*" (as in 2:15), would have been more appropriate, but the use of the verb "*vayashken*" recalls the word "*mishkan*," "tabernacle," where the Divine Presence hovers over the cherubim.

- **Rivers:** In Eden, four rivers babble through the garden and flow on to water the rest of the world (2:14). Various prophets foretell of a river that will flow forth from the Temple to water the rest of the land (see Joel 4:18; Zech. 14:8). The most prominent, of course, is Ezekiel, who describes the mighty streams of water that will issue forth from the Temple and bring healing and fertility to everywhere it reaches:

  > As I came back, I saw on the bank of the river a great many trees on the one side and on the other.... Wherever the river goes, every living creature that swarms will live, and there will be very many fish, once these waters reach there. It will become fresh; and everything will live where the river goes.... On the banks, on both sides of the river, there will grow all kinds of trees for food. Their leaves will not wither nor their fruit fail, but they will

> bear fresh fruit every month, because the water for them flows from the sanctuary. Their fruit will be for food, and their leaves for healing. (Ezek. 47:7–12)[109]

The divine healing properties of the waters produce trees whose fruit and leaves bring life and health to all who eat of them;[110] its associations with the Garden of Eden speak for themselves.

- **The holy mountain:** Ezekiel relates to the Garden of Eden in his prophecies, and many read his descriptions as a reflection of the Eden tradition (and the expulsion from Eden).[111] Ezekiel holds that the garden is at the top of the holy mountain: "With an anointed cherub as guardian I placed you; you were on the holy mountain of God" (Ezek. 28:14), and this draws another parallel between Eden and the Temple, which is built on a mountaintop.
- **The place of worship and sacrifice:** Man, placed in the Garden of Eden, has a role and a purpose: "And the Lord God took the human and placed him in the Garden of Eden to work it and care for it (*le'avdah uleshamrah*)" (2:15). The sages in Genesis Rabba 16:5 read this verse as an allusion to the sacrificial service, based on the connection to "*le'avdah uleshamrah*" in the verses of "You shall serve (*taavdun*) God on this mountain" (Ex. 3:12), and "Take care (*tishmeru*) to sacrifice to Me in its due time" (Num. 28:2), and some even read this as the plain meaning of the text.[112] Man's role in the garden is parallel to his role in the Tabernacle and Temple.

109. For our purposes, it makes no difference if Ezekiel refers to an actual spring that flows from Jerusalem (as held by B. Z. Luria, "The History of the Water Supply in Ancient Jerusalem," *Sinai* 28 [1951]: 9–18), or – as most scholars hold – he refers to a prophetic vision of the future.
110. The chiastic structure of this prophecy emphasizes the blessing that these waters bring to all they reach. For further discussion, see Jonathan Grossman, "'Structural Ambiguity' in Ezekiel 33–38," *Beit Mikra* 49 (2004): 212–216.
111. See a summary of opinions and relevant debates in Day, *From Creation to Babel*, 47–49.
112. Cassuto, *From Adam to Noah*, 122 (based on parallels with other creation accounts); Wenham, "Sanctuary Symbolism." Cassuto's motive for this interpretation is that toil was given to humanity only after his sin and expulsion from Eden. See also Hart, "Prologue," 332.

- **Divine Presence:** In the Garden of Eden, God's perpetual presence is expressed through the evocative verb "*mithalekh*": "Then the man and his wife heard the voice of the Lord God as He was walking (*mithalekh*) in the garden in the cool of the day" (3:8). This verb is also used to describe God's presence in the Tabernacle: "I will establish My abode in your midst.... I will be ever present (*vehithalakhti*) in your midst" (Lev. 26:11–12).

Based on these connections, some perceived the Garden of Eden as the location of the ancient Temple, even claiming that its geographical location was in Jerusalem, on the top of Mount Moriah. I interpret this close connection as figurative rather than literal.[113] There is no explicit mention of the words "temple" or "tabernacle" in Genesis, no explicit hint to the altar or sacrifice, and the sages' interpretation of "to work it and take care of it" should be read as a symbolic, not concrete, identification.

The significance of this profound connection has dramatic implications for the course of history, as represented in this story. Why does God choose to guard the Tree of Life with cherubim, rather than cut it down? If humanity is never to return to the garden, why does God go to the trouble of stationing cherubim with fiery swords to guard the way? The end of the story, therefore, seems to anticipate future return to the garden. Even if humanity is banished for now, there is vital importance to the concept of an existing haven, of a site where the Tree of Life grows, and God walks through the garden in the cool of the day.

The expulsion from the Garden, and then from Eden, become the opening act of an intricate, winding story. The next act sees Israel building the Tabernacle, which restores God's presence to reality itself. In this divine dwelling place, the cherubim do not guard the way to the Tree of Life, keeping Israel out; on the contrary, their wings are lifted and the Tree of Life rests within the Ark, inviting all who wish to taste of it:[114]

---

113. Day, *From Creation to Babel*, 31.

114. As the wise one states about wisdom in Proverbs: "It is a tree of life to those who hold on to it and its supporters are happy" (3:18) – and the wisdom of the Torah is contained within the Ark and the cherubim watch over it, but do not prevent its supporters from following the Torah.

> See, I set before you this day life and prosperity, death and adversity.... I have put before you life and death, blessing and curse. Choose life, if you and your offspring would live, by loving the Lord your God, heeding His commands, and holding fast to Him. For thereby you shall have life and shall long endure upon the soil that the Lord swore to your ancestors, Abraham, Isaac, and Jacob, to give to them. (Deut. 30:15–20)

Another act in the "Saga of the Cherubim" takes places when the Divine Presence departs from the Temple. Ezekiel describes how the cherubim carry the Divine Chariot on their backs and bear the Divine Presence away from the Temple:

> And a cherub stretched out his hand among the cherubs to the fire that was among the cherubs; he took some and put it into the hands of him who was clothed in linen, who took it and went out.... The cherubs ascended; those were the creatures that I had seen by the Chebar Canal.... Then the Presence of the Lord left the platform of the House and stopped above the cherubs. And I saw the cherubs lift their wings and rise from the earth, with the wheels beside them as they departed; and they stopped at the entrance of the eastern gate of the House of the Lord, with the Presence of the God of Israel above them. They were the same creatures that I had seen below the God of Israel at the Chebar Canal; so now I knew that they were cherubs. (Ezek. 10:7–20)

On the eve of the destruction of the Temple, God leaves His house, borne away on the Divine Chariot carried by the cherubim, and heads towards the east. This scene is obviously tragic, but it conceals a vein of hope: God does not leave the cherubim to guard His House with a fiery sword. Israel are cast out from Israel as Adam and Eve were cast out from Eden, but this time the Divine Presence accompanies them. God does not remain behind in the Temple, but follows Israel to their place of exile, as "the People of Israel are so beloved that the Divine Presence accompanies them to every place of exile."[115]

115. Numbers Rabba 7:10, and other parallel sources.

Cain's story (and its connection to the sin of Eden) remains open and undecided. His fate may be reexamined upon the birth of Seth, which concludes the chapter. The very birth of Seth – "another child in place of Abel, for Cain killed him" – reopens Cain's file, and casts Cain's line under scrutiny.

The Family of Cain and the Line of Seth (4:17–5:32)

The story of crestfallen, fratricidal Cain continues with his departure from "the presence of the Lord" (4:16). This description traces the character's movement as he makes his way out of Eden – the land around God's garden where he brought his offering and murdered his brother – eastward to the land of Nod.

Cain's departure "out of the presence of the Lord" is not merely geographical, of course, but religious, recalling Jonah's flight "out of the presence of the Lord" when he attempts to avoid God's mission (Jonah 1:3). As many commentators note there (especially Ibn Ezra), Jonah's escape is not merely geographical; it expresses his eschewal of God's word, his evasion of dialogue with God. Cain can be seen in a similar light: once he murders his brother, he can no longer remain in God's presence. The protagonist who invents the very idea of bringing a sacrifice to God, of drawing close to him through an offering (which is in the very name "*korban*" from the root K-R-B, "to draw close"), is banished and distanced from God's presence.

The previous chapter posited that Cain's line is recorded not only in order to keep track of the disgraced hero, but to keep an eye on the sinner whose fate may be subject to change upon the birth of a new son to Adam and Eve.

Cain's line is not presented in what will become the usual format of the chosen sons of Genesis, and this may hint to his dynasty's fate. Nonetheless, the basic model is retained, where the generations are listed and culminate with the birth of three sons in one generation, each of whom represents its own culture (this will be the case with Seth's line, which culminates in the birth of Noah's sons, Shem, Ham, and Japheth, and with Shem's line, which concludes with the birth of Terah's sons, Abram, Nahor, and Haran).[1]

The model is not merely similar, however – there is striking, intriguing similarity between the names of Cain's line and that of Seth:[2]

1. Adam	
	2. Seth
	3. Enosh
2. Cain	4. Kenan
3. Enoch	5. Mahalalel
4. Irad	6. Jared
5. Methujael	7. Enoch
6. Methushael	8. Methuselah
7. Lamech: Jabal, Jubal, Tubal-cain (Naama)	9. Lamech
	10. Noah: Shem, Ham, Japheth

1. In a different context I proposed that ending the line of Seth with the birth of Terah's three sons intentionally recalls the lines of Cain and Seth, but also the first three sons of Adam, out of whom one was killed, just as Haran died before his father (Grossman, *Abram to Abraham*, 69).
2. Skinner, *Genesis*, 138. See also Benno Jacob, *Das Erste Buch der Tora: Genesis* (Berlin, 1934), 167–168.

There are seven generations in Cain's line and ten in Seth's; these symbolic numbers suggest that these patterns were designed with intent. The striking similarity of each family's names is even greater – not always identical in regard to order or sound (Cain's Enoch is the third generation from Adam while Seth's Enoch is the seventh, for example; Irad is not identical in sound to Jared), but the similarity is obvious.

Some disregard the importance of these similarities,[3] but there is no such phenomenon in any other dynasties listed in Genesis. Rather, these parallels invite comparison between the lines because Seth's line constitutes an alternative to Cain's. As we already noted, Seth's birth draws attention to Cain's sin once more, and calls his lightened sentence into question.

THE LINE OF CAIN

Cain's dynasty continues for seven generations, a number which, as Westermann notes, symbolizes totality, wholeness.[4] Not necessarily in a moral sense – far from it! – but Cain's family is presented to the reader as a complete, whole entity. Adam's line, through Cain, can be compared to the seven days of creation – a completed project, open to scrutiny. Cain's line, however, does not culminate with a sense of "rest," as the creation of the world concludes with Sabbath. Rather, "rest" will feature in the tenth generation of Seth's line.

What information is provided about this family? The reader knows much about Cain – about the reason for his name, his profession, and his dark history – but after this murder, he begins life anew as the first builder of a city: "And Cain knew his wife and she conceived and

3. This position has two variations. Some argue that aside from the two similar names, there is no real similarity between the dynasties, especially as one is seven generations and the other is ten (Mathews, *Genesis*, vol. 1, 281, though he does concur that their juxtaposition invites moral comparison between Cain's Lamech and Seth's Enoch, who were both the seventh generation). Others claim that there is similarity between the names, but this has no literary significance, as there is a well-known prevalence of similarity between names in ancient Near Eastern genealogical lists and royal dynasties (David T. Bryan, "A Reevaluation of Gen 4 and 5 in Light of Recent Studies in Genealogical Fluidity," *ZAW* 99 [1987]: 180–188).
4. Westermann, *Genesis*, vol. 1, 324.

gave birth to Enoch. And he built a city, and he named the city Enoch after his son" (4:17). Despite the initial confusion about whether "he built" refers to Cain or Enoch, the verse's end clarifies that Cain built the city and called it by his son's name.[5] The root of the name Enoch, *ḥanokh*, is related to the building of buildings and cities (the *ḥanuka* of a building means "dedication"), but Cain seems to name his city after his son in order to release the city from his own curse. By dedicating the city to the next generations, he can justify the idea of permanent residence for his children when he himself has been cursed to wander.[6] Either way, Cain is not just a murderer – he is a social revolutionary, as the construction of a city has profound civil and political implications.[7] Though it is but one step for a man, it is a giant leap for mankind. The building of the first city in human history recalls the *Epic of Gilgamesh*, when Enkidu – the wild man born of the field – undergoes a process of civilization which culminates with his arrival in Uruk, the great city, where he encounters King Gilgamesh (Tablet II).[8] Having left the idyllic paradise of Eden, humans have already begun to cover themselves with clothes, and they must work for their living. Now, the next generation leaves soil and field for city life. Just as the first step, the departure from God's garden, is depicted as the result of rebellion and punishment, Cain builds his city following his own sin and expulsion. Once again, failure and sin lead to progress and development, and this progress does not end with Cain, but extends beyond him.

The next few generations are mentioned only by name. The next characters fleshed out by narrative details are Lamech and his sons, the last generation of Cain's line. The brief narrative about Lamech himself

5. Cassuto holds that Enoch, not Cain, builds the city (Cassuto, *From Adam to Noah*, 230).
6. Another valid reading is that of the Midrash that naming a city after a person is a human attempt to build a lasting monument, and thus to secure one's place in history. The Midrash mocks those who name cities after themselves (Genesis Rabba 23:17). It is interesting that Cain, who murders his brother, is also the first to recognize a person's transient nature, and the first to attempt to overcome this by naming a city after his son.
7. The link between murder and building a city recalls the prophecy of Habakkuk: "Woe to he who builds a town with blood, and founds a city with injustice" (2:12).
8. Compare to Blenkinsopp, *Creation*, 85.

is vague and cryptic, but this obscurity only serves as further characterization of Cain's line and the portrayal of this doomed family.

Above all, Lamech's family is notably creative. All three sons, born of two different wives, develop a different branch of technology. Ada gives birth to Jabal, "the father of those who live in tents and raise livestock," and to Jubal, "the father of all who those who play the lyre and pipes" (4:21). Both sons are founding fathers, "who founded the art" (Ibn Ezra). One develops the science of husbandry, which perhaps means he developed the art of leading the herd, or of using other animals to guide the flock, or, as Rashi and Radak suggest, that he was the first to lead the herd away from his own home for grazing, or, as Yehuda Kiel proposes, he may have been the first to breed and raise cattle. The second son invents music – he is the first to identify notes, chords, and harmony; as Ibn Ezra points out (and only about this son), "this is great wisdom indeed."[9] Zillah's son, Tubal-cain, does not disappoint either – he "forged all kinds of tools of copper and iron" (4:25). He is not described as the "father" of metalwork, but the narrative context certainly implies that he is the founder of ironmongery.[10] This marks a new, revolutionary stage of civilization, and even hints to the beginning of the Iron Age (which is also linked to urbanization).

How should the reader respond to these descriptions? Some interpret these details in a negative light. Rashi, citing Genesis Rabba, condemns the creativity of this family: "The father of those who live in tents and raise livestock – the Midrash states that [this refers to] those who build temples for idol worship, and stir [divine] jealousy," while his brother "took up lyre and flute to play for pagan deities."[11] This criticism presumably extends from their family connection, from their descent from the "devilish" Cain, but some modern scholars also argue that these cultures are presented in a negative light in themselves.[12] These

9. Note that the ancient world considered music as a reflection of natural order. This is especially true of the Greeks, who perceived music as a reflection of the harmony within reality.
10. Some attempt to insert the phrase "he was the father of" about Tubal-cain as well, see Gunkel, *Genesis*, 53.
11. Rashi on Gen. 4:20.
12. Hauret, "Réflexions pessimistes et optimists."

critical views, I believe, project too many preconceptions on the text. This is a family of Einsteins, of Shakespeares, of Newtons, and an unbiased reading of these verses inspires nothing but awe at the sheer diversity of creative genius in a single family. In other ancient cultures, inventions of these kinds are ascribed to the gods, so accrediting music and metalwork to human hands is a subtle jab at these pagan myths. Moreover, the Bible's fondness for wandering shepherds makes it hard to perceive the descendants of Cain, the founder of this lifestyle, in a critical light. Cain's descendants are also recognized for inventing the concept of music, one of humanity's highest forms of expression, which is used to soothe the soul and praise God. And all this is aside from their role in industrial development. We can only imagine this family sitting around the dinner table, casually sharing their strokes of genius. So, there is no reason to read these descriptions with a negative eye, aside from preconceptions that Cain's descendants, too, will be cursed. On the contrary, it seems that Cain's side of the family is responsible for most of humanity's progress – ironically, progress that was born of Cain's forced divorce from the soil.

It seems that creativity and progress, however, were not the only things happening around the dinner table. Another cryptic event is reported about Lamech and his family – Lamech's song to his wives (4:23–24).

This song comprises three brief stanzas, the first being an opening that invites his wives to listen, and then two stanzas that anaphorically open with the word "*ki*," "for":

> Adah and Zillah, hear my voice / wives of Lamech, listen to my words.
> For a man I killed for wounding me / a young man for injuring me.
> For if Cain is avenged seven times / then Lamech seventy-seven times.

From this brief passage, it is clear where Lamech's sons inherited their capacity for innovation. Lamech, the first to take two wives, is also the first to compose poetry. These three short stanzas include the three kinds of poetic parallelism that characterize all the biblical poetry to come. The first stanza is a classic parallelism, synonymous parallelism:

> [1] Adah and Zillah, [2] hear [3] my voice
> [1] wives of Lamech, [2] listen [3] to my words.

In the second stanza, the second hemistich completes the first:

> [1] a man [2] I killed [3] for wounding me
> [1] a young man [3] for injuring me

And the third is arranged in a chiastic parallelism:

> [1] If seven times, [2] avenged is [3] Cain
> [3] then Lamech, [1] seventy-seven times.

Is Lamech, then, the father of poetry, just as his son Jubal is the father of music? The creative atmosphere, however, darkens when the actual poetic content is explored. The most straightforward reading sees the poem as an ode to the proud hunter, back from the hunt. In fact, documentation of these hunting songs can be found in the book of Job, which describes a wild ass that is so elusive that it will never hear the proud cheers of the hunter: "It scorns the tumult of the city / it will never hear the cheers of the driver" (Job 39:7). Not only animal hunters are lauded with these songs; soldiers were also lauded as they returned from the battlefield: "The laughing women echoed each other, chanting, Saul has thrashed thousands, and David – myriads!" (I Sam. 18:7; see also David's lament for Saul and Jonathan, II Sam. 1).

In this context, Lamech's song can be understood thus:[13] Lamech returns home and proudly displays his new injuries to his wife, declaring, "You should have seen the other guy," meaning that he killed the man who inflicted these wounds upon him. He continues that if the head of the family, Cain, was granted special protection by God from all those who threaten him, he himself exceeds this as he will take revenge

13. As proposed, for example, by Gunkel, *Genesis,* 53–54.

"seventy-seven times" over against anyone who harms him. If we take into account the fact that his son invented the art of working with iron and bronze, his own sword may have struck fear into the heart of anyone who saw it.[14] Moreover, his song is lusty with heavy use of the first person: "*my* voice," "*my* words," "*I* killed," "wounding *me,*" "injuring *me.*" This may well be a reflection of "Lamech's cruel egotism."[15]

Does the biblical text support Lamech's pride? Hermann Gunkel writes that indeed, his song can be read as a shout of praise for the local hero. However, this reading disregards the song's biblical context. While some ancient cultures would have regarded such a declaration as a sign of greatness, it is hard to claim that boasting of killing concurs with general biblical philosophy, especially when the song is placed in the mouth of one of the descendants of Cain, who murdered his brother.[16]

While the seventh generation of Cain's line is awash with creativity, the men of that generation seem to strike terror into the hearts of all those around them. Progress, music, and science are part of their culture, but so is celebration of death and murder; this combination may seem surprising at first, but the mere mention of recent European history should serve as sufficient proof that vicious, cold-blooded mass murderers often enjoyed a good symphony along with their morning tea.

Cain's descendants, then, inherited their ancestor's murderous streak along with his creative prowess, and both qualities seem to culminate with the seventh generation of his dynasty. The text is strewn with hints that this generation will see the end of the line. All three of Lamech's sons are named with the verb root Y-B-L, which recalls the name Abel, who was murdered by their ancestor Cain. Moreover, the tension between Abel and Cain is brought to the surface once more in

---

14. More than two hundred years ago, von Herder proposed reading Lamech's song as "a song of praise for the sword" (Johann Gottfried von Herder, *Vom Geist der Ebräischen Poesie: Eine Anleitung für die Liebhaber derselben, und der ältesten Geschichte des menschlichen Geistes* [Deßau, 1782], 309).
15. Wenham, *Genesis*, 114.
16. Therefore, while Gunkel is correct in understanding the poem in the general context of blood vengeance, Johannes Pedersen, who disagrees with Gunkel, is also correct that the song resonates with negative aggression more than bravery (Pedersen, *Israel, Its Life and Culture* [Oxford, 1953], vol. 2, 380).

the name of his third son, "Tubal-cain."[17] The recollection of the first generation through the names of the final generation is expressed openly in Lamech's song: "If seven times avenged is Cain, then Lamech seventy-seven times" (4:24). Lamech sets himself in parallel to Cain, and it emerges that they have much in common. The Midrash, cited by Rashi, brings Cain's life to an end through the murderous culture he imbued in his own descendants:

> How was Cain killed?... His great-grandson Lamech, the seventh generation, was blind, and when he went out to hunt his son would hold his hand. When he saw the horn of an animal, he would call out, "I see an animal," and he would draw his bow against it and kill it. Once, he saw Cain's horn between two hills but he did not see Cain himself, and said, "I see the horn of an animal." He drew his bow against him and killed him. And when he went to take it, the young one said, "It is my own elder!" He thrust out his hands in regret and struck the young one's head and killed him by mistake.... Then, all three of them remained in one place: Cain, killed, the young one, killed, and Lamech, blind.[18]

Cain himself is killed by the very culture he created. The midrash goes on to describe that "at that moment the ground opened up its mouth and swallowed four families: Enoch, Irad, Methujael, and Methushael." That is, Lamech's act brought Cain's entire line to its demise. As Robert Robinson aptly notes, the description of a dynasty is usually an expression of the continuity of life; here, Cain's line hints to death and loss of life again and again.[19]

---

17. Compare to Jacob, *Genesis*, 148–149.
18. *Tanḥuma, Bereshit*, 11. See this tradition in James Kugel, *Traditions of the Bible: A Guide to the Bible As It Was at the Start of the Common Era* (London and Cambridge, MA, 1998), 164–167.
19. Robert B. Robinson, "Literary Functions of the Genealogies of Genesis," *CBQ* 28 (1986): 600n8.

This, then, is the portrait of Cain's line: a dynasty rich with invention and creativity, but also tainted with murderous rage and threat; a culture that does not hesitate to eliminate its rivals, even if they are their brothers.

After the reader encounters this dynasty, they are introduced to the line of Seth. The births of Seth and his son Enosh are mentioned even before chapter 5 – the generations of Seth – as a conclusion for the story of Cain: "Adam again knew his wife, and she gave birth to a son and called his name Seth, saying, 'God has granted me another child in place of Abel, for Cain killed him.' And Seth too had a son, and he named him Enosh. Then people began to call on the name of the Lord" (4:25–26). Various scholars have questioned the inclusion of Seth's birth within Cain's story, especially considering the systematic presentation of Seth's line in the next chapter.[20] I believe that its inclusion hints to Seth's status as an alternative to Cain. The juxtaposition of the birth of Seth with the end of Cain's line invites comparison between the two dynasties. Their comparison, indeed, already begins with these verses, and continues into the next chapter.

THE LINE OF SETH

What do we know about the line of Seth? Firstly, the etymology of his name can be compared to that of Cain's name: "Adam again knew his wife, and she gave birth to a son, and called his name Seth (*Shet*), saying,

20. One classic solution in scholarship was to claim that the verses about Seth's line at the end of chapter 4 and the genealogical list in chapter 5 come from different sources. Others challenged this claim. Knohl notes that in these verses, Adam is referred to as "Adam" rather than as *ha'adam*, "the man," which deviates from the accepted scholarly divisions. Moreover, the name "God" is used in verse 25, which is not characteristic of the posited source of chapter 4 (Knohl, *Biblical Beliefs*, 148). Knohl himself attempts to reconstruct what he believes is the original formulation: "And Lamech knew his wife again and she bore a son. And he called his name Noah, saying, 'This one will comfort us from our work and the painful toil of our hands from the ground that was cursed by the Lord.' Then they began to call on the name of the Lord" (ibid., 149). According to this suggestion, Noah is the offspring of Cain, not Seth! While this does solve some textual issues, there is absolutely no basis for this version in any ancient translations, and is therefore merely speculation.

'God has granted (*shat*) me another child in place of Abel, for Cain killed him.'" Like Cain, Seth is named by his mother.[21]

Following both births, Eve acknowledges God as the source of her fertility, but a different relationship with God is reflected in each name. With Cain's birth, Eve expresses her partnership with God, as if the two of them are equal partners bringing a child into the world: "I have produced a man with God" (4:1). While, as noted, this need not be read as criticism of Eve's attitude, the difference between this and her attitude following the birth of Seth is nonetheless striking. After Seth is born, she characterizes herself as the recipient and God as the giver: "God has granted me another child." As Cassuto notes, "On the first occasion, she gloried in her creative power and her collaboration with the Lord; this son she now regards purely as a gift vouchsafed to her by Heaven."[22] Is this difference reflected in the two different dynasties? Do Cain and his descendants see themselves as creators alongside God, while Seth and his sons perceive themselves as God's servants? I believe that other discrepancies between the two dynasties support this reading. This can be seen from a closer look at Seth's line:

- **Enosh** – "And Seth too had a son, and he named him Enosh. Then people began (*huḥal*) to call on the name of the Lord" (4:26). This information is provided as the conclusion of the story of Cain and Abel (as part of chapter 4, before the "generations of Seth" in chapter 5). Some of *Ḥazal* and medieval commentators interpret the word "*huḥal*," "began," in a negative sense, as derived from the word "*ḥol*," "profane." Pseudo-Jonathan translates to this effect, and Rashi explains: "Then it

21. Garsiel comments that this verse has intentional alliteration that echoes Seth's name: "And Adam again knew his wife (*et ishto*), and she gave birth to a son, and called his name (*et shemo*) Seth (*Shet*), saying, 'God has granted (*shat*) me…" (Garsiel, *Midrashic Names*, 57).

22. Cassuto, *From Adam to Noah*, 246. Yael Shemesh adds that while in the naming of Cain, the focus is on the father ("I have produced a *man* with God"), in the naming of Seth, the focus begins to be on offspring ("For God has granted me another *child*"). Now, Seth will be the line that continues. See Shemesh, *Mourning in the Bible: Coping with Loss in Biblical Literature* (Tel Aviv, 2015), 172.

became common to name people and idols with the name of the Holy One, blessed be He, to make them idols and to call them deities."[23] Yet in other places in the Bible, "calling on the name of God" is wholly positive. It suffices to mention that Abraham "built an altar to the Lord and called on the name of the Lord" (12:5), and that Zephaniah envisions that at the end of days, "I will make the peoples pure of speech, so that they all call on the Lord by name and serve Him with one accord" (Zeph. 3:9). This verse also seems to express a positive development between God and humanity. Ibn Ezra suggests that in this generation, "they began to pray," others suggest that people began to give their children theophoric names (Bekhor Shor), or perhaps they began to engage in theology and the glorification of God's name: "Then the righteous of that generation began to preach God's name to the masses" (Sforno). Alongside these possibilities, an entirely different one emerges: it was then that people began to refer to God using the Tetragrammaton, the four-letter divine name, *YHWH*. Until this point, biblical characters only refer to "God" as "*Elohim.*" This is especially salient in the Eden narrative, when the narrator refers to God with the Tetragrammaton, but the serpent and the woman call him "*Elohim*" (3:1, 3, 5). However, there is one anomaly in this theory, which is that though Eve says "God (*Elohim*) has granted me another son" at the end of the chapter – which contrasts with the next verse where people begin to call on the name of the Lord (*YHWH*)[24] – after Cain's birth she expresses, "I have produced a man with the Lord (*YHWH*)" (4:1). Some diachronic scholars point to this verse as a sign that the story of Cain and Abel is not in its proper chronological place immediately after the expulsion from Eden.[25] Some ancient translations, such as the Septuagint and the

23. Rashi on Gen. 4:26.

24. Benno Jacob counted and found that the name "*Elohim*" appears 40 times by the end of chapter 4; the combination "*YHWH Elohim*" appears 20 times, and "*YHWH*" alone appears 10 times (all in chapter 4) – a total of 70 times (Jacob, *Genesis*, 156).

25. Day, *From Creation to Babel*, 38.

Vulgate, replace the name "YHWH" with "*Elohim*,"[26] and if we adopt this reading, the problem is solved. In any case, use of the Tetragrammaton is apt following Cain's birth, as an expression of Eve's feeling of closeness to God. The name "God" generates a sense of distance between God and His creations, which is inconsistent with the high emotion expressed after Cain's birth.

In any case, "calling on God's name" seems to reflect the beginning of a new religious relationship between God – YHWH – and His creations.

- **Enoch** – The text deviates from its technical, formulaic pattern with the birth of Enoch in the seventh generation: "When Enoch had lived sixty-five years, he became the father of Methuselah. After he became the father of Methuselah, Enoch walked faithfully with God for three hundred years and had other sons and daughters. Altogether, Enoch lived a total of 365 years. And Enoch walked with God and then was no more, because God had taken him" (5:22–24). Enoch is famously the subject of many legends and midrashim. Certain Second Temple sects perceived him as a figure deeply entrenched in astrology and astronomy – presumably because he lived for 365 years, the number of the solar year.[27] In any case, the unique character of Enosh is evident from the unique description of his life and death. It is twice mentioned that he "walked with God" – a description unique to his character in this chapter – and it is not stated that he actually died, but rather, "he was no more, for God had taken him." In contrast to other members of the dynasty in this chapter, the name of God appears three times in the description of Enoch's character. Moreover, Enoch is the seventh generation – while the number seven is always symbolic, this is even more significant considering that Cain's line only endures for seven

26. Moshe A. Zipor, *The Septuagint Version of the Book of Genesis* (Ramat Gan, 2005), 102–103.
27. On these traditions, see Kugel, *Traditions*, 177–178. Kugel does not ascribe this to the number of years of Enoch's life (however, see p. 191). For traditions that associate Enoch with the art of writing, see Kugel, *Traditions*, 175–177.

generations.[28] Even without delving into the cryptic details of the text, it is clear that Enoch is characterized in an extraordinarily positive light; a man who "walks with God" is certainly a positive figure, especially in Genesis, where this expression also describes Noah, and Abraham is commanded: "*Walk before Me* and be blameless" (17:1).

Given his obvious virtue, then, his unexplained, untimely end is all the more surprising. Radak understands the expression "and was no more" as a swift, sudden death: "It says, 'and he was no more,' for he did not become ill and had no pain upon his death, and it never occurred to his generation that he would die halfway through his life, rather than living as long as his contemporaries; they did not realize this until he was dead. That is why it says, 'and he was no more.'"[29] Therefore, the first death in the Bible (apart from Abel's murder) awakens a sense of unease; it is clear that there is no correlation between virtue and lifespan. On the contrary, Rashi and others explain that his early death is linked to his righteousness.[30] The second thing that emerges from this episode is that even early death – perhaps, especially early death – is in the hands of God: "And he was no more, for God had taken him."[31] His early death may even be hinted to through the precise formulation of his life. Usually, the descendant's years are written with the plural verb "*vayeheyu*," "all the years of his life *were*," but Enoch's years are described with a verb in the singular form "*vayehi*," as if to reflect his shortened

28. See further in Jack Sasson, "A Genealogical 'Convention' in Biblical Chronology?" *ZAW* 90 (1978): 175; Gary A. Rendsburg, "Notes on Genesis XV," *VT* 42 (1992): 266–268.
29. Radak on Gen. 5:24.
30. Rashi on Gen. 5:22.
31. Genesis Rabba expresses reservations regarding the idea that Enoch did not die but instead was taken up to the heavens like Elijah. This is clearly out of concern that Enoch would be embraced as an archetype of Christian belief, considering that the midrash involves "heretics": "The heretics asked R. Abahu, 'Where do we find actual death for Enoch?' He said to them, 'Why?' They said to him, 'It says he was taken, just as Elijah was taken.' He said to them, 'If you explain the word "taken" this way, then what of Ezekiel, where it says, 'I am about to take your beloved ones by plague'?" (Genesis Rabba 25:1).

lifespan. In this genealogical list, Lamech's life is also described with the verb "*vayehi*." Though Lamech's life is over twice as long as Enoch's, his 777 years are relatively brief, compared to all ten generations. Excluding Enoch and Lamech, the first members of Seth's line lived an average of 930 years. Given that, Lamech's life was about 150 years shorter than most of his ancestors'.[32]

Though no reason is given for Enoch's untimely end, the focus on his character effectively divides Seth's line into a set of seven generations and a set of three generations. Enoch marks the end of one age, and Noah the end of another. This division reinforces the connection between Enoch and Noah. Besides the similar letters of their name, both characters are said to have "walked with God": Enoch "walked with God" (5:22), while "with God walked Noah" (6:9). No other character is described in this way, and the fact that this rare expression appears in the seventh and tenth generations of Seth's line can hardly be coincidental. As mentioned, the purpose of this connection is first and foremost structural, calculated to divide Seth's line into a set of seven generations that ends with Enoch, and a set of three generations that ends with Noah.[33]

- **Noah** – The final generation to receive special narrative attention is, of course, the tenth generation, Noah. As noted earlier, like Enoch, he is described as a person who walked with God, but this characterization is developed even further. Not only does he walk with God; he is "a righteous man, blameless in his generation" (6:9) and a partner in a covenant with God: "I will

32. Rabbi Menashe Viner proposes that this theory can determine which version of Gen. 9:29 is correct. The Masoretic text has *vayehi* in singular form, while other versions, such as the Yemenite Torah scrolls, has *vayeheyu*, in the plural. Given that Noah's lifespan is long, the Yemenite Torah scrolls must be correct.
33. This is not the only case of a biblical list that can be divided into seven and three. See the examples brought by Rendsburg, "Notes," and the Ten Plagues of Egypt can also be added to this list, as they can be divided into a set of seven (blood-hail) and three (locust-death of the firstborns). See Scott B. Noegel, "The Significance of the Seventh Plague," *Biblica* 76 (1995): 532–539; Grossman, "Ten Plagues."

establish My covenant with you" (6:18, as well as the covenant of the rainbow at the end of the Flood narrative).

Noah is already singled out at birth, when his father gives a reason for his name. As the first of the line, Seth's name is given with an etymology, and now, with the tenth generation, this circle is closed. In order to build up to this etymology, the regular genealogical formula is already broken when Lamech bears a son, where the usual "X lived Y years and begat Z," becomes instead, "Lamech lived eighty-two years and begat *a son*" (5:28). This deviation moved Rashi to interpret "a son," *ben*, as a hint to "building," *binyan*: "And he begat a son – and from him, the world was *built*."[34] While there may be an etymological connection between *ben* and *binyan*,[35] in this case, this deviation allows the name of Lamech's son to be postponed until the next verse, where it is announced together with its etymology: "He named him Noah (*Noaḥ*) saying, 'This one will comfort us (*yenaḥamenu*) in the labor and painful toil of our hands caused by the ground the Lord has cursed'" (5:29). This etymology, of course, draws attention to the figure of Noah, but its actual content is significant in itself.

Why does Lamech name his son "Noah"? What makes him so certain that he will be the one to bring humanity relief from its bitter toil? Many point out that Lamech is referring to God's curse of the ground following the sin in Eden, and this is likely, given the similar language of the relevant verses. God curses the land thus: "**Cursed is the ground** because of you; through *painful toil* will you eat of it all the days of your life" (3:17). Lamech echoes this language when he names his son: "This one will comfort us in the labor and *painful toil* of our hands caused by **the ground the Lord has cursed**." The question, however, still remains – what makes Lamech think that his son is the chosen one?[36]

34. Rashi on Gen. 5:28.

35. For such a position (as well as reservations with it), see Herbert Haag, "*Ben*," TDOT 2: 149 (he also suggests there that the word for "son" in Aramaic, "*bar*," is related to the word "*livro*," "to create").

36. Skinner is convinced that the comfort Lamech refers to is the cultivation of the vineyard and the invention of wine (Skinner, *Genesis*, 133).

Some suggest that Noah was the inventor of the plow, so that tilling the earth became infinitely easier in his time: "This one will comfort us – he will allow us to rest our hands from painful toil. Until Noah came, they did not have plowing instruments, and he invented them; until then, the earth brought forth thorns and thistles when wheat was planted because of Adam's curse, but in Noah's day they subsided. This is the meaning of 'comfort us' – he will allow us to rest."[37] This reading, of course, assumes that Lamech was a prophet who knew that his newborn son would revolutionize agriculture. Ibn Ezra indeed first suggests this, but alternatively proposes that his name was changed when his talent emerged.[38] Radak suggests that Lamech's words are not a prediction but a prayer, an expression of hope that their suffering would come to an end through his son.[39]

It is somewhat unconvincing, however, to assume that this etymology is derived from information that is not provided in the text itself. I wish to take a completely different direction, one that explains why Lamech is convinced that a change will come to the world with his son's birth. A careful calculation of the ages listed in the text yields a chronological timeline that measures history from the dawn of time – from the creation of the first man. If we add up their ages, it turns out that Lamech, Noah's father, was born in the 847th year since the world's creation, while Noah, who was born when Lamech was 182, was born in the year 1056. If so then Noah, it emerges, was the first of Seth's descendants who was born after Adam's death. Given that Adam lived for 930 years (5:5), he was still alive at Lamech's birth, but died 126 years before Noah's birth. As Rashbam points out,

37. Rashi on Gen. 5:29.

38. See Kiel, *Genesis*, 148, who also refers to the Vilna Gaon, who regularly comments that biblical etymologies should not be understood as the names given at birth, but only after a certain time, when the child's character emerges.

39. Radak on Gen. 5:29.

> This was the first birth since Adam's death, and he was therefore called Noah, saying, "May this one correct the corruption of that one." It is an expression of prayer – "May he give us rest," as in, let us rest from him, that is, may he bring us relief and ease.[40]

Adam's death brought new hope into the world. He was the one who unleashed God's curse: "Cursed is the ground *because of you*; through painful toil will you eat of it *all the days of your life*" (3:17). Though this curse can be read as a general declaration to all of humanity, it can also be understood as a temporary state that will only plague Adam and his descendants during his own lifetime. As long as Adam walks the earth, it remains stubborn, unwilling to yield its fruit without springing up thorn and thistle; but now that Adam has returned to the earth from which he was taken, the mollified soil will treat his descendants kindly. The name of Lamech's son is an expression of hope that the curse will now be lifted, that they will no longer have to suffer painful toil in order to extract their daily bread from the ground.[41]

Later, I will question whether Lamech's expectations are fulfilled. For now, though, Noah's name brings tidings of hope for humanity as the replacement of the first generation, whose sin unleashed curse upon the ground.

A further detail draws attention to Noah's unique character. Noah does not produce a son at the same age as his ancestors, who became

40. Rashbam on Gen. 5:5. It is interesting that Bekhor Shor sees Cain's curse as the curse referred to by Lamech. He explains that Cain's descendants perish with the Flood during Noah's time, bringing an end to that curse. Even if Rashbam's suggestion is more convincing, there is still room to consider Bekhor Shor's suggestion, given that the line of Seth is an alternative to Cain's descendants, who perish in the Flood.

41. See also Yitzhak Moshe Emanueli, *Genesis – Commentary and Insights* (Tel Aviv, 1978), 105. The Netziv was aware of the possibility of intentional ambiguity (for examples, see Jonathan Grossman, "Ambiguity in the Biblical Narrative and Its Contribution to the Literary Formation" [PhD diss., Bar-Ilan University, 2006], 18), and here, too, he claims that Noah's name hints to two different roots, N-Ḥ-T and N-Ḥ-M: "And for this reason his name is only two letters long, without the third letter, so that it can hint to both roots. And the meaning of '*yenaḥamenu*' is also double, [not only in the meaning of N-Ḥ-M, comfort, but] also the meaning 'he will bring us rest,' as Rashi suggests" (*HaEmek Davar* on Gen. 5:29).

fathers for the first time between the ages of 65 (as Mahalalel and Enoch were) and 182 (as Methuselah was). Rather, he was five hundred years old at the birth of his sons, moving the sages to cite the verse, "In old age, they still yield fruit, remaining lush and fresh" (Ps. 92:15) in reference to him.[42] This postponement is perceived in the Midrash as part of a divine plan:

> Rabbi Yudin said, "Each generation bore sons at the age of one hundred or two hundred, but this one bears sons at the age of five hundred? It is because God said, 'If they are wicked, I do not wish that they will be destroyed in the water; but if they are righteous, it will inconvenience him as he will have to build many arks.' So God withheld his fertility until he was five hundred years old."[43]

A broader look at the book of Genesis reveals that later birth is generally a sign of being elected by God. It is no coincidence, for example, that Nahor produces twelve sons with no apparent difficulty, while Sarah's infertility and the question of Abraham's heir is a central motif in the Abraham cycle. Just as Isaac's birth is obviously a miraculous sign of divine intervention, the birth of Noah's sons when Noah is at the ripe old age of five hundred should also be read as a sign of divine intervention and election.[44]

To summarize the scant narrative information related about the line of Seth, every detail is concerned with its relationship with God. In the third generation, they began to call on the name of the Lord; in the seventh generation Enoch walks with God; and in the tenth generation, a blameless righteous man also walks with God and forms a covenant with Him. In contrast, the line of Cain "begins with killing and ends with a song of praise about bloodshed. The line of Seth begins with praise

42. Genesis Rabba 26:32.
43. Ibid.
44. This was suggested to me by my son Ro'i, and I thank him for it. He also suggests that the birth at old age is another connection between Noah's covenant and Abraham's covenant with God (see below for the discussion regarding this). Since both covenants include a blessing for fertility, I think his suggestion is correct that the births at old age are also connected to the covenants.

for God – 'for God has granted me another son' (4:25) and ends with a prayer to God: 'May this one comfort us' (5:29)."[45] It is worth noting that the name of the dynasty's founder, Seth, is also related to the comfort and consolation of the loss of Abel, who was murdered by his own brother, while Noah, the tenth of the line, is linked to comfort and relief from the ground's curse. Thus, Seth's family is presented as the world's consolation for the two sins that led to humanity's downfall. There is also a strong sense of religious awakening over the generations. Beginning with calling on the name of God, Seth's descendants then walk with God and pray to God, and there is no doubt that Noah's relationship with God elevates this process to a new level.

Seth's dynasty, then, is clearly and obviously favored over the line of Cain. One culture is linked to bloodthirsty power and threat to its surroundings, while the other walks with God. Cain's case is reopened, and the new verdict is clear: the culture he has born is entrenched in blood and death. While this brutal vitality does result in some positive progress, such as the birth of art and science, a culture based on murder nonetheless has no right to exist. The fate of both dynasties can already be traced in the pattern of each lineage. The line of Seth is introduced through an orderly formula, with lists of data that anchor it within history, while Cain's clan is listed in rapid succession, with little concrete information, giving it a sense of fleeting transience.[46] Note that not only the name *Adam*, Seth's father, becomes a general synonym for humanity, but the name of his son, Enosh, does as well – the word "*enosh*" appears as a noun throughout the Bible and is generally translated as "mortal" (see Deut. 32:26, and many other examples).[47]

If so, it emerges that while Cain himself is not punished with the death penalty usually given to murderers in the Bible, his descendants uphold a violent culture that celebrates death; and because there is now an alternative dynasty in the world, Cain's line ultimately receives the death penalty. The Flood wipes out every last one of his descendants,

45. Emanueli, *Genesis*, 106.

46. Some claim that traces of conflict can be detected between the two dynasties in the slight differences between their sons' names (Mahalalel versus Mehujael, for example). See Yoav Barzilai et al., *Genesis-Exodus: Pages for Study and Teaching* (Herzog College: Alon Shvut, 1999). I am hesitant to accept this claim.

47. Jacob, *Genesis*, 151.

and only Seth's descendants populate the world anew. Not a single person alive today is descended from Cain.

In this context, it is intriguing to note the midrash that Naama – Tubal-cain's sister – is Noah's wife.[48] This is presumably how the midrash deals with the surprising mention of Naama in Cain's genealogical list, as daughters seldom feature (due to the fact that once they married, they were considered part of their husband's family). Even if the sages suggest this in order to justify her mention, it nonetheless results in the literary preservation of Cain's genes – his blood is perpetuated even after most of humanity, including all his male descendants, is wiped out. In this way, while the violent culture of Cain's family is eradicated, and its name is erased without a trace, a spark of Cain's creativity lives on through Naama, bringing light and music into the world.

THE HOPE OF A NEW GENERATION

Are Lamech's hopes realized through his son? The etymology of Noah's name should be read, as noted, as an expression of hope that the ground is no longer cursed. The bitter truth is that Noah's contemporaries would no longer suffer from the cursed ground – they would simply be washed away. The cruel disparity between his generation's hopes and their ironic fulfillment can be traced through the language in the text:

- **The ground's curse in Eden:** "Cursed is the ground (*arura ha'adama*) because of you; through painful toil (*be'itzavon*) will you eat of it all the days of your life" (3:17).
- **The birth of Noah:** "This one will comfort us (*yenaḥamenu*) in the labor and painful toil (*ume'itzvon*) of our hands caused by the ground the Lord has cursed (*min ha'adama asher ererah Hashem*)" (5:29).
- **On the eve of the Flood:** "The Lord saw how great had become the wickedness of humankind on earth, and that every

48. "R. Aba son of Kahana said, 'Naama was the wife of Noah, and why was she called "Naama"? Because her deeds were pleasing.' Others say that it was a different Naama – as she would make pleasing sounds on the tambour for idol worship" (Genesis Rabba 23:3).

inclination of the thoughts of the human heart was solely evil all the time. The Lord regretted (*vayinaḥem*) that He had made man on earth, and He was pained (*vayetatzev*) to his very heart. And the Lord said, 'I will wipe out the human race I have created from the face of the earth – from man to beast to creatures that crawl and to the birds of the sky – for I regret (*niḥamti*) that I have made them" (6:5–7).

The root N-Ḥ-M reflects a change in situation. Noah's father hopes that he will bring them from painful toil to comfort and relief. What actually happens is that God regrets the creation of humanity – N-Ḥ-M not in a positive sense of comfort and consolation, but in a negative sense of regret and pain – and the roots N-Ḥ-M and E-TZ-V in these verses show the ironic gap between humanity's hopes for a better future and the disaster that washes all hope and all future away.[49]

But the complex dance between God, man, and soil does not end with this tragedy. A further scene takes place immediately after the Flood, and its language hints that this drama is but another scene in a show that will go on:[50]

- **At the end of the Flood**: "And the Lord smelled the pleasing aroma, and the Lord said in His heart, 'Never again will I curse the ground because of humans, because the inclination of the human heart is evil from his youth'" (8:21).

On the eve of the Flood, God is "pained to His very heart," and now, He "said in His heart"; while before, "every inclination of the thoughts of the human heart was solely evil all the time," God now states that "the inclination of the human heart is evil from his youth." On the eve of the Flood, human hopes are dashed with ironic cruelty, but now, there is new hope: "Never again will I curse the ground because of humans (*ha'adama ba'avur ha'adam*)."

49. Given that the etymology of Noah's name ("this one will comfort us") is ironically turned about from "comfort" to "regret," the text offers an alternative meaning to his name immediately after God's regret: "And Noah (*Noaḥ*) found grace (*ḥen*) in the eyes of the Lord" (6:8).

50. See also Kiel, *Genesis*, 149.

> There is no doubt that this phrase refers to the ground's curse in Eden – "Cursed is the ground because of you (*arura ha'adama ba'avurekha*)."[51] There is even room to debate whether God's explicit mention of *"ha'adam,"* "humans," hints to the first man, to Adam, where his name is parallel to the "you" in "because of you."

The tragic scene of the Flood, then, ends with a spark of hope that Lamech's prayer will indeed be fulfilled. I will explore how the state of the ground becomes disentangled from human sin in my discussion of the Flood narrative, but for now, I wish to point out that eventually, Lamech's prayer is answered, even if he himself does not live to see it.

This pattern – of high hopes shattered by catastrophe and devastation that nonetheless reach poignant fulfillment – can be hesitantly applied to the birth of the State of Israel. At the beginning of the century, global national awakening sparked a new yearning for Zion, but these proud hopes were followed by the greatest tragedy and slaughter in modern Jewish history. And yet, as the dense, tragic cloud of ashes settled, a new state was born, against all odds, against all expectations.

The Birth of Humanity

The establishment of humanity is a series of false starts. The first generation born to Adam and Eve is an attempt to develop the world through their two sons: one to work the soil, and one to lead the animals. While this division may offer a sense of partnership, of "two are better than one," this dichotomy quickly leads to envy, anger, and tragedy. It also leads to civilization and technology, but this progress is coupled with discord, power struggles, and bloodlust. An alternative dynasty arises with the birth of a new son, Seth, which marks the beginning of a different humanity, a humanity deeply connected to God.[52]

---

51. Regarding the use of a different root for "cursed" – K-L-L rather than A-R-R – see Vermeulen, "Blessing and Cursing," 125.
52. See further in Brigitte Kahl, "And She Called His Name Seth (Gen. 4:25): The Birth of Critical Knowledge and the Unread End of Eve's Story," *Union Seminary Quarterly Review* 53 (1999): 19–28. She claims that Seth's birth is the rebirth of humanity, of virility without violence.

What is the meaning of this first attempt, the purpose of the line of Cain? The text could have easily jumped from chapter 1 to chapter 5. The connection between them is indicated in the text itself, with chapter 5 opening with language redolent of the first creation narrative: "This is the book of the generations of Adam. On the day God created humankind, in the likeness of God He made him. Male and female He created them and blessed them and named them humankind on the day when they were created" (5:1–2). This verse strongly recalls the description of humanity's creation: "So God created humankind in his own image, in the image of God He created him; male and female He created them" (1:27). Chapter 5 is a fulfillment of God's blessing of fertility, as humanity increases for ten generations. All this indicates that chapter 5 continues where chapter 1 leaves off, while chapters 2–4 parenthetically tell of two mortifying lapses in human history – the sin of Eden and Abel's murder. Why are these stories included, instead of a majestic narrative sweep from humanity's divine origin to the line which will one day produce Abraham?

The answer is evident in the arrangement of chapters 1–11 in their entirety: failures and failings also leave their mark on reality. Human history is also subject to its members who break the law, not only to those who keep it. Cain's story is tragic, worse than tragic: it is the story of a brother who murdered his brother and has no right to exist on the face of the earth. Yet Cain was also the first to bring an offering to God, the first to build a city, and his descendants invented music, science, and technology. Does it take a certain ruthlessness, a certain disregard for the law, to create something new? Are those who stay firmly within the bounds of the law unable to think out of the box? I do not believe that this is the sweeping conclusion of these stories, but at the beginning of creation, human progress and development – both moral and religious – is achieved through the breaking of boundaries, leaving the new earth marked with the fingerprints of their unstable creators, creators too unstable to remain on earth.

Sons of God and Daughters of Man: On Flesh and Spirit (6:1–4)

One of the strangest episodes in the book of Genesis – and, arguably, the entire Bible – is the story of the "sons of God" who lusted after the daughters of man, producing "the heroes of old, men of renown." These mysterious "sons of God" are often interpreted as angels, which would explain why their coupling with human women results in the birth of Nephilim – that is, giants.[1] Yet the real surprise lies in the fact that a tale so redolent of pagan myth managed to make its way into the Bible at all.

1. The Septuagint already identifies the Nephilim with the giants, and this reading has been widely accepted throughout history, especially due to the words of the spies in Numbers: "And there we saw the Nephilim, the sons of the giants of the Nephilim" (Num. 13:33). See Ron Hendel, "The Nephilim Were on the Earth: Genesis 6:1–4 and Its Ancient Near Eastern Context," in *The Fall of the Angels*, ed. C. Auffarth and L. T. Stuckenbruck (Leiden, 2004), 21–22. He believes they are called "Nephilim" because they "fell" (*naphlu*) during the Flood.

In an attempt to temper these mythical overtones, various commentators have proposed that the "sons of God" are not angels, but men referred to as "the sons of God." There are three main variations of this approach:

- "Sons of God" refers to judges, men of authority (or their sons). This reading can already be found in some midrashim, and it is widely accepted by medieval commentators.[2] The use of the word *elohim* as a synonym for rulers is certainly possible (as seen in Gen. 23:6, Ex. 4:16, and more); moreover, in the ancient world, rulers often perceived themselves as gods, or as descended from divinity, which could conceivably lead to the use of language that rulers and kings used themselves.[3] According to this reading, the text is mockingly referring to these leaders with their own pompous language. These haughty leaders believed that their "divine" status allowed them to do as they please. The noble class would freely take any pretty women from the lower classes, the "daughters of man."

  There are two main problems with this prevalent reading. Firstly, from a linguistic perspective, it is problematic to assume that the "sons of God" against "the daughters of man" hints to an interclass struggle. Why should "daughters of man" refer to the lower class? Even after reading Psalm 49:3: "Sons of man *(benei adam),* sons of people *(benei ish),* rich and poor together," it is hard to claim that this is the plain meaning of our verse.

  Another problem lies in the interpretation of the plot, according to this reading. What is wrong with the nobility's actions? The expression, "And they took wives for themselves," is the usual biblical description of marriage (see, for example, Gen. 24:67;

2. This is Ibn Ezra's first interpretation.
3. Meredith Kline, "Divine Kingship and Genesis 6:1–4," *Westminster Theological Journal* 24 (1961): 187–204. Of course, it must be taken into account that even if there were lone kings who claimed that they were descended from divinity, this is not such a prevalent phenomenon and there are no known kingdoms who referred to themselves as "the sons of God" (David J. A. Clines, "The Significance of the 'Sons of God' (Gen. 6:1–4) in the Context of Primeval History [Gen 1–11]," *JSOT* 13 [1979]: 33–46).

Ex. 6:20, 23; Ruth 4:13). There is nothing unusual about the higher classes taking beautiful wives from the lower classes. Some argue that this is a polemic against polygamy,[4] while others hold that it alludes to the custom of *jus primae noctis*, "the right of the first night," where the local ruler seizes brides on their wedding night: "As they were making her beautiful for her husband, the ruler would come in and sleep with her first."[5]

Another interpretation of this reading is that they took wives from "whomever they pleased" and forced them into marriage: "With brute force and a strong hand they would kidnap peoples' daughters as wives, thus destroying world order completely"[6] – that is, they seized women for marriage without consent or anything in return. Nahmanides suggests they may even have seized married women. This would explain why their actions are criticized, and as Rabbi Yaakov Medan has shown, this inappropriate practice is prevalent in Genesis as well as beyond it.[7] Yet even so, this is absent from the text itself. It is unconvincing to claim that the actual problem with their actions is missing from the narrative and must be filled in by the reader.

- "Sons of God" refers to descendants of Seth's line who took wives from Cain's line, the "daughters of man."[8] This reading

4. Kline, "Divine Kingship," and similarly A. R. Millard, "New Babylonian 'Genesis' Story," *Tyndale Bulletin* 18 (1967): 12.
5. Genesis Rabba 26:6. See John Walton, "The Sons of God in Genesis 6:1–4," in *The Genesis Debate*, ed. R. Youngblood (Nelson, 1986), 184–209. The Talmud also states on this: "The hegemon would lie with her first" (Ketubot 3b). This custom is already documented in the *Epic of Gilgamesh*: "He mates with the lawful wife; He first, the groom after" (Tablet II, lines 61–70). It is intriguing that Enkidu expresses disgust at this phenomenon: "Enkidu blocked the door to the wedding with his foot, not allowing Gilgamesh to enter" (ibid., 98–99), which reveals that there have always been those who are opposed to this dreadful custom.
6. Bekhor Shor on Gen. 6:2.
7. Rabbi Yaakov Medan, "The Book of Bathsheba," *Megadim* 18–19 (1993): 87–90.
8. This is Ibn Ezra's third interpretation. And see, for example, Leroy Birney, "Exegetical Study of Genesis 6:1–4," *JETS* 13 (1970): 45–47; James E. Coleran, "The Sons of God in Genesis 6,2," *Theological Studies* 2 (1941): 488–509; John E. Hartley, *Genesis* (NIBC: Peabody, MA, 2000), 96. This reading is prevalent in classic Christian exegesis (Julius Africanus, Augustine, Luther, Calvin).

also eliminates any elements of divinity from the scene, but its advantage over the first is that it interprets the verses within their immediate narrative context. The previous scene dealt with the dynasty of Seth, whose members "began to call on the Lord" and who "walk with God," justifying their description as "sons of God" (as opposed to Cain's line).[9]

Alternatively, some hold that the opposite is true, and that "the sons of God" refers to Cain's descendants, while "the daughters of man" are of Seth's line.[10] They have also pointed out a connection between the sons of God *seeing* how beautiful (*tovot*) the daughters of man are, and how Eve *sees* how good (*tov*) the forbidden fruit appears (3:6). Just as Eve lusts (*taava*) for the forbidden fruit, the sons of Eve, Cain's descendants, lust for the daughters of Seth. Yet neither of these interpretations does much to justify the particular choice of the phrases "the sons of God," and "the daughters of man." These terms reflect a deeper, more inherent difference between them, rather than just a difference in ancestry.[11]

- "Sons of God" can also theoretically be read in a figurative sense, as the servants of God (like the common expression "the sons of the prophets"), whereas "the daughters of man" reflect the rest of humanity.[12] This, too, dispels any trace of mystic atmosphere. Yet this reading is not convincing. Firstly, the term "daughters of man" does not easily exclude believers from what is usually a general reference to humanity. Secondly, why should

9. Birney, "Exegetical Study."
10. Eslinger, Lyle, "A Contextual Identification of the *bene ha'elohim* and *benoth ha'adam* in Gen 6:1–4," *JSOT* 13 (1979): 65–73, and this has also been proposed to me by Rabbi Yaakov Medan in a private exchange. My friend, Dr. Yoshi Farjun, brought my attention to the midrash mentioned by Rabbi Kasher: "And the sons of God saw – these were the sons of Cain, who were good looking and tall…" (Kasher, *Torah Shelema,* vol. 2, 371).
11. J. Scharbert, "Traditions Redaktionsgeschichte von Gen. 6, 1–4," *BZ* 11 (1967): 66–78; Lothar Ruppert, *Genesis I: Gen 1,1–11,26* (FzB 70: Würzburg, 1992), 272–279; Day, *From Creation to Babel,* 78. Sven Fockner, "Reopening the Discussion: Another Contextual Look at the Sons of God," *JSOT* 32 (2008): 435–456.
12. This is Ibn Ezra's second interpretation. Fockner, "Reopening the Discussion."

> marriage between people who worship God and people who do not produce supernatural, giant offspring? The same is true, of course, of any argument which interprets "the sons of God" and "the daughters of man" as two sets of mortal beings.

These interpretations are calculated to dispel the mythological, decidedly unbiblical atmosphere that hovers around the verses if the characters are read as angels. Yet such a reading is prevalent and ancient. It is described in I Enoch (ch. 10 and onwards) and the book of Jubilees (4:22; 5:1); it also crops up in several midrashim, in the Talmud, and in the Zohar. Modern scholars have also embraced this reading, as it fits in with the language and plot. Elsewhere in the Bible, the expression "sons of God" refers to angels and the heavenly hosts, especially in the book of Job, where the members of the Heavenly Court gather around God: "One day the sons of God presented themselves before the Lord, and Satan also came along with them" (1:6; 2:1; see also Dan. 3:25). In Job 38:7, "the sons of God" refers to the celestial bodies.

From the point of view of plot, it certainly seems more likely that "the sons of God" describes a non-human entity, for their cohabitation with human women results in the birth of supernatural offspring, "the men of renown," and perhaps the Nephilim, the giants (who appear again in Num. 13:23, though this reading is subject to interpretation – see below). The meaning of this episode is difficult to grasp if "the sons of God" refers to the ruling class, the nobility.

Yet the reading that "the sons of God" are angels is not without its own difficulties. Firstly, there is no other biblical context in which divine beings have any trace of sexuality, or any means of cohabiting with humans. Other biblical angels are otherworldly, unearthly beings, characterized in a completely different light, which makes this episode all the more jarring.[13] In fact, while the phrase "the sons of God" is usually associated with divine beings, it is nonetheless a rare term – angels appear throughout Genesis, but they are generally referred to as

13. The strange portrayal of "the sons of God" in this story has led Hendel to claim that this is precisely the narrative objective: to depict the cosmic confusion which led to the Flood (Hendel, "Nephilim," 20).

"*malakhim*," "angels," or "*anashim*," "men." Why are these divine beings portrayed so differently, and described with a different name?[14] The book of Jubilees refers to these figures as "angels of God" (ch. 5), but this is not the name used in Genesis.[15]

There is, however, another detail that should be taken into account, one with dramatic implications for the identification of "the sons of God."[16]

THE PLACEMENT OF VERSE 3

The placement of verse 3 is surprising: "Then the Lord said, 'My spirit will not abide in man forever, since he is but flesh. His days will be a hundred and twenty years.'"[17] At first glance, this verse seems to interrupt the logical narrative flow. The report of the heroes' birth (v. 4) ought to follow the report of relations between the sons of God and the daughters of man (v. 2), before God evaluates the situation (v. 3),

14. They are not serving as God's messengers in this narrative, so that the term "*malakhim*," most essentially meaning messengers, is less appropriate. For that reason, this particular expression may have been chosen, as it expresses their status within reality without connection to their usual role.
15. Hendel claims that the phrase "sons of God" may have been borrowed from the Ugaritic language, where this expression literally referred to the children of El ('bn il'), and this sense may have developed in Hebrew meaning "angels." He shows that one of the chief gods, named "El," is "the father of the sons of El" (Hendel, "Nephilim," 18). However, it is problematic to claim that the Bible would adopt such a pagan phrase, given its usual reservations against polytheism.
16. The narrative has a certain ancient pagan feel (see especially Paul D. Hanson, "Rebellion in Heaven, Azazel, and Euhemeristic Heroes in 1 Enoch 6–11," *JBL* 96 [1977]: 195–233; David L. Peterson, "Gen. 6.1–4, Yahweh and the Organization of the Cosmos." *JSOT* 13 [1979]: 47–64; Kraeling, "Significance and Origin"). At the same time, the story's unique nature is evident even from an initial reading: it refers to "the sons of God," not to "the gods," and as Cassuto ("The Sons of God") and Sarna have emphasized (*Genesis*, 45), the children born of these unions are not immortal. I will discuss this further below.
17. For the reading that the word "*beshagam*," "since he is but..." is referring to the sons of God, and is related to the word "*beshgaga*," "mistake," see Otto Gruppe, "War Genesis 6:1–4 ursprünglich mit der Sintflut verbunden?" *ZAW* 9 (1889): 146–147. On the proposal that this word is intentionally ambiguous, see Christensen, "Janus Parallelism." Kraeling, "Significance and Origin," 199, is loath to interpret *beshagam* in this sense.

but the present form of the sequence dictates otherwise: first, the sons of God lie with the daughters of man, then God sees this and makes a decree to limit human lifespan and strength ("My spirit will not abide in man forever"), and only after that does the reader hear of the birth of supernatural heroes. In the words of Harold Ginsberg, "This verse is clearly out of place, for it ought not to come immediately after verse 2, but after verse 4,"[18] or, in the words of Alexander Rofe: "Regardless of the interpretation of this verse, one thing is clear – it disrupts the sequence."[19] It is no wonder that some rearrange the verses in question, or omit verse 3 altogether, to solve the problem.[20]

How, then, can this sequence be explained?[21] Yitzchak Marzel suggests two possible contributions:

> Verse 3 is in its correct place, for two purposes. One, contact between the sons of God and the daughters of man is immediately evaluated; there is no postponement of God's justice. Two, to clarify that the "men of renown" are weak people whose maximum lifespan is 120 years. There is no reason to admire them or deify them. Their weakness stems from their limited lifespan.[22]

18. Harold Louis Ginsberg, *Encyclopedia Biblica*, s.v. "Nephilim," vol. 5, 897.
19. Alexander Rofe, *Angels in the Bible: Israelite Belief in Angels as Evidenced by Biblical Traditions*, 2nd ed. (Jerusalem, 2012), 54.
20. As already proposed by Wellhausen (*Die Composition Des Hexateuchs Und Der Historischen Bucher Des Alten Testaments*, 3rd ed. [Berlin, 1899], 307–309), and many following him. See, for example, Kraeling, "Significance and Origin"; Wolfram Herrmann, "die Gottessöhne," *ZRGG* 12 (1960): 242–251; Westermann, *Genesis*, vol. 1, 366; Darshan, "Sons of God," 158–159. Bartelmus claims that as there is no parallel to verse 3 in the book of Enoch, it should be considered a very late addition (Bartelmus, *Heroentum in Israel*, 151–193). Others have shown that the style and composition of the verse testify to its belonging to the narrative. See John J. Collins, "The Sons of God and the Daughters of Man," in *Sacred Marriages: The Divine-Human Sexual Metaphor from Sumer to Early Christianity*, ed. M. Nissinen and R. Uro (Winona Lake, 2008), 260.
21. John Day proposes that the narrative separation of the birth of the Nephilim and the relations between the sons of God and the daughters of man softens the mythical atmosphere that accompanies the story (Day, *From Creation to Babel*, 91).
22. Yitzchak Marzel, "The Sons of God and the Daughters of Man: Development and Annihilation," *Beit Mikra* 27 (1982): 215.

Before I come back to Marzel's suggestion, which fits with the main narrative objective, I first wish to point out that the particular order of verses may well touch upon the essence of this narrative, and the identity of the sons of God.

To clarify this issue, I wish to explore verse 4, which describes – as generally assumed – the offspring of the sons of God and the daughters of man:[23] "The Nephilim were on the earth in those days and also later, when the sons of God came to the daughters of man and had children by them. They were the heroes of old, men of renown."

While it is usually assumed that these Nephilim are the children of this coupling, it does not actually state that they were "born" from them, but rather that they "were" in the land – "were" in the sense of "came into being," as in, "In those days, in the same year that the sons of God married women from the daughters of man, they were in the land – that is, they came into the land ... the Nephilim."[24] That is, verse 3 is only out of sequence if we assume that the Nephilim are *born* from the sons of God and the daughters of man.

If we dismiss this assumption, then a more straightforward reading presents itself: this description is simply important background information for the narrative. The Nephilim were in the land "at that time" – during the time when the story took place.[25] Compare this, for example, to Genesis 12:6: "And Abram passed through the land to the place of Shechem, to the Oak of Moreh. And the Canaanites were then in the land."[26] The Canaanites were obviously there at the time of Abram's journey, not *as a result* of his journey. Our own verse should be read in the same way: the Nephilim were in the land when this story was taking place. If not for this description, the reader would not be able to understand the story. Before God appears to Samuel, for example, the narrator explains: "In those days, the Lord's word was precious; vision was hardly rampant" (I Sam. 3:1). Without this explanation, the reader might

23. This approach is already evident in the book of I Enoch 7:2, and in Jubilees 5:1, and many propose that this is the plain meaning of these verses.

24. Ginsberg, "Nephilim," 897.

25. Compare to von Rad, *Genesis,* 111; Childs, *Myth,* 56–58; Seebass, *Genesis I,* 189, 191; Day, *From Creation to Babel,* 82–83.

26. Similarly, see Gen. 13:7.

not understand why it does not occur to Samuel that God is speaking to him. Therefore, the narrator explains: "In those days (perhaps unlike your own time, dear reader), the Lord's word was rare indeed." Here, too, in order to understand the story, the narrator takes care to inform the reader that in those days, there were Nephilim around. At some point they disappeared, but at that time, dear reader, they were still around.

Based on this reading, another possible conclusion is that the sons of God mentioned in the stories are in fact the Nephilim themselves, and for this reason, the narrator takes care to mention them. It is worth repeating that until this point, there is no mention of any descendants born from the coupling described in verse 2, so it is problematic to assert that the Nephilim are necessarily the offspring of the sons of God. Rather, this detail seems to clarify the scene itself – the sons of God, the Nephilim, once lived in the land, and took wives from the daughters of man.

According to this reading, then, the "sons of God" are not angels. Rather, they seem to be some kind of mythical race, a different race than humans – they are giants, some other kind of sentient beings.[27]

The ancient world, as reflected in literary traditions both biblical and extra-biblical, was fascinated with giants. In the Bible, there is testimony to the presence of giants in the land of Canaan,[28] not to speak of the famous confrontation between David and Goliath (I Sam. 17), which implies that giants were incorporated in armies and served as a special deterrent; they were not only larger and stronger, but were perceived to have bodily differences: "And yet another war broke out, in Gath. There was a man of gigantic proportions, who had six fingers and six toes on his hands and feet, twenty-four in all" (II Sam. 22:20). Various legends from all over the

27. For the debate whether this is a reference to giants in general or a specific race of giants, see Kraeling, "The Significance and Origin," 204 (he inclines towards the latter reading).

28. See Num. 13:22, 28; Deut. 2:10, 20–21; 3:11; Josh. 15:14; Judges 1:20; Amos 2:9. Scholars are divided as to whether there is clear evidence of giants in ancient times. Taub claims there was never such a thing, and that this refers to tribes who had very long necks because of the rings they wore around them. Weisman, in contrast, shows that there is documentation of people who were 3.2 meters tall who lived in the Middle East. See Max Sussman, "Sickness and Disease," *ABD* 6: 13.

world attempt to trace the origins of these giants. Greek mythology in particular has extensive descriptions of the descendants who were born to Uranus and Gaia, such as the three Hecatoncheires, meaning the "Hundred-Handed Ones," who were giants with a hundred hands, as well as the one-eyed Cyclops,[29] and the Titans – a race of giants, led by Cronus, who ruled the earth for generations.[30] No culture is too small to contain a giant or two tucked away in its literary traditions,[31] and giants have continued to plod their way into contemporary literature, whether hidden away in dark forests or working as groundskeepers in certain magical boarding schools.

This background is relevant for our discussion too, as it turns out that in the ancient world, giants roamed the world, and were considered heroes, men of renown. The giant Goliath, for one, certainly struck fear into the hearts of the people:

> Then the go-between of the Philistine forces came forth; his name was Goliath, of Gath, and he was six cubits and a span tall…. And the Philistine concluded, "I challenge the ranks of Israel today: give me a man, and let us duel!" When Saul and all of Israel heard the Philistine's speech, they were seized with panic and terror. (I Sam 17:4–11)

---

29. *The Odyssey* tells of Odysseus' encounter with the cyclops Polyphemus in the land of Cyclops. These creatures are characterized as cultureless individuals who do not live in a community, produce any form or art, nor work in agriculture. They do not practice the art of seafaring either, which was one of the most salient features of Greek culture. They also rejected Greek hosting etiquette, as is clear from Odysseus' encounter with Polyphemus. Rather, they lived in caves, and ruled over their wives and children as they deemed fit.
30. Cronus was the leader of the Titans until his son, Zeus, overthrew him at what marked the end of the Titan age and the rise of Olympus, whose pantheon was then led by Zeus.
31. Before Greek mythology there have also been references to giants, albeit few references. Especially worthy of mention is Ubelluris/Upelluri, a Hittite mountain of a god who supports the western edge of the sky on his shoulders. According to the myth "Song of Ullikummi": "When they built the heavens upon me, and the earth, I knew nothing / When they divided the heavens from the earth with a knife, I did not know this either / Now my right shoulder pains me a little, but I do not know who is this god" (he refers to the god that Ea mentioned to him before; ANET, 125). In Hurrian mythology, Ubelluris the giant has a different function, and he is known as "the dreaming god."

The description that "the Nephilim were in the land" at that time clarifies who these sons of God are; they are giants who took human wives for themselves, and the children born of these unions were far mightier than regular men.

There is one obvious disadvantage to this reading, however – why are the Nephilim initially referred to as "the sons of God"? Were these giants especially close to God?[32] Rather, we can take another use of the word here, "*elohim*," into account. *Elohim* is sometimes used to connote something huge, immense, colossal. Nineveh, the big city, is described as "a great city, immense (*l'elohim*), three full days' walk across" (Jonah 3:3), and as Radak comments there: "In order to emphasize something's vast size, one can liken it to God, such as 'mountains of *El*' (Ps. 36:7), 'cedars of *El*' (Ps. 80:11), 'the flame of *Ya*' (Song. 8:6)." Ralbag interprets this way for "the sons of God" as well: "They are giants, and they are described as sons of God to convey their size and strength, just like 'mountains of *El*.'"[33]

It is true that, according to this reading, the giants are called by two different names in verse 4: "The *Nephilim* were on the earth in those days and also later, when *the sons of God* came to the daughters of men and had children by them." However, the use of two different terms does not pose any difficulty to this suggested reading. First, the phenomenon of different names used for the same character, even in the same sentence, is common in the biblical narrative,[34] which tends to prefer variegation (in contrast to the common style in Ancient Eastern literature). Many examples of this tendency exist. It suffices to cite several from Genesis alone: "With the coming of dawn, the *angels* urged Lot [...] When he hesitated, the *men* grasped his hand" (Gen. 19:15–16);

32. Even if the aforementioned myths give this impression, it is difficult to believe that the Bible would adopt this view. On the contrary, some modern scholars claim that these ancient giants had a certain kind of deformity or disease. See, for example, the Anchor Bible Encyclopedia, where giants are discussed in the context of "disease," and the sub-entry of "deformities" (Sussman, "Sickness and Disease," 13). If this is true, it is unlikely that they would be referred to as "the sons of God."
33. Ralbag on Gen. 6:2.
34. Nahmanides already made this methodological point in his commentary to Gen. 30:40, citing as an example: "Now Jacob had pitched his tent in the *hill country*, and Laban with his kinsmen camped in the *hill country of Gilead*" (Gen. 31:25).

"And the *child* grew and was weaned, and Abraham made a great feast on the day that *Isaac* was weaned" (Gen. 21:8); "two of Jacob's sons, *Simeon and Levi,* Dinah's brothers, took their swords [...] *The sons of Jacob* came upon the dead bodies and looted the city" (Gen. 34:25–27); "Then ten of *Joseph's brothers* went down [...] So *Israel's sons* were among those who went to buy grain" (Gen. 42:3–5).

In some instances, the translators sought to facilitate easier reading by using the same English term for different synonymous words, as in: "The sheep (*hakevasim*), on the other hand, Jacob kept apart, and he made these animals (*hatzon*) face the streaked or completely dark animals of Laban" (Gen. 30:40).

Thus, repeating the term "sons of God" and then using the variant term "Nephilim" should not surprise us. Moreover, if we view these two nouns as terms that underscore different qualities of the giants, then this would conform with a common phenomenon in biblical narrative. In this regard, Adele Berlin cites the following remarks of Uspenskey:

> In a literary work, one character may be called by several different names or designated by a variety of titles. Frequently, different names are attributed to one and the same person in a single sentence or in closely connected passages.[35]

As Berlin proceeds to demonstrate, the usage of a variety of terms often serves a specific literary function. In our case, too, we may posit several different theories as to the benefit of using different terms in reference to the giants. The reader's interest is piqued by the mention of these legendary creatures, and recognizes them by their familiar name. But as the verse continues in describing how these giants would take the daughters of men for wives, who then bore heroes, it is appropriate to revert to the names that were used at the beginning of the story. These immense giants would take the daughters of men for wives – this seems to convey that it went on for centuries, for as long as the Nephilim were in the land – and thus the famous giants, the men of renown, were born. The change in their name, from "the sons of God" to "Nephilim," which is derived

35. A. Berlin, *Poetics and Interpretation of Biblical Narrative* (Sheffield 1983), 59–60.

from the root N-P-L,[36] may reflect the change in their status after they take the daughters of man for themselves: from self-important, mighty beings, to fallen figures who become weak and mortal and fleeting.

Even if we adopt this reading, however, a nagging question lingers: Why was this story incorporated into the book of Genesis, just before the grand story of the Flood? How does it contribute to the overall plot? While this describes union between two different kinds of beings – between giants and men – this can hardly be seen as a sin in itself, and there is no real expression of divine anger or punishment.

In order to understand the scene's contribution, I wish to point out connections between these four brief verses and the Flood narrative. Some scholars deny any connection between the first four verses of the chapter and the Flood narrative (which they posit begins only in 6:5), while others read this scene as an introduction to the Flood narrative, even claiming that these lines contain the sin which led to the world's destruction.[37] I favor the latter approach, given the textual connections between these two scenes. I will lead up to these connections through a discussion of how exactly these "daughters of man" are portrayed in the text.

Beautiful or Good?

The daughters of man are described as "*tovot*," which attracts the attention of the sons of God. What exactly does "*tovot*" mean in context? Largely understood as "beautiful," this reading is certainly logical – beautiful women attract male attention. Nonetheless, some read this adjective as a moral trait: the sons of God perceived that the daughters of man were virtuous. This reading may be surprising, but it is based on a convincing argument: on its own, the word "*tov*" does not mean

36. "The term itself almost certainly means 'fallen ones', whether morally fallen in the general sense or fallen from heaven in a more specific sense" (R.F. Youngblood, "Giants," *NIDOTTE*, vol. 4, 678).

37. Kraeling, "Significance and Source." From a different direction, Hendel ("Of Demigods and the Deluge: Toward an Interpretation of Genesis 6:1–4," *JBL* 106 [1987]: 13–26), and Darshan, ("Sons of God") reach a similar conclusion that perceives these verses as an introduction to the Flood narrative.

"beautiful" anywhere else in the Bible. When a woman is described as beautiful, she is described as *"tovat mareh,"* literally, "good-looking."[38] There is room to debate what exactly Samson's Philistine father-in-law means when he tries to convince Samson to marry his wife's sister instead of his own wife, who has been given to another Philistine: "Is her sister not better (*tova*) than her?" (Judges 15:2). If we adopt the accepted reading that "better" means "prettier," this is an example of the word "*tov*" meaning "beautiful" on its own, so that this is feasibly the case in our context.[39]

Even if we do accept this accepted meaning, the question still remains as to why the regular expression is reduced to "*tov*" alone. I believe this is related to the narrative structure and its connection with the next scene – the beginning of the Flood (6:5–8):[40]

1. When *humans began to increase* in number over the earth and daughters were born to them, *the sons of God* saw that the daughters of man were *tovot*, and they took themselves wives from *whomever* (*kol*) they chose.
2. Then the Lord said, "My spirit will not abide in man forever, since he is but flesh. His days will be a hundred and twenty years."

---

38. See Gen. 24:16; 26:7; II Sam. 11:2; Esther 1:11; 2:2–3; 2:7; Nahum 3:4 has "*tovat ḥen*." See van Wolde, *Words Become Worlds*, 73–74; Idem, *Stories of the Beginning*, 113; Carol M. Kaminski, "Beautiful Women or 'False Judgment'?: Interpreting Genesis 6:2 in the Context of the Primeval History," *JSOT* 32 (2008): 457–473. Kaminski adds that this was the sons of God's mistake: they assumed that the daughters of man were morally worthy of them, but were mistaken, as the continuation of the story reveals. Marzel claims that the adjective "*tovot*" refers to their fertility (Marzel, "Sons of God"), but he does not explain his basis for this reading.
39. Day, *From Creation to Babel*, 81. It is worth noting that in Judges, there is extensive play with the words "*tov*" and "*ra*," which may have led the narrator to omit the full expression and use just "*tova*." See Grossman, *Ambiguity*, 56–58. There may also be room to debate regarding the description of the sheaves in Pharaoh's dream (Gen. 41:5, and later on in the chapter).
40. Compare to that proposed by Mathews, *Genesis*, vol. 1, 322. He proves the cohesion of 6:1–8, also based on connections between this unit and chapter 5, Seth's line. I do not think these connections are convincing enough to serve as proof.

3. The Nephilim were on the earth in those days and also later, when the sons of God came to the daughters of man and had children by them. They were the heroes of old, men of renown.

The next verses introduce the narrative of the Flood:

1. *The* Lord saw how the wickedness of humankind on earth *had increased,* and that *every* (*kol*) inclination of the thoughts of the human heart was solely evil *all* (*kol*) the time.
2. The Lord regretted that He had made man on earth, and He was grieved to His very heart. And the Lord said, "I will wipe out the human race I have created from the face of the earth – from man to beast to creatures that crawl and to the birds of the sky – for I regret that I have made them."
3. But Noah found favor in the eyes of the Lord.

The opening of these scenes is strikingly similar. Just as the sons of God *see,* God *sees*; the sons of God see how "good" the daughters of man are, while God sees how "evil" man has become. And while humanity "increases" in the first scene, humanity's evil "increases" in the second, and there is even use of the all-inclusive word "*kol,*" "all," in the opening of both scenes.

In order to encourage the connection between the two scenes, the regular expression *"tovat mareh"* may have been shortened to just "*tovot*" in order to contrast with the "evil" of man in the second scene. This does not mean that "*tovot*" necessarily means moral goodness in the first scene. Rather, it implies that the usual phrase for beauty has been shortened in order to encourage the connection between the scenes.

FLESH VERSUS SPIRIT

It is not only the two opening lines that are parallel to each other; the two scenes also unfold similarly. After the sons of God "see" the women and take them for wives, God makes a decree: "My spirit will not abide in man forever" – moving away from the original, ideal state. This decree limits human power and reduces his life to a mere one hundred and twenty years. Similarly, once God "sees" what is happening on earth,

He is moved to make another decree that will unleash death upon the world. This time, not only will human life be reduced to one hundred and twenty years, but life will be wiped out altogether: "I will wipe out the human race I have created from the face of the earth." Both scenes then conclude with a similar third component: despite God's decree, there is some saving grace. Despite humanity's reduced lifespan, there are still heroes, men of renown. Despite humanity's impending doom, Noah has found favor in the eyes of God, and he will be saved.

These structures strongly imply that the story of the sons of God serves as a prelude to the Flood, the first step in God's destruction of the world. As I noted in the introduction, the opening verse of the narrative hints to the creation of humanity: "When humans began to increase in number over the earth and daughters were born to them" (6:1), seems to be a fulfillment of God's blessing to humanity following its creation: "Be fruitful and multiply, and fill the earth and subdue it" (1:28).[41] Now, indeed, humanity is becoming many, but this increase seems to be leading to an unexpected result: to disorder and evil. From this perspective, the story of the sons of God should not be discussed as an isolated unit, but rather as an introduction to the Flood narrative. The story of the giants is yet another example of God's disappointment in His world. In what sense is the story of the giants who take human wives an example of corruption that leads to the Flood? The answer may lie in the final verse of the opening scene: "These are the heroes of old, men of renown" (6:4). These "heroes" are celebrated as the peak of human physical glory, and they are admired heroes, men of renown. Yet, this physical celebration comes at the price of a different kind of quality: "My spirit will not abide in man forever, since he is but flesh." In this story, flesh and spirit are two irreconcilable elements; when flesh is increased, spirit is reduced. Humanity revels in its mighty, physically powerful heroes, but the text hints that God's vital spirit diminishes, rather than grows, within their powerful frame. The concept of "*shem*," "renown," "fame," or literally, "name," will be a recurring motif over the next narratives. The story of the giants, "men of renown," is in dialogue with the Tower of

41. See further in Turner, *Announcements*, 28. After the Flood, God repeats this blessing to Noah, albeit with some important changes.

Babel narrative, where humanity seeks out a *shem* for themselves (11:4). Yet in contrast with these two stories, it is Abraham – the descendant of *Shem* – who takes center stage as one who seeks not his own name, but to "call on the name of the Lord" (12:8).[42] It is Abraham, calling on God's name, whose own name becomes great (12:2), while the mighty heroes and the tower builders scatter and fade away.

The story of the sons of God is essentially an introduction to the Flood because in it, flesh is elevated above spirit, and the "name" of humanity is elevated above the "name" of God. In contrast to these heroes stands Noah, who is unique because he has found favor in the eyes of God. He does not achieve a "name" through strength and power, but through his relationship with God.[43]

The motif of *shem* appears in four different acts within the unit that opens the book of Genesis, forming a kind of chiastic structure:

- "Then they began to call on the name of the Lord (*shem* YHWH)" (4:26).
- "They are the heroes of old, men of renown (*shem*)" (6:4).
- "Let us make a name (*shem*) for ourselves" (11:4).
- "And he built an altar there to the Lord, and called on the name of the Lord (*shem* YHWH)" (12:8).

The line of Seth is chosen because it began to call on the name of the Lord, and Abraham is chosen because he called on the name of the Lord; meanwhile, the heroes of old and the tower builders fade away because they focus on glorifying their own, fleeting name.

Reading this story as a prelude to the Flood narrative, and as an expression of tension between flesh and spirit, also illuminates humanity's new lifespan: "And the Lord said, 'My spirit will not abide in man forever, since he is but flesh. His days will be a hundred and twenty years" (6:3). How can the number "one hundred and twenty" be understood? Some suggest that there will be another one hundred and

42. Hendel, "Nephilim," 16.

43. In the context of this discussion, it is interesting that Noah names his son "Shem," and that this son is the one in whose tents God will dwell (Gen. 9:27).

twenty years until the Flood before humanity is wiped out. This reading is reflected in the Qumran scrolls, some ancient translations,[44] and even some midrashim, such as: "Every one hundred and twenty years, Noah would plant cedar trees and chop them down. When they asked him, 'Why do you do so?' he answered them, "the Master of the world told me He will bring a flood to the world."[45] The advantage of this reading is that it explains why people still had long lifespans after the Flood, as Ibn Ezra explains:

> Some say that it is the lifespan for everyone, and if some live longer, they are in the minority, while this refers to the majority. Yet this cannot be true, as Shem lived for six hundred years, and all the generations after him lived for many years. It was in Peleg's time that the years began to diminish. And from David's time until today, seventy or eighty years. And the truth is what Onkelos said, that humanity was given a deadline, just like the meaning of "in forty days": if they repent they will be saved, but if they do not repent they will die.[46]

Nonetheless, despite Ibn Ezra's claims, the most convenient reading is that God responds to the relations between "the sons of God" and the "daughters of man" by shortening the human lifespan. This is expressed through the phrase, "*his days will be* one hundred and twenty years." This seems to be an ongoing description, consistent with the broader context of the formation of human culture. From now on, people will live for a mere one hundred and twenty years, not a thousand.[47] While after the

44. In Targum Neofiti, Targum Onkelos, Pseudo-Jonathan, *Mekhilta DeRabbi Yishmael,* and Sanhedrin 108a.
45. Genesis Rabba 30:7. Some modern scholars also favor this direction, such as Hamilton, *Genesis,* 269; Helge S. Kvanvig, "Gen. 6:1–4 as an Antediluvian Event," *SJOT* 16 (2002): 79–112; Fockner, "Reopening the Discussion."
46. Ibn Ezra on Gen. 6:3; similarly, Kiel, *Genesis,* 156n85. Many commentators favor this interpretation, such as Rashi, Radak, Bekhor Shor, and Ralbag.
47. See Jacob Klein, "The 'Bane' of Humanity: A Lifespan of One Hundred and Twenty Years," *Acta Sumerologica* 12 (1990): 58–70. Childs (*Myth,* 54) claims that Herodotus presents a similar view (*History,* 1:163; 3:23) but Day disagrees and argues that this

Flood people still lived for several centuries, the lifespan of people born after the Flood grows noticeably shorter (Shem lives for six hundred years, while his son Arpachshad lives for 438). A second turning point occurs in Peleg's lifetime, from over four hundred years to around two hundred, and people's lifespans begin to dwindle until Moses himself dies at precisely the age of one hundred and twenty (Deut. 34:7).

Therein lies the rub: spirit cannot endure within flesh for very long. God's spirit does not abide human flesh. Here is the tension between the upper world and the lower world, between flesh and spirit. Is the abridgment of the human lifespan a correction, a *tikkun*, for this tension, or merely a result? This story can be read in a certain ironic light: the union between these "sons of God" and "daughters of man" does not extend human life by bringing them closer to immortality; rather, it shortens it.[48] A giant of a man does not live longer; rather, his vast frame burns his life force more quickly. Yet beyond this irony, beyond the contempt for human aspirations of immortality, certain *tikkun* is contained in these verses.

First of all, the abridgement of human life is mentioned within a certain context in Genesis. Much has been written about the relationship between the biblical Flood narrative and other ancient Semite flood traditions. Without delving into this discussion, the story of the Flood is documented in two Akkadian epics: the *Epic of Gilgamesh* (Tablet XI) and the *Atrahasis*.[49] As many have noted, a careful comparison between

---

does not refer to the reduction of the human lifespan (*From Creation to Babel*, 92n38). I concur with Day; Herodotus does not mention one hundred and twenty years as a brief lifespan, but as a long life.

48. See a slightly different formulation in Cassuto, "The Sons of God"; Marzel, "Sons of God."

49. The more common comparison is to the Flood story in the *Epic of Gilgamesh*. Nonetheless, Tikvah Frymer-Kensky claims that the story is more structurally similar to that of *Atrahasis*. She, among many others, holds that these comparisons reveal more disparities than similarities, and that the biblical narrative should be read as a polemic (Frymer-Kensky, "What the Babylonian Flood Stories Can and Cannot Teach Us About the Genesis Flood," *Biblical Archaeology Review* 4 [1978]: 32–41). A similar claim has been made by Richard M. Davidson, "The Genesis Flood Narrative: Crucial Issues in the Current Debate," *Andrews University Seminary Studies* 42 (2004): 49–77.

the three Flood narratives reveals fundamental disparities between them. While the biblical Flood narrative has a moral objective, the Mesopotamian Flood narratives are concerned with gods and human mortality.[50] Both Mesopotamian Flood stories conclude with the gods' decision to limit human lifespan; if not by an all-consuming flood, then by other means. In *Atrahasis*, humanity becomes mortal (prior to the Flood, humans, like gods, were immortal), and is additionally sentenced with various afflictions that will limit the growth of the population, such as infertility, infant mortality, and more.[51] In the *Epic of Gilgamesh*, human life is not shortened, but various disasters promise to limit human strength and lifespan:[52]

> Instead of your bringing on a flood,
> Let the lion rise up to diminish the human race!
> Instead of your bringing on a flood,
> Let the wolf rise up to diminish the human race!
> Instead of your bringing on a flood,
> Let famine rise up to wreak havoc in the land!
> Instead of your bringing on a flood,
> Let pestilence rise up to wreak havoc in the land!

Besides other profound differences between the accounts, in Genesis, human lifespan is limited *before* the Flood (6:3), while in the other two stories, the length and quality of human life is presented as a compromise: never again will a flood be used to wipe out the human race, but the gods will find other ways to keep irritating human noise down to a minimum.[53] In the Bible, God is also troubled by humanity, not by

---

50. See, for example, the discussions of Grintz, *Uniqueness and Antiquity*, 42–45; Sarna, *Understanding Genesis*, 39–62; Day, *From Creation to Babel*, 61–76. Day focuses on the Flood narrative mentioned by Berossus (3rd century BCE), which Josephus compares to the biblical account (*Antiquities*, 1:11–12).
51. *Atrahasis*, Tablet III, lines 316–333.
52. *Epic of Gilgamesh*, Tablet XI, lines 186–193.
53. This difference may stem from a different disparity: Noah is told of the Flood in advance, in contrast to the Mesopotamian Flood stories, where one of the gods breaks his friends' vow and hints about the oncoming Flood.

its bothersome noise, but by its distorted values, by its prioritization of flesh over spirit. Human admiration of physical strength is what leads to a shortened lifespan. This gives the sense that humankind is responsible for its own moral choices and the outcomes of these choices, in sharp contrast to the Mesopotamian tradition, which gives the impression that humanity is some kind of irritating buzzing nuisance, whose lifespan is shortened to give the gods some peace and quiet. According to the biblical tale, humans have moral responsibility; the Mesopotamian accounts dehumanize humanity and strip humans of their moral accountability.

But how does shortening the human lifespan serve as a *tikkun,* or at least encourage *tikkun,* for distorted moral values? I imagine that for a person who lives for a thousand years – practically "forever" (v. 3) – time is not quite so precious. There is no pressing need to "find the time," to "make time" – there is all the time in the world. A person who lives for a thousand years can choose a dozen different professions, marry again and again – or safely postpone something until "tomorrow," for there are endless centuries of tomorrows stretching out before him. There is no pressing need to fix the world today, to make moral progress today – there will always be more time. Humanity's lifespan is greatly decreased on the eve of the Flood, when the dominant zeitgeist is "from whomever they chose" (v. 2). Once time becomes precious, choices become more precise and more significant. Awareness of mortality leads to soul-searching, to conscious choices, to catalyzed achievement – for now, for the first time, time is pressing.

The Flood: Destruction and Re-Creation (6:5–9:7)

There is no doubt that the Flood narrative is the most dramatic turning point of the pre-Abraham narratives of Genesis. The world, though its creation is so carefully described in the first chapters of the Bible, is completely washed away, and a new world is created in its place. This total destruction and re-creation, however, is far from smooth – the narrative is as choppy as the rising sea, to the extent that various scholars argue that the Flood narrative is fused from two different textual traditions, like the two different creation accounts in the first two chapters of the book. While this position is compelling, convincing, and well supported in the text, there are also strong, equally compelling arguments that despite its apparent inconsistencies, the story is unified and harmonious. With each side presenting half a picture, the following pages will seize the rope by both ends and read the Flood narrative as two distinct threads, but two threads that are woven together, warp and weft that form a single tapestry.

To this end I will first survey the central issues that challenge a simple, continuous reading of the Flood narrative.

DIFFERENT NAMES OF GOD

Throughout the Flood narrative, the narrator flits back and forth between "God" (*Elohim*) and "the Lord" (YHWH). While this is not an actual problem or contradiction, it is nonetheless unusual in the context of the book of Genesis – most stories use one or the other. In these chapters, however, both names appear intermittently, without clear reason why one or the other is chosen.[1] Genesis Rabba already mentions this phenomenon, as Rashi writes at the beginning of chapter 8:

> And God remembered – this is the name of the attribute of judgment, which is changed to mercy through the prayers of the righteous. But the wickedness of the wicked transforms the attribute of mercy to judgment: "And the Lord saw how great had become the wickedness…"; "And the Lord said, 'I will wipe out,'" even though that name is the attribute of mercy.[2]

According to this reading, the Flood narrative uses two divine names to reflect two divine attributes: judgment and mercy. They alternate throughout the story to show how wickedness transforms mercy to judgment; this explains why the name of the Lord, which is usually associated with mercy, is used in verses of anger and punishment.

1. Cassuto attempts to explain this alternation thus: *Elohim* is the default name and the Tetragrammaton is always used in particular circumstances – in the context of sacrifices (including the gathering of pure animals before the Flood, and offering them up at the end), and in the statement "and the Lord sealed them in," which reflects an especially intimate gesture on the Lord's part (Umberto Cassuto, *A Commentary on The Book of Genesis: From Noah to Abraham*, trans. Israel Abrahams [Jerusalem, 1964], 35–36). However, in another place Cassuto proposes replacing "the Lord" with "Noah" in the verse, "And the Lord sealed them in" (Umberto Cassuto, *La Questione della Genesi*, trans. M. E. Hartom [Jerusalem, 1990], 36). See our discussion on this opinion below. For another explanation of why God's names alternate, see Robert E. Longacre, "The Discourse Structure of the Flood Narrative," *Society of Biblical Literature: Seminar Papers* 10 (1976): 255–258 in particular.
2. Rashi on Gen. 8:1, based on Genesis Rabba 33:3.

DUPLICATION

The reader encounters more problematic issues than God's shifting names – the story is riddled with duplication and repetition. When the story is read from the beginning, the reader learns how God instructs Noah to build "an ark of gopher wood" (6:14) for the purpose of preserving every animal species on earth, "From the birds of each kind, and from the animals of each kind, from all that crawl on the ground of each kind – two of each shall come to you to stay alive" (6:20). Noah is also told to prepare provisions for himself, his family, and for the animals (6:21), and the reader is then told that Noah carries out these instructions: "And Noah did so. According to all that God commanded him, so he did" (6:22). Noah receives orders and immediately executes them: he builds an ark, gathers two of each animal species, and prepares provisions for them all.

Yet as soon as Noah "does so," God turns to him once again, and once again warns him that He is about to bring a flood: "For in seven days I will bring rain on the earth for forty days and forty nights, and I will blot out from the face of the ground every existing thing I have made" (7:4). Moreover, God repeats the order to bring every kind of animal on board – yet this time, with different specifications: Noah must gather seven of every "clean" animal and only two of each "unclean" animal. Rather than ask God what to do with his arkful of animals, or why God seems to have changed His mind, the narrator reports that Noah once again "did according to all that the Lord commanded him" (7:5).

Not only are these two passages – 6:13–22 and 7:1–6 – repetitive, they actually contradict each other. According to the first command, Noah must bring two of every species, while according to the second, he must bring seven pairs of certain species.

These are not the only snags in the text. When the rain begins to fall and Noah boards the ark, there is also a sense of superfluous, awkward repetition. We can divide the verses into two parts (7:6–9 / 7:10–16) according to their various components:[3]

3. It is worth emphasizing that the prevalent diachronic division into sources does not resolve all the issues, as I will discuss below.

1. **The beginning of the Flood "upon the earth" and Noah's age:** And Noah was six hundred years old when the flood of waters was upon the earth.
2. **Noah and his family board the ark:** And Noah and his sons and his wife, and the wives of his sons with him, went into the ark because of the waters of the Flood.
3. **The animals board the ark:** The clean animals, and the animals that are not clean, and the birds, and all that crawls on the ground, came two by two to Noah, to the ark, male and female, as God had commanded Noah.

1a. **The beginning of the Flood "upon the earth" and Noah's age:** And after seven days, the waters of the Flood came upon the earth. In the six hundredth year of Noah's life, in the second month, on the seventeenth day of the month, on that day, all the wellsprings of the great deep burst, and the floodgates of heaven were opened. And the rain fell upon the earth for forty days and forty nights.

2a. **Noah and his family board the ark:** On that very day, Noah, and Shem, Ham, and Japheth, Noah's sons, and Noah's wife together with the three wives of his sons, went into the ark.

3a. **The animals board the ark:** They [entered] with all the beasts of every kind, all the cattle of every kind, all crawling creatures that crawl upon the earth of every kind, and all the flying creatures of every kind, every bird, every winged animal. They came to Noah to the ark, two by two, all flesh that had within it the breath of life. Those that came, male and female of all flesh they came, as God had commanded him, and the Lord then sealed him in.

The repetition in these verses is salient: each narrative element appears twice, and in the same sequence. There are also semantic differences between the two descriptions: the first sequence (1–2) refers to a "flood," whereas the second (1a) describes how the wellsprings of the deep burst open and the floodgates of heaven open.

The description of the actual Flood also comes in waves of repetition (17–24):

> (17) And the flood was forty days upon the earth, and the waters increased and lifted the ark, and it rose above the earth.
> (18) And the waters surged and increased greatly upon the earth, and the ark drifted on the surface of the waters.
>
> (19) And the waters surged greatly, greatly upon the earth, and they covered all the high mountains under all the heavens.
> (20) Fifteen cubits upward the waters surged, and the mountains were covered.
>
> (21) And all flesh that moved upon the earth perished – the birds, the cattle, the beasts, and all crawling creatures that crawl upon the earth, and all humankind.
> (22–23) All in whose nostrils was the breath of life, everything on dry land, died. All existence on earth was wiped out, from humans to cattle to crawling things to the birds of the sky, they were wiped out from the earth.[4]

These verses contain no contradictions, only stark repetition. This repetition may be for the sake of poetic impact: the verses depict the scene gradually, back and forth, as the waves of the Flood gradually rise and the ark rocks back and forth on the swelling waters. As Cassuto writes:

> [T]he use of repetition and verbal parallelism is a common feature of the literary style of the ancient East generally and of the

4. It is interesting to note the process that reaches a climax in this verse: God decrees: "I will wipe out the human race I have created from the face of the earth – from man to beast to creatures that crawl and to the birds of the sky – for I regret that I have made them" (6:7). When announcing this decree to Noah, God reiterates this idea with slight changes: "For in seven days I will bring rain on the earth for forty days and forty nights, and I will blot out from the face of the ground every existing thing I have made" (7:4). The verse that describes the actual destruction combines these two versions: "All existence on earth was wiped out, from humans to cattle to crawling things to the birds of the sky, they were wiped out from the earth" (7:23). On one hand, this lists the parties that are wiped out in detail ("from humans to cattle") as mentioned in the first decree, while on the other hand, all "existence" is wiped out – as in God's message to Noah. Compare to Cassuto, *From Noah to Abraham*, 95.

> Bible in particular; and any one who wishes to remove from the Scriptural texts all that is in harmony with this practice is simply closing his eyes to a basic and characteristic trait of these passages.[5]

CONTRADICTIONS

As already noted, "God" commands Noah to gather two of each species, while "the Lord" tells him to gather seven of each "clean" animal. There are additional contradictions in the text. One such example is the duration of the Flood. Initially, the Flood is expected to last for forty days and forty nights: "For in seven days I will bring rain on the earth for forty days and forty nights" (7:4); and indeed, "the rain fell upon the earth for forty days and forty nights" (7:12). However, the storm only subsides after one hundred and fifty days; God remembers Noah only after "the waters surged upon the earth for a hundred and fifty days" (7:24). Only then, "God remembered Noah and all the beasts and all the cattle that were with him in the ark. And God sent a wind over the earth, and the waters subsided. And the wellsprings of the deep and the floodgates of heaven were closed, and the rain from the heavens ceased" (8:1–2). It is not that the rains fall for forty days but it takes one hundred and fifty days until the water drains away.[6] Rather, the verses imply that the storm itself rages for one hundred and fifty days – for five months and not just a month and a half (see also 8:3).[7] The plot unfolds thus: the waters rose for one hundred and fifty days (7:24) and eventually reached a height of fifteen cubits above the highest mountains (7:20), and from this day onwards – the seventeenth day of the seventh month – they subsided."[8]

There are other smaller issues which may or may not be actual contradictions, such as the fact that the dove was unable to land "for there was water all over the face of the earth" (8:9), even though it was

5. Cassuto, *From Noah to Abraham*, 38. He also claims there that this is not mere repetition, but "whenever the text reverts to a given subject it tells us something new." See also Cassuto, *Genesis and Its Structure*, 283–297.
6. As proposed, among others, by Cassuto, *From Noah to Abraham*, 102; Wenham, *Genesis*, 298.
7. As emphatically claimed by John Emerton, "An Examination of Some Attempts to Defend the Unity of the Flood Narrative in Genesis," *VT* 37 (1987): 402–404.
8. Gunkel, *Genesis*, 146.

already reported that "in the tenth month, on the first of the month, the tops of the mountains appeared" (8:5).[9]

The next scenes also contain elements of contradiction. At first, it seems that Noah attempts to determine for himself whether he can leave the ark. "At the end of forty days" he opens the ark window and sends the raven and dove to see if the waters have subsided; in this way, he learns that the waters have dried up (8:6–14). Immediately after, however, it emerges that Noah leaves the ark following divine revelation: "And God spoke to Noah, saying: 'Leave the ark, you and your wife and your sons and your sons' wives with you'" (8:15–16). Rabbi Zev Weitman takes this a step further and claims that according to the storyline that incorporates the name "the Lord," it initially seems clear that the Flood will last for forty days, so Noah knows precisely when to begin checking whether the water has subsided. However, according to the second thread, which uses the name "God," there is no promise that the Flood is temporary. On the contrary – Noah only knows that the land is about to be destroyed, and it is not at all clear that the earth will ever be habitable. According to this reading, the ark may be his new permanent home:

> Noah is brought into the ark, which preserves the memory of a lost world within it – the handiwork of God. Perhaps, for him, this ark is but a microcosm, a tiny world that houses the righteous one whose acts saved him from the fate of his generation, but were insufficient to be a shield for them, too, when God decided to destroy His world.[10]

With abundant divine mercy, however, God takes pity on Noah and everyone crowded together with him in the ark.[11] After one hundred

9. Cassuto shows that this "contradiction" can also be found in the *Epic of Gilgamesh*, and claims that "the dove is sent to see… if there were other places that were above the surface on the water, and as there were not yet other peaks that rose about the surface of the water, the dove had no choice but to return back from where it had been sent" (Cassuto, *Genesis and Its Structure*, 293).
10. Rabbi Zev Weitman, "The New Creation," *Alon Shvut* 78 (1980): 28.
11. Ibid.

and fifty days, the Flood comes to an end, but until a divine order allows him to leave the ark and settle upon dry land once more (8:16–17), he does not find out for himself whether it is safe to leave the ark.

The story also contains two different conclusions – in each one, God/the Lord expresses that never again will the world be destroyed by flood. The Lord catches the fragrance of the sacrifices Noah offers up and says in His heart: "Never again will I curse the ground because of humans, because the inclination of the human heart is evil from his youth. And never again will I destroy all that lives as I have done. As long as the earth endures, seedtime and harvest, cold and heat, summer and winter, day and night shall not cease" (8:21–22). Later on, God forms a covenant with His creations: "I will establish My covenant with you, that never again will all flesh be cut off by waters of a flood, nor will there ever again be a flood to destroy the earth" (9:11), and spreads the rainbow across the sky as a sign of this covenant.

The double closure generated from this double conclusion seems to close two narrative circles at once – the opening of each thread seems to correspond to a parallel conclusion:[12]

First Introduction: 6:5–8	**First Conclusion: 8:20–22**
The Lord saw how great had become the wickedness of humankind on earth, *and that every inclination of the thoughts of the human heart* was solely evil all the time. The Lord regretted that He had made man on earth, and **He was grieved to His very heart**.	And Noah built an altar to the Lord, and he took from all the clean animals and from all the clean birds, and offered burnt offerings on the altar. And the Lord smelled the pleasing aroma, and the Lord **said in His heart**, "Never again will I curse the ground because of humans, *because the inclination of the human heart is evil from his youth*. And never again will I destroy all that lives as I have done.

12. See, for example, in Breuer, *Pirkei Bereshit*, vol. 1, 205.

Second Introduction: 6:12–17	**Second Conclusion: 9:11–15**
As for Me, I am about to bring *floodwaters on the earth to destroy all flesh* that has the breath of life within it from under the heavens.	I will establish My covenant with you, that never again will *all flesh be cut off by waters of a flood*, nor will there ever again be a flood to destroy the earth.

These repetitions and contradictions are solved at once if we adopt the theory that this narrative is a fusion of two different stories, or of two different descriptions of the Flood. Modern scholarship refers to two difference sources, while Rabbi Mordechai Breuer defines them as two different aspects. Just as there are two creation narratives, one after the other, there are two parallel accounts of the world's destruction and renewal. Within this paradigm, the concept is practically obvious: if the world's creation is described from two different perspectives, of course its destruction and recreation will be explored from both of these perspectives.

What is the nature of these two accounts of the Flood? Rabbi Breuer aptly opens his discussion of these chapters by pointing out the two instances of divine vision:[13]

- "The Lord saw how great had become the wickedness of humankind on earth" (6:5).
- "And God saw the earth, that it was corrupted, for all flesh had corrupted its way upon the earth" (6:12).

These introductions reflect the character of each different narrative. One, featuring the Lord, focuses on human sin – the Lord sees "the wickedness of humankind." The second, which uses the name of God, focuses on the "earth" and on "all flesh" – God sees how every living being participates in the earth's destruction, and from this the sages derive that even the animals were guilty of this destruction.

According to this approach, the two interlaced narratives cannot be reconciled, and each thread should be read on its own. In fact, each thread is almost complete, comprising a beginning, an end, and several

13. Breuer, *Pirkei Bereshit*, vol. 1, 136.

vital narrative elements.[14] Each begins with the reason for the Flood, continues with preparations for the Flood, as well as a description of the Flood itself and how Noah boards the ark, and concludes with God's promise never to destroy the world again.

Once again, this approach can be justified given that there are two different accounts of creation – corresponding with the two accounts of the world's destruction and renewal. The reality created in chapter 1 is washed away in the Flood, and to be more precise, the human history that begins in chapter 2 is drowned as well. Both the world and the history of its human population then begin anew.

Based on this dichotomy, we can also point to Noah's different role in either thread. He finds favor in the eyes of "*the Lord*" (6:8), and the Lord singles him out as the sole righteous soul of his generation: "Then the Lord said to Noah, 'Go, you and all your household, into the ark, *for you alone have I seen righteous before Me in this generation*" (7:1). In contrast, *God* preserves Noah so that humanity will not become utterly extinct: "But I will establish My covenant with you, and you will enter the ark – you and your sons and your wife and your sons' wives with you" (6:18). The covenant God speaks of here is the covenant of the world's existence, which is, in many senses, parallel to the covenant of the rainbow at the end of the story (which I will discuss in context of the general narrative structure). Noah is chosen to preserve the human race because he is "a righteous man, blameless in his generation," but the focus is on the world's continuity, and for this purpose God instructs him to build the ark as a temporary nature reserve for all the species that will populate the world once more after the waters subside. And indeed, in "God's" narrative, the animals march up in pairs themselves: "Two of each *shall come to you to stay alive*" (6:20); they "came two by two to Noah, to the ark, male and female, as God had commanded Noah" (7:9); "They came to Noah to the ark, two by two, all flesh that had within it the breath of life. Those that came, male and female of all flesh they came, as God had commanded him" (7:15–16). In "the Lord's" narrative, in contrast, Noah must gather members of each species to him

14. See a comprehensive, well-structured division in Westermann, *Genesis*, vol. 1, 395–398; Barzilai, *Genesis-Exodus*, 18–19.

and bring them to the ark: "Of every clean animal, *you shall take* seven pairs, males and their mates, and two of every animal that is not clean, a male and its mate" (7:2). In this respect, too, it is clear that one narrative documents the survival of the species (the animals come to Noah *to stay alive*), while the other focuses on Noah's righteousness as the reason for his survival, and even the animals who survive do so thanks to Noah's actions. This also explains the number of animals Noah is commanded to take in each account: only one female and one male of each kind is necessary to perpetuate the species, while *the Lord* orders the preservation of extra members of each pure species. The differentiation between pure and impure is relevant to the world of the righteous, religious person, and indeed, at the Flood's end Noah builds an altar to the Lord, takes "from all the clean animals and from all the clean birds," and offers "burnt offerings on the altar" (8:20).

A Unified, Harmonious Narrative

While the story reads fruitfully and meaningfully when unraveled into two separate strands, it can also be read as a unified, harmonious whole. Before focusing on this approach, however, I will point out five difficulties that challenge the former reading:

1. It is agreed that 6:5–8 present the prelude to the Flood according to the thread that features the Lord. I wish to focus on verse 7: "And the Lord said, 'I will wipe out the human race I have created from the face of the earth – from man to beast to creatures that crawl and to the birds of the sky – for I regret that I have made them.'" Even when "man" is the focus, it emerges, the animals will be destroyed together with him – there is no point to a world without humanity, which is consistent with the view presented in the second creation narrative. However, the order of the creatures mentioned in this verse forms a striking chiastic parallel with the first creation narrative in chapter 1: humans, animals, creeping things, and birds of the heavens. This hardly seems coincidental, and this seems to be in direct dialogue with the first creation narrative. And indeed, these animals will be mentioned again later on, in sections that are ascribed to

the "God" narrative (7:14). In fact, not only does the order of creatures in 6:7 recall the first creation story, but the language is also reminiscent of chapter 1 – the root B-R-A, in "I have created" is also associated with Genesis 1 but not 2 (which uses "the Lord").[15]

2. When Noah, his family, and the animals have finished boarding the ark (according to the verse associated with the name "God"), *the Lord* shuts the door behind them: "Those that came, male and female of all flesh they came, as God had commanded him, and *the Lord* sealed them in" (7:16). This curious detail has baffled commentators and scholars alike: given the use of the name "the Lord," it can hardly be ascribed to the "God" narrative strand, but on the level of plot, it is a direct continuation of the previous verses – once everyone is finally on board, the door is sealed behind them.

   Even scholars who usually shy away from emending the text have felt compelled to change the name "the Lord" to "Noah," so that the verse reads "and Noah sealed them in."[16] Cassuto justifies this change thus: "There is no justification for God to have sealed the ark, when it would have made more

---

15. Compare to Grintz, *Uniqueness and Antiquity*, 130, and see Rabbi Breuer's attempts at dealing with this surprising confusion (Breuer, *Pirkei Bereshit*, vol. 1, 157–159). It is no wonder that some felt compelled to claim that this verse was added at a later stage (David M. Carr, *Reading the Fractures of Genesis: Historical and Literary Approaches* [Louisville, 1996], 57, and similarly, Jean-Louis Ska, "The Story of the Flood: A Priestly Writer and Some Later Editorial Fragments," in *The Exegesis of the Pentateuch: Exegetical Studies and Basic Questions* [FAT 66: Tübingen, 2009], 1–22). Another example of a similar problem that stems from dividing the narrative into two sources is the combination, "*re'aḥ niḥoaḥ*," "pleasing aroma," in 8:21–22, which we cannot elaborate upon here, but see further in Grintz, *Uniqueness and Antiquity*, 130. I will note that Terry Fenton in a lecture in Basel in the summer of 2001, found this issue so problematic that he proposed that the verses of Noah's offering and the sweet savor God smells indeed belongs to the E narrative, in contrast to what is accepted in research. His view has been rejected as all else points to this unit belonging to the J narrative (Day, *From Creation to Babel*, 124n3). The combination of terms belonging to both threads in a single verse supports the notion that the text forms one cohesive unit.
16. As even held by Cassuto, *Genesis and Its Structure*, 36.

sense for Noah to close it from the inside,"[17] but this argument is inherently flawed. Even the Babylonian flood narratives are concerned with the issue of closing the door to the ark, and a comparison between the two accounts is fascinating. According to the *Epic of Gilgamesh*, when the Babylonian hero Utnapishtim finishes building the ark, he boards it and then summons "the caulker of the boat," Puzur-Ammurri, to seal the door from the outside, and in exchange he gives him "the edifice and all it contained."[18] As Shifra and Klein note, there is certain cruel irony in giving the sailor such generous payment for his labor when the innocent victim will never actually enjoy it; this detail is but another "cynical deception" on Utnapishtim's part.[19] Noah's ark, too, needed to be sealed in from the outside, but rather than exploit innocent victims, there is emphasis that the Lord Himself seals Noah in.[20]

In any event, it is incorrect to state that "it would have made more sense for Noah to close it from the inside." Vast wooden ships obviously needed sealing (with tar or clay) to waterproof them from the stormy seas, and who else could seal the ark from the outside, if none but its passengers were meant to survive the Flood? How can those who hold that the narrative is composed of two separate strands explain that "the Lord" seals Noah in after he has boarded the ark at "God's" command?

3. In general, even though most of the narrative can be split into two, there are nonetheless verses and passages that are clearly dependent on, or a direct continuation of, verses that are ascribed to the other source. This is especially salient in the description of the ark's construction. Even though it only appears in the "God" narrative, the "Lord" narrative relates

17. Cassuto, *Genesis and Its Structure*, 37n102.
18. *Epic of Gilgamesh*, Tablet XI, lines 97–98.
19. Shifra and Klein, *In Those Distant Days*, 279.
20. The Septuagint translates "*ba'ado*," as "from the outside of it": "And God sealed off the ark from the outside" (Zipor, *Septuagint*, 137). This is also how the Septuagint translates other instances of the word "*be'ad*" (Gen. 20:18; Judges 9:51; Job. 1:10), but in this case, this translation is logical: the ark needs to be sealed from the outside.

to the ark as a given entity: "Then the Lord said to Noah, 'Go, you and all your household, into the ark, for you alone have I seen righteous before Me in this generation'" (7:1). This order is given to Noah immediately following the description of the ark's construction (as commanded by *God*) and the sequence therefore reads seamlessly, but if the two threads were separated, then according to the "Lord" narrative, where did this ark suddenly come from? Until this point, there is no mention of it at all in the "Lord" thread. A subtler example is the mention of the ark's window, through which Noah sends the raven and dove: "And so it was that at the end of forty days Noah opened the window of the ark that he had made" (8:6). This detail assumes that the reader has already heard about this window, whose construction ("Make a skylight for the ark")[21] is indeed specifically mentioned in God's (not the Lord's!) instructions to Noah. The construction of this skylight-window is only mentioned in the narrative that features God, and it is only used in the narrative featuring the Lord.[22] This, too, reflects certain interdependence of the two threads; they are not fully extricable.

4. Even if this does not constitute absolute proof of the story's unity, the Babylonian flood story has elements which are parallel to the "Lord" thread (birds are sent forth to check whether the waters have dried up, and sacrifices are brought at the flood's end), as well as elements which are parallel to the "God" thread (the ark is sealed with tar, and it comes to rest at the top of a tall mountain).[23] While the elements of the Babylonian epic are not, or need not, be entirely congruent with the biblical account, the fact that a parallel narrative

21. See Kiel's debate on this matter (*Genesis*, 175, 199).

22. There is room to debate whether there is a reason for the change of name, from "*tzohar*," "skylight," to "*ḥalon*," "window."

23. Archibald H. Sayce, *Early History of the Hebrews* (New York, 1897), 126; Grintz, *Uniqueness and Antiquity*, 131–132. See also Gordon J. Wenham, "Method in Pentateuchal Source Criticism," *VT* 41 (1991): 106 (and the references to Shea and Miller in n23 and n24).

includes details from both biblical threads strongly implies that only the combination of both threads constitutes a narrative whole.[24]

5. While the fifth point I wish to mention does not directly challenge the notion of two separate narrative threads, it nonetheless encourages the possibility of a unified, harmonious reading. While the dates mentioned in the story are generally ascribed to the "God" strand, all the chronological details provided in the other account, such as the forty days and the certain count of weeks, integrate seamlessly with these dates:[25]

- On the seventeenth of the second month, "All the wellsprings of the great deep burst, and the floodgates of heaven were opened" (7:11).[26]
- After the flood begins, "The waters surged upon the earth for a hundred and fifty days" – that is, five months, from the second month to the seventeenth of the seventh month.
- And indeed, the next date provided in the narrative is the seventeenth of the seventh month, when the waters begin to subside and the ark comes to settle on Mount Ararat. That is, one hundred and fifty days after the rain begins to pour, the ark comes to rest on Mount Ararat.
- About two and a half months later, on the first of the tenth month, "the tops of the mountains appeared" (8:5).
- At this point in the story, after forty days Noah opens the window of the ark and sends the raven and the dove

24. In the cynical words of Sayce: "If the document hypothesis were right, there would be only two ways of accounting for this fact. Either the Babylonian post had before him the present 'redacted' text of Genesis, or else the Elohist and Yahvist must have copied the Babylon story upon mutual understanding that the one should insert what the other omitted. There is no third alternative" (Sayce, *Ancient History*, 125–126).
25. Gerhard Larsson expresses this similarly in "Remarks concerning the Noah-Flood Complex," *ZAW* 112 (2000): 75–77.
26. The adjacent verse reports that the rain fell for "forty days and forty nights" (v. 12), and according to this, the Flood ceased forty days after the seventeenth of the second month, which is the twenty-seventh of the third month.

(8:6–8). After a week he sends the dove out again (8:10). And another week later he sends the dove out a third time (8:12). Scholars who divide up the Flood narrative into two assume that these forty days are counted from the beginning of the Flood, but those who read the story as a whole say that Noah sends the dove after an additional forty days, which are counted from the time that the mountaintops are visible.[27] According to this count, from the time the ark settles on the first of the tenth month, another forty days and then three weeks brings us to the first of the twelfth month.

- One month later, "in the first month, on the first day of the month," Noah sees that "the water had dried up from the earth," and he is therefore able to remove "the covering of the ark" (8:13).
- The final date provided in the story jumps ahead to the twenty-seventh of the second month, when only then "the earth was completely dry." Exactly one year and ten days after the rain begins to fall – one full solar cycle[28] – the earth is finally dry once more, and Noah and his fellow passengers are able to leave the ark.[29]

---

27. See especially Cassuto, *Genesis and Its Structure,* 296; Gordon J. Wenham, "The Coherence of the Flood Narrative," *VT* 28 (1978): 336–348; Wenham, "Method."
28. See also Cassuto (*Genesis and Its Structure,* 296), unlike Barré, who claims that both narratives are based on an annual cycle that was 360 days long (Lloyd M. Barré, "The Riddle of the Flood Chronology," *JSOT* 41 [1988]: 3–20). Frederick Cryer claims that the thread that features God's name is based on the lunar cycle of 354 days, a solar calendar of 365 days, and a calendar of 360 days (Frederick H. Cryer, "The Interrelationships of Gen 5,32; 11,10–11 and the Chronology of the Flood [Gen 6–9]," *Biblica* 66 [1985]: 241–261). On various chronologies for the Flood narrative in the Apocrypha (reflecting different fundamental positions), see Moshe Zipor, "The Flood Chronology: Too Many an Accident," *Dead Sea Discoveries* 4 (1997): 207–210.
29. According to the book of Jubilees, Noah left the ark on "the first of the third month" (6:1). This intentionally recalls the reception of the Torah on Mount Sinai, and that verse continues: "And he built an altar on that mountain," and later on, the connection to Mount Sinai is explicit. In this way, the book of Jubilees connects the rainbow covenant with the covenant of Sinai.

From a chronological perspective, read in full, the story reads logically, at a pleasing symbolic pace, documenting the destruction and rebirth of the world over the course of a year. Despite certain repetition and specific contradictions, the narrative ultimately emerges as a coherent, cohesive, and logical whole.[30]

6. There are further proofs that the two narrative threads are not so easily disentangled, but I wish to turn to the most convincing argument that the story should, in fact, be read as a single, unified whole: the narrative structure.[31] If the narrative is arranged in a complex, organized structure, then this supports the hypothesis that the text is one unified work that should not be split into two parallel accounts.[32] The narrative structure can be described thus:[33]

   A. Double opening:

      a. The Lord's decision to bring a Flood: "The Lord saw how great man's wickedness had become…and He was grieved to His very heart" (6:5–12).

---

30. See further in Yoshinobu Endo, "The Structure of the 'Genesis Flood Narrative' and the Documentary Hypothesis," *Exegetica* 10 (1999): 1–18.
31. Cassuto already notes that the Flood narrative comprises twelve sections that are arranged in a chiastic structure (Cassuto, *From Noah to Abraham*, 30). My proposed structure differs slightly from his own.
32. Wenham, "Method." Compare to Bernhard Anderson, "From Analysis to Synthesis: The Interpretation of Genesis 1–11," *JBL* 97 (1978): 23–39.
33. Wenham himself divides the narrative into thirty (!) scenes, with "God remembered Noah" at the center (8:1), thus forming a concentric structure (Wenham, "Method," 338). See also Emerton's criticism of this division (Emerton, "An Examination of Some Attempts to Defend the Unity of the Flood Narrative in Genesis," *VT* 38 [1988]: 6–11). Dorsey, for example, proposes a concentric structure that begins with "These are the *toledot* of Noah" (6:9–10) and ends with the verses that repeat Noah's sons (9:18–19), which are largely considered the introduction to the next scene, of Noah's drunkenness (Dorsey, *Literary Structure*, 52). Dorsey's proposal was also adopted by Cotter, who explained that 6:1–8 should be read as a single unit describing the eve of the Flood, whereas the story itself begins in 6:9 (Cotter, *Genesis*, 53). This was also adopted by Elchanan Samet, who uses Dorsey's structure and holds that the narrative begins in 6:9 (Samet, *Studies in the Weekly Parasha*, Series 3 [Jerusalem, 2013], 39–42). He defines the verses before 6:9 as a transitive link between the genealogical lists and the Flood narrative. The basis for this (surprising) delineation is that the formula "*eleh toledot*" always introduces a new unit.

b. Building an ark and gathering all living beings in order to "establish a covenant": "Take for yourself every food that is eaten and store it with you, and it will be for food for you and them" (6:13–22).

B. Noah and his fellow passengers board the ark: "Go, you and all your household, into the ark" (7:1–9).[34]

C. The Flood begins, and the world is destroyed: "All the wellsprings of the great deep burst, and the heavens were opened... and the mountains were covered" (7:10–24).

C1. The end of the Flood and the renewal of the world: "And the wellsprings of the deep and the floodgates of heaven were closed... the tops of the mountains appeared" (8:1–4).

B1. Noah and his fellow passengers leave the ark: "Leave the ark, you and your wife..." (8:15–20).

A1. Double ending:

a. The Lord's decision to never bring a Flood again: "And the Lord said in His heart... because the inclination of the human heart is evil from its youth" (8:20–22).

b. "The establishment of a covenant" with all flesh: "Every moving thing that lives shall be for you as food" (9:1–17).

This structure aptly reflects the movement of the plot: the first half describes the preparations for the Flood and the destruction of the world, while the second half portrays the end of the Flood and the beginning of a new world. The Flood narrative is not only the end of an era, but the beginning of a new one.

34. Dorsey (*Literary Structure*, 52) and Samet (*Studies* 3, 62) add that it is emphasized that seven pairs of pure animals and birds enter the ark together with him, with their parallel sacrifice in the second half of the narrative (according to the proposed structure, at the end of component B1). Samet even shows that both sections contain the verb "to take" (7:2; 8:20).

There is, of course, room to explore each component of this structure and its counterpart in depth, but for the purpose of this discussion, it suffices to point out the perfect, orderly symmetry of this structure. Theoretically, it is possible to claim that this structure is largely based on verses that are ascribed to the "God" narrative, so that this structure does not support the narrative's unity. However, the narrative in its entirety progresses at an orderly pace, according to its general chiastic structure, and the verses associated with the "Lord" thread integrate flawlessly into this structure without any noticeable deviation. Overall, the narrative is cohesive and unified.

In light of this, we come to a complex conclusion: these chapters do contain a double description of the Flood narrative, continuing the double creation accounts of the first two chapters of Genesis. Unlike the creation narratives, however, these threads, each colored with their own emphases and objectives, are woven into a single, cohesive, harmonious account; their narrative components are interdependent, each providing part of the whole picture.

While the two threads woven into a single unit, 7:1–10, can theoretically be distilled into two parts according to the divine name used in each section ("the Lord" in 1–5 and "God" in 6–10), when read together, this passage functions like a classic biblical sequence of a divine order and its execution:[35]

---

35. Nechama Leibowitz discusses the significance and contributions of this structure in her studies. See especially her methodological comment in *Genesis*, 513–518, and see Amos Frisch's discussion of her method in "A Chapter in Nechama Leibowitz's Approach: On 'Repetition Structure' in Biblical Narrative," in *Pirkei Nechama: Prof. Nechama Leibowitz Memorial Volume*, ed. M. Ahrend, R. Ben-Meir, and G. Cohn (Jerusalem, 2001), 313–323. For a comprehensive study of this structure and its various contributions, see Meir Sternberg, "Repetition Structure in Biblical Narratives: Strategies of Informational Redundancy," *Literature* 25 (1977), 109–150.

Noah's Instructions (1–4)	**Their Execution (5–10)**
Then the Lord said to Noah, "Go, you and all your household, into the ark, for you alone have I seen righteous before Me in this generation.	And Noah did according to all that the Lord commanded him. Noah was six hundred years old when the flood of waters was upon the earth. And Noah and his sons and his wife, and the wives of his sons with him, went into the ark because of the waters of the Flood.
Of every clean animal, you shall take seven pairs, males and their mates, and two of every animal that is not clean, a male and its mate. Of the birds of the sky also, seven pairs, male and female, to keep seed alive on the face of all the earth.	The clean animals, and the animals that are not clean, and the birds, and all that crawls on the ground, came two by two to Noah, to the ark, male and female, as God had commanded Noah.
For in seven days I will bring rain on the earth.	And after seven days, the waters of the Flood came upon the earth.

While there are certain disparities between the instructions and their execution (especially in relation to the pure animals), these are eclipsed by the similarity and harmonious correspondence between the verses: Noah carries out his orders in full, even if the instructions are issued by "the Lord" but carried out under the watchful eye of "God." These narrative threads, then, are woven into a single, cohesive whole.

This leads us to another question: if the two creation accounts are listed separately, one after another, then why are the two corresponding Flood narratives woven into one story? Even those who firmly favor the theory that these are two separate sources have no choice but to admit that the narrative presentation differs greatly from that of the double creation account, in that they are fused together, not divided into two separate chapters.

THE FIRST WORLD AND THE SECOND WORLD

This, in turn, leads to one of the underlying themes and objectives of the story. There is one fundamental question that accompanies the entire narrative: Is there a difference between the prediluvian world and the postdiluvian world? Does the Flood truly wash away the old and bring something new in its wake? The story opens with the Creator's disappointment in humanity: "The Lord regretted that He had made man on earth, and He was grieved to His very heart. And the Lord said, 'I will wipe out the human race I have created from the face of the earth – from man to beast to creatures that crawl and to the birds of the sky – for I regret that I have made them'" (6:6–7). If so, then why did God renew the world, rather than destroy it completely? Noah's descendants will fill the earth once more, and who can guarantee that their moral world will change for the better? What is the story's inner logic? Does anything truly change after the Flood?

In seeking out differences between the old world and the new, we stumble upon a challenging paradox related to the status of humanity. The text seems to encourage two opposite readings, and over the next few pages, I will attempt to reconcile these views and thereby define humanity's new status within the order of creation.

THE HUMBLING OF HUMANITY

There is one striking difference between the old world and the new: in the new world, humans are permitted to eat animals. Some argue that there is no explicit statement that the prediluvian population was prohibited to eat animals,[36] but the most straightforward reading is that all living creatures were vegetarians:

> Then God said, "I give you every seed-bearing plant on the face of all the earth and every tree that has fruit with seed in it. They will be yours for food. And to all the beasts of the earth and all the birds in the sky and all the creatures that move along the

36. N. Rabban, "The Problem of Eating Meat in Genesis," *Tarbiz* 21 (1949): 25–29. He holds that Gen. 1:29 differentiates between humankind, who are to eat "seed–bearing plants" and animals, who are to eat "green plants." Ralbag already went in this direction, and wrote emphatically against the belief that Adam was not allowed to eat meat: "This is a blatant lie, anyone with any sense should avoid it" (on Gen. 1:29–30). Based on his claim, it seems he was motivated to avoid the idea that God changes His mind after the Flood, when eating meat is obviously permitted.

> ground – everything that has the breath of life in it – I give every green plant for food." And it was so. (Gen. 1:29–30)

In contrast, Noah is given divine permission to eat animals: "Every moving thing that lives shall be for you as food. Like the green plants, I give you everything" (9:3).[37] As Rashi states, based on Sanhedrin 59b: "I did not permit Adam to eat meat, only plants, but to you, 'like the green plants,' which I gave to Adam, 'I give you everything.'"[38]

The killing and eating of animals is limited in two ways, which reflects the complexity of this new world order:

- "But you shall not eat meat with its lifeblood (*benafasho damo*) in it" (9:4). Rashi takes this to mean that meat should not be consumed while the animal still has its life force within it, that is, while it is still alive – the prohibition of *ever min haḥai*. Only dead animals may be eaten; eating an animal that is still alive is an act of unforgivable cruelty.[39] Nahmanides disagrees and holds that this prohibition means that blood itself may not be eaten: the flesh together with its *nefesh* means its blood, as *nefesh* means blood.[40] This is also the prevalent view in modern scholarship:[41] humans are granted permission to eat animal flesh, but the consumption of its blood is forbidden. The prohibition of blood consumption appears several times in the Torah, in various contexts.[42] In Genesis, Noah is told not to eat the blood because the "animal's spirit" or "life force" is contained

37. Some commentators claim that already here, only certain animals may be eaten, but not all (for example, Ḥizkuni and Rabbenu Baḥya). However, a straightforward reading seems to suggest that this general language is not coincidental: "*Every* moving thing that lives shall be for you as food. Like the green plants, I give you *everything*." According to this, it seems that all creatures are now permitted for consumption.
38. Rashi on Gen. 9:3.
39. This direction is also favored by Westermann, *Genesis*, vol. 1, 464.
40. Nahmanides reads "blood" as an explanation for "lifeblood, spirit." He openly disagrees with Rashi, although his commentary on 1:29 shows identification with Rashi's interpretation.
41. For example, von Rad, *Genesis*, 127–128.
42. See Lev. 7:26 and on; Deut. 12:16, 24; 15:23.

in its blood. This is similar to the formulation in Deuteronomy: "But make sure that you do not partake of the blood; for the blood is the lifeblood, and you must not consume the lifeblood with the flesh" (Deut. 12:23). While an animal's body is now acceptable for eating, its spirit, its life force, is still off limits – in biblical thought, this force is contained within its blood.[43] This seems to be calculated to keep human audacity in check; a person may not consume another life, only its flesh.[44]

- "And for your lifeblood I will demand an accounting; from every beast I will require it. And from humankind, from every man toward his brother, I will demand an accounting for human life. Whoever sheds the blood of man, by man shall his blood be shed, for in the image of God He made humankind" (9:5–6). This is the prohibition of murder. The first explicit prohibition of murder is presented in the context of eating: it is permissible to kill any creature for the purpose of eating – any creature, that is, except for human beings, who must not be killed.[45]

How can this change be understood? If God intended for people to be vegetarians – as the first humans were – then why are they suddenly permitted to eat animals after the Flood? If, on the other hand, the consumption of animals is entirely permissible, then why was it only permitted after the Flood, rather than granted to Adam along with his dominion over the animal kingdom at the time of creation?

The most common explanation perceives this change as a result of Noah's rescue of the world's animals during the Flood. The animal

43. In contrast to the claim of Henning Graf Reventlow, "Sein Blut komme über sein Haupt," *VT* 10 (1960): 311–327

44. I believe that blood represents life, as opposed to those who hold that it symbolizes death (Leon Morris, "The Biblical Use of the Term 'Blood,'" *JTS* 3 [1952]: 216–226). See Canon Lindsay Dewar's response to Morris' suggestion in "The Biblical Use of the Term 'Blood,'" *JTS* 4 (1953): 204–208.

45. This is also true on the other hand, and the claim of *Tosafot* (Sanhedrin 56b), that before the Flood it was permissible to eat an animal that had died on its own, may be correct. The focus of this prohibition is on the killing, on taking the soul away for the purpose of food.

kingdom was saved by Noah and his ark, and now they are indebted to their savior, even for the purpose of being eaten. As Nahmanides writes:

> When they sinned, and He destroyed the ways of all flesh from upon the land, it was decreed that they would be wiped out in the Flood. When Noah saved them in order to preserve the species, He gave him permission to slaughter and eat them, for they existed because of him.[46]

There are various formulations of the theory that "they all should have been lost, but they remained in existence because of Noah, and for this reason he was given this advantage over them."[47] This reading, however, is problematic – is it logical that because Noah saved the animals, he now has permission to destroy them? In a sense, the opposite would have been more suitable: from now on, it should have been humanity's responsibility to care for and preserve the animals, just like Noah did in the ark.

Rather, it seems more appropriate that this change reflects a change in status, either the status of animals, or the status of humankind. Rabbi Tamir Granot has suggested that after the Flood, animal life was reduced to the status of plant life, rendering them suitable for consumption: "The new order stems from the election of a smaller group [humanity], based on their unique common denominator – that they were created in the image of God – which excludes the larger group [other animals].[48] According to this reading, after the Flood, humanity's unique connection to God was celebrated, and their responsibility expanded. Animals do not share this spark of divinity with humans, and the new disparity between animals and the humans allows humans to eat the animals. This theory is supported by the similar language that equates animals with plants: "Every moving thing that lives shall be for you as food. Like the green plants, I give you everything" (9:3).

---

46. Nahmanides on Gen. 1:29.
47. Rabbi Shabtai Bass, *Siftei Ḥakhamim* on Gen. 9:3.
48. Tamir Granot, "What Changed After the Flood?" Virtual Beit Midrash of Yeshiva Har Etzion, http://www.etzion.org.il/en/what-changed-after-flood.

This is an interesting argument, but I believe that various hints scattered throughout the narrative encourage the opposite reading. A close bond between Noah and the animals is evident throughout the Flood narrative; human and animal are juxtaposed time after time. This is true not only in regard to sin: "And God saw the earth, that it was corrupted, for all flesh had corrupted its way upon the earth" (6:12), but also when Noah and the animals board the ark: "And Noah and his sons and his wife, and the wives of his sons with him, went into the ark because of the waters of the Flood. The clean animals, and the animals that are not clean, and the birds, and all that crawls on the ground, came two by two to Noah, to the ark" (7:7–9), as well as when they leave the ark: "Leave the ark, you and your wife and your sons and your sons' wives with you. And every living thing of all flesh that is with you, the birds, the cattle, and every crawling thing that crawls upon the earth – bring them out with you" (8:16–17). The phrase "bring them out *with* you" hints to an ongoing connection between Noah and his family and the animals that will continue even after they have left the ark. Further hints of this human-animal bond are scattered in the text, and I will point them out below.

For now, I wish to draw attention to two surprising turns of phrase that describe the animals. God refers to the pairs of animals using the expression "*ish ve'ishto*," which literally means "man and his wife": "Of every clean animal, you shall take seven pairs, man and his wife (*ish ve'ishto*), and two of every animal that is not clean, man and his wife (*ish ve'ishto*)" (7:2). This phrase is generally used to describe human relations and it is surprising to find it applied to animals – the phrase "*zakhar u'nekeva*," "male and female," which is used elsewhere in the Flood narrative, is far more suitable. Indeed, the Septuagint (and other ancient translations) replaces this expression with the more obvious "seven of each, *male and female*."[49] This anthropomorphizing phrase seems to be calculated to bring the animal world closer to the human

49. Zipor, *Septuagint*, 135. Prof. John Wycliffe of Oxford, in his ancient translation of the Bible into English (the first of its kind, preceding the King James translation by about two hundred years), chose to ignore the words *ish* and *ishto*, and translated the verse as if it states "male and female" – "Of all clean living beasts, thou shalt take (with thee) by seven and by seven, male and female."

world, to subtly create a bond between Noah, his family, and the animals that are about to share such close quarters for over a year.

A similar use of unexpected language is used to describe how Noah and the animals leave the ark: "So Noah emerged, and his sons and his wife, and his sons' wives with him. Every animal, every crawling thing and every bird, everything that moves upon the earth, *in their families*, came out from the ark" (8:18–19). The first chapter of Genesis describes different kinds of animals, different species, but the word used is "*min*," "kind," or "species," not the more human "*mishpaḥot*," "families." The use of another phrase usually associated with humans rather than animals also serves to bridge the gap between the human world and the animal world.[50]

Moreover, this arises from the plot itself: human and animal emerge from the ark together. Most of humanity, and most of the animal world, were washed away as one: "And the Lord said, 'I will wipe out the human race I have created from the face of the earth – from man to beast to creatures that crawl and to the birds of the sky'" (6:7), and now the survivors of each set foot upon the newly dried earth together: "And God remembered Noah and all the beasts and all the cattle that were with him in the ark" (8:1). God recalls Noah and the animals at the very same time, in a single thought. Neither Noah's wife nor his sons are recalled at that moment – just Noah and the animals. It is no wonder, then, that the rainbow covenant is formed with "all flesh" – an expression that, in the Flood narrative, encompasses both human and beast, all living things.[51] In the new postdiluvian world, human and animal set foot upon the earth together, at the same time.

The status of animals does not change after the Flood; therefore, something must have changed in human status. To determine the nature of this change, we can compare the language of the world's creation and its re-creation after the Flood, with particular focus, of course, on the creation of humankind and the human's new role after the Flood.

50. Mathews could be correct in that the word "families" may anticipate the next chapter, the description of the families of Shem, Ham, and Japheth. There, this word is used repeatedly (Mathews, *Genesis*, vol. 1, 390). This, of course, emphasizes the connection between humans and animals even further.

51. See further in John Olley, "Mixed Blessings for Animals: The Contrasts of Genesis 9," in *The Earth Story in Genesis*, ed. N. C. Habel and S. Wurst (Sheffield, 2000), 130–139, and below, in my discussion of the rainbow covenant.

<table>
<tr><th>The Creation of the World (Gen. 1)</th><th>The Re-Creation of the World (Gen. 8)</th></tr>
<tr><td>And the spirit (ruaḥ) of God hovered over the waters.</td><td>And God sent a wind (ruaḥ) over the earth, and the waters subsided.</td></tr>
<tr><td>So God made the space separating the water beneath from the water above the space.</td><td>And the wellsprings of the deep and the floodgates of heaven were closed, and the rain from the heavens ceased.</td></tr>
<tr><td>And God said, “Let the water under the heaven be gathered to one place, and let dry land appear.”</td><td>And the waters continued to diminish until the tenth month. In the tenth month, on the first of the month, the tops of the mountains appeared.</td></tr>
<tr><td>trees bearing fruit containing seed according to their kinds.</td><td>and look, there was a freshly picked olive leaf in its mouth.</td></tr>
<tr><td>Let there be lights in heavenly space to separate the day from the night.</td><td>And the dove returned to him towards evening.</td></tr>
<tr><td>and let birds fly above the earth across the space of heaven.</td><td>He sent out the dove, but it did not return to him again.</td></tr>
<tr><td>And God said, “Let the land produce (totze) living creatures according to their kinds: the livestock, the creatures that move along the ground, and the wild animals, each according to its kind.” And it was so.
God made the wild animals according to their kinds, the livestock according to their kinds, and all the creatures that move along the ground according to their kinds.</td><td rowspan="2">“Leave (tze) the ark, you and your wife and your sons and your sons’ wives with you. And every living thing of all flesh that is with you, the birds, the cattle, and every crawling thing that crawls upon the earth – bring them out with you, and let them swarm on the earth and be fruitful and multiply on the earth.” So Noah emerged (vayetze), and his sons and his wife, and his sons’ wives with him. Every animal, every crawling thing and every bird, everything that moves upon the earth, in their families, came out (yatzu) from the ark.[52]</td></tr>
<tr><td>So God created humankind in his own image, in the image of God He created him; male and female He created them.</td></tr>
</table>

52. Joshua Berman comments on the comparison between restoring people to dry land and the first creation: “The distinction between male and female in the creation of humankind (1:27) is retained in the world’s rebirth, as Noah is commanded: ‘Leave the ark, you and your wife, your sons and your sons’ wives with you’ (8:16)” (Berman, “Who in His Goodness Renews,” 11).

God finished on the seventh day His work that He had made, and *ceased* on the seventh day...God blessed the seventh day and made it holy.	And Noah built an altar to the Lord... And the Lord smelled the pleasing aroma, and the Lord said in His heart, "Never again will I curse the ground because of humans, because the inclination of the human heart is evil from his youth. And never again will I destroy all that lives as I have done. As long as the earth endures, seedtime and harvest, cold and heat, summer and winter, day and night shall not *cease*.
God blessed them, saying, "Be fruitful and multiply, and fill the earth and subdue it. Have dominion over the fish of the sea and the birds of the sky and over every living creature that moves on the ground."	And God blessed Noah and his sons, and said to them, "Be fruitful and multiply, and fill the earth. And fear and dread of you shall be on all the animals of the earth, and on all the birds of the sky, on all that moves on the ground and on all the fish of the sea. Into your hand they are given.
Then God said, "I give you every seed-bearing plant on the face of all the earth and every tree that has fruit with seed in it. *They will be yours for food.*	Every moving thing that lives *shall be for you as food.* Like the green plants, I give you everything.

The re-creation of the world after the Flood is clearly in dialogue with the original creation in the first chapter of Genesis. Even without division into days, each stage of creation in echoed in the process of the world's renewal, from the moment the floodwaters begin to recede.[53] God sends a wind to dry up the waters and the mountaintops emerge,

53. Covering the world in water reverts it to the state of the second day of creation; for this reason, it is clear why there is no need to echo the creation of light and darkness, which was never harmed in the first place. Samet suggests reading the words "land" and "water" as key words in the Flood: "In the Flood narrative the boundaries are broken between 'water' and 'land' and the previous arrangements are cancelled, with the waters once again returning to cover the land, as it was before creation" (Samet,

just as dry land emerges from the primordial waters at creation. The newly sprouted olive leaf in the dove's beak recalls the first sprouting of vegetation.[54] Indeed, the narrator emphasizes that the branch was "freshly picked," as Bekhor Shor writes, "so that it was obviously stripped off a tree and not from a branch that [the dove] found floating on the water."[55]

The allusion to the next stage of creation is subtler: the creation of the celestial bodies may be hinted to in the surprising detail that the dove came back "towards evening." There are no temporal details at all until this point of the narrative, so scholars and commentators have made various attempts to justify this phrase. Some read this as an expression of speed, that the dove found a newly sprouted tree that same day and did not have to fly far to find one,[56] while others, on the contrary, see it as a sign of delay – that the new vegetation was so plentiful that the dove was able to linger until the evening before it was necessary to return to the ark.[57] Either reading is feasible, but this detail may serve a different purpose altogether: for the first time in the narrative, there is recognition of the difference between night and day. For almost a year, the ark has been tossing upon the waves, with dark, streaming torrents obscuring the light of day. Huddled in the belly of the ark, when was the last time that Noah, his family, and the animals saw the light of the sun? For the first time, there is clear distinction between day and night:

Studies 3, 56). Even if one claims that the words "water" and "land" are too common to be key words, he is still correct that the boundaries between the two, and between dry land and sea, have been abolished.

54. There is room to debate why the creation of plants is represented specifically through an olive leaf. This may be due to the tree's special durability – perhaps this led to its survival throughout the Flood – or it may be an indication that even olive trees were already visible on the surface of the water, even though the olive tree is not a tall species. Radak on Gen. 8:11 proposes two additional explanations: "Why did it bring from the olive tree? Perhaps it was the closest to where the ark was, or perhaps because the olive has leaves all year round."
55. Bekhor Shor on Gen. 8:11.
56. Radak on Gen. 8:11: "On the day it came to him, towards the evening."
57. Ḥizkuni on Gen. 8:11: "And Noah knew that the waters had receded – because it waited to come back until the evening." Gunkel debates whether this symbolizes God (*Genesis*, 65), but such a claim seems exaggerated.

the dove returns to the ark towards evening, when the sun is setting. Once again, the sun and the moon, and the day and the night they rule, become a relevant part of life on earth. It is no coincidence, either, that the dove is the harbinger of this return to reality; birds (and fish) were the first living creatures to see the light of the newly created sun on the morning of the fifth day.

Humans and animals emerge from the ark and set foot on dry land together. While both were created on the sixth day, a distinction can be drawn between this scene and the original sequence of creation. When the world is created, animals and humans are each created through their own divine act of speech, and humans are created last of all, "in the image of God." In contrast, after the Flood, humans and animals are presented as a single unit – God orders them to alight at the same time, and indeed, they leave the ark together. The difference between the old world and the new seems to be related to the salient disparity between God's blessing to the first man and the blessing to Noah, and in turn, the difference between what constitutes food for each of them:

God's Blessing to the First Man	God's Blessing to Noah
Be fruitful and multiply, and fill the earth *and subdue it.*	Be fruitful and multiply, and fill the earth.
Have *dominion over* the fish of the sea and the birds of the sky and over every living creature that moves on the ground.	*And fear and dread of you shall be on* all the animals of the earth, and on all the birds of the sky, on all that moves on the ground and on all the fish of the sea. Into your hand they are given.

The two blessings are similar, and both seem to describe dominion over the animals; after all, is there any real difference between "dominion" over them and commanding their "fear and dread"?[58] Actually, there *is* a difference between these two formulations. While both point to

58. And indeed, Cassuto writes: "The benison vouchsafed to the first man is confirmed and renewed in identical terms" (*From Noah to Abraham*, 124).

humanity's mastery over the animal world, the particular form of this mastery is completely different.

Some read the transition from "dominion" to "fear and dread" as an increase of human mastery over animals – expressed, of course, in the newly granted permission to kill them for food. In the words of Moshe Weinfeld: "The control granted to humans over animals after the Flood is absolute: not only does he have dominion over them, but he is allowed to eat them, just like the plants that he ate until now."[59]

However, it seems more likely that the opposite reading is correct. The first man is told "to subdue" the earth, but this element is absent from the blessing to Noah.[60] How will this have bearing upon humanity's position within reality? The human's new role is alluded to in the Midrash: "Fear and dread of you – fear and dread were restored, but dominion was not restored."[61] According to this midrash, Noah and his generation were only granted part of the original blessing – their dominion over the animals was *not* restored.[62]

In the Bible, the verb "*lirdot*," to have dominion, signifies rule and government, and usually appears in a neutral sense, of a leader ruling his people (though it carries a more negative connotation in Modern Hebrew). For example, we learn that King Solomon "had dominion (*rodeh*) over the whole region to the west of the River.... He had peace on every surrounding border, from Dan to Beersheba, Judah and Israel dwelled in safety, each person in the shade of his grapevine and fig tree, all the days of Solomon" (I Kings 5:4–5). Solomon controls the entire region, but this does not mean that his subjects suffer – on the contrary,

---

59. Moshe Weinfeld, *Olam HaTanakh: Genesis* (Tel Aviv, 1993), 64. This was also expressed by Rabbi David Zvi Hoffmann.

60. The Septuagint was troubled by this omission and fills in the blessing to Noah to make it parallel, "*kai katakyrieusate autes*," "and dominate it."

61. Genesis Rabba 34:12.

62. This omission, too, was filled in in several manuscripts of the Septuagint. While in the Masoretic version, God concludes His blessing to Noah and his sons with these words: "As for you, be fruitful and multiply, increase greatly on the earth and multiply in it (*urevu ba*)," in the aforementioned manuscripts of the Septuagint, instead of "*urevu ba*," "multiply in it," the words "*uredu ba*," "and have dominion over it" appear (Zipor, *Septuagint*, 157). In this way, this translation completes the missing "dominion."

they enjoy peace, safety, and prosperity.[63] The first man is not ordered to "dominate" the land in a negative sense; rather, he is granted privilege that goes hand in hand with responsibility. As Rav Kook explains:

> Anyone possessing intellectual and philosophical facilities knows that the "dominion" mentioned in the Torah – "have dominion over the fish of the seas and the birds of the sky" – does not refer to the oppression of a tyrant, who abuses his people and his subjects in order to achieve his own personal whims. Heaven forbid that an ugly law of enslavement such as this should be sealed with eternal approval in God's world, who is good to all, and has compassion over all His creations.[64]

Moreover, I am not certain that Nahmanides is correct in defining "dominion" as "doing as they wish with animals and crawling things" in order to help people with their work.[65] This "dominion" seems to mean the responsibility that comes with leadership, as opposed to the privileges of leadership. God blesses the first man with the power of leadership over all the world's animals; he must take care of them and serve as their ambassador in God's world. In chapter 1, this dominion is presented as humanity's ultimate purpose: "Let us make man in our image, in our likeness, *so that he may have dominion* over the fish of the sea and the birds of the sky, over the livestock and all the wild animals, and over all the creatures that move along the ground" (1:26). By ruling over the animal kingdom, humanity fulfills the divine spark within it, as a representation of God within His world: "You have made him a little less than divine, and adorned him with glory and majesty / You have made him master of Your own handiwork, laying the world at his feet" (Ps. 8:6–7). In contrast, Noah is not blessed with this element of dominion; instead, he is granted fear and dread over the animal kingdom. After

63. The aforementioned midrash that claims that Noah and his sons were not granted dominion claims that this dominion was restored in the days of Solomon, as implied in the cited verse (Genesis Rabba, ibid.).
64. Rabbi Abraham Isaac Kook, *A Vision of Vegetarianism and Peace* (Jerusalem, 1965), 9.
65. A position adopted by Rabbi Yehuda Shaviv, "'Rule' in its Earliest Meaning," *Megadim* 22 (1994): 26.

the Flood, humanity is no longer the king of the world, alhough he has been imprinted with superior wisdom and skill which causes all the animals to fear his wily traps and lethal bow. From now on, the deer will fear the lioness, and the mouse will fear the snake, due to their strength and speed, and all the beasts of the world will fear humanity for its ability to hunt them down with weapons. The world may have been re-created after the Flood, but things are not as they were before. Man is no longer the "king" of the world, even though all fear him.

In light of this essential difference, the different consequence of each blessing is clear. After the first man is blessed with dominion over the world, he is provided with plants and fruits and seeds to eat: "Then God said, 'I give you every seed-bearing plant on the face of all the earth and every tree that has fruit with seed in it. They will be yours for food'" (1:29). As long as the crown rests upon his head, man may not eat any of his subjects. The king's role is to ensure social order in his kingdom, to guarantee wellbeing, safety, and justice for all. After the Flood, however, humanity is stripped of its dominion; humankind, it turns out, is not fit to reign over God's world. Humans are still at the top of the food chain, and the animals will fear them, but this is mere dread, not reverence for a ruler.

The disparity is more apparent when comparing how "God's image" comes into play in each scene.[66] In chapter 1, humankind is fit to rule over the world because it was created in the image of God: "Then God said, 'Let us make man in our image, in our likeness, so that he may have dominion over the fish of the sea and the birds of the sky, over the livestock and all the wild animals, and over all the creatures that move along the ground'" (1:26). In contrast, when the world begins anew after the Flood, humankind's spark of divinity is mentioned as the reason that murder is forbidden; people are a protected species, protected by their creation in God's image: "And for your lifeblood I will demand an accounting; from every beast I will require it. And from humankind, from every man toward his brother, I will demand an accounting for human life. Whoever

66. Compare to Bernd Janowski, "Die lebendige Statue Gottes: Zur Anthropologie der priesterlichen Urgeschichte," in *Gott und Mensch im Dialog*, ed. M. Witte (Berlin/New York, 2005), 183–214.

sheds the blood of man, by man shall his blood be shed, for in the image of God He made humankind" (9:5–6). Rather than serving as its crown of dignity, as the driving force behind its unique, dignified place in the world, humanity's spark of divinity has become its saving grace, its mark of Cain, ensuring its protection within the new Darwinian world order.

In this light, the permission to eat animal flesh is a reflection of human failure, recognition of human limitations and the inclination of the human heart, which is "evil from youth" (8:21). After the Flood, the role of humanity changes; the world begins anew, but this time, man will not steer it. He remains the world's most highly evolved creature, and all tremble before him, but he has been dethroned, and he is no longer their king. He may be the strongest, most capable creature, but he has joined the rest of the animal world in their struggle for survival.

Humankind's new place is reflected in the blurring of the boundaries that were established between human and animal in the first creation account. There, the verb "*bara*," "create," is applied intensely to humanity's creation, differentiating man and woman from the animals, created on the same day, yet with a different act of speech, a separate act of creation. After the waters of the Flood dry up, however, human and animal leave the ark at the same time. Humans, the most advanced land mammals of them all, begin to repopulate the earth at the same time as their fellow land mammals. As I already suggested, the use of the anthropomorphizing phrases "man and wife" and "according to their families" not only serves to elevate the status of animals, but includes them within the same category as humans, which has implications for the human world no less than for the animal world. In the old world, humanity was "created" separately; in this postdiluvian reality, the human is on equal footing with the rest of creation.

The fall from this pedestal also has positive implications: from now on, the world will not suffer as a result of human sin. As the world's leader, every human act and decision directly affects the world itself. When Adam sins, the ground itself is cursed. When humanity fails, the whole world fails along with it, as God declares on the eve of the Flood: "The Lord regretted that He had made man on earth, and He was grieved to His very heart. And the Lord said, 'I will wipe out the human race I have created from the face of the earth – from man to beast to creatures that crawl and to the birds of the sky'" (6:6–7). God's fury at humanity automatically extends to everything under humanity's dominion. After the Flood, this connection is severed. Now that humanity no longer rules the world, God declares: "Never again will I curse the ground because of humans, because the inclination of the human heart is evil from his youth. And never again will I destroy all that lives as I have done" (8:21). I have already mentioned how these verses function as a framework for the narrative, that on the eve of the Flood, God mourns "in His heart" and decides to wipe out humanity (and his world along with him), while at its end, God declares "in His heart" that never again will the earth suffer for human sin. Humanity will go on sinning – "the inclination of the human heart is evil from his youth" – but the world itself will not be punished as a result of his sins. From now on, humanity alone will bear the brunt of its sins, but the world is no longer under its jurisdiction, and the world will be spared.

This change is in poignant dialogue with Lamech's prayer at the birth of Noah. He wishes for the ground's curse to come to an end and his prayer is ultimately fulfilled, but not as he anticipated. In W. W. Jacobs' famous story, "The Monkey's Paw," Herbert wishes for a large sum of money and his parents indeed receive it – but as compensation for Herbert's death. Lamech wishes for the soil's curse to come to an end and this indeed comes to pass – but it is fulfilled through the world's destruction by Flood and the divorce between humanity and the earth.

In this light, God's reconciliation with humankind at the Flood's end takes on an air of tragedy, of resignation. God does not forgive humanity for its first failed attempt, and humanity does not promise to try better next time; there is no compassionate, loving statement of reconciliation and renewal. Rather, God grimly accepts that the human inclination is evil from its youth and confiscates the human's scepter so that he does not do any more harm, and the world will be safe from his evil inclination.

Nonetheless, the divorce between the human and his world is not the final, tragic word. Within the broader expanse of biblical historiography, the Flood is only a brief intermission, to be followed by two new stages which mitigate the bleak atmosphere of the Flood's end: the election of Abraham and his descendants, and the prophetic vision of the end of days.

The Election of Abraham and His Descendants

Divine disappointment in humanity and its role has stripped it of its crown, but God has not completely despaired of finding human representatives to rule over the world in His name. From now on, responsibility will be confined to a certain family line, which will eventually found a nation, bearing God's name on its banner for all the world to see. As a result of the new world order following the Flood, Abraham and his descendants are elected as God's chosen people. The discourse of nationality that bursts into reality only after the Flood is profoundly connected to this process. At the beginning of Genesis, there is no need for different nationalities or different languages. Adam is not the father of seventy nations, but Noah is. After the world's birth, it seemed that humanity would rule as one over the animals, that together, it would "subdue the earth." This attempt failed, and now God switches over to His contingency plan: creating seventy nations from Noah and his sons, and electing a single nation who will lead the world in God's ways. All the families on earth will be blessed through Abraham and his chosen seed.

And indeed, Abraham's descendants will be involved in a complex, conscious dialogue with the question of eating animals. The most salient example can be found in Leviticus 17, which penalizes anyone who slaughters an animal outside of the camp. The law implies that whoever kills an animal solely for eating is considered guilty of murder: "If anyone of the house of Israel slaughters an ox or sheep or goat in the camp, or does so outside the camp, and does not bring it to the entrance of the Tent of Meeting to present it as an offering to the Lord, before the Lord's Tabernacle, bloodguilt shall be imputed to that man: he has shed blood; that man shall be cut off from among his people" (Lev. 17:3–4). While this episode contains nuances of fear of sacrifice to demonic entities outside the camp, the connotations of "bloodguilt shall be imputed to that man: he has shed blood" cannot be overlooked. Like Rashi's harsh words on that verse: "It is as though he has shed human blood, for which one deserves the death penalty." This law implies that the concept of sacrifice to God poses a possible solution to the issue of killing animals for food. An animal sacrificed as a wellbeing offering is first and foremost an offering to God, and in such a case, a person is able to partake of its flesh as well. This law suggests that the killing of animals solely for the purpose of eating is "bloodshed," but when offering an animal to God, its blood is not spilled but gathered in a vessel and sprinkled over the altar.[67]

While this law is emended in Deuteronomy 12, and Jewish law ultimately permits the slaughter of animals for food, the underlying principle of the prohibition in Leviticus 17 reveals much about the Torah's complex attitude towards animal slaughter. Noah is permitted to eat animals after the Flood, but Abraham's descents develop and maintain a dialogue with this toleration, even restricting it in certain ways.[68]

The End of Days: A Vision of Vegetarianism and Peace

Ideally, humanity would have retained its leadership and remained herbivorous. Nonetheless, the Bible does not preach the virtues of a meat-free lifestyle, just as it does not preach the virtues of walking around naked like Adam and Eve before their sin, in the ideal world in the Garden of Eden. Similar to the Eden model, the prediluvian world represents an ideal state that humanity is not yet able to maintain, so the Creator is "forced" to shift the universal paradigm and bring humankind through a process that will hopefully lead to the ideal place that was expected from it at creation.

And indeed, in several places throughout the Bible, there are certain hints that the world will one day revert to its herbivorous state. In our imperfect world, humans are permitted to eat animals, but if the world reaches an ideal state, then all animals – including humans – will once again subsist on plants, fruits, and seeds. This is alluded to in several prophecies:

---

67. Jan Joosten also proposed reading Lev. 17 in this way, in "Réflexions théologiques sur Lévitique 17," *Revue d'Histoire et de Philosophie Religieuses* 93 (2013): 145–156.

68. It is worth noting that pure animals that may be eaten but cannot be brought as sacrifices have a special law regarding the covering of their blood with earth (Lev. 17:13). Even though these animals may be killed for the sake of food, their blood should not be left uncovered to cry out to God.

> The wolf shall dwell with the lamb, the leopard lie down with the kid, the calf, the beast of prey, and the fatling together, with a little boy to herd them. The cow and the bear shall graze, their young shall lie down together, and the lion, like the ox, shall eat straw. (Is. 11:6–7; cf. Is. 65:25)

Commentators have argued whether this prophecy will be fulfilled in a literal sense or a symbolic sense.[69] It is even more difficult to determine whether humans, too, will stop eating animal flesh, but this reading is certainly possible. If we adopt the interpretation that Isaiah's vision will be fulfilled in a literal sense, and that humans, too, will stop eating meat, then this idea aptly reflects the beginning of Genesis. At the end of days, the world will return to its ideal state, and animals and humans alike will eat only from "seed-bearing plants on the face of all the earth and every tree that has fruit with seed in it" (Gen. 1:29).

HUMANITY'S CONNECTION WITH GOD

On one hand, humankind falls from its pedestal in the wake of the Flood; people are no longer the rulers of the animal kingdom, but just another one of God's creatures. On the other hand, a careful comparison of the world's renewal with its initial creation reveals that humanity is far more intimately involved with the world's re-creation – to the point that God and humankind effectively renew the world together.

This is salient in the fact that Noah is the one who builds the ark and gathers the animals to preserve them from extinction. Moreover, if

69. See the argument between Maimonides and Rabbi Abraham ben David (Raavad) about the character of the "end of days." Maimonides writes: "Do not think that in the days of the Messiah there will be any change in the ways of the world, or that what was established at creation will change – the world will continue in its ways, and what it says in Isaiah, that "the wolf will lie with the lamb," is a figurative parable, meaning that Israel will live peacefully alongside the wicked of the world who are compared to a wolf and a tiger…" ("Laws of Kingship," 12:1). Raavad objects, "But in the Torah (Lev. 26:6), it says: 'And I will remove the wild beasts from the land.'" Meaning, the blessings of *Parashat Beḥukkotai* already imply that carnivorous animals will literally cease their hunting. A similar debate exists among modern scholars regarding the interpretation of the prophecy in Isaiah. See, for example, Franz Delitzsch, *Biblical Commentary on the Prophecies of Isaiah*, vol. 1, trans. J. Martin (Edinburgh, 1890), 286.

the emergence from the ark is their symbolic rebirth, then Noah is the one who delivers them from their wooden womb and sends them off to their new lives. In parallel to the biblical expression for offspring, "*yotze yerekh,*" literally meaning, "the issue of one's thigh/loins,"[70] the animals Noah restores to the land are "*yotze hateva*" (9:10), "the issue of the ark." They are born anew, and Noah is the one who brings them forth into the world. This is also keenly reflected in the scene where Noah sends the dove through the window of the ark, in which Noah is characterized as a parent sending his or her child out into the world.

NOAH, DOVE, AND RAVEN

Forty days after the rains have ceased to fall, Noah decides to gauge the state of the world by sending out a raven and a dove. While the ark does have a "skylight" (6:16), a "window" (8:6), Noah can only look out to his immediate surroundings, the region of Mount Ararat, and he is curious to know whether the waters have dried up in more distant areas. Noah manages to explore his surroundings through these birds.

As mentioned, this stage seems somewhat superfluous – immediately afterwards, God appears to Noah and orders him to leave the ark. That is, even after Noah determines that the ground has indeed dried up, Noah waits for God's word before leaving the ark. If the narrative is divided into two separate sources, then according to the source featuring the name of the Lord, Noah uses the birds to determine whether he can leave, while according to God's story, Noah does nothing but sit and wait before God eventually orders him to set foot on land. However, as discussed at length, the narrative is arranged as a continuous, coherent story. Read thus, Noah and God emerge as joint partners in their decision to leave the ark and begin life anew on the flood-washed earth. After Noah determines that the waters have dried up, he is ready to leave the ark. At this point God appears to him, approves of his decision, and blesses the departing passengers: "Leave the ark, you and your wife and your sons and your sons' wives with you. And every living thing of all flesh that is with you ... and be fruitful and multiply on the earth" (8:15–17). The seamless sequence of

70. Gen. 46:26; Ex. 1:5; Judges 8:30.

events characterizes Noah and God as partners: Noah decides that he can leave the ark, and God enables it and blesses all those who leave the ark. While God is their Creator, Noah is their deliverer. In chapter 1, God commands the earth to bring the animals forth: "Let the land bring forth (*totze*) living creatures according to their kinds" (1:24), yet God effectively creates them, "God made the wild animals according to their kinds" (1:25). After the Flood, Noah is the one who brings the animals forth into their new reality: "Leave the ark.... And every living thing of all flesh that is *with you*, the birds, the cattle, and every crawling thing that crawls upon the earth – *bring them out with you*, and let them swarm on the earth and be fruitful and multiply on the earth" (8:16–17). Noah – the representative of humankind – is the one who sees the animals reborn; he is God's partner in creation in the new world.[71]

In this new world, unlike the old, humanity participates in its re-creation. A human builds the ark that will save all living creatures from extinction. A human cares for them all as they rock within the wooden womb that floats upon the waters. A human determines the best time for their delivery and rebirth (in contrast to the words of the mishna that "without your consent you were formed; without your consent you were born"[72]). At the same time, however, this human does not create himself. He is not the master of this new world, and he submits to the divine order that tells him precisely when to leave the safety of the ark. Ultimately, God is the one who blesses His creations to be fruitful and multiply on the earth, and Noah and his family are included among the recipients of this blessing. I will refer back to this point in the context of Noah's drunkenness and the blessing and curse he utters to his sons.

Based on these ideas, I wish to explore the verses depicting how Noah sends off the raven and dove (8:6–13). This unit is divided into four stages:

---

71. It may be that Rashi himself (on 8:17) alludes to this tension in his interpretation of the difference between the text and the Masoretic reading, the *keri* and the *ketiv*: "*Hotze* is written, but *hayetze* should be read. *Hayetze* means, tell them to come out; *Hotze* means, if they do not want to come out, make them come out yourself."

72. Avot 4:22.

1. 8:7: Noah sends the raven (which does not provide any information).
2. 8:8–9: Noah sends the dove for the first time (and learns that there is still "water all over the face of the earth").
3. 8:10–11: Noah sends the dove a second time (and learns that "the waters had receded from the earth").
4. 8:12–14: Noah sends the dove a third time (and does not return, prompting Noah to remove the ark's cover and see that "the water had dried up from the earth").

Through this process, Noah and the reader learn that the waters gradually dry up.[73] The raven is the clear odd one out in this section; the process actually begins when Noah sends the dove for the first time, while the raven contributes nothing to Noah's knowledge of the situation.

It seems that the raven serves little purpose within the narrative; its only function is as a foil to the dove. This contrast is apparent from the moment Noah sends them – it merely states that "[Noah] sent out a raven" (8:7), while the reason Noah sends the dove is elaborated in the text itself: "Then he sent out a dove from him to see whether the water had receded from the surface of the ground" (8:8). There are several intriguing differences between these descriptions:

- While Noah "sent the raven," he sends forth the dove "*from him.*"[74] This generates a sense of closeness between Noah and the dove, and almost implies that the dove is leaving him, that the two are being separated.

73. From this perspective, the pattern of this section is consistent with a typical biblical pattern pointed out by Yair Zakovitch, which he calls "three and four" – that is, after three attempts, there is a change with the fourth attempt. The success on the fourth attempt in this passage comes as no surprise; on the contrary, the reader anticipates it, given that the land is gradually drying up.

74. In the Septuagint: "And he sent out the dove after him," instead of "from him." It is difficult to understand precisely why the Septuagint uses this word (see, for example, Skinner, *Genesis*, 156; Zipor, *Septuagint*, 148), but it may reflect the translator's surprise with the very use of the word "from him" and an attempt to illuminate it.

- More importantly, the purpose of the raven's mission is not reported at all – upon a first reading, the reader has no idea why it is being sent out. Is the raven being released from the ark, or is Noah enlisting its help? The reason for its departure only becomes apparent when the dove is sent "to see whether the water had receded from the surface of the ground" (8:8). In retrospect, this must have been the reason that Noah sent the raven as well, but the very fact that this information is only revealed the second time is surprising; it would have been more logical to relate this information the first time Noah sends out a bird.[75]

Both differences create the impression of closeness between Noah and the dove; this contrast implies that Noah himself is debating whether the raven can be trusted with its mission – to the extent that the reason for his departure is not even mentioned. In contrast, Noah trusts the dove, and the reason for its mission is described at length.[76]

The contrast between the birds grows even more extreme upon their return. The raven does not come back to Noah; the meaning of the vague description, "It flew back and forth until the water had dried up from the earth," is given to debate. Rashi understands that the raven did not even set out on its mission, but rather "kept circling around the ark."[77] Radak, among others, suggests that the raven set out to find corpses, as Noah expected, but it never went back to Noah to relay the information; it may or may not have found dead bodies. Many others claim that the raven never returned to the ark at all.[78] In any case, there was certainly a

75. As expected, this omission is filled in the Septuagint, which also describes the purpose of the raven's mission: "And he sent the raven to see if the waters had receded" (Zipor, *Septuagint*, 147). As often is the case, however, this addition obscures the original narrative intentions.
76. This also hints that Noah was never going to gather any information from the raven; he only learned whether "the waters had receded" from the dove.
77. Rashi on Gen. 8:7. Rashi further explains why the raven would not fly far from the ark: "He was afraid that he would take his mate." Meaning, Rashi, following Sanhedrin 108b, is suggesting that the raven was afraid that Noah would take his mate for himself, and he therefore refused to go very far. This strange midrash will be given textual basis below.
78. See, for example, J. Gottsberger, "*Yatzo VaShov* in Genesis 8,7," *BZ* 6 (1908): 113–116.; Westermann, *Genesis*, vol. 1, 447.

lack of communication between Noah and his first scout, which prompted him to send the more communicative dove, as Radak explains: "The dove has the capacity to bring information back to its sender."[79]

Unlike the raven, the dove's return to the ark is described in detail: "But the dove found no resting place for its foot, and it returned to him, to the ark.... And he stretched out his hand and took it and brought it back to him into the ark" (8:9). This verse is charged with emotion.[80] Firstly, there is a clear sense of closeness between Noah and the dove in the double description "and it returned to him, to the ark." The dove does not merely return to the ark for technical reasons, but to him, to Noah, to the man who sent him. Noah's action is also surprising: "He stretched out his hand and took it and brought it back to him into the ark." This long, descriptive verse does not advance the plot in any way – the previous verse already related that the dove returned to the ark. Some commentators suggest that Noah took the dove in his hands in order to examine it. For example, Bekhor Shor explains that he took it "to check its feet and wings to see if he could find any mud or dirt, and whether there were any leaves in its beak, in order to understand whether the waters had abated."[81] Rather than describe a technical inquiry, however, this verse seems calculated to awaken associations of tenderness and closeness: Noah sends out his hand to bring the dove in. It could have flown in by itself, but Noah sends out his hand towards it. If the words "and he took it (feminine) and brought it (feminine) back to him" were about a woman, not a bird, then read out of context, this suggestive sequence might have been taken for a description about marriage. The language and form of this verse strongly evokes biblical descriptions of marriage, such as, "And Isaac *brought her into* the tent of his mother Sarah *and he took* Rebekah as his wife, and he loved her" (Gen. 24:67),

79. Radak on 8:7–8.

80. I discuss "associative meanings" that accompany this scene at other opportunities. See Grossman, *Text and Subtext*, 71. On the subtlety in the description of the dove's return, see Skinner, *Genesis*, 156.

81. Bekhor Shor on Gen. 8:9. Interestingly enough, Josephus describes the dove returning with an olive leaf in its beak thus: "It returned to him, dirtied with mud" (Josephus, *Antiquities*, 1:11). The birds in the story of *Atrahasis* also return from the Mesopotamian flood with mud on their feet.

"And there, Judah saw the daughter of a Canaanite; her name was Shua, *and he took her and came to her*" (Gen. 38:2), and, above all, "And in the evening *he took* Leah his daughter *and brought her to him*, and he came to her" (Gen. 29:23).[82] Indeed, this last verse and our verse under discussion are the only two instances of the exact phrase "*vayave ota elav*," "And he brought her to him," in the Bible.

To load romantic associations of marriage and intimacy onto Noah's relationship with the dove would certainly be an exaggeration; yet, even if unexpected, these associations cannot be overlooked completely. They create a subtle sense of closeness between Noah and the dove, in sharp contrast to the brief, technical description of the raven. Compare the text's description of the raven's "return," "it flew back and forth," to that of the dove's return, "and it returned *to him*."

This bond is hinted to in a covert etymology of Noah's name in this scene. As mentioned earlier, the meaning of Noah's name has already been explored twice in the text. With his birth, his father explicitly declares the reason for his name: "He named him Noah saying, 'This one will comfort us in the labor and painful toil of our hands caused by the ground the Lord has cursed'" (5:29). According to Lamech's prayer, Noah's name is related to comfort, to consolation. On the eve of the Flood, another etymology is implied in the text:

> The Lord regretted (*vayinaḥem*) that he had made man on earth, and He was pained to his very heart. And the Lord said, 'I will wipe out the human race I have created from the face of the earth – from man to beast to creatures that crawl and to the birds of the sky – for I regret (*niḥamti*) that I have made them.' But Noah (*Noaḥ*) found favor (*ḥen*) in the eyes of the Lord. (6:6–8)

These verses present tension between most of humanity, whose creation God regrets (*naḥem*) and Noah (*Noaḥ*) who finds favor (*ḥen*) in the eyes of God. "*Ḥen*," "favor," spelled "*ḥet-nun*," is the reversal of "*nun-ḥet*," "*Noaḥ*." This is a device that is found elsewhere in the Bible, such as in

82. Another example of the imagery of marriage: "And Boaz *took* Ruth and she became his wife, and he *came* to (had relations with) her" (Ruth 4:13).

I Chronicles 11:45: "And Joha (*vaYoḥa*) his brother (*aḥiv*), the Tizite" – "And Joha," "*v-y-ḥ-a*," is "his brother," "*a-ḥ-y-v*," backwards.[83] Before the Flood, however, the most straightforward etymology of Noah's name has yet to appear. When Noah sends out the dove, a third etymology is tucked away in the text: "But the dove found no resting place (*manoaḥ*) for its foot" (8:9). This implicit etymology comes the closest to the literal meaning of Noah's name[84] – outside of the ark, there is no resting place for the dove's feet,[85] but inside the ark, Noah awaits its return, holding out his hands to serve as a perch for its weary feet, and brings her inside to him.

Nahmanides is sensitive to these romantic nuances in these lines and notes with characteristic sharpness: "But the dove found no resting place – that was good for it."[86] This addition is taken from Naomi's words to Ruth: "Daughter, I must seek out rest (*manoaḥ*) for you, so it will be good for you" (Ruth 3:1). Naomi hopes for "rest" – in the form of a good marriage – for her widowed daughter-in-law.[87]

If so, the description of Noah's bond with the dove reaches a climax upon the dove's first return to the ark. When Noah sends it out a second time, this connection gradually weakens. Gradually, the two grow apart. The first time Noah sends out the dove, he sends it "from him," whereas the second time, "he again sent out the dove from the ark" (8:10) – not from him, but merely "from the ark," which conveys less

83. There is room to debate whether this is intentional palindromic wordplay or coincidence. Other examples of palindromes can be found in Gen. 27:31; Gen. 44:34; Num. 31:16; Deut. 19:6; I Kings 13:32.

84. Jacob, *Genesis*, 220; Kiel, *Genesis*, 202. Kiel surmises that the verse "And the ark *came to rest* (*vayanaḥ*) in the seventh month, on the seventeenth day of the month, on the mountains of Ararat" (8:4) is also playing on Noah's name (ibid., 198).

85. Compare to: "Yet even among those nations you shall find no peace, nor shall your foot find a place to rest (*manoaḥ*)" (Deut. 28:65).

86. Nahmanides on Gen. 8:9.

87. In the book of Ruth, the word "*menuḥa*," "rest," is especially associated with marriage, as Naomi tells her widowed daughters-in-law in chapter 1: "May the Lord grant that you find rest (*menuḥa*), each woman in the house of her husband" (1:9). It is therefore likely that the "rest" she refers to before Ruth goes down to the threshing floor is in implicit dialogue with the "rest" she spoke of in chapter 1. See further in Grossman, *Ruth*, 203.

closeness between them. The gap widens with the dove's second return; whereas the first time, the dove returns "to *him*, to the ark," upon its second return, "the dove came to him." The dove still returns to Noah, but the omission of the double expression of return, of the ark, is less evocative. The dove is not "coming back to him, coming back home"; it is merely "coming back to him," and there is no description of Noah bringing the dove back inside, allowing it to rest on his own hands.[88]

By the third time, there is no depiction of closeness between Noah and the dove, as if they are preparing to part for good. There is no mention of flying away "from him," or even "from the ark," and, of course, "his dove, his perfection," never returns, so the two figures part ways forever.

Using the raven as a foil to the dove is not surprising, especially given the biblical associations with the dove, with its ability to make its way back to its nest, to its family. For example, when Isaiah speaks of Israel's return to its land, he declares: "Who are these that float like a cloud, like doves to their cotes?" (Is. 60:8).[89] These connotations may well be connected to the ancient practice of using doves as carriers, as Radak proposes in his interpretation:

> When Noah saw that he had learned nothing from the raven, he sent the dove. For the dove has the capacity to bring information back to its sender.... It also has a natural yearning to return to its nest. This led to the practice of kings of raising doves in their royal homes, to send them away to distant places with a message tied to their wings, and it would return to its sender with a reply tied to its wings.[90]

88. It may also be suggested that the time the dove returns, "*le'et erev*," "evening-time," recalls the word for raven, "*orev*," hinting that following the dove's return, Noah and the dove will begin to grow apart, until it grows as distant as the raven.
89. Do these connotations play a part in the midrash that the prophet Jonah, whose name is the same Hebrew word for dove, will flee away from God but eventually return to his role?
90. Radak on Gen. 8:7.

In contrast to the dove's strong homing instincts, however, the raven is associated with the opposite characteristics – a creature who does not have a permanent habitat, a wilderness bird that flies from deserted place to deserted place. When Isaiah describes the total destruction that awaits Edom (perhaps as a symbol of all enemy nations), he pronounces: "Jackdaws and owls shall possess it; great owls and ravens shall dwell there. He shall measure it with a line of chaos, with weights of emptiness" (Is. 34:11).[91] The fact that ravens are the creatures that sustain Elijah with bread and meat (I Kings 17:6) is related not to their innate kindness, but to the fact that Elijah is hiding out in an isolated, hidden place, devoid of human company. Therefore, it is wild, solitary ravens who bring food to the wild, solitary Elijah.[92]

The difference between these birds is also reflected in their song – the dove is associated with sweetness and softness, as in Hezekiah's prayer, where his voice gradually grows weaker as his sickness overcomes him: "I cried out until morning.... I piped like a swift or a swallow, I moaned like a dove" (Is. 38:13–14).[93] In contrast, the raven has a rough, coarse caw: "He provides animals with food, to the young ravens who call out" (Ps. 147:8).

In general, the dove is associated with human communication, whereas the raven represents the wild and the desolate where his hollow call rings out. The lover in Song of Songs refers to his beloved as "my dove, my perfection," while the only lover linked to the raven, "that grim, ungainly, ghastly, gaunt, and ominous bird of yore," is probably Edgar Allan Poe's Lenore.

---

91. Later on, the prophet says: "There, too, the lilith shall repose, and *find herself a resting place*" (34:14).

92. The sages of Genesis Rabba, and Rashi in their footsteps, draw a connection between Noah sending the raven and ravens feeding Elijah: "Until the waters dried up – the raven was prepared for a different mission 'once the waters dried up,' when the rains ceased in Elijah's time, as it says, 'And the ravens would bring him bread and meat'" (Rashi on Gen. 8:7). This connection is based on a contrast: the raven does not fulfill its mission during the Flood of Noah's time, but it does during the famine of Elijah's time.

93. See also Nahum 2:8; Is. 59:11; Ezek. 7:16.

The contrast between the raven and the dove is reinforced at the narrative's end, when Noah "took from all the clean animals and from all the clean birds, and offered burnt offerings on the altar" (8:20). The raven is an unclean species, excluded from Noah's gift to God, but if Noah took from *all* the clean birds, then the dove was certainly offered up on the altar, serving as a connection between Noah and his Maker. And indeed, doves will play a significant role in several offerings and related mitzvot, unlike the unclean raven.[94]

What is the meaning of this comparison, of the narrative tension between the two birds? And how does the subtle bond between Noah and the dove, and their gradual separation, contribute to the reading of this narrative?

Noah's connection with the dove recalls family relationships, and this seems to be the main objective of these associations. As Philo describes, leaving the ark is a kind of birth, a kind of rebirth; the ark is like a womb that gives birth to all the creatures of the world:[95]

> Over the course of the Flood, the ark serves as a protective womb, enveloping those inside from the destruction that rages without. In the ark, no doubt, certain relationships are formed between the creatures.[96]

From this perspective, the dove leaving the ark is like a child leaving its mother, while Noah, of course, is like a parent sending his or her child off into the world. The dove must learn to leave its mother, to leave the cradling protection of the ark. The dove must be born and grow up.

---

94. Cassuto (*From Noah to Abraham*, 107), claims that not only does the dove's sacrifice stand in the background of its successful mission, but it is also linked to the fact that the dove, unlike the raven, may be eaten (Lev. 11:15). Westermann debates whether this criterion is relevant here (Westermann, *Genesis*, vol. 1, 447).
95. In his (somewhat scandalous) book on Moses, Freud writes that the ark Moses is placed in represents the womb: "The abandonment in the ark is an unmistakable symbol of birth: the ark – the mother's womb, the waters – the amniotic fluid" (Freud, "Der Mann Moses und die monotheistische Religion," in *Selected Works in Hebrew*, trans. R. Ginsburg, vol. 7 [Tel Aviv, 2009], 20).
96. Pnina Galpaz-Feller. *VaYoled: Relations between Parents and Children in Biblical Stories and Laws* (Jerusalem, 2006), 16.

The gradual detachment between the dove and the ark, between the dove and Noah, is the gradual detachment that occurs between every growing child and his or her parents, until they become established as an autonomous person. At first, the dove cannot find rest anywhere but in its mother's arms. Next, the dove makes real contact with the outside world, bringing an olive leaf in its beak. And finally, it breaks away from the ark, from the wooden womb that protected it, and is born anew, accompanied with God's blessing: "Be fruitful and multiply on the earth."

As mentioned, in Genesis 2 the animals come before Adam to see if they are fitting to be his "helpmates," but they are not able to meet this need. Adam's rejection of the animals precedes the creation of the first woman, who is his perfect mate. It was proposed there that the snake is stung by this rejection, and tempts them into sin out of revenge, so that the story ends with tension between humans and animals: "Enmity will I set between you and the woman, and between your offspring and hers" (3:15). But now, as Noah leaves the ark together with the animals he has saved, any such tension has dissipated, and humans and animals leave the womb together as one big happy family.[97]

Noah, then, is presented as the one who restores the animals to land, sending them off as a parent who has cared for them during their vulnerable youth. He is God's partner in the renewal of creation, and this idea is manifest in several other narrative elements.

I briefly mentioned above that from a linguistic perspective, at least, the beginning of the new world is parallel to the rest of the seventh day of the first creation. The key verb root for "rest" of the first creation, SH-B-T, is echoed in God's promise to the world after the Flood: "As long as the earth endures, seedtime and harvest, cold and heat, summer and winter, day and night shall not cease (*yishbotu*)" (8:22). However, the crucial difference between the day of rest granted at the end of the first creation and the end of the world's rebirth is that after this rebirth, God is appeased and makes this promise as a result of Noah's sacrifices: "And the Lord smelled the pleasing aroma, and the Lord said in His heart, 'Never again will I curse the ground because of humans, because

97. Even if this does not refer to an actual "helpmate," the text may be hinting to the semantic field of love and marriage in the description of Noah's separation from the dove.

the inclination of the human heart is evil from his youth. And never again will I destroy all that lives as I have done'" (8:21). Humanity is what leads to God's reconciliation with the new world, and just as Noah sent the dove, Noah is the one who moves God to promise that the new world will endure, even if He fails to state that this new world is "very good." In the words of Joshua Berman:

> In contrast to the first creation, which is entirely executed by God, in the process of its rehabilitation, the human plays a wider role. Noah is the one who builds the ark.... He is the one who sends the birds out on their mission, he is the one who receives the olive branch, who sees that the land has dried up, who goes down himself and brings the animals out of the ark, and he is the one who offers up the sacrifices.[98]

Berman sees this human involvement as atonement for the sins of the old world, and therefore summarizes the human's role thus: "Noah is the high priest who carries out the holy service of the repentance process and the rehabilitation of the world."[99]

I wish to propose a different reading of humankind's role, and to this end I will fast-forward to the next scene – the story of Noah's vineyard and drunken state. I will argue below that this brief episode simultaneously concludes the Flood narrative and introduces the story of the Tower of Babel. Just as God plants a garden – the Garden of Eden – immediately after creating the world, Noah plants a vineyard after the world's rebirth. This connection has different elements of significance, which I will discuss below, but in the context of our discussion I wish to point out that Noah, not God, plants the vineyard after the Flood. In Eden, God curses those who deserved to be cursed (the serpent), while in the vineyard narrative, Noah is the one who pronounces a curse against the guilty party (Ham). Following the birth of the world, God is the one who makes the new soil sprout and bloom; with the world's rebirth, Noah is the one who replants the gardens that have been

98. Berman, "Who in His Goodness Renews," 14.
99. Berman, ibid.

washed away. And the power of blessing and curse, too, is transferred to the sphere of humanity, who, in this new world, is presented as God's partner in re-creation.

HUMANITY'S STATUS: PARTNER WITHOUT A CROWN

The conclusion is that humankind is presented as God's partner in the new world. But this partnership is surprising, given that we saw how humanity is humbled, not elevated, following the Flood. How can it be that he is awarded the place of God's partner in re-creation *after* he has lost the crown of "dominion over the fish of the sea"?

At first glance, this seems to be a contradiction, but in fact, this is a precise reflection of humankind's new status in the postdiluvian world.[100] Before the Flood, God gave free rein to humanity, with full dominion over the world. In light of its miserable failure – "the earth was full of violence" – God was forced to remove humanity from its lofty position, and from this point on, people must prove themselves worthy through their actions, not through an official position of power. This change recalls the process of the Magna Carta (a charter of rights that King John of England was forced to grant to his barons in 1215). Until this point, the king had exercised absolute power by divine right over his subjects; now, following this agreement, he would remain the first and most powerful man in the kingdom – so long as his deeds proved that he was not exploiting his power for his own interests, against the wishes of the nobility. Before the Flood, God created the world alone, and humankind was appointed ruler over a reality that already existed. Under such circumstances, humankind did not feel any obligation towards this reality, but employed it solely for its own ends. After the Flood, however, God allowed humankind to be a partner in creating reality anew; this participation, this responsibility, compels humankind to act responsibly towards the environment he helped create. From now on, he feels obligation towards the animals he saved and the world he replanted, not just towards himself and his own needs. Humanity may

100. In 2016, I taught a course entitled "Diachronic and Synchronic Readings of Genesis" at Bar-Ilan University. I raised this debate to the participants and the above suggestion was proposed by Dr. Udi Shevach. I owe him my thanks.

have been stripped of its crown, but slowly, surely, through careful partnership with the Creator, and hard work and responsibility through its own actions, it has the power to work its way back up to the top, to rightfully regain its crown.

> Judaism considered the *imago* element to be not a gratuitous grant bestowed upon man but rather a challenge to be met by man; not as an endowment fashioned by God but rather as a mission to be implemented, as a *hyle,* formless matter to be molded by man. Perhaps the central norm in our ethical system is related to *Imago Dei,* to be like God, reflect His image, become a Divine being, live like a creature who bears resemblance to its Maker.[101]

101. Soloveitchik, *Family Redeemed,* 7.

The Covenant of the Rainbow: Growth and Fulfillment (9:8–17)

After Noah offers up sacrifices, God decides that He will never destroy the earth again. God makes this declaration to Himself, "in His heart": "And the Lord smelled the pleasing aroma, and the Lord said in His heart, 'Never again will I curse the ground because of humans, because the inclination of the human heart is evil from his youth. And never again will I destroy all that lives as I have done'" (8:21). Some read this as a vow rather than a statement,[1] but even if so, God does not pronounce it to anyone else. This declaration is reiterated at the narrative's conclusion, sounded out loud to humanity, in the covenant of the rainbow. While these endings conclude the two threads of the Flood

1. Shevuot 37a. See also Lorberbaum, "Rainbow," 514–515. See also Rashi on Gen. 8:21: "Something repeated twice is an oath, as it says, 'As I swore after the waters of Noah,' and we did not find an oath, only it was repeated twice – for something repeated twice is an oath."

narrative similarly (to the effect that the world will never be destroyed again),[2] this repetition is not detrimental to the sequence; after God decides never to destroy the world again, He informs Noah of this decision and forms a covenant with him.

The text refers to God's commitment never to destroy the world as a "*brit*," a "covenant." In the Bible, this term can signify a one-sided commitment,[3] but it is more convenient to read it as a mutual agreement. Even if this contract is formed between two unequal parties (such as a feudal contract), it is colored with tones of mutual commitment. Is there any element of human commitment in the covenant of the rainbow, or does its fulfillment rest solely with God?

Reading the covenant in context, aspects of human commitment can be found. As Rashi implies, "Noah was afraid to engage in reproduction, until the Holy One, blessed be He, promised him that He will never destroy the world again, and so He did."[4] Before the covenant, God blesses (and, perhaps, commands) Noah and his sons to be fruitful and multiply, to begin the world's population anew: "And God blessed Noah and his sons, and said to them, 'Be fruitful and multiply, and fill the earth.... As for you, be fruitful and multiply, increase greatly on the earth and multiply in it'" (9:1–7). This is no easy task; Noah and his sons leave the ark to set foot upon the eroded soil of a devastated world. Decayed corpses of humans and animals litter the drowned heaps of vegetation. Is there any purpose in starting anew – what if another flood should ravage the earth? How can Noah and his sons bear to bring new life to such a bleak world? At first, "be fruitful and multiply" is presented as a blessing: "And God blessed Noah and his sons," but by the end of the section, it sounds like an order: "As for you, be

2. Some see in the conclusion featuring the name of the Tetragrammaton more total commitment that the world will not be destroyed, while the story in God's name only commits to no more floods – the world can theoretically still be destroyed by fire, for example (Sibley Towner, "Genesis 9:8–17," *Interpretation* 63 [2009]: 168–171).
3. See, for example, Pancratius Beentjes, "Partner-Partij-Paniek: De Bijbelse Notie 'Verbond' en zijn Problemen," *Collationes* 21 (1991): 287–300. He reaches the conclusion that the word "covenant" should be understood in the sense of "commitment" or "festive promise." He discusses the rainbow as an example.
4. Rashi on Gen. 9:9.

fruitful and multiply, increase greatly on the earth and multiply in it." There is no contradiction between the two formulations, but this subtle shift reflects the characters' emotional state. A blessing is not enough; the weary survivors must be actively ordered to start a family in order to ensure the future of humankind.[5]

The covenant of the rainbow, then, is the other side of the coin: Noah and his family must carry on and bring new life into the world despite the painful desolation around them. God, on His part, promises that He will never wipe out their world again, that this new life will never suffer from such total destruction. Some analyze the verses in context even further, and argue that this covenant is fully mutual, and God will not destroy the world on the condition that humanity, on its part, refrains from murder, and commits to executing justice against any who break this pact: "Whoever sheds the blood of man, by man shall his blood be shed" (9:6).[6] According to this reading, the covenant is reexamined in Isaiah 24, when the prophet hints that it has been violated: "For the earth was defiled under its inhabitants, because they transgressed teachings, violated laws, broke the ancient covenant" (24:5).[7] I find this reading far-fetched; I do not think the covenant of the rainbow should be seen as a fully mutual covenant. Its main focus is God's promise never to bring another flood, but its context does show that humanity, in turn, commits to sustaining the world through bearing children, while God commits to preserving the world that humanity builds. Yair Lorberbaum claims that this covenant is necessarily one-sided, as God also makes this promise to the animals: "The covenant cannot be other than one-sided, as God's commitment is toward 'every living creature that is with you, the birds, the cattle,' and so on, as well as toward the land itself."[8] Given that the other side's

5. Compare to Radak on Gen. 9:9: "And 'I' adds to what He said, 'As for you, be fruitful and multiply.' That is, you deal with populating the world, and I, too, will maintain its existence, that the world's population will never be wiped out again."
6. On the chiastic structure of the verse, see, for example, Anthony R. Ceresko, "The Chiastic Word Pattern in Hebrew," *CBQ* 38 (1976): 305.
7. Steven D. Mason, "Another Flood? Genesis 9 and Isaiah's Broken Eternal Covenant," *JSOT* 32 (2008): 177–198.
8. Yair Lorberbaum, "The Rainbow in the Cloud: An Anger-Management Device," *The Journal of Religion* 89 (2009): 521–522.

condition is merely to exist – to be fruitful and multiply – then animals, too, can also be committed members of this pact. This is not a binding legal contract, of course, but rather a symbolic covenant that presents both sides as responsible for the world's existence. Every living creature will reproduce, and God, on His part, will not destroy the world. This is subtly reflected by comparing the opening part of the covenant with the order to be fruitful and multiply two verses earlier: "*As for Me*, look, *I* am establishing My covenant with you" (9:9), which is preceded two verses earlier with: "*As for you*, be fruitful and multiply, increase greatly on the earth and multiply in it" (9:7).[9] Thus, both parties must commit to the world's continuity.

The covenant of the rainbow can be divided into three parts, three divine speeches. Three titles divide the unit into three short speeches (vv. 8–11; 12–16; 17):

> **(8–11):** *And God said to Noah and his sons with him*, "As for me, look, I am establishing My covenant with you and your offspring after you, and with every living creature that is with you – with the birds, the cattle, and every beast of the earth with you, from all that came out of the ark to all the beasts of the earth. I will establish my covenant with you, that never again will all flesh be cut off by waters of a flood, nor will there ever again be a flood to destroy the earth."
>
> **(12–16):** *And God said*, "This is the sign of the covenant that I am giving between Me and you and every living creature that is with you, for all future generations. My bow I have given in the clouds, and it shall be a sign of the covenant between Me and the earth. When I bring clouds over the earth and the bow is seen in the clouds, I will remember My covenant between Me and you and every living creature of all flesh, and never again shall the waters become a flood to destroy all flesh. When the bow is in the clouds, I will see it and remember the everlasting covenant between God and every living creature, all flesh that is upon the earth."

9. Cassuto, *From Adam to Noah*, 128.

> (17): *And God said to Noah,* "This is the sign of the covenant I have established between Me and all flesh upon the earth."

The difference between the first two speeches is obvious. The first speech is God's promise that a flood will never destroy the world again. This is the main content of the covenant and God's commitment, and it is addressed not only to humankind, but to all living creatures, every living thing that was washed away in the Flood.[10] In this section, there is no mention of the rainbow.

However, the main subject of the second speech is the rainbow. There is no content of the actual covenant, but the token of its fulfillment: "When I bring clouds over the earth and the bow is seen in the clouds, I will remember My covenant." Does God really need a reminder? Is there any fear He might forget? Cassuto suggests that the main purpose of this "reminder" is for humanity:

> The sign will be of greater service to mankind than to God.... The fact that the Bible tells us here that God *announced* to them the sign implies that it is to them that the announcement is important. They will always see the sign, and this constant observation will be a sign and token of the promise of God, who remembers the covenant.[11]

Others, however, read the text more literally – as an actual reminder for God:

> Even before its establishment as a symbol filled with significance, the rainbow is intended to serve God as a kind of instrument for controlling His own wrath. To use another, albeit anachronistic,

10. On God's inclusion of the animals, see Simon De Vries, "God's Provision for the Well-Being of Living Creatures in Genesis 9," in *Literary Encounters with the Reign of God*, ed. S. H. Ringe and H. C. Paul (Atlanta, 2003), 89–103; Olley, "Mixed Blessings." As I already commented, this seems to be related to the bond that was formed between human and animal after the Flood.
11. Cassuto, *From Noah to Abraham*, 139. Emphasis in the original.

> term: the rainbow is a mechanism for anger management, which God created as a device for controlling His anger.[12]

As is typical with such debates, there is merit to both sides of the argument. If people also have certain obligation towards this covenant, then the sign is also intended as a reminder for them. If the world ever looks up at the stormy skies and fears that another flood is coming, the rainbow will be a soothing reminder of God's promise. It is no coincidence that the rainbow stretches from the sky down onto the earth; it is an arc of color that joins heaven and earth, God and humanity, together.

However, the literal reading, that the rainbow serves as a sign for God, also has weight. The most convincing proof for this reading is the slight variation of the introductions to the two speeches. God makes the first speech to Noah and his sons: "And God said to Noah and to his sons with him" (9:8). This speech is addressed to Noah and his family, and it is imperative that they hear what He has to say. Thanks to God's promise, they can now raise families without fear that at any given moment, the waters of the deep will come bursting up from the ground to engulf them all. Humanity needs to hear this promise, to hear this reassurance. The second speech, however, is not addressed to anyone; it opens with "And God said" (v. 12).[13] God's first speech constantly focuses on His addressees: "I am establishing My covenant *with you and your offspring after you*, and with every living creature that is *with you* – with the birds, the cattle, and every beast of the earth *with you*, from all that came out of the ark to all the beasts of the earth. I will establish my covenant *with you* ..." (vv. 9–11). In contrast, the second speech focuses on God's role: "*My* bow *I* have given in the clouds, and it shall be a sign of the covenant between Me and the earth. When *I bring* clouds over the earth and the bow is

12. Lorberbaum, "Rainbow," 524. Abrabanel linked this debate to the question of whether the word "*uritiha*," in reference to "seeing" the rainbow, refers to God seeing it or to everyone seeing it in general. See his commentary on Genesis 9.
13. Radak, who believes that the sign was for human purposes (like Cassuto), felt a need to add the recipients. He writes on Gen. 9:12: "And God said – its meaning is, to Noah and his sons. This is the sign that I am giving you so that you will not be afraid of a flood of water when I bring rain upon the earth."

seen in the clouds, *I will remember* My covenant between Me and you and every living creature of all flesh, and never again shall the waters become a flood to destroy all flesh. When the bow is in the clouds, *I will see it and I will remember* the everlasting covenant" (vv. 13–16). In this speech, God and His remembrance is the focus; the rainbow will move God to remember His promise. Just as a person dons his tzitzit or winds his tefillin around his arm as a physical reminder of his connection with God, the rainbow breaking through the clouds is a physical reminder for God, of the covenant He formed with all living creatures.

But what about the third speech, the speech that makes no obvious contribution, the speech that seems to be entirely repetitive? This brief speech, just one verse long, seems to be an official conclusion for the covenant, and the second speech in particular (as Radak, for example, argues).[14] The similarity between the beginning of the second speech and the third speech creates a clear framework:

> "This is the sign of the covenant that I am making between Me and you and every living creature that is with you, for all future generations." (v. 12)

> "This is the sign of the covenant I have established between Me and all flesh upon the earth." (v. 17)

As often happens in the case of literary frameworks, there are certain fundamental differences between the opening and the conclusion. Here, a certain process develops over the course of the covenant, and culminates in the brief closing speech. This process is related to the animals' place within this covenant:[15]

> (9–11) As for Me, look, I am establishing My covenant with you and your offspring after you, and with every living creature

14. Radak on Gen. 9:17: "He repeated this to Noah a third time to encourage him and to make a complete promise to him."
15. Westermann treats this development differently (*Genesis*, vol. 1, 472).

> that is with you – with the birds, the cattle, and every beast of the earth with you, from all that came out of the ark to all the beasts of the earth. I will establish My covenant with you, that never again will all flesh be cut off by waters of a flood, nor will there ever again be a flood to destroy the earth."
>
> (12) And God said, "This is the sign of the covenant that I am making between Me and you and every living creature that is with you, for all future generations."
>
> (13) "it shall be a sign of the covenant between Me and the earth."
>
> (15) "I will remember My covenant between Me and you and every living creature of all flesh, and never again shall the waters become a flood to destroy all flesh."
>
> (16) "I will see it and remember the everlasting covenant between God and every living creature, all flesh that is upon the earth."
>
> (17) And God said to Noah, "This is the sign of the covenant I have established between Me and all flesh upon the earth."

Initially, in verses 9–11, there is a sense that Noah's family is the focus of the covenant, while the animals are included as appendages, only included as part of God's promise because of humankind: "And with every living creature *that is with you* – with the birds, the cattle, and every beast of the earth with you … I will establish My covenant with you, that never again will all flesh be cut off." "All flesh" will be safe, thanks to the covenant that God is forming with Noah and his family.

The next stage, verse 12, which focuses on the sign of the rainbow, also maintains the idea that "all flesh" will be spared because of the covenant between humanity and God. Here, too, it states: "This is the sign of the covenant that I am making between Me and you *and* every living creature *that is with you.*" At this stage, it is even theoretically possible to think that the covenant only includes animals who are part of human culture, as in, only the animals that are "with you."

The next stage, verse 13, sees a significant change, even if only an implicit one. The covenant is between God and "the earth," a formulation that could apply to any creature of the earth.

Two verses later, God establishes that the covenant is "between Me and you *and* every living creature." Here, the animals' involvement does not depend on humans; they are included within the covenant with a simple, unconditional "and." Both humans and animals are equally part of God's covenant; one is not secondary to the other.

The fifth stage, verse 16, sees a real change – animals are not only presented in equal standing to humans, but they are included within the same category – people and animals are both defined as "every living creature, all flesh that is upon the earth." Both people and animals are "living creatures," and the covenant therefore applies to them equally. Note that this formulation combines the two previous stages: the covenant's members are "living creatures" (the term used in verse 12) who are "upon the earth" (which refers back to verse 13).

This end of this process is reflected in the final verse of the covenant, verse 17. Here, both people and animals are referred to together as "all flesh upon the earth." Not "all living creatures," the language used until now – the focus is on their flesh, their physical being. Their physical existence, the sense of their feet standing on firm ground, will always be guaranteed, as opposed to solely because of the life-spirit within them.[16]

Therefore, the third speech acts not only as the conclusion of the covenant, but also an advancement of it. This may indeed explain why it deserves its own introductory speech, "And God said to Noah," instead of representing the end of the second speech.

ESTABLISHING THE COVENANT AND ITS SIGN

I believe that there is a further development in the third speech, one which justifies referring to this lone verse as a "speech" in itself. In order to discuss this development, I first wish to explore the expression "*lehakim brit*," "to establish a covenant," which features throughout the first speech, thus establishing a linguistic framework: "Look, I am establishing

16. This development is consistent with the language used after the Flood, as mentioned above, in my analysis of the Flood narrative.

My covenant with you.... I will establish My covenant with you." What does this verb, "*lehakim*," "to establish" or "set up," mean in the context of a covenant? Is there any difference between it and the common term "*likhrot brit*," which literally means "to cut" a covenant (as used in this sense for the first time in the "covenant of the pieces" with Abram in Genesis 15:18)?

Many scholars hold that there is a substantial difference between *lehakim* and *likhrot* – that the former verb means "to uphold, to fulfill" an existing covenant rather than to form a new one, with emphasis on the fulfillment of existing terms. They believe that *lehakim* used in the expression *lehakim brit* retains its usual meaning, such as: "Would He speak and not act, promise and not fulfill (*yekimena*)" (Num. 23:19); "Her husband Elkanah said to her, 'Do what seems best to you; stay behind until you wean him. Only may the Lord fulfill (*yakem*) His word'" (I Sam. 1:23); "On that day, I will fulfill (*akim*) all that I have spoken against Eli and his house" (I Sam. 3:12).[17] In these verses, and many others, the verb *lehakim* means to fulfill an existing commitment.

If so, then *lehakim brit* has the same sense as *lehakim davar*, meaning to fulfill someone's word or promise, as in: "But it is because of their wickedness that the Lord your God is dispossessing those nations before you, and in order to fulfill the word (*hakim et hadavar*) that the Lord made to your fathers, Abraham, Isaac, and Jacob" (Deut. 9:5). And, it has the same sense as "*lehakim shevua*," "to fulfill an oath," as in: "For to you and your descendants I will give all these lands, and I will fulfill the oath (*vehakimoti et hashevua*) I swore to Abraham your father" (Gen. 26:3). To "fulfill" a covenant is not to form it anew, which would be *likhrot brit*, but to fulfill an existing covenant. One of many proofs for this distinction can be found in Deuteronomy (whose main theme is the covenant formed on the plains of Moab). Throughout the book, the verb *likhrot* appears again and again in the sense of establishing a new covenant,[18] but in just one verse, the book deviates from its usual language and uses the verb *lehakim* – "Remember that it is the Lord your God who gives you the power to get wealth, in order to fulfill the covenant (*hakim et brito*)

17. See also I Kings 2:4; Jer. 29:10; 33:14; 34:18.

18. Such as Deut. 5:2; 5:3; 7:2; 28:69; 29:13.

that He made on oath with your fathers, as it is this day" (Deut. 8:18). This refers to an existing covenant, made with Israel's ancestors, not to a new covenant, and therefore *lehakim* is suitable.[19]

This reading is logical and illuminates many verses in the Bible, with one exception: the covenant of the rainbow. God seems to be forming a brand-new covenant with all flesh after the Flood, so understanding the verb *lehakim* as the fulfillment of an earlier covenant is problematic. This has led some to argue that the term also refers to the formation of a new covenant.[20] However, does the first theory need to be dismissed? Some scholars have suggested that God is referring to an earlier covenant which is not explicitly mentioned in the text, though this is unlikely and unconvincing.[21] Equally unconvincing is the theory that this covenant is a continuation of what God tells Noah on the eve of the Flood: "But I will fulfill My covenant with you, and you will enter the ark, you and your sons and your wife and your sons' wives with you" (6:18).[22] While this verse does make an important contribution, as I will shortly discuss, this reading does not actually solve the problem, since this verse, too, uses the verb *lehakim*, implying that here, too, God is referring to an earlier covenant. So, the problem is moved back earlier, and the question still stands: Which existing covenant is God promising to fulfill?

---

19. It may be that Rashi has this intent in his commentary on Gen. 9:11: "And I will fulfill – I will give My covenant fulfillment." See also Jer. 34 – the combination of the verb *likhrot* in verses 8, 13, and 15, as well as the use of *lehakim* in verse 18. The proposed distinction also clarifies the use of both verbs throughout the book of Ezekiel. The verb *likhrot* discusses new covenants in 17:13, 34:25, 37:26, while the verb *lehakim* relates to the fulfillment of the covenant of Sinai (16:60; 16:62). The topic of oaths made by women, discussed in Numbers, can also be included within this discussion, as the verb *lehakim* there refers to whether the woman's father or husband allows her vow to be fulfilled (Num. 30:2–17).
20. For example, Paul Williamson, *Abraham, Israel and the Nations: The Patriarchal Promise and Its Covenantal Development in Genesis* (JSOTSup 315; Sheffield, 2001), ch. 6; Day, *From Creation to Babel*, 123–136.
21. William Dumbrell, *Covenant and Creation: A Theology of the Old Testament Covenants* (Exeter, 1984), 26. Wenham, similarly, writes that it seems that God had already formed a covenant with Noah that was not mentioned in the text (*Genesis*, 175).
22. Hamilton, *Genesis*, 316.

One possible suggestion is that God is referring back to the decision He made in His heart – that He will never destroy the world again. He had already reached this decision and is not stating it for the first time – hence the use of the verb *lehakim* rather than *likhrot*. He now forms a covenant with the world in order to fulfill the decision He already made in His heart.

Nonetheless, out of all the suggestions made in this context, I find Jacob Milgrom's the most likely. He suggests that the expression "*lehakim brit*" is suitable here because God is referring back to the creation of the first man and His blessing as a kind of commitment to preserve the existence of humankind, and now He is renewing His covenant through Noah and his family,[23] similarly to the words of Jeremiah: "Thus says the Lord: If I have not made My covenant with day and night, if I have not appointed the laws of heaven and earth…" (Jer. 33:25). This reading is supported by the aforementioned use of the verb "*lehakim*" at the beginning of the Flood narrative: ""But I will *fulfill* My covenant with you, and you will enter the ark, you, and your sons, and your wife and your sons' wives with you" (6:18). The fact that God is about to destroy the world moves Him to declare that He will not wipe out humanity completely – He will *fulfill* His covenant to perpetuate humanity through Noah, his wife, and their sons.[24]

Whether or not we adopt this explanation, the verb used throughout the first speech is "*lehakim*." In the second speech, another verb makes an appearance – "*latet*," "to give": "And God said, 'This is the sign of the covenant that I am giving (*noten*) between Me and you…. My bow I have given (*natati*) in the clouds." This verb is rare in the context of covenants,[25] but it is nonetheless suitable, as God is not using it to

23. Jacob Milgrom, *Leviticus 17–22* (AB: New York, 2000), 2343–2346. His second suggestion is also interesting – that the verb refers to his sons (the covenant was formed with Noah, but they need to fulfill it).

24. Cassuto, *From Noah to Abraham*, 68. Other ancient commentators who interpret thus (Rabbi David HaEdni, Abravanel, Netziv) are mentioned in Elchanan Samet, *Studies in the Weekly Parasha*, Series 2 (Jerusalem, 2004), 23–25.

25. Compare to another exception, God's words about Phineas: "Therefore, say, I hereby give (*noten*) him My covenant of peace" (Num. 25:12).

refer to the actual covenant, but to the *sign* of the covenant itself.[26] There are several verses that use the verb *latet* in reference to signs, such as: "If there appears among you a prophet or a dream-diviner and he gives you a sign or a portent" (Deut. 13:2); "Now, please swear to me by the Lord – for I have shown you loyalty – that you, too, shall be loyal to my father's house; give me a true sign" (Josh. 2:12); "Therefore, my Lord will give you a sign – look, the young woman is with child and about to give birth to a son" (Is. 7:14). In these contexts, the verb "*latet*" has a similar meaning to the verb "*lasim*," to put or to set – the sign is not given over to another entity, but is set up in a certain place to serve as the reminder of a promise to be fulfilled. Rahab ties a scarlet thread in her window to remind the spies of their promise to save her; God spreads a rainbow across the sky to recall His own promise.

If so, the different verbs reflect the different focuses of each speech: the covenant is "fulfilled," "upheld," while the sign of the covenant is "given" to serve as a reminder for the covenant's fulfillment. This difference leads to another, more important distinction for our purposes: a covenant is fulfilled between two parties, while a sign need only be "given" for one party. The tefillin worn on the forehead are for all to see, while the sages believed that the tefillin worn on the arm should be covered by a person's sleeve; the Bible states, "and it shall be *for you* as a sign on your arm" (Ex. 13:9), which is interpreted to mean, for *you* and not for others. The first speech focuses on both parties – a covenant has no meaning if it is one sided – and it therefore makes sense that it emphasizes God's audience and not just God Himself: "And God said to Noah and to the sons who were with him…" (9:8).

In contrast, the second speech, while addressed to the recipients of God's promise, is nonetheless relevant without any audience. The sign's purpose is to remind God of His promise to never bring another Flood. As Lorberbaum eloquently puts it, God is setting a reminder for Himself: "I will remember My covenant between Me and you….

26. I believe John Day is incorrect when he brings Genesis 9:12 as a proof that the verb *latet* also refers to the covenant (Day, *From Creation to Babel*, 123n1). Rather, this verb refers to the sign of the covenant. Cassuto also debates whether the verb *natan* refers to the covenant or to its sign (Cassuto, *From Noah to Abraham*, 135).

When the bow is in the clouds, I will see it and remember the everlasting covenant" (9:15–16). Aptly enough, the introduction of this speech only mentions God and omits His addressees: "And God said" (9:12).

However, in light of this division, it emerges that the sign of the covenant has a further role: "And God said to Noah, 'This is the sign of the covenant I have established between Me and all flesh upon the earth'" (9:17). In this brief concluding remark, the verb *lehakim* refers to the sign of the covenant itself!

It may be that this verb refers to the covenant itself, as in, "This is the sign – for the covenant I have established," but a more straightforward reading implies that the verb is linked to the actual sign of the covenant. This suggests that the sign itself serves a purpose beyond that of reminding God of His promise – with the third speech, the rainbow is colored as a sign for all flesh upon the land as well. The rainbow will spread across the sky to calm human fears that each rainstorm will turn into another cataclysmic Flood, that each time rain falls, life on earth will be washed away once more. The rainbow will curve across the sky for humanity's sake, too, but this only becomes evident with the third speech, at the very end of the unit. This explains why the third and final speech is introduced with "And God said *to Noah*" (9:17).

The structure of the unit outlines the covenant in several stages, like a legal contract. The first stage lays out the "conditions" of this covenant, where God promises humans and animals that the world will never be destroyed again. The second stage describes the sign that God will use in order to remember this promise. And the third stage describes how this sign is also relevant for the recipients of this promise. Through this process, the rainbow that stretches from heaven to earth becomes a collective reminder, for God in heaven and for all creatures on earth.

THE RAINBOW CONNECTION

Why was the rainbow chosen to symbolize God's promise that rain from the sky would never again turn into a flood? The medieval commentaries debate whether the verse implies that this is the first time a rainbow ever appears in the sky (Ibn Ezra and Radak) or whether God chose to charge an existing phenomenon with new meaning (Nahmanides). Either way, the question of why the rainbow was chosen as a symbol of this renewed covenant remains.[27] Among the various suggestions, one likely explanation is that the shape of the rainbow, its curve from the sky to the ground, represents the connection between heaven and earth,[28] but the most widely accepted interpretation is that of Nahmanides:[29]

> The reason for this sign is that the rainbow was not shaped so that its ends reach up towards heaven, so that it would seem as if heaven is shooting towards the earth – "And He sent His arrows and scattered them" to the earth (cf. Ps. 18:15) – but He made it the opposite shape, to show that heaven will not shoot towards the earth. And this is the way of fighters – they turn their bows around when they call for peace against whoever is against them, when they have no intention of shooting arrows against them.[30]

Nahmanides compares the rainbow to a bow and arrow. Not only does its shape recall the archers' weapon of war (which may be the source

27. Ellen van Wolde claims that the "bow" in question is not a rainbow, but a bow of war – it was common for Mesopotamian gods to be represented with a bow in their hand (van Wolde, "One Bow or Another? A Study of the Bow in Genesis 9:8–17," *VT* 63 [2013]: 124–149). As the full expression is "bow in the clouds," her claim is problematic, although there is no effective difference between the readings, as the rainbow seems to be alluding to the weapon of war. Paul Kissling writes similarly, though he eventually concludes that it is a multifaceted symbol that expresses different aspects (Kissling, "The Rainbow in Genesis 9:12–17: A Triple Entendre," *Stone Campbell Journal* 4 [2001]: 249–261). Kilmer makes the interesting suggestion that the goddess Nintu's necklace of sapphires (made from flies) that she dons so as not to forget the flood (*Atrahasis*, Tablet III, lines 273–275) can be compared to the rainbow (Anne D. Kilmer, "The Symbolism of the Flies in the Mesopotamian Flood Myth and Some Further Implications," in *Language, Literature, and History: Philological and Historical Studies Presented to Erica Reiner*, ed. F. Rochberg Halton [AOS 67: Winona Lake, 1987], 175–180). This suggests that the rainbow is chosen for its beauty, like a necklace that hangs in the sky.
28. Michael Ferber, *A Dictionary of Literary Symbols*, 2nd ed. (Cambridge, 2007), 166.
29. As shown by Yosef Ofer and Jonathan Jacobs, *Nahmanides' Torah Commentary Addenda Written in the Land of Israel* (Jerusalem/Alon Shvut, 2013), 113. See their discussion on the connection between Nahmanides' interpretation of the rainbow's meaning and the question of whether the rainbow existed since creation or whether it was created for this covenant.
30. Nahmanides on Gen. 9:12.

of the rainbow's name, "*keshet be'anan*" literally meaning "a bow in the cloud"),[31] but it echoes the biblical notion that God fights by shooting arrows down from the heavens.[32] Even if this is only true in a figurative sense, the rainbow can still be characterized as God's weapon – turned backwards as a symbol of truce.[33]

Moreover, this sense of reconciliation is reflected not only through the bow's shape, but through its sheath of cloud. The rainbow is never referred to as just a bow; throughout the covenant, it is always associated with clouds: "My bow I have given in the clouds... when I bring clouds over the earth and My bow is seen in the clouds... when the bow is in the clouds" (9:13–16). The cloud is a prevalent biblical symbol of covering and concealment, as in, for example, "The Presence of the Lord dwelled on Mount Sinai, and the cloud hid it for six days" (Ex. 24:16). Or, compare this to Ezekiel's prophecy about Pharaoh: "I will cover the sky and darken its stars; I will cover the sun with clouds and the moon shall not give its light" (Ezek. 32:7). The symbol of the covenant is not just an upturned bow; it is a bow covered in cloud, sheathed, concealed, obscured. In the ancient Near East, bows were sometimes broken as rites of peace when forming a treaty,[34] so that the image of a bow sheathed in cloud is an apt symbol of peace and reconciliation.

---

31. K. L. Younger, "*Keshet*," *NIDOTTE* 3: 1004.
32. Compare to the words of Abrabanel (on Gen. 9): "It is called 'bow' because it is shaped like a semi-circle... forming a kind of warrior's bow, and the text might be describing the sun here as a bow because the ancients all referred to the sun's rays as 'arrows' and to the sun as 'God's bow,' as rays emanate from the sun like arrows from a warrior's bow." Concerning the bow and arrows as weapons in Greek literature, see Ferber, *Literary Symbols*, 166. Also, see further there about the development of the symbol of the bow in later literature. He concludes his survey thus: "If so, the bow became the chief symbol of the rivalry between science and poetry" (ibid., 167).
33. This is also the most accepted approach in modern scholarship, since Wellhausen. There have been attempts to read the bow as a warning to humanity against wasting the world's resources for individual benefit, but this idea has not caught on. See a discussion in, for example, Udo Rüterswörden, "Der Bogen in Genesis 9, Militärhistorische und traditionsgeschichtliche Erwägungen zu einem biblischen Symbol," *Ugarit-Forschungen* 20 (1988): 247–263. He also brings evidence of the biblical connection between the rainbow and the bow as a weapon.
34. Nahum M. Waldman, "The Breaking of the Bow," *JQR* 69 (1978–9): 82–88. See also Zech. 9:10.

Nonetheless, God's flooding of the world is not portrayed as an onslaught of arrows shot from a bow. There are other places in the Bible where such imagery is used, such as the destruction of Sodom, when fire comes down from the sky and "the sun came out against the land" (Gen. 19:23), as if launching an attack.[35] In the Flood narrative, the world is flooded with water from above and from below; the text does not invoke war imagery at all. The symbol of an upturned, cloud-sheathed bow as a sign of truce is not consistent with God's method of destruction.

Another possibility emerges from the rainbow's shape. Rather than symbolizing the arc of the archer's bow, the rainbow's arc may be a reflection of the sky's reconstruction, of the supportive arch that is set in place following the Flood. The Flood, after all, is portrayed as the "sky falling down," as the boundaries set between land and water at creation being swept away, as the floodgates of heaven opening and drowning the earth. At the Flood's end, these boundaries are reinstated: "And the wellsprings of the deep and the floodgates of heaven were closed, and the rains from the heavens ceased" (8:2). Now, with His promise never to flood the earth again, God reveals a glimpse of the rebuilt sky, of the shimmering arc that supports the rebuilt heavens. Now the upper waters are safely stored away, and never again will they pour down to drown the earth. The rainbow, then, is a visual expression of the new, reinforced, secure structure of the heavens.[36] While this is one possible reading, as mentioned above, the rainbow's full biblical name, "the bow in the clouds," supports the first suggestion that it is like a weapon, not to mention that domes and arcs only became prevalent during the Roman period, so it is problematic to project this imagery onto the biblical text.

---

35. For a broader discussion of this verse see Grossman, *Abram to Abraham*, 314–316. For the option that Deborah's song also has military connotations, "Thus may all Your enemies perish, O Lord, and may His friends be like the rising sun" (Judges 5:31), see ibid., 516n42.
36. This interesting idea was proposed by Laurence A. Turner, "The Rainbow as the Sign of the Covenant in Genesis ix 11–13," *FT* 43 (1993): 123. A similar, but subtler, formulation can be found in Kissling, "Rainbow," 259–260.

The Covenant of the Rainbow and the Covenant of Circumcision

The rainbow also plays another role in the development from God's covenant with Noah to the covenant of circumcision with Abraham; indeed, many have discussed the connection between these two covenants.[37] In the context of the discussion about eating animals, I mentioned that this postdiluvian reality reflects the new world order in which not all humans are invited to rule the world, but that a single nation will be chosen to do so (this nation will be chosen after the next unit, when humanity is divided into nationalities).

This is inherently connected to the relationship between the two main covenants in the book of Genesis: the rainbow is the symbol of the first (Gen. 9), and circumcision is the symbol of the second (Gen. 17). I have shown elsewhere that a comparison of the two conveys that the two covenants are profoundly connected yet dramatically different,[38] and with the reader's permission, I will bring this comparison again in order to reveal yet another shade of the rainbow's significance:

The Covenant with Noah (Gen. 9)	**The Covenant with Abraham (Gen. 17)**
As for you, be fruitful and multiply, increase greatly on the earth and multiply in it	I will multiply you greatly... And I will make you very, very fruitful
As for me, look, I am fulfilling My covenant with you and your offspring after you	And I will fulfill My covenant between Me and you, and your offspring after you

37. See especially Nahmanides on Gen. 9:12–13; Sean E. McEvenue, *The Narrative Style of the Priestly Writer* (AnBib 50: Rome, 1971), 170–171; Cassuto, *Genesis and Its Structure*, 41–43; Renate Brandscheidt, "Schöpfung im Bund: Die Schöpfungs und Bundeskonzeption in der priesterlichen Urgeschichte," *Trierer Theologische Zeitschrift* 123 (2014): 1–21; Menachem Leibtag, "The Significance of Circumcision on the Eighth Day," *Alon Shvut* 130 (1991): 93–100 (the latter two contributed to this comparison regarding the creation narrative as well).

38. Grossman, *Abram to Abraham*, 244–247.

and with every living creature that is with you – with the birds, the cattle, and every beast of the earth with you, from all that came out of the ark to all the beasts of the earth. I will establish My covenant with you	
for all future generations	throughout their generations, as an everlasting covenant
My bow I have given in the clouds, and it shall be a sign of the covenant between Me and the earth.	And you shall circumcise the flesh of your foreskin, and it shall be a sign of the covenant between Me and you
I will see it and remember the everlasting covenant	throughout their generations, as an everlasting covenant

Beyond these linguistic connections, God opens His conversation with Abraham with the words, "Walk before Me and be blameless" (17:1), which, of course, is in dialogue with the description of Noah as a "righteous man, blameless in his generation; Noah walked with God" (6:9). Additionally, just as the covenant of circumcision is fulfilled "on the very day that God had spoken to him" (17:23), Noah enters the ark "on that very day... as God had commanded him" (7:13–16).[39]

While many of these parallel phrases are typical covenant discourse,[40] these narratives also share a further, unique connection. The significance of this connection is especially related to the differences

39. Alexander proposed relating the revelation at the end of the Binding of Isaac to this connection. He suggests that the covenant of circumcision has a conditional feel and these blessings only become definite after he withstands the trial of sacrificing his son. Therefore, he holds that the revelation at the end of this scene is related to the covenant of circumcision, and both should be compared, together, to the covenant of the rainbow (Thomas Desmond Alexander, "Genesis 22 and the Covenant of Circumcision," *JSOT* 25 [1983]: 17–22).

40. And indeed, scholars have pointed out linguistic formulae that characterize covenant narratives. See George E. Mendenhall, "Covenant Forms in Israelite Tradition," *BA* 17 (1954): 50–76; Moshe Weinfeld, "The Covenant of Grant in the Old Testament and

between the covenant, differences that reflect the process that humanity undergoes over the generations between Noah and Abraham. There are four main components that differ between the two covenants, thus revealing this development:

1. **The covenant's participants:** The covenant of the rainbow is formed with "all flesh," which includes all of humanity and even animal life as well. This is emphasized throughout the covenant narrative, not only when the covenant is first announced (9:9–10), but also when the symbol is revealed (9:12, 15–16), and even during its brief conclusion (9:17). As we have already discussed, the fact that all living creatures are part of this covenant is so crucial that the inner development of the covenant can be traced through this perspective.[41] In contrast, the covenant of circumcision is only formed with Abraham and his descendants. While Abraham will become "the father of many nations" (17:4), the language of the covenant focuses on Abraham alone: "And I will set a covenant between Me and you" (17:2). Not only are animals excluded, but any humans who are not descended from Abraham are excluded as well.[42]
2. **The site of the covenant:** Noah's covenant is established with focus on "the earth" – that is, the entire world. God makes a pact with all living creatures, wherever they may be on the earth.[43]

in the Ancient Near East," *JAOS* 90 (1970): 184–203; Dennis J. McCarthy, *Treaty and Covenant: A Study in Form in the Ancient Oriental Documents and in the Old Testament* (Rome, 1978).

41. McEvenue shows how more participants are gradually included in the covenant over the course of the first speech (*Narrative Style*, 73). As I have shown, this broadening continues over the next two speeches.
42. Westermann, however, claims that the covenant of circumcision reflects a universal approach similar to that expressed in Gen. 12:3 ("and in you all the families of the earth shall be blessed"), as in both places, the blessing is presented as affecting many nations. While Abraham is indeed blessed as one who will become "the father of many nations," unlike Gen. 12:3, Abraham himself will be the father of these nations, so this still reflects a blessing to an individual rather than a universal blessing.
43. Cassuto famously reads a typological number of keywords within a narrative as proof of the unit's cohesion, especially seven or multiples of seven. In his analysis of

Abraham's covenant, however, is formed within certain geographical boundaries: "And I will give to you and your offspring after you the land in which you are sojourning, *all the land of Canaan* as an everlasting heritage. And I will be their God" (17:8). This juxtaposition implies that the land of Canaan is granted to Abraham and his descendants as part of this covenant, and their special connection with God will be perpetuated through this land. As Rashi already notes: "And *there,* 'I will be [your] God,' but whoever lives out of the land, it is as if I am not their God."[44]

3. **Human commitment:** While the geographical area relevant to the covenant shrinks, the human's duty to God grows. All that is expected of humanity in the covenant of the rainbow is to reproduce for the purpose of maintaining the world's existence; this requirement is, after all, inherent to human and animal nature. In contrast, God makes religious demands of Abraham, moral and physical requirements which are not necessarily natural to human nature: besides enduring the pain of circumcision, Abraham must "walk before God and be blameless" in order to become God's chosen people (17:1). Whatever the precise meaning of this phrase, it clearly exacts moral and religious effort on Abraham's part, efforts that go far beyond natural biological tendencies.[45]

---

the covenant of the rainbow, he mentions the triple repetition of the phrase "on the earth" (vv. 14, 16, 17) as well as the three mentions of the "bow in the clouds" (vv. 13, 14, 16), and the seven occurrences of the word "covenant" in this passage (Cassuto, *From Noah to Abraham,* 135). I have expressed my reservations towards this approach elsewhere (Grossman, *Text and Subtext,* 116–146), but precise numbers aside, the word "covenant" is clearly a keyword in this passage. The word "earth" appears in this unit in completely different contexts, but the final count of seven appearances is probably not coincidental. The phrase "all flesh" is no less salient in this section for appearing "only" five times. The term "earth" is salient in this unit, regardless of number.

44. Rashi on Gen. 17:8, according to the Yemenite manuscript. This is quoted in Avraham Grossman, *Rashi,* trans. J. Linsider (Oxford, 2012), 178, and see there for a broader discussion of Rashi's special attitude towards the land of Israel as is reflected in this interpretation.

45. See further in Grossman, *Abram to Abraham,* 225–227. There, I proposed: "From here [the covenant of circumcision and on], Abraham's relationship with his God is presented as a closer relationship, as two who share an intimate bond, as two who

4. **Ultimate responsibility:** Who is ultimately responsible for the fulfillment of each covenant? Whoever is responsible for the covenant's sign. Whereas God is the one who spreads the rainbow across the sky: "My bow *I* have given in the clouds, and it shall be a sign of the covenant between Me and the earth" (9:13), it is up to Abraham and his descendants to fulfill the sign of their covenant: "And God said to Abraham, 'As for you, you shall keep My covenant, you and your offspring after you, throughout their generations. This is My covenant which *you* shall keep between Me and you, and *your offspring* after you: every male among you shall be circumcised. And *you* shall circumcise the flesh of your foreskin, and it shall be a sign of the covenant between Me and you'" (17:9–11).

These four differences all stem from a single root. The covenant formed with Noah is a "natural" covenant, regarding existence itself. All living creatures are included in this covenant, and in order to fulfill it, all they must do is simply survive, simply exist. The covenant of circumcision with Abraham, however, represents a higher way of life, a covenant built upon the first covenant of mere survival. With this covenant, Abraham commits to a higher moral and religious standard of life, and only a specific group is included – the same group that accepts Abraham's God as their God. In order to show their religious commitment to this covenant, it is man, not God, who is responsible for the fulfillment of its sign; when each son is eight days old, it is the parents who will declare, through circumcision, that the God of Israel is their God, and that fertility and life comes from Him. These religious declarations are missing, of course, from the covenant of the rainbow, which is formed with all flesh, even animals.

There is also development on God's part: In the first covenant, His promise is not to destroy the world, which is effectively passive. With Abraham's covenant, however, He plays a more active role. Rather than

stay together." And indeed, this covenant is a central axis in the broader Abraham narratives, marking the turning point of Abraham's relationship with his Maker (ibid., 505–513).

"live and let live," He tells Abraham *how* to live, and forms a more intimate bond with him. God changes Abraham's name, like the emperors who rename their most loyal subjects as a sign of their protection (like Pharaoh, who gives Joseph another name when he becomes his second in command), and all this in order to "be God to you and your offspring after you" (17:7). Focusing on a single family allows for an intimate connection that cannot be maintained when all of humanity – and every living creature besides – is included within the covenant.[46]

In light of this, a further symbolic meaning of the rainbow emerges in parallel to the symbol of circumcision.[47] Clouds bring rain and make the earth fruitful, but in the Flood narrative, there is so much outpouring of rain that the world's very existence is threatened. I previously suggested that the rainbow is covered, sheathed, by the cloud, but the opposite can also be suggested: "My rainbow I have given in the clouds" (9:13).[48] The rainbow only emerges when sunlight breaks through the clouds; that is, the rainbow usually signifies the end of a storm. The rainbow, in a sense, limits the fertile power of the rainclouds. Similarly, the reproductive organ is obviously related to human fertility, and this virility, this reproductive power, must also be marked with a holy

---

46. Rabbi Itamar Eldar pointed out to me that this process is parallel to the connection between the creation of the world and the building of the Sanctuary (on this connection see, for example, Nechama Leibowitz, *Studies in Shemot – Exodus*, trans. A. Newman [Jerusalem, 1983], 475–482). A limited divine revelation in a defined area allows a revelation to which the whole world can be subjected.
47. The connection between these covenants has surprising expression in Ezekiel's vision of the Heavenly Chariot – there is glowing fire below the loins, and Ezekiel compares this glow to that of the rainbow: "From what appeared as his loins up, I saw a gleam as of amber – what looked like a fire encased in a frame; and *from what appeared as his loins down, I saw what looked like fire.* There was a radiance all about him *like the appearance of the bow which shines in the clouds on a day of rain,* such was the appearance of the surrounding radiance" (Ezek. 1:27–28). Based on this, Bekhor Shor on Gen. 9:13 likens the rainbow to divine revelation: "My bow – it is a great symbol, for the rainbow is the figure of God's glory, as recorded in Ezekiel… when the heavy rains fall, I bring a figure of glory before you, so that you will accept the Divine Presence, and if I had wished to destroy you I would not show you My glory, as it is not the royal way to appear before enemies who are disgraced before him."
48. Mathews, for example, writes that the colorful rainbow, as seen from the earth, pierces the threatening darkness of storm clouds. (*Genesis*, vol. 1, 410).

covenant. The rainbow is parallel to the act of circumcision because both signify that the sweeping force of fertility must be kept in check, thus testifying to the covenant between the world and God.[49] The covenant of the rainbow, concerned with the natural world's existence, is signified by a natural phenomenon related to rain; the covenant of circumcision, concerned with human moral and religious values, is etched upon the human body itself – or, more precisely, upon the bodies of the sons of Abraham, who are committed to walking before God.

49. Sandra Jacobs claims that at Qumran, there were not many symbols of the covenants of the rainbow or of circumcision, as both were associated with sexuality, and these cults downplayed sexuality within their culture (Jacobs, "Expendable Signs: The Covenant of the Rainbow and Circumcision at Qumran," in *The Dead Sea Scrolls in Context: Integrating the Dead Sea Scrolls in the Study of Ancient Texts, Languages, and Cultures*, ed. A. Lange, E. Tov, and M. Weigold [Leiden, 2011], 562–575).

Noah's Vineyard: Family Curse and National Blessing (9:18–29)

Finally, in the last story of Noah's life, the reader hears Noah's voice before he steps off the stage. In a surprising twist, the righteous, blameless one who walks before God is the first person in the world who falls into a drunken, naked stupor in his tent.

Typical of the brief, terse biblical text, more is hidden than revealed in these few lines. Why does Noah become drunk? Does Noah deliberately drink himself into forgetfulness, or does he inadvertently become the first person to learn of the intoxicating, humbling effects of wine?[1]

The most fundamental question that accompanies this brief episode, however, does not touch upon the nature of drunkenness itself, but rather on its connection to nakedness. Noah's nakedness is the main motif of the story and its main complication, and its resolution determines who will be cursed and who will be blessed; who, having

1. Day, *From Creation to Babel*, 147–150.

survived the Flood, will also survive the wrath of the father. What is the meaning of the connection between drunkenness and nakedness? Drunkenness in general may result in different reactions; it is the form that Noah's drunkenness takes – nakedness – that serves as the narrative objective of these brief lines.

The beginning of this interpretative journey, of course, begins with the definition of the narrative unit. This is not always such a complicated task,[2] but in this case, there are reasons to read this narrative as the conclusion of the Flood narrative on one hand, and on the other, as the introduction of a new unit – the story of the dispersion of the nations and the Tower of Babel.

This story can be considered the conclusion of the Flood narrative, as it relates the death of its protagonist, Noah, with the usual formula that accompanies the reader through the first ten generations of human history: "And Noah lived after the flood, three hundred and fifty years. And all the days of Noah were nine hundred and fifty years, and he died" (9:28–29). Following the story of his drunkenness, Noah dies at the ripe old age of 950. These verses conclude the long unit that begins with "the book of the generations of humankind." Moreover, Noah's death also concludes the shorter unit that opens with "the generations of Noah," who begets "three sons, Shem, Ham, and Japheth" (6:9–10). The history of Noah ends with the story of his drunkenness, the blessing and cursing of his sons, and his death. Only then does a new "*toledot*," a new history, begin: "And these are the generations of the sons of Noah, Shem, Ham, and Japheth; sons were born to them after the Flood" (10:1). This new beginning also seems to indicate that the previous episode serves as the conclusion of Noah's story – the story of the Flood.

On the other hand, subtle textual details hint that this narrative is shaped as the beginning of the dispersion of the nations: "The sons of Noah who came out of the ark were Shem, Ham, and Japheth, and *Ham was the father of Canaan*. These three were the sons of Noah, and *from them the whole earth spread out*" (9:18–19). This certainly anticipates the diffusion of the new population over the face of the earth, chapters

2. On the complexity of demarcating biblical narratives, see Yairah Amit, *Reading Biblical Narratives* (Tel Aviv, 2010), 24–31; Grossman, *Text and Subtext*, 182–218.

which also conclude with a similar expression: "From there the Lord scattered them over all the face of earth" (11:9). This generates a strong literary framework for three consecutive units: Noah's drunkenness (the end of ch. 9); the dispersion of the nations (ch. 10); and the Tower of Babel (the beginning of ch. 11).[3] While the thematic connection between the first two units has yet to be determined, the language and structure certainly encourage the reading of this narrative as the first part of the next section.

This brief episode opens with Noah's sons ("The sons of Noah who came out of the ark were Shem, Ham, and Japheth…") and concludes with Noah's death. This generational overlap allows it to function as a narrative nexus that looks both behind and ahead, a Janus narrative that simultaneously concludes and opens two different sections.[4] These lines focus on Noah as the protagonist of the previous narrative, and at the same time anticipate how Noah's sons' actions in this scene will shape the future of the world's population.

This requires a double analysis, of course: a reading of the episode as the conclusion of Noah's life story and the story of the Flood; and as the story of his sons and the nations that will be born from them.

NOAH'S VINEYARD AS THE CONCLUSION OF THE FLOOD NARRATIVE

As mentioned, reading these verses as the conclusion of the Flood narrative directs the spotlight upon Noah, the tenth generation of humankind. This context invites scrutiny of Noah's actions in this scene.

Planting and Drinking

> And Noah began to be a man of the ground, and he planted a vineyard. And he drank from the wine and became drunk, and lay uncovered inside his tent (9:20).

After the Flood, Noah reconnects with the newly dried earth and becomes a farmer. The first thing he does is plant a vineyard: "And Noah began to be a man of the ground, and he planted a vineyard." Does this

3. Cassuto, *From Adam to Noah*, 141–143.
4. On this phenomenon, see Grossman, *Text and Subtext*, 193–196.

description contain any hint of criticism towards Noah? Some sages viewed this in a negative light: "And Noah began (*vayaḥel*) to be a man of the ground – because he needed the ground, he grew profane (*ḥulin*). R. Yehuda son of R. Shalom said: At first 'he was a righteous man, blameless,' and now he is but a 'man of the ground.'"[5] This midrash points out the ironic transformation from "*ish tzaddik*," a "righteous man," to "*ish ha'adma*," a "man of the ground." Genesis Rabba also notes:

> Three had a passion for agriculture, and no good was found in them: Cain, Noah, and Uzziah. Cain was a "worker of the ground"; Noah became a "man of the ground"; Uzziah had "farmers and vinedressers in the hills and in the Carmel because he loved the ground" (I Chr. 26:10).[6]

There is no mistaking the negative tone of this midrash. Through the description "man of the ground," Noah is compared to Cain, who murdered his brother. Together with Cain and Uzziah, Noah is defined as someone whom "no good was found in them" (other versions contain the description "no use"). Overlooking how Noah built an ark to save his family and the animals, this midrash focuses on the end of the life, when he becomes a "man of the ground" and brings no further benefit to the world; perhaps he even sets it back.

Keeping in line with this midrash, Rashi goes a step further and criticizes Noah's decision to plant a vineyard rather than any other crop: "He made himself profane, for he should have planted something else first."[7]

Noah's actions, however, can be read in a different light. The first verse, in fact, invites positive expectations: the verb *vayaḥel* does not stem from the root Ḥ-O-L, "profane," but from the root H-Ḥ-L, "began,"[8] which reflects new beginnings in a new world. Noah is starting anew,

5. *Tanḥuma, Bereshit* 13.
6. Genesis Rabba 36:20.
7. Rashi on Gen. 9:20, following Genesis Rabba. Some believe that Rashi was a vintner, and if so, his criticism of Noah is particularly intriguing (although in all likelihood, Rashi was involved in a trade unrelated to wine).
8. Compare to our above debate about Enosh's generation: "And Seth too had a son, and he named him Enosh. Then people began to call on the name of the Lord" (4:26).

reconnecting with the ground after so many months spent floating above it. This verb often symbolizes new hope: after Samson's hair is shaved and his strength is lost, "the hair on his head began (*vayaḥel*) to grow back as soon as it had been shaved" (Judges 16:22), hinting that his miraculous strength, too, will be restored. The description "Solomon began (*vayaḥel*) to build the House of God in Jerusalem.... He began (*vayaḥel*) to build on the second day of the second month in the fourth year of his reign" (II Chr. 3:1–2) anticipates the dawn of a shining new era. These examples, of course, do not prove that every instance of the word *vayaḥel* is inherently positive, but they certainly illustrate that this opening verse need not be read in a negative light.

Moreover, the description "*ish ha'adama*," "man of the ground," also raises positive associations. It can be read as a statement of Noah's skill, as Ibn Ezra writes: "He knows how to work the ground, and this is great wisdom."[9] Noah's new vocation, in fact, can be read as a fulfillment of the etymology his father Lamech expresses at his birth: "He named him Noah saying, 'This one will comfort us in the labor and painful toil of our hands caused by the ground the Lord has cursed'" (5:29). Noah is forced to spend most of the narrative closed up in an ark upon the water, but now he can finally embrace his destiny and return to the ground, to work it and bring hope and relief to humankind.

In fact, Noah's description as a "man of the ground" serves as a reprise of humanity's original creation: "And the Lord God formed man of dust from the earth" (2:7). This comparison unearths an important parallel, as there, too, following man's creation, God plants a garden in the newly created world: "And the Lord God planted a garden in Eden in the east" (2:8). Noah's planting echoes God's own sequence of actions: once he sets foot upon the newly dried earth (in parallel to the first creation of man), Noah then plants the earth, just like God did.[10] I will return to this comparison, which ties in with the heart of the narrative objective.

9. Ibn Ezra on Gen. 9:20.
10. In several stories of rebirth, the hero's near-death and rebirth takes place in the vicinity of plants or trees, which seem to function as symbols of regrowth and rebirth after the end of a previous life (for an analysis of this motif in Ishmael's rebirth in Genesis and Hermann Hesse's *Siddhartha*, see Jonathan Grossman and Sara Daniel, "'Like Arrows in the Hand of the Warrior, So Are Youths': Reading Ishmael's Expulsion

There is also room to challenge Rashi's criticism of planting a vineyard. In several places in the Bible, planting a vineyard is considered a positive act. In wartime, a man who has just planted a vineyard is exempt from fighting and may return home to tend to it: "Is there anyone who has planted a vineyard but has never harvested it? Let him go back to his home, lest he die in battle and another harvest it" (Deut. 20:6). In that context, the planting of a vineyard is considered parallel to building a house or marrying one's betrothed. Isaiah likens Israel to God's vineyard: "For the vineyard of the Lord of hosts is the house of Israel / and the men of Judah are the seedlings he planted for His delight" (Is. 5:7). In that context, Isaiah would not have used these metaphors had their connotations been negative. In Song of Songs, too, the vineyard is a place of hope and growth and beauty (for example, 7:12). Above all, wine is granted its own special blessing and place in religious celebration. As mentioned before, it may be that through planting a vineyard, Noah fulfills his destiny as the one who brings relief to humankind; now, people will be able to forget their sorrows through wine.[11]

Rabbi Itamar Eldar suggested to me that Noah's new title and the first crop he plants are related: the phrase "*ish ha'adama*," "man of the ground," is unique, and expresses a certain harmonious bond between man and soil. A person who is enslaved to the cursed earth, who must sweat for his daily existence, will not plant a vineyard; he will plant grain to produce bread. To plant a vineyard is a luxury, something only undertaken when the ground is fertile and yielding to human touch. In Eden, man is God's gardener, who tends to His lush fruit trees; therefore, Noah's planting of a vineyard transports the reader back to the prelapsarian days of Eden, when tending the soil was not drudgery but delight.

This optimistic opening, however, does not last long, and the next verse already describes Noah's humiliation: "And he drank from the wine and became drunk, and lay uncovered inside his tent" (v. 21). Even here, however, Noah's downfall is described gradually, as drinking wine is not

in Genesis 21 in light of Hermann Hesse's *Siddhartha*," *Hebrew Studies* 57 [2016]: 73–91). Here, too, the world's rebirth after the Flood is associated with the planting of a vineyard, which symbolizes regrowth and renewal.

11. Skinner, *Genesis*, 133.

inherently negative (see Jotham's parable in Judges 9:13, for example, or the poetic celebration of Psalm 104:15's "wine to cheer the heart of man, oil to make the face shine"[12]). Even drunkenness is not necessarily presented as negative in the Bible, as described in Proverbs: "Give strong drink to the hapless and wine to the embittered. Let them drink and forget their poverty, and put their troubles out of mind" (Prov. 31:6–7). Nonetheless, the biblical attitude towards drunkenness is more complex, and Habakkuk's criticism is especially apt in this context: "Woe to you who make others drink to intoxication as you pour out your wrath, in order to gaze upon their nakedness!" (Hab. 2:15). The prophet's criticism is directed against drunkenness that leads to nakedness. Needless to say, this prophecy is in strong dialogue with our narrative. Noah's drunkenness results in nakedness, and even though he is contained within his tent,[13] this kind of drunkenness is not looked upon kindly: "For even the blameless righteous man whose virtue saved the whole world was led to sin by wine; he was led to disgrace, to the cursing of his own descendants."[14] Once again, the con-

---

12. The Talmud's commentary on this verse is interesting: "Rabba raises a contradiction: It is written: '[And wine that] gladdens (*yeshamaḥ*)' [which could be read] 'makes crazy,' but we read it as '*yesamaḥ*,' 'gladdens.' [The resolution is,] if one merits, it gladdens him [*mesameḥo*]; if he does not merit, it makes him crazy [*meshamemehu*]" (Sanhedrin 70a). This is the Talmud's text as we have it, but there is a more logical version based on the *Yad Ramah*'s commentary: the word *yeshamah* (with a *heh* instead of a *ḥet*) was the written version of the Psalms of the *Amora'im*, but was read with a *ḥet* as *yesamaḥ*, leading Rabba to claim this. As he writes, "*Yeshamah* is written with a *heh* but it is read as *yesamaḥ* with a *ḥet*: if he is worthy, [meaning] he only drinks enough for bodily pleasure, it gladdens him; if he does not merit, and he drinks too much and becomes drunk, it makes him crazy, from the language of SH-M-H, as in 'Be appalled, heavens (*shomu shamayim*)' (Jer. 2:12), or 'And I will destroy (*vahashimoti*) the land' (Lev. 26:32)." Even if the plain meaning of the verse in Psalms praises wine, the ambivalence that Rabba presents is also evident in the Bible itself.
13. I will mention Rabbi Samson Raphael Hirsch's reading below, that Noah became drunk outside his tent – perhaps even together with his sons – but when he felt that he was losing control, he managed to reach his tent, and uncovered himself there. If Noah indeed attempted to hide his disgrace, then Ham emerges as even more villainous, as a voyeur who deliberately invaded his father's privacy. See further below.
14. Nahmanides on Gen. 9:26–27. Deborah Sweeney and Julia Asher-Greve explore the symbolism that accompanies nudity in Egyptian and Mesopotamian art. One of their conclusions is that nudity, especially in context of war, is associated with loss, defeat, humiliation, and death. In religious contexts, however, it is a cultic symbol, often of

nection between drunkenness and nakedness is central to the narrative objective, and I will later discuss this in comparison to the story of Eden.

If so, while the first verse anticipates a positive story, the second verse shatters these expectations when Noah falls into a drunken stupor. Admittedly, however, any criticism of Noah is eclipsed by the narrative evaluation of his sons. After all, this episode opens with: "The sons of Noah who came out of the ark were Shem, Ham, and Japheth, and Ham was the father of Canaan. These three were the sons of Noah, and from them the whole earth spread out" (9:18–19). Noah could have easily been mentioned along with his sons, especially given the fact that the narrative opens with focus on his actions. His omission in the first line, therefore, is calculated to direct the reader's focus to his sons, rather than to the father: Noah's actions are only described in order to determine which of his sons are blessed, which are cursed, and how it all came about. The next scene – the sons' reactions to their father's nakedness – is therefore the most important scene in the narrative, and the key to understanding its objective.

I will discuss these reactions in the next part of our analysis, as this scene is the introduction to the dispersal of the nations. For now, in the context of Noah's characterization in the narrative, I wish to focus on Noah's response when he awakens from his drunken stupor and learns what his sons have done. Firstly, the fact that Noah immediately regains control of the situation is admirable in itself, in comparison, for example, to Lot, who also becomes drunk after his home is destroyed, and whose drunken state is exploited by his daughters.[15] For two nights, Lot "did *not know* when she lay down or when she rose," and he never

---

fertility and abundance. One intriguing observation is that in ancient Egypt, nudity was often used to signify reincarnation and renewal of the body in the next world (Sweeney and Asher-Greve, "On Nakedness, Nudity, and Gender in Egyptian and Mesopotamian Art," in *Images and Gender: Contributions to the Hermeneutics of Reading Ancient Art*, ed. S. Schroer [OBO 220: Fribourg and Göttingen, 2006], 125–176). Here, nakedness is clearly associated with disgrace, although its dialogue with the Eden narrative also lends it a dimension of rebirth, of the newly created Adam and Eve walking about in God's garden.

15. Many have noted this connection. See, for example, Brad Embry, "The 'Naked Narrative' from Noah to Leviticus: Reassessing Voyeurism in the Account of Noah's Nakedness in Genesis 9.22–24," *JSOT* 35 (2011): 427–429.

reacts to his daughters' deeds; from the reader's perspective, he never emerges from his drunken stupor. In contrast to the implied criticism of Lot,[16] Noah awakens and immediately "*knew* what his youngest son had done to him" (9:24), curses those who deserve to be cursed, and blesses those who deserve to be blessed.

Thus, a complex picture of Noah emerges from this scene: Initially, it seems that Noah is following in the footsteps of his Creator by planting the newly re-created world. He then becomes drunk and sprawls naked in his tent, subject to his sons' mercy, but he soon emerges from this shameful state and seizes the family reins once more, doling out blessings and curses.

This process is crucial for the understanding of this scene as the conclusion of the Flood narrative. Its objective is inherently related to its place within the text: Noah is an active participant in the re-creation of the world and plants a vineyard, transporting the reader back to Eden, to the planting of the world's first garden upon the newly dried soil. This parallel serves to illuminate why Noah becomes drunk in this scene, and why nakedness plays so central a role – as it does, of course, in the Eden narrative. This connection is already hinted to in the Talmud:

> "And Noah began to be a man of the ground, and he planted a vineyard".... The Holy One, blessed be He, said to Noah: Noah, shouldn't you have learned from Adam the first man, whose [banishment from the Garden of Eden] was caused only by wine? This is in accordance with the opinion of the one who says that the tree from which Adam the first man ate was a grapevine. As it is taught: Rabbi Meir says: The tree from which Adam the first man ate was a grapevine, as nothing except wine brings trouble upon a person.[17]

According to this reading, the Tree of Knowledge was a grapevine, and Noah followed in Adam's footsteps without learning from his mistakes.

---

16. I have developed this elsewhere. See Grossman, *Abram to Abraham*, 356–364; Grossman, "Associative Meanings in the Character Evaluation of Lot's Daughters," *CBQ* 76 (2014): 40–57.
17. Sanhedrin 70a–b.

Even if we reject the claim that the Tree of Knowledge was a grapevine, in both cases the protagonist is led to sin by the fruit of a tree, and the two plots share many common elements besides:[18]

Man and Woman in Eden	Noah in His Tent
And God blessed them, and said to them, "Be fruitful and multiply, and fill the earth and subdue it. Have dominion over the fish of the sea and the birds of the sky and over every living creature that moves on the ground." Then God said, "I give you every seed-bearing plant on the face of all the earth and every tree that has fruit with seed in it. They will be yours for food."	And God blessed Noah and his sons, and said to them, "Be fruitful and multiply, and fill the earth. And fear and dread of you shall be on all the animals of the earth, and on all the birds of the sky, on all that moves on the ground and on all the fish of the sea. Into your hand they are given. "Every moving thing that lives shall be for you as food. Like the green plants, I give you everything."
The Lord God formed a human from the dust of the *ground* and breathed into his nostrils the breath of life, and the human became a living being. The Lord God *planted* a garden in Eden in the east, and placed there the human He had formed.	And Noah began to be a man of the *ground*, and he *planted* a vineyard.
She took of its fruit and ate it, and she gave some also to her husband who was with her, and he ate.	And he drank from the wine and became drunk

18. On this analogy, see especially Devora Steinmetz, "Vineyard, Farm, and Garden: The Drunkenness of Noah in the Context of Primeval History," *JBL* 113 (1994): 193–207.

And the two of them were naked, the man and his wife, and they were not ashamed.	and lay uncovered inside his tent.
And the woman *saw* that the fruit of the tree was good for food and enticing to the eye and lovely to look at... and she gave some also to her husband who was with her, and he ate.	And Ham, the father of Canaan, *saw* his father's nakedness and told his two brothers outside.
And the eyes of both of them were opened, and they *knew* they were naked	Then Noah woke from his wine and *knew* what his youngest son had done to him.
And He said... *Cursed* are you.	And he said, "*Cursed* be Canaan,
Your longing will be for your husband, and he will rule over you.	a servant of servants shall he be to his brothers."
The Lord God made garments of skin for Adam and his wife and clothed them.	Then Shem and Japheth took a garment, and the two of them laid it on their shoulders and walked backward and covered their father's nakedness.
And *placed* (*vayashken*) east of the Garden of Eden cherubim.	May God enlarge Japheth, and *let him dwell* (*vayishkon*) in the tents of Shem.

Additionally, based on the language of each scene, the expulsion from Eden, which concludes the Eden narrative (3:22–24) can be compared to the dispersion of the nations all over the world, which concludes the vineyard narrative (10:1–11:9).[19] God's concern at humanity's potential power is voiced in each scene (I will explore the specific connection between Eden and the Tower of Babel later on, in my discussion of the Tower of Babel):

19. As proposed by Steinmetz, "Vineyard, Farm, and Garden," 197–198.

Humankind's Expulsion from Eden (3:22–23)	**The Dispersion of the Tower Builders (11:6–8)**
And the Lord God said, "Man has *now* become like *one of us*, knowing good and evil. *Now, he* must not be allowed to reach out his hand and take also from the Tree of Life and eat, and live forever.	And the Lord said, "*Now,* they are *one* people and with one language, and this is what they have begun to do. *Now* nothing they intend to do will be impossible for them.
So the Lord God banished him from the Garden of Eden to work the earth from which (*misham*) he had been taken.	From there (*misham*) the Lord scattered them over all the face of earth.

The parallel between the Garden of Eden and Noah's vineyard illuminates the function of Noah's nakedness. Noah is the first person in human history to become drunk, and in his inebriation he is stripped of his cognitive abilities and his clothes. This, of course, reflects humanity's state in the Garden of Eden: Adam and Eve have not yet acquired knowledge, and they walk about naked and unashamed. Their eyes are only opened once they have eaten the forbidden fruit. In contrast, Noah's eyes close as a result of his drinking, and he degenerates back into humanity's primal, unknowing, naked state. The sexual undertones that color the story of Eden are also present in this scene: Noah's nakedness not only symbolizes the shedding of human culture, but hints to a sexual dimension that is played out through Ham's reaction, as I will discuss below. In this way, the garden and eating from the Tree of Knowledge is parallel to the vineyard and drinking wine, but whereas the former leads to knowledge and covering up, the latter leads to drunken stupor and uncovering. Noah's eyes are only opened once more when he recovers from his inebriation to find himself naked beneath the covering Shem and Japheth placed over him.

In order to discuss the meaning of this comparison, I will first point out the dynamic interchange of the characters and their roles within the narrative. Some have claimed that an analogy can only be considered intentional if the characters from one scene are compared to the same characters from the other scene throughout the narrative (for example, Adam could only be compared with Noah if the comparison follows from the beginning of each scene to its end). If this were indeed the case, this comparison would not withstand their criteria.[20] However, I believe that such dynamic analogies (such as Adam first being compared to Noah, then to Ham, etc.) should not be considered a disadvantage; on the contrary, this often contributes to the narrative objective. In such a case, these shifting comparisons hold the key to the meaning of the analogy itself.[21]

Who is Adam's parallel in the story of Noah's vineyard? First and foremost, Noah himself: Noah is the one who drinks and becomes drunk and naked, just as Adam and Eve were the ones who were naked, and just as Adam and Eve ate from the Tree. However, the actual sinner in the second story is Ham, whose sight, like Eve's, leads him to sin: "And Ham, the father of Canaan, *saw* his father's nakedness," parallels, "And the woman *saw* that the fruit of the tree was good for food."[22] And just as the sinner (or his son) is cursed fiercely because of his sin in Noah's narrative: "Cursed be Canaan" (9:25), so too the sinners themselves (in the serpent's case) and the ground that they live upon is cursed because of their sin.

The stages of the sin of Eden, then, are divided between Noah and Ham: Noah drinks (in parallel to Adam and Eve's eating), while Ham sins (in parallel to their sin). In the Eden narrative, the themes of knowledge and sexuality are woven together; in Noah's story, they are divided between Noah, who loses his knowledge and clothing, and Ham, whose sin is related to sexuality. This distinction is neither coincidental nor marginal; rather, it allows for a further distinction, one closely tied with the significance of this comparison. In the Eden narrative, God

20. Paul R. Noble, "Esau, Tamar, and Joseph: Criteria for Identifying Inner-Biblical Allusion," *VT* 43 (2002), 219–252.

21. Regarding these definitions, see Jonathan Grossman, "'Dynamic Analogies' in the Book of Esther," *VT* 59 (2009): 394–414. Rabbi Amnon Bazak refers to this as an "interchangeable parallel" (Bazak, *Parallels*, 198). For more examples, see Grossman, *Text and Subtext*, 364–368.

22. Perhaps, in parallel to Ham's action, "And he told his two brothers outside," the "telling" in the Eden narrative can be placed: "And He said, 'Who told you that you are naked?'" (3:11).

punishes the sinners who ate from the Tree of Knowledge, but God is not an active player in Noah's story. Because Noah does not sin, he himself is able to confront the sinner, curse whoever is deserving of curse, and bless whoever is deserving of blessing.[23]

Noah, not God, cultivates the soil after the world's re-creation; Noah, not God, distributes reward and punishment. And, maintaining this pattern, Shem, not God, covers Noah's nakedness. In the Garden of Eden, Adam and Eve try to cover their nakedness with fig leaves, but this does not suffice, and eventually God "made garments of skin for Adam and his wife and clothed them" (3:21). While Noah enters his tent, this outer covering does not suffice, and Ham still sees his father's nakedness, moving Shem and Japheth to take a garment and cover their father properly. Once again, human initiative takes the place of God's actions; people take responsibility and correct their own mistakes. It is no wonder, then, that Noah blesses Shem that God will one day dwell within his tents; by showing respect and compassion for his father, Shem is essentially emulating God.[24]

Noah, if so, is stripped of his knowledge and his clothing, and reverts to the prelapsarian state of humankind. Ham sees his father's nakedness and shames him by telling his brothers. Will curse and punishment follow sin, as it did in the world before the Flood? The answer comes swiftly: in this new world, sin (which here, too, is connected to sexuality) does not go unpunished – but this time, humans are not only the sinners. Humans also decree punishment, and moreover, they also attempt to correct the sin themselves. They do not only cause damage and corruption; they take initiative into their own hands, and seek to fix the damage and corruption caused by their fellow humans.

For the first time, humanity is not one uniform group; not all people must suffer on account of one person's sin. Only Ham, the father

23. Steinmetz, "Vineyard, Farm, and Garden." On Noah, utterer of blessing and curse, as God's representative in the story, see also Vermeulen, "Blessing and Cursing," 124–125 (and n38 for further discussions).

24. The analogy between Adam's family and his sons and Noah's family and sons does not end there, and we will discuss this further in the next scenes (Cain and Abel; the nations' dispersal) in the analysis of chapter 10; there, too, we will note the similar process of responsibility transferred from God to humankind.

of Canaan, sins in this scene, and only he is cursed, while the ones who correct his sin are blessed. In fact, the blessing that issues forth from Noah's mouth is also revolutionary: for the first time, man, not God, is the one to pronounce a blessing. Until this point, God has bestowed five blessings;[25] in this narrative, Noah pronounces both blessings and curses. Moreover, until this point, God has blessed humanity, while here, humanity blesses God Himself: "Blessed is the Lord, God of Shem" (9:26). It seems that not Shem, but God, is the recipient of Noah's blessing – indeed, the God of Shem.[26]

Cautiously, tentatively, I will hesitantly propose that a surprising parallel between Noah and God emerges from the language of the text. At first, Noah is uncovered in his tent: "He lay uncovered *in his tent*" (9:21). At the end of the story, Noah pronounces a blessing that God will reveal Himself in Shem's tent: "May God enlarge Japheth, and let Him dwell *in the tents* of Shem" (9:27). Although some interpret Japheth as the subject of "let him dwell,"[27] the verb *shakhen* is generally associated with God, with the Divine Presence (*Shekhina*), leading most

25. Gen. 1:22; 1:28; 2:3; 5:2; 9:1.

26. Some modern translations have attempted to translate according to different vocalization here, such as "*Elohai*," "my God," resulting in: "Blessed by the Lord my God be Shem" (NRSV, RSV), but these translations are not convincing. After the word "Blessed," the name of the blessed always appears, as shown by Day, *From Creation to Babel*, 142.

27. As Pseudo-Jonathan translates, "The Lord shall beautify the borders of Japheth, and his sons shall convert and dwell in the schools of Shem," and Genesis Rabba and others present a similar reading. This is especially salient in translations that add Japheth as the explicit subject of the verse, such as "May God extend the territory of Japheth; may Japheth live in the tents of Shem" (Mathews, *Genesis*, vol. 1, 414), though he himself wonders whether Japheth's descendants were ever close to the borders of Israel, and he does not find a solution (ibid., 424–425). If we adopt the accepted solution since Wellhausen that the Philistines were descended from Japheth, this would solve the problem, but it seems that Gen. 10:14 sees them stemming from a different source (it depends on the identification of the Philistines mentioned there). On this confusion, see also Westermann, *Genesis*, vol. 1, 494, who eventually despairs of identifying three national groups descended from Noah's three sons. Modern scholarship generally considers Japheth the subject of *veyishkon* (see Day, *From Creation to Babel*, 144). On this expression as a symbol of peace and blessing, see John P. Brown, "Peace Symbolism in Ancient Military Vocabulary," *VT* 21 (1971): 1–23.

commentators (such as Rashi, Ibn Ezra, and Radak)[28] to interpret the blessing thus: God will expand and bless Japheth, but He will actually dwell among the tents of Shem. The double mention of the tent (which has only appeared once in the biblical text until this point) serves as a narrative framework that encourages reading Noah as the human hand of God, who plants, blesses, and curses.

The analogy between the Eden narrative and the story of Noah's vineyard brings out the meaning of this episode as a conclusion to the Flood narrative. After the world is renewed, a vineyard is planted – parallel to the planting of the Garden of Eden after the world's creation. Noah, like Adam and Eve before their sin, is also stripped of his knowledge and his clothing. In planting the vineyard, Noah takes over God's role, a transferal of responsibility that continues to the end of the story, when, like God, he bestows blessing and punishment. In between, however, Noah reverts to the naked, ignorant status of Adam and Eve in the Garden of Eden, which leads to sexual sin, parallel to eating from the Tree of Knowledge.

In this way, this brief episode completes the story of the world's renewal after the Flood. Humanity's status changes in the new world; less honor and more responsibility is placed on its shoulders. Noah's actions reflect this change. In this story, he is no longer the blameless righteous character he was before the Flood; he uncovers himself in his tent, and his sons witness his shame. Noah, however, is not like Adam, who shies away from responsibility; not only does he plant a new garden after the Flood, but he also takes the power of blessing and curse into his own hands, and uses them well.[29]

---

28. See especially Walter C. Kaiser, *Toward an Old Testament Theology* (Grand Rapids, 1978), 37–39; Hamilton, *Genesis*, 326.

29. The next stage in this context is Abraham's election, and the language of blessing is salient in God's first revelation to him, even giving him the impression that the blessings are being given to him at his responsibility, in the words of Rashi (on Gen. 12:2): "The blessings are given in your hand." See also Genesis Rabba 39:11, and see further in Grossman, *Abram to Abraham*, 87–91.

NOAH'S VINEYARD AS THE INTRODUCTION TO THE DISPERSION OF THE NATIONS

Surprisingly, this episode opens with a focus on Noah's sons. Though Noah could have easily been mentioned along with them, the text seems to intentionally focus on Noah's sons rather than upon Noah himself: "The sons of Noah who came out of the ark were Shem, Ham, and Japheth, and Ham was the father of Canaan. These three were the sons of Noah, and from them the whole earth spread out" (9:18–19). The story of how the world's population spread out over the world, then, begins here, and the brief story of Noah's drunkenness is deliberately inserted here, between the introduction to how "the whole earth spread out" and the genealogies of Shem, Ham, and Japheth that begin in the next chapter. (If the narrative is renamed "The Story of Canaan's Curse" or "Noah's Sons' Blessing and Curse," then the whole episode seems to integrate more seamlessly into the narrative sequence.) These brief lines offer insight into the characters of the three men whose descendants will repopulate the entire world; like Cain and Seth, the characteristics of each son will be embodied in their genealogical lines. I will shortly argue that the qualities and cultures of each son are subtly reflected in the seemingly technical genealogical lists of chapter 10; these qualities and the cultures they engender are encapsulated in the story of Noah's vineyard, Canaan's curse, and the blessing of Shem and Japheth.

"And Ham, the Father of Canaan, Saw His Father's Nakedness and Told His Two Brothers Outside" (9:22)

What, exactly, is Ham's sin? Though crucial to the understanding of the narrative, his actual deed is not at all clear from the verses. The verb "saw" can be read in a literal sense, but it may hint to some kind of action. In the Talmud, Rav and Shmuel dispute precisely this point: "Rav and Shmuel [disagreed]: One says that he castrated [Noah] and one says he sodomized him" (Sanhedrin 70a). Both Rav and Shmuel agree that "he saw" is just a euphemism for some kind of sexual corruption. What moved the *Amora'im* to look beyond the literal meaning of the word? Such a reading is presumably based on two details: firstly, when Noah wakes up, he "knew what his younger son had *done* to him" – this implies that something had actually been done to him; secondly, the harsh curse he utters against Ham and Canaan has led readers throughout history to assume that something dark indeed must have moved Noah to unleash so harsh a curse against his own son. It would be hard to justify his reaction if all Ham did was smirk at his father's drunken state and tell his brothers of it.[30]

Some commentators favor the reading that Ham castrated his father,[31] claiming that Ham wished to prevent his father from fathering any more children. However, out of the two readings presented in Sanhedrin, it seems more likely that Ham "cohabited" with him. "Seeing" a person's nakedness is used as a euphemism for sexual relations in several places in the Bible, such as Leviticus 18 ("the uncovering of nakedness") and especially: "If a man marries his sister, the daughter of either his father or his mother, so that he *sees her nakedness* and she *sees his nakedness*, it is a disgrace; they shall be excommunicated in the sight of their kinsfolk. He has *uncovered the nakedness* of his sister; he shall bear his guilt" (Lev. 20:17). Alongside the verb "he has uncovered (*gila*) the nakedness of his sister," the expression "sees her/his nakedness" is explicitly used as a euphemism for sexual relations. This supports the reading that Ham lay with his father Noah, whose nakedness was already *uncovered* in the previous verse. Another option is that Ham took advantage of Noah's drunken state to lie with his father's wife, who is considered Noah's "nakedness." This reading reinforces the parallel between this episode and the story of Lot's daughters (Gen. 19): both Noah and Lot drink wine and their children take sexual advantage of them in their drunken state.

In the context of discussing Canaan's curse I will develop this possibility, but for now, I will note that despite the obvious incentive to interpret Ham's "seeing" figuratively, a literal reading is still possible: that is, Ham disrespectfully looked upon his father's nakedness, and not only did he fail to cover him up, he also went to tell his brothers of this amusing

30. John Bergsma and Scott Hahn, "Noah's Nakedness and the Curse on Canaan," *JBL* 124 (2005): 39–40.

31. See Robert Graves and Raphael Patai, *Hebrew Myths: The Book of Genesis* (London, 1963), 122–124. See also Cassuto, *From Noah to Abraham*, 150.

spectacle.[32] The Bible's sensitive attitude to sexual purity, especially within the family unit, may justify Noah's harsh reaction. What Ham did was publicize Noah's disgrace, instead of discreetly and respectfully covering it up.

The claim that Noah's reaction is disproportionate to Ham's offense still stands – perhaps Ham was in the wrong place at the wrong time, and his surprise momentarily overcame his good sense.[33] But in these primordial tales of how the world came into being, each detail has enormous repercussions; each minute aspect of a forefather's character will serve as the blueprint for his descendants' culture, and there is no room for momentary lapses of judgement or coarse behavior. An act of murderous rage will give birth to a culture that glorifies brute strength and bloodshed; a moment of crass disrespect will spawn a dynasty of sexual corruption.

Shem and Japheth's actions present the correct alternative to Ham's response: "Then Shem and Japheth took a garment, and the two of them laid it on their shoulders and walked backward and covered their father's nakedness, their faces turned backward so as not to see their father's nakedness" (9:23). Not only do Shem and Japheth avert their eyes from their father's nakedness, they cover him while facing backward. Without any explicit laws of modesty, despite being utterly alone in the world, with no one to witness or judge their actions, the brothers instinctively understand that they should not look upon their father's nakedness. Interestingly, there is no explanation of why their father's nakedness is off-limits in the text, and the brothers do not explain or attempt to justify their meticulous actions. In this way, this becomes an underlying premise of the narrative: looking upon the father's nakedness is forbidden, based on an intuitive grasp of modesty and paternal respect.

There is room to debate whether the singular form of the verb "took" – *vayikaḥ* instead of *vayikḥu* – lays emphasis on the first person

32. See further in Embry, "The Naked Narrative." This reading is reflected in Exodus Rabba 30:5: "The Holy One, blessed be He, said: Ham, the father of Canaan, did not strike, but only saw, and now he and his sons are slaves forever, so he who curses and strikes – how much more so."

33. Rabbi Samson Raphael Hirsch's reading (on Gen. 9:22) is interesting in this context, as I discuss above: "He entered the tent, desiring to visit his father in a private space, and came to see his father when drunk." Ham did not merely stumble upon his father; his sin began with an invasion of his private space.

who is mentioned, which, in this case, is Shem.[34] In the words of the Midrash: "Rabbi Yochanan said: Shem initiated this deed, and then Japheth came and obeyed him; therefore Shem was granted a tallit, and Japheth a garment."[35] There are other biblical sources where the singular form of the verb is clearly calculated to prioritize the first character over the latter (such as Num. 12:1). In any case, Shem is later given clear preference over Japheth without any obvious explanation in the text, so the singular form of the verb may serve to subtly illuminate Shem's initiative.

Ham or Canaan

As soon as Noah stirs, he regains control of the situation and puts his sons in their proper place. The first to suffer his wrath, however, is not Ham – who actually does the dirty deed – but his grandson, Canaan. This detail is not marginal or coincidental, and it is certainly not any kind of textual corruption, because Canaan is mentioned again and again throughout the narrative. With the first mention of Noah's sons, Ham is specifically described as "the father of Canaan" (9:18). This epithet is used once again when Ham sees his father's nakedness: "And Ham, the father of Canaan, saw" (v. 22). Upon waking, Noah's first response is to curse Canaan (v. 25) who is mentioned once more when Noah blesses Shem and Japheth – poor Canaan, who is presumably no more than a young infant at the time, will be their servant (v. 27).

The focus on Canaan is surprising because there is no obvious reason for this focus at all. Noah's inexplicable shift to Canaan has baffled commentators and scholars for generations, yielding a vast range of possible solutions. Some claim (such as Ibn Ezra) that Canaan tagged along

---

34. This syntactic phenomenon is also found in rabbinic literature (see, for example, Mishna Yevamot 12:6; Eduyot 10:3; Eiruvin 10:10, and more), and there, too, there is room to debate whether the first person mentioned is more significant. Wilhelm Gesenius discusses this phenomenon and illustrates with other examples from the Flood narrative: "And Noah and his sons and his wife, and the wives of his sons with him, went (*vayavo*) into the ark" (7:7); "So Noah emerged (*vayetze*), and his sons and his wife, and his sons' wives with him" (8:18). See Gesenius, *Hebrew Grammar*, trans. A. E. Cowley, 2nd ed. (Oxford, 1910), 468.

35. Genesis Rabba 36:9. There are different versions of their respective rewards in different versions of the midrash; what is clearly implied is that Shem's reward was greater than that of Japheth.

with his father and somehow participated in his sin,[36] while others offer explanations for why Canaan is punished despite the fact that Ham is the one who sins (see especially Rashi, Nahmanides, and Radak).[37]

A particularly intriguing explanation has been proposed by modern scholars. I have already mentioned that some hold that Ham's sin was to sleep with his father's "nakedness" – that is, with Noah's wife. Based on this, some have suggested that Canaan was the child born from this incestuous act between Ham and his mother, leading Noah to curse the bastard product of Ham's sin.[38] Though fascinating, this reading is difficult to swallow. If Ham had indeed slept with his mother, the mention of Noah's nakedness a verse before would be superfluous, and it is unlikely that Shem and Japheth would be granted such a fervent blessing for simply not sleeping with their mother. The sequence of events also challenges this reading, as Noah curses Canaan as soon as he wakes up, when (according to this view) he was only just conceived.

The solution to this problem seems to be closely related to the narrative placement: the story of Canaan's curse as the introduction to the dispersal of the nations. Canaan, of course, is of unparalleled importance to biblical history, given that Abraham, of Shem's seed, will inherit Canaan's land in the future. The focus on Canaan, rather than his father, is calculated as a comment on the nature of Canaanite culture, as inherited from Canaan's father. As repeated time and again, Ham is Canaan's father – Canaan shares his father's nature, his father's disrespect for his

36. Some have proposed emendations of the text, see especially Wellhausen, *Die Composition*, 12–13; Skinner, *Genesis*, 182; von Rad, *Genesis*, 131–132; Day, *From Creation to Babel*, 140–141. This claim is based – besides the obvious expectation that Ham, not Canaan, ought to be the subject of the curse – on the definition of the sinner as the "younger son." While it does not seem that Ham is indeed the youngest, perhaps this verse reflects an approach that Canaan is Noah's youngest son, which solves the issue. I will relate to the language of the verse below.

37. According to Rashi, Ham castrates his father so he will not be able to have a fourth son, whereas Canaan is Ham's fourth son. Nahmanides holds that Canaan is Ham's oldest son who was born shortly before Ham's sin, so Noah curses Canaan so that all of Ham's descendants will be cursed. Radak writes (on Gen. 9:20): "God saw that Canaan's descendants would be evil, so He placed a curse in Noah's mouth, for he was a prophet, and his curse came true."

38. Bergsma and Hahn, "Noah's Nakedness."

own father, his father's tendency towards sexual perversion. In the Torah, Canaan exemplifies sexual corruption, especially incest: "You shall not copy the practices of the land of Egypt where you dwelt, or of the land of Canaan to which I am taking you, nor shall you follow their customs" (Lev. 18:3). Two of Ham's sons are held up as a warning for Israel – Egypt and Canaan. These nations are not merely corrupted by usual desire; sexual recklessness and lechery are part of their religious rituals, part of their customs – Israel must not "follow their customs." At the end of the list of sexual prohibitions, it is emphasized that the Canaanites were expelled from their land because of their sexually perverted culture: "For all those abhorrent things were done by the people who were in the land before you, and the land became defiled. So let not the land spew you out for defiling it, as it spewed out the nation that came before you" (Lev. 18:27–28).

While scholars are divided in regard to the extent of ancient Canaan's sexual corruption, all concur that there *was* certain corruption, as is also evident from the sin of Baal Peor (Num. 25). One striking example is the ritual copulation between the Babylonian high priest and the high priestess prostitute during the climax of the Babylonian New Year Akitu festival, which was celebrated annually in the month of Nisan.[39] The words of R. Yehuda (citing Rav) in Sanhedrin aptly reflect the sexually perverted conventions of ancient pagan ritual: "Israel knew that idol worship was not genuine – they would only worship idols to allow themselves sexual relations in public."[40] Some justifiably claim that this explains why the verb "*liznot*," "to stray," is often used in conjunction with worship of the Baal – the verb *liznot* is derived from the same root as the word "*zona*," "prostitute," and ritual prostitution was central to Baal worship.[41] Baal, the chief god of the Canaanite pantheon,

39. About this festival, see Johannes C. de Moor, *New Year with Canaanites and Israelites* (2 vols.), Kampen, 1972. It was also a central place of wine drinking (Johannes C. de Moor, "*Baal*," *TDOT* 2: 190), which once again connects wine with sexuality.

40. Sanhedrin 63b.

41. M. J. Mulder, "Baal in the OT," *TDOT* 2: 198. See also Maimonides, *Guide for the Perplexed*, III:37. There, Maimonides states that forbidden mixtures are related to a prevalent Canaanite custom: "They also mention that when one species is grafted upon another, the bough that is meant to be grafted ought to be held in the hand

was the storm god, bringer of clouds and rain, so he was also associated with fertility (especially fertility of the soil, but human fertility as well). Sexuality and fertility therefore played a central role in Canaanite ritual.

This background is crucial for understanding Noah's focus on Canaan. Even if Ham was the one who looked upon his father's nakedness, the text takes advantage of this event to draw attention to Canaanite culture; Canaan (as well as his older brother, Egypt) inherited his father's sexually perverse nature.[42]

To this end, I believe, the narrator employs the deliberately obscure expression: "And he knew what his younger son had done to him" (9:24). This description of Ham is puzzling, as he is usually presented as Noah's middle son. Nahmanides claims that the sons are mentioned not in order of their birth, but according to other factors,[43] while Cassuto adds that biblical cadence usually saves the longest word for the end of the list, so that even though Japheth is the eldest (as emerges from 10:21), he will always be mentioned last.[44]

However, while this expression can be justified on a technical level, its use is nonetheless surprising, as until this point, Ham is always referred to by name. Noah's reaction also uses explicit names – Canaan, Shem, Japheth. Why does the narrator suddenly describe Noah's reaction without using Ham's name? Rashi, following the sages, suggests that the expression does not reflect Ham's relative age, but his lack of virtue: "His younger son – the most reviled and disgraced, as in 'I have

---

of a beautiful girl and of a man who has come into her in a disgraceful manner that they describe and that the woman must graft the bough upon the tree while the two are performing this act."

42. Egyptian debauchery is discussed in Ezek. 16:26: "You played the whore with your neighbors, the lustful Egyptians; you multiplied your harlotries to anger Me." The story of Joseph and Potiphar's wife is also indicative (Gen. 39), as well as Abram and Sarai's descent to Egypt (Gen. 12), that the Bible saw Egypt as a place of sexual corruption. In ancient Egypt, marriage between siblings was acceptable, especially in the royal court; moreover, sexual relations between other family members, such as a father and daughter, were not taboo (see Milgrom, *Leviticus 17–22*, 1518–1519).

43. Nahmanides on Gen. 6:10 (see also his commentary on 9:24). He claims that Japheth is the eldest, then Shem, then Ham; the same view is held by Rabbi Samson Raphael Hirsch.

44. Cassuto, *From Noah to Abraham*, 165.

made you small amongst the nations, disgraced."[45] Bekhor Shor suggests that this refers to Shem, rather than to Ham: "He made greater efforts for the mitzva, so it should not come as a surprise that the younger son received a greater blessing than the elder."[46] I believe that this nameless description does refer to Ham, but its anonymity allows for a smoother transition between Ham's action and Noah's reaction, which is voiced against Canaan. Had the verse stated, "And he knew what Ham had done to him," then his subsequent curse of Canaan would have been even more awkward. The nameless description preceding Noah's curse eases the shift from Ham, the sinner, to Canaan, who is cursed.

The focus on Canaan in this narrative, of course, anticipates the future biblical focus on the land of Canaan, and some scholars have shown that there is special focus on Canaan in the next chapter as well. The geographical borders of Canaan's territory are described in detail: "The border of the Canaanites was from Sidon toward Gerar as far as Gaza, and in the direction of Sodom, Gomorrah, Admah, and Zeboiim, as far as Lasha" (10:19), while the description of where Noah's other grandchildren settled is less specific. The special focus on Canaan, of course, is based on the special status of Israel's future land. In the words of Cassuto, the description of its borders is not "objective geographical, purely for learning's sake, but forms a link in the chain of interconnected sections of which the book of Genesis is composed."[47]

If so, all three units concerned with "the dispersal of the nations" are connected through a single theme:

Firstly, the story of Noah's drunkenness portrays the characters of each of Noah's sons, the three branches of humanity, through the actions of their forefathers.[48] Shem – the father of Abraham and his descendants – emerges as a sensitive, modest figure with respect for his father. Through this, he is granted God's presence in his midst.[49] Japheth

45. Rashi on Gen. 9:24.
46. Bekhor Shor on Gen. 9:24.
47. Cassuto, *From Noah to Abraham*, 212.
48. Cassuto, *From Noah to Abraham*, 149.
49. The poet of Psalms may have been playing with Noah's blessing to his sons in order to describe Israel dwelling securely in its land: "He expelled nations before them, settled the tribes of Israel in their tents, allotting them their portion by the line" (Ps. 78:55).

is blessed in the name of God (*Elohim*), not with the special Tetragrammaton unique to Israel, and this expresses his less intimate connection with the Lord. However, unlike his brother Ham, his is not a culture of corrupt sexuality, and he follows Shem's lead to protect their father's honor. Ham, in contrast to his brothers, is characterized as a sexually perverse figure whose corruption will taint the culture of his descendants, particularly the line of his son Canaan.

The second act of this scene depicts the geographical dispersion of the nations descended from Noah's three sons (ch. 10). As mentioned, this unit, too, focuses on Canaan; this time, the focus is geographical, rather than cultural-etiological. As I will propose in my discussion of chapter 10, here, too, Ham's descendants are characterized in an inferior light to Noah's other descendants – as a slave to his brothers.

The third unit concluding the saga of the nation's dispersal is the Tower of Babel narrative, an etiological narrative of why the nations are scattered, and why there are different languages. While there is no explicit focus on Canaan, the names and places mentioned in the story hint to its connection with the descendants of Ham. Moreover, the Tower of Babel narrative serves as a prelude to Abraham's election, which follows shortly after.

In short, the purpose of this saga is not merely to relate the dispersal of the nations, but to depict the moral tension between the sons of Ham and the sons of Shem. The moral choices of their ancestors serve to justify what is to come, to justify why one nation is entitled to dispossess another. The fierce, mighty Nimrod does this (10:8–10), but why should the modest, venerable descendants of Shem – in whose midst God dwells – drive out the Canaanites? The text already plants the answer to this question along with the very dawn of nationality: Canaan is cursed because he follows in the footsteps of his corrupt father, Ham.

The text' s presentation of the sons of Noah as their descendants' moral archetypes is also expressed in the biblical etymologies of their names. "Japheth" ("*Yefet*") is explicitly described in terms of expansion: "*Yaft Elohim LeYefet*," "May God enlarge Japheth" (9:27).[50] Whether this "enlargement" is related to general blessing, to the specific increase of his

50. Garsiel, *Midrashic Names*, 60.

descendants or their land, or to both, as Radak writes, "God will expand his borders and his blessing,"[51] it is interesting that Japheth is portrayed in so positive a light. Though he is overshadowed by Shem (as reflected in the blessing that "he will dwell in the tents of Shem"), the obvious enmity towards Ham is directed towards Ham alone. In the next chapter, we learn that Japheth has seven sons and seven grandchildren, a symbolic hint to the fulfillment of his blessing.

The meaning of Ham's name is not explicitly mentioned in the narrative. Bekhor Shor notes the wordplay between the name Canaan and the root K-N-A, meaning to submit: "He will be submitted (*nikhna*) to everyone; he was cursed through his name, just as the others were blessed through their name."[52] The meaning of Ham's name, however, may also be planted in the narrative; several scholars have commented that the word "Ham" has two meanings in ancient Egyptian: "royalty" and "slave." While it is generally problematic to project wordplay from other languages onto the biblical text, such a reading is more easily justified when the narrative is concerned with the origin of nations such as Canaan and Egypt, especially when the word "slave" is in such profound dialogue with Canaan's curse,[53] and Ham is the father of Egypt (10:6). This idea once again connects the son's fate with the father's sin: Ham's very name hints to his son's end.

The sages also characterize Ham and Canaan as the archetypal fathers of slavery: "R. Yaakov bar Zavdi said: For what reason can a slave go free at the price of an eye or a tooth? From this: 'And he saw... and he told' (9:22)."[54] R. Yaakov here holds that a slave is set free if his master removes his eye or his tooth, for at that moment, the slave severs his

51. Radak on Gen. 9:27.

52. Bekhor Shor on Gen. 9:25.

53. Gary A. Rendsburg, "Wordplay in the Hebrew Bible: An Eclectic Collection," in *Puns and Pundits: Wordplay in the Hebrew Bible and Ancient Near Eastern Literature,* ed. S. B. Noegel, 137–162 (Bethesda, MD, 2000), 143–144. See also Grossman, *Text and Subtext,* 66–69.

54. Genesis Rabba 36:9. See also the version in *Midrash Tanḥuma* (ed. Buber), *Noaḥ,* 21: "R. Yehuda bar Shalom said in the name of R. Yaakov bar Zabdi, who said in the name of R. Abahu: Ham saw with his own eyes and told with his mouth, therefore the Holy One, blessed be He, said if a slave is struck in his eye or his tooth he will be set free, as it says, "If a man strikes [the eye] of his slave."

connection with Ham, the father of all slaves. Ham used his eyes, his sense of sight, and his mouth, his speech, for sin: "And Ham, the father of Canaan, *saw* his father's nakedness and *told* his two brothers outside." When a slave's function of sight or speech is compromised, he or she is no longer associated with Ham.

I believe that Ham and Canaan's punishment is an expression of Noah's sense that this branch of the family cannot be left to its own devices. Through his vulnerable state, Noah learns that both Shem and Japheth – especially the former – can be trusted, but the younger son, Ham/Canaan, must be given over to his brothers' control. In the next chapter, as I will show, it is Ham who attempts to rule over his brothers, which reflects his struggle to shake off his father's curse.

Is the meaning of Shem's name also reflected in Noah's blessing, "Blessed be the Lord, the God of Shem"? While this is doubtful, it is nonetheless worth pointing out two details in this context. Firstly, in the Bible, the meaning of the name "Shem" is not merely "name"; it expresses eternity, stability, memory, and resurrection. This is evident, for example, in the book of Ruth, when the word *shem* is a keyword that expresses the revival of the family line after it is almost wiped out.[55] Moreover, the word is sometimes used as a reference to God, given its connotations of eternity and stability, such as: "May the Lord answer you in time of trouble, the name of Jacob's God keep you safe" (Ps. 20:2). The speaker does not mean that God's name will elevate the speaker, but that God Himself will come to his aid, as is evident from the parallelism. The phrase "to establish His *name* there" in Deuteronomy refers to the Divine Presence dwelling in the Sanctuary. Therefore, Shem's name links him closely and intimately with God, who is blessed in the narrative along with Shem, through Shem.

If this is so, then this episode is part of the narrative sequence woven throughout Genesis 1–11. Before the ten generations between Adam and Noah are listed, we learn that "And Seth too had a son, and he

55. See Gavriel Chaim Cohen, "Naming in the Book of Ruth," *Studies in Bible and Interpretation* 2 (1986): 151–160; Bezalel Porten, "The Scroll of Ruth: A Rhetorical Study," *Gratz College Annual* 7 (1978): 24; Kristin Moen Saxegaard, *Character Complexity in the Book of Ruth* (Tübingen, 2010), 57–63; Jonathan Grossman, "Stability and Surprise in the Book of Ruth's Exposition," *Beit Mikra* 60 (2015): 213–215.

named him Enosh. Then people began to call on the name of the Lord" (4:26). Calling on the name of the Lord is an explicit theme in the text; with Seth's line, humanity began to call on the name of the Lord, but how does this develop? Like the line of Cain, which is wiped out in the Flood, and the line of Seth, which survives through Noah, there are two parallel axes: the builders of the Tower of Babel seek to glorify their *own* name (11:4), while Abraham, descended from Shem, travels through the land of Canaan, calling on the name of the Lord (12:8). Shem's name, therefore, reflects not only the eternity, the stability of his line, but his profound connection with God, whose name he and his descendants will invoke.

Besides these hints, subtle wordplay connects Shem's blessing with Japheth's blessing: "Blessed is the Lord, God of Shem (*Elohei Shem*)...May God enlarge Japheth, and let him dwell in the tents of Shem (*ahalei Shem*)" (9:26–27). Shem's blessing opens with *Elohei Shem* and Japheth's blessing ends with *ahalei Shem*.[56] This subtle use of anagram is not merely aesthetic; it ties the two blessing together so that Shem is blessed once again in Noah's blessing to Japheth.

The saga of the nations' dispersal unfolds in two stages: first Shem is chosen (and Ham is rejected), and later on, Abraham is chosen out of Shem's descendants. Shem is chosen because of his modesty and respect, and later on, out of those with proper sexual morality, Abraham will be chosen to call upon the name of God.

WEAVING THE TWO NARRATIVE CIRCLES TOGETHER

To reiterate, the story of Noah's vineyard is a nexus between two eras: it marks the end of the Flood narrative and Noah's life, and it introduces the beginning of the next age, of the dispersal of his descendants around the world. Though both Noah and his sons are born before the Flood, Noah is a product of the old world, while his sons represent the future of the new world.

56. See, for example, in Mathews, *Genesis,* vol. 1, 424. Like many other scholars, he understands "he will dwell in the tents of Shem" as referring to Japheth, and notes the contrast between Japheth, who is invited into, and Ham, who is expelled from, the home of Shem.

This definition is reflected through the description of his death, which falls back into the formulaic pattern of Seth's lineage from Genesis 5. In this chapter, Seth's genealogy follows this pattern:

a. X lived 105 years and begat Y.
b. X lived 807 years after the birth of Y, and had other sons and daughters.
c. Altogether, X lived 912 years, then he died.

This formula is also used to describe Noah's life – although the beginning of the formula and its end are separated by the Flood narrative and the world's renewal:

a. "When Noah was five hundred years old, he became the father of Shem, Ham, and Japheth" (5:32).
b. "And Noah lived after the flood, three hundred and fifty years" (9:28).
c. "And all the days of Noah were nine hundred and fifty years, and he died" (9:29).[57]

The fact that the end of Noah's life echoes the pattern from the "old world" firmly designates him as part of the "old world," as part of the first ten generations that followed Adam. Nonetheless, there are certain deviations from the usual formula, which reflects the upheaval in his life: rather than "and X lived Z years after the birth of Y, Noah "lived for three hundred and fifty years *after the Flood*." Other descendants' lives are defined by the birth of their first child, but Noah's life is defined by the Flood: the first part of his life was before the Flood, and the second

57. Different Masoretic manuscripts differ on the singular or the plural form of "*vayehi/veyehyu*," "[all the days of Noah] was/were." The Aleppo Codex and Yemenite scrolls have the plural form (as do the Septuagint, the Samarian Pentateuch, and the Syriac), unlike the accepted Masoretic text. It seems that Onkelos, as well, had the plural form in his text of the Bible (see the discussion in Posen, *Onkelos*, 206–207). As I note above, if the plural form is associated with longer life, then the Yemenite version is preferable; but the singular form is also justified, as his life is renewed "after the Flood," when lives become shorter.

part of his life takes place after the Flood. The second part of his life is not defined by his sons;[58] they are part of the new world, a world of many nations. Noah belongs to the old world, where son followed father, and all of humanity was one.

Noah's association with the old world is also expressed through the textual pattern of ten generations: there are ten generations between Adam and Noah, and ten generations between Noah and Abraham. A mishna in Avot gives the impression that there are ten generations in each sequence:

> Ten generations from Adam to Noah, to let you know how slow God is to anger: throughout the generations they increasingly provoked Him, until He brought the Flood upon them. Ten generations from Noah to Abraham, to let you know how slow God is to anger: throughout the generations they increasingly provoked Him, until Abraham came and received all the reward which could have been theirs.[59]

Though this mishna presents the two counts as equal, Abraham is not, in fact, the tenth generation after Noah, but the tenth generation after Shem. Noah, therefore, marks the end of the first ten generations, while his sons begin a new era, the second set of ten generations that culminate in the birth of Abraham.[60]

Why, then, does the story of Noah's drunken state connect the end of the Flood narrative and the beginning of the new age? The first circle, Noah's story – loss of knowledge, nakedness, new human initiative after the Flood – concludes the saga of the Flood, Noah's personal odyssey of "this one will bring us comfort." The second circle, the story of Noah's sons – seeing nakedness, curse, and the redefinition of the relationship between the three brothers – introduces the story of the dispersal of the nations. These two narrative focal points are interwoven

58. See further in Grossman, *Text and Subtext*, 171.

59. Avot 5:2.

60. The list's design also hints to another possible division that begins with Noah and ends with Terah, as I will discuss below.

just as the two eras are interwoven at their seams – in this way, the text presents the story of the nation's dispersal as yet another consequence of the Flood. These are not merely juxtaposed; they are interwoven, blurred together by Noah's drunken state. The story of the nations' dispersion marks a new era in history, but it is an era born of the old world – as its corrective, as an attempt to re-create the old world in a different way. After the idea of a united "humanity" fails, "nationality" is born in its place. This is a direct result of the understanding that human hearts are evil from their youth – the world cannot progress, cannot even survive, through a universal appeal to humankind. Nationality is born once the moral is distilled from the immoral, once Noah awakens and distinguishes the good from the bad. Only once this distinction is made can one line of humanity set off along a new path – to the path that leads to the name of God.

The Dispersal of the Nations: Three Families, Seventy Nations (Ch. 10)

A new age has begun. Birth begins anew upon the earth: "These are the generations of the sons of Noah, Shem, Ham, and Japheth; sons were born to them *after the Flood*" (10:1). These are the children of a new era; an era when families become nations. Families become nations only after the Flood, only after God has despaired of humanity's universal morality. Because the human heart is evil from its youth, from now on the world will only make moral progress through one nation – or, to be more precise, through a single family line. To this end, there is a need for differentiation between different branches of humanity.

Three elements are raised again and again throughout the chapter, three elements that serve to differentiate between the different nations: "by their families" – ethnic distinction; "by their languages" – that is, cultural differences expressed through their different tongues; and "their lands," the geographical areas where each one settles (Japheth – v. 5; Ham – v. 20; Shem – v. 31). These definitions touch upon the different characteristics of a "nation," and for this reason, at the end of the analysis of this chapter, I will refer to several recent debates among political science scholars to see how these discussions illuminate the biblical text.

THE DISPERSION OF THE THREE SONS OF NOAH: A UNIQUE CULTURE?

Apart from the ethnic identity of each son's descendants, does the narrative hint to any cultural differences between the various branches of humanity? Firstly, it is worth remembering that "the various arts were, largely, professional secrets of each family or tribal unit, which were concentrated in special quarters,"[1] so that the connection between family-tribal segregation and artistic-professional segregation in the chapter is not surprising. Indeed, we can also point out different cultural differences between the various ethnicities. First of all, "Each had its own language for its clans in their nations" (10:5) – here the Hebrew word *leshonot* is used, as opposed to the word *safa* in the Tower of Babel narrative.[2] The difference between spoken languages is not merely a semantic issue; it touches upon deep cultural differences. Even without delving into theories about the relationship between thought and speech, and how language itself shapes thought, a people's language is inherently connected to its culture. This is due to the technical needs of specific peoples (for example, not every musical instrument has a name in every language, as not all instruments are played all over the world) and to the characteristics specific to their region. One famous example, of course, is that the peoples indigenous to the northern circumpolar regions have many words for snow, based on its thickness, whiteness, and state, whereas for most English speakers, just two words suffice: snow and sleet. While this claim is not strictly true,[3] the principle nonetheless remains intact.

1. Yohanan Aharoni, *Carta Bible Atlas* (Jerusalem, 1964), 19.
2. On the relationship between "*safa*" and "*lashon*," see below, and see Cassuto, who refutes the idea that these different terms are the result of different sources (Cassuto, *Genesis and Its Structure*, 90–91). I will discuss his argument below, in the context of the Tower of Babel narrative.
3. Geoffrey Pullum, *The Great Eskimo Vocabulary Hoax and Other Irreverent Essays on the Study of Language* (Chicago and London, 1991), 159–171. He refutes the scholarly claims that the Eskimo people have many different words for snow.

Arabic has separate words for maternal and paternal aunts and uncles, which may reflect a certain *hamula* – clan – lifestyle with significantly different relationships with the maternal and paternal sides of the family. Hebrew has a wide range of verbs for harvesting various crops. In the Bible, the root K-TZ-R is used to describe the harvest of wheat and barley, and B-TZ-R for harvesting grapes. Even more verbs are used in rabbinic literature: "Laborers who were plucking (*oderim*) figs, or plucking (*goderim*) dates, or harvesting (*botzerim*) grapes, or harvesting (*mosekim*) olives, they may eat and they are exempt [from separating tithes]" (Bava Metzia 89b). This array of verbs reflects the cultural immersion in farming, as well as the land of Israel's special gift of fruit.[4]

Beyond the claim that languages are formed by their speakers' needs, some took this concept a step further and argued that language itself influences its speakers' conscious and actually affects thought – the principle of linguistic relativity. This theory was widely discussed at the beginning of the twentieth century, and while it is less accepted today,[5] there is nonetheless a certain relationship between a nation's culture and its language, a relationship which is not one-directional: "Members of a community or social group do not only express experience; they also create experience through language."[6] This idea, of course, raises curious questions about words which exist in one language but not another. The word "*schadenfreude*," which exists in Hebrew and German describing joy at someone else's misfortune, does not exist in English; the German word "*fernweh*," which expresses longing and nostalgia for somewhere

4. See T. Katzir, "A Holiday Harvest," *The Academy for the Hebrew Language*, 2010, http://hebrew-academy.org.il.
5. See Guy Deutscher, *Through the Language Glass: How Words Colour Your World* (London, 2010); Deutscher, *The Unfolding of Language: An Evolutionary Tour of Mankind's Greatest Invention* (New York, 2005).
6. Claire Kramsch, *Language and Culture* (Oxford, 1998), 3. (This is a central argument she uses again and again.) In this context, I especially wish to mention Joshua Fishman, who has devoted many articles to this idea. See, for example, Fishman, *Reversing Language Shift: Theoretical and Empirical Foundations of Assistance to Threatened Languages* (Clevedon, 1991). In this study, he emphasizes that language and culture "symbolize each other." See also the extensive study by Karen Risager, *Language and Culture Pedagogy: From a National to a Transnational Paradigm* (Languages for Intercultural Communication and Education 11: Clevedon, 2006).

the nostalgic person has never been, was only born in this language, and it lacks an English or Hebrew equivalent. Does this reflect a common German experience, or does its very existence heighten awareness and prevalence of such a phenomenon? Certain words are obviously connected to a certain culture, such as the Spanish word "*sobremesa*," which expresses the light chatter that follows a meal, while the diners have already left the table but the conversation is still flowing (along with tea and nuts). With no precise English equivalent, this word is obviously derived from Spanish dining habits, but does the fact that this practice has been given a concrete name perpetuate the phenomenon itself? Further insight can be garnered by exploring words on the verge of culture, which may or may not characterize the nature of the language and its speakers. For example, the Swedish word "*lagom*" is translated as "moderate," whereas its precise meaning in Swedish is more accurately defined as "just the right amount." Are such precise words inherently conducive to precision and moderation in its speakers? Does the fact that Russian has a special word for the emotion felt towards a person once loved but loved no longer (*razbliuto*) reflect that Russian speakers experience more turbulent relationships, and more separations, than the rest of the world? Does this word, perhaps, heighten their awareness of this poignant experience?[7]

There are endless examples of such words, and for our purposes I wish to clarify that the description that the different nations descended from Noah's sons speak different languages hints to a certain cultural distinction between them.

Beyond the differentiation expressed through language, the description of each nation covertly reflects the different cultural-economic focuses of each of Noah's descendants. In this context, Bustenay Oded encourages the comparison of this chapter with the end of Cain's line – the sons of Lamech:

---

7. The reader is invited to draw his or her own conclusions about the fact that in Japanese, there is a special term (*bakku-shan*) for a girl who is considered beautiful – so long as she is seen from behind; that Indonesian has a word (*mencomot*) for stealing little things that the thief has no use for, but does so for the fun of it; that a specific Spanish word (*tuerto*) means someone who can only see in one eye; and that only Yiddish has a "*schlimazel*."

> And Adah gave birth to Jabal; he was the father of those who live in tents and raise livestock. His brother's name was Jubal; he was the father of all who those who play the lyre and pipes. As for Zillah, she too had a son, Tubal-cain, who forged all kinds of tools of copper and iron. The sister of Tubal-cain was Naama. (4:20–22)

Cain's line ends with the three sons of Lamech, whereas humanity begins anew with the three sons of Noah; just as Lamech's sons are differentiated by their skills and way of life – the wandering shepherd, the cultured musician, and the industrial metalworker – Noah's sons, too, each follow a separate path, a distinct way of life.[8] Unlike the explicit descriptions in chapter 4, Noah's sons' descendants are not so clearly categorized, but their characterizations can be gleaned from the text.

The chapter's introduction retains the familiar order of Noah's sons: "These are the generations of the sons of Noah, Shem, Ham, and Japheth; sons were born to them after the Flood" (10:1). Their geographic distribution, however, is described in reverse order: the first son mentioned is Japheth, then Ham, and finally Shem.[9]

JAPHETH

Japheth's unique lifestyle and profession is easily traced in the concluding formula of his genealogy, which deviates from that of his two younger brothers: "From these the maritime nations spread out in their lands. Each had its own language for its families in their nations" (10:5). Japheth is the only brother who settles on islands, which suggests that his descendants are naval merchants and experienced sailors. One of Japheth's grandsons is Tarshish, the son of Javan (v. 4), whose ships are famous in the biblical world: "For the Lord of hosts has ready a day

---

8. Butsenay Oded, "The Table of Nations (Genesis 10) – a Socio-cultural Approach," *ZAW* 98 (1986): 14–31. He takes note (ibid., 19) of the term "father" that is used to describe Lamech's sons, and which appears again in chapter 10 in regard to Shem (10:21).
9. Radak may be correct in that the text wanted to juxtapose the descendants of Shem with the Tower of Babel narrative and Shem's genealogy that follows (Radak on Gen 11:6).

against all that is proud and arrogant, against all that is lofty, so that it is brought low… against every soaring tower, and every mighty wall, against all the ships of Tarshish" (Is. 2:12–16),[10] and for this reason, Tarshish was famed for its trade and treasures: "For the king had a fleet in Tarshish, at sea with Hiram's fleet; every three years, the fleet would come from Tarshish, loaded with gold and silver, ivory, monkeys and parrots" (I Kings 10:22), "Let kings of Tarshish and the islands pay tribute, kings of Sheba and Seba offer gifts" (Ps. 72:10), and many other examples.[11]

Moreover, Nahmanides saw Japheth's settlement of the islands as a fulfillment of Noah's blessing to him, that his inheritance expands because his naval expertise opens up the whole world to him:

> And the meaning of "from these the maritime nations spread out in their lands" is that the sons of Japheth were island dwellers and they were separate from each other, each one of his sons living on a different island by himself, with their lands far from each other, and this is their father's blessing, who said: "May God enlarge Japheth," as they were many, widely spread all over the earth. But the sons of Ham were all close together on the land, and it therefore says, "The border of the Canaanites was from Sidon… their lands and nations," and the same with the sons of Shem.[12]

In this way, Noah's blessings begin to be fulfilled; with his glorious ships, Japheth has the whole world at his fingertips. The first of the brothers chooses a certain vocation, a certain lifestyle: Japheth settles on the islands and becomes a nation of voyagers, sailors, and merchants.

HAM

The narrative description of Ham's descendants deviates from the technical, formulaic nature of this chapter. Beyond the anomalous description

---

10. See also I Kings 22:49; Is. 23:1; 23:14; 60:9; Ezek. 27:25; Ps. 48:8.
11. On Tarshish, see David W. Baker, "Tarshish," *ABD* 6: 331–333. See also his etymological discussion of the name possibly being related to the cleansing of metal. Regarding its geographical location, see Day, *From Creation to Babel*, 154–165.
12. Nahmanides on Gen. 10:5.

of Canaan's borders, which is of course related to the special biblical focus on the land of Canaan, there is a further, striking deviation – the story of Nimrod, the son of Ham's eldest son, the only character who is significantly fleshed out in this genealogical chapter:

> And Cush fathered Nimrod, the first on the earth to be a mighty warrior. He was a mighty hunter before the Lord. That is why it is said, "Like Nimrod a mighty hunter before the Lord." (10:8–9)

> The beginning of his kingdom was Babylon, along with Uruk, Akkad, and Calneh in the land of Shinar. From that land Asshur went out and built Nineveh, Rehoboth-Ir, Calah, and Resen between Nineveh and Calah; that is the great city. (10:10–12)

Nimrod's unique character is already evident in the description of his birth: "And Cush fathered Nimrod." The previous verse cites a list of Cush's sons, but Nimrod is not mentioned: "The sons of Cush: Seba, Havilah, Sabtah, Raamah, and Sabteca. The sons of Raamah: Sheba and Dedan" (10:7). The seven descendants mentioned here (five sons and two grandsons) do not include Nimrod, whose birth is only related in the next verse. Assuming that the "Cush" in question is the same in both verses,[13] Nimrod is clearly set apart from his brothers. Is this a positive evaluation of Nimrod that directs a favorable spotlight upon him (as Radak notes)? Does this hint that Nimrod's family did not see him as a legitimate son? In either case, he certainly stands apart.

Nimrod is hailed as the "first to be a mighty warrior (*gibor*)." Nahmanides seems to be justified in associating this quality with the establishment of the first kingdom, as a natural leader who is the first to organize and control a military.[14] The term "mighty hunter" should be understood in a similar sense, as Josephus describes: "A bold, violent, forceful man."[15]

13. This can be debated. For evidence that this refers to the same Cush, see Samuel Abramsky, "Nimrod and the Land of Nimrod," *Beit Mikra* 25 (1980/81): 15n54.
14. In contrast to Ibn Ezra's interpretation (on Gen. 10:8) that his might was related to hunting animals. Rashi, unlike Ibn Ezra, sees this as a negative evaluation.
15. Josephus, *Antiquities*, 1:113.

He may have hunted down those who dared oppose him (other warriors, or even his subjects, hinting to his nature as a fierce dictator), or his victims may have been wild animals, which was a sign of royal strength and bravery in the ancient world, as is evident, for example, from the series of reliefs depicting King Ashurbanipal hunting lions (from 668–630 BCE).

Above all, Nimrod is characterized through the description of his kingdom: "The beginning of his kingdom was Babylon, along with Uruk, Akkad and Calneh in the land of Shinar" (v. 10).[16] The word "kingdom" occurs only once in this chapter, in relation to Ham's descendants. Nimrod is the world's first conqueror, the first to control the surrounding areas through force in order to establish an empire. This is evident from his birth somewhere in Africa, as part of Ham's clan, followed by his campaign to Mesopotamia, which he conquers and dominates, becoming the world's first emperor.

There have been many attempts to identify the figure of Nimrod with an ancient historical king. Some see him as the archetype of the Mesopotamian king, such as Hammurabi, Gilgamesh, Sargon, and Naram-Sin of Akkad. Others associate him with an Egyptian pharaoh (such as Amenhotep III), or with an Assyrian leader (Tukulti-Ninurta I, who reigned between 1243 and 1207 BCE).[17] Other scholars perceive him as a demythologization of the Babylonian god Ninurta (the god of war and hunting), reduced in Genesis to a king of flesh and blood.[18] These theories, however, remain in the realm of speculation; there may have been an actual historical king behind the biblical figure, but his specific identity has no bearing on the narrative objective. Nimrod is the "first" warrior, the first conqueror, the first hunter – he founded the

16. The parallel description in Chronicles only mentions that Nimrod "began to be a mighty one (*gibor*) in the land" (I Chr. 1:10), without the description of his conquest.
17. Speiser, *Genesis*, 72.
18. Karel van der Toorn and Pieter W. van der Horst, "Nimrod Before and After the Bible," *HTR* 83 (1990): 1–29. There are several details with this claim, first and foremost that Ninurta is not described as the builder of cities, which is a fundamental part of Nimrod's characterization. Some claim that Ninurta's biblical name is "Nisrokh," as in: "He was worshipping in the temple of his god, Nisrokh" (II Kings 19:37; Is. 37:38). See Mathews, *Genesis*, vol. 1, 449n75.

world of war, of conquest, of domination. He is the "first" king. With the birth of nationality, the struggle for mastery of a certain region and its resources is born as well. The birth of nationality gives rise to the birth of international politics.[19] And indeed, archaeological study has shown that the first ancient kingdoms rose to power in Mesopotamia:

> Under such circumstances the first mighty kingdoms rose up; those who managed to impose a single, organized regime on their settlement and even set out to spread their dominion beyond their own borders. Here, one after another, Sumer and Akkad, Mitanni, the Hittites, and the Arameans mounted the historical stage.... Compared to them, Egypt was closed and consistent in its development, and as the generations marched on the only thing that changed was the Pharaonic dynasty in power, from the earliest days of the kingdom...until the latest.[20]

In the context of this chapter this issue has further significance: it is Ham (or his son Canaan) who is cursed and designated for slavery by his father, yet Ham produces the first empire, the first conqueror. The curse, as mentioned, focuses on Canaan, so that the streak of power and domination issuing forth from another of Ham's descendants can be justified, but nonetheless, Nimrod's campaign of conquest may hint to an attempt to shake off the ancestral curse that haunts their dynasty.

Nimrod represents the lifestyle of Ham's descendants: permanent settlement in organized cities, kingdoms and politics. This is especially evident in the next verses: "From that land Asshur went out and built Nineveh, Rehoboth-Ir, Calah, and Resen between Nineveh and Calah;

---

19. The sages generally see Nimrod in a negative light, as a rebel against God. For example: "Then they began – R. Simon said: This language is used in three places, implying rebellion. Then they began to call on the name of the Lord; 'And it was when man began'; he began to be a mighty one" (Genesis Rabba 23:9). The Midrash also accuses Nimrod of being the king who cast Abram into the fiery furnace. It could be that the very establishment of earthly rule is seen as a slight against heavenly rule.
20. Aharoni, *Atlas Carta*, 12.

that is the great city" (vv. 11–12).[21] The sons of Ham are credited with building empires, with founding the "great city" of Nineveh! Such details are only presented about Ham's line, which implies that in this respect, they are distinguished from their brothers.[22] The descendants of Shem and Japheth may also have built cities, but there is no indication of this in this chapter; Ham is the son characterized as the great urban developer, the founder of empires.

SHEM

Last, but not least, comes Shem. Is there any particular characterization of Shem's line in these verses? The first clue lies in the emphasis on family: the introduction to Shem's line already associates it with one of its descendants, and one of Shem's brothers: "To Shem also, sons were born. He was the father of all the children of Eber, the brother of Japheth, the eldest" (v. 21). I will discuss the possible meanings of the word "father" below – not all of them are strictly related to being the father of the family – but the unusual association with his brother certainly shows his strong connection with his family, at least this brother. Shem's connection with "Japheth, the eldest" is consistent with the concept that the eldest brother is the head of the family line, the head of all the brothers.[23] Similarly, we find "Utz, his firstborn, and Butz, his brother" (Gen. 22:21), and, "Aaron took Elisheba, daughter of Amminadab and sister of Nahshon, as his wife" (Ex. 6:23). This alone justifies Shem's association with Japheth, but in the wider context of the narrative, this detail serves a further purpose. Noah blesses Japheth that he will "dwell in the tents of Shem" (Gen. 9:27), a blessing that draws the two brothers together, while Ham is excluded; and through the explicit mention of Shem's connection with Japheth in this chapter, Noah's blessing is fulfilled. A similar fraternal bond is

21. On the preferred reading that Nimrod is the subject of the sentence, the builder of Nineveh (rather than a person by the name of "Ashur"), see Abramsky, "Nimrod," 3–4.

22. On the establishment of the cities mentioned in this verse and the beginning of the "royal city" in Mesopotamia, see A. Leo Oppenheim, *Ancient Mesopotamia: Portrait of a Dead Civilization* (Chicago, 1964), 109–142. On the connection between Nimrod and the founding of the Mesopotamian royal city, see Abramsky, "Nimrod."

23. Cassuto, *From Noah to Abraham*, 218.

emphasized once again among Shem's descendants: "To Eber two sons were born. The name of one was Peleg, for in his time the earth was divided, and his brother's name was Joktan" (v. 25).

But Shem's family line is not only closely associated with family in this respect. This chapter presents three generations of Japheth's line and four generations of Ham's line, while a full six generations of Shem's line are listed (up to the thirteen sons of Joktan). Beyond its subtle emphasis on family, this chain is an expression of perpetuation and continuity. It is Shem's line that goes on and on for six generations and concludes with the birth of thirteen great-great-great-grandsons, the promise of further generations, of exponential growth. Shem's very name hints to eternity, to immortality through the birth of children who will bear the name of the family line forever.

In a certain sense, this stability is in dialogue with the stable settlement of Ham's descendants, who seek permanence and continuity through the construction of fortified cities and powerful kingdoms – kingdoms that, they believe, will endure forever. This implied tension between the sons of Ham and the sons of Shem may also be manifest in a further element of Shem's lifestyle reflected in these verses.

Bustenay Oded proposes that the introductory verse to Shem's line already hints to their lifestyle: "To Shem also, sons were born. He was the father of all the children of Eber" (v. 21). What does this mean? As we shortly learn, Eber is indeed one of his great-grandchildren, but why is he singled out and anticipated right away? Ibn Ezra believes that this is because this descendant will be the ancestor of Abraham: "The reason for 'the father of all the children of Eber (*Ever*)' – to inform that he is the father of the Hebrews (*Ivrim*), of whom there is no one higher, and the Lord is his God. As it is written, 'Thus says the Lord, the God of the Hebrews (*Ivrim*).'"[24] He writes even more explicitly elsewhere: "And there is no doubt that the meaning of 'Abram the Hebrew (*Ivri*)' (Gen. 14:13), is that he was of the sons of Eber, as in, 'the father of all the sons of Eber,' the opposite of 'and Ham is the father of Canaan.'"[25] Nahmanides disagrees with the reading that this verse refers to Shem's great-grandchild:

24. Ibn Ezra on Gen. 10:21.

25. Ibid., Ex. 21:2.

> The meaning of "the father of all the sons of Eber (*Ever*)" – he was the father of all those who dwell on the other side (*ever*) of the river, the place of Abraham's origin. It does not make sense that this mention of "*ever*" refers to the name of the man who was Peleg's father, for why should he be connected to him?[26]

A reference to one particular descendant – in this case Eber – generations before his birth is puzzling indeed.

Based on the formula "the father of all…" that appears in chapter 4, I would like to make a completely different suggestion. In chapter 4, the meaning of this phrase pointed to a new cultural or occupational reality. Jabal is "*the father* of those who live in tents and raise livestock" (4:20) – he invented a new form of shepherding, and is considered the "father" of this science. His brother Jubal is "the father of all those who play the lyre and pipes" (4:21) – once again, he is the founder, the inventor, of a new science, a new concept in the world. If so, then we can adopt Oded's reading that "the father of all the sons of *Ever*" does not refer to the individual Eber, but to a new form of life – to people who wander, who are "*ovrim*," who "cross" and "pass on" – who move from place to place. Like the island-dwelling, seafaring sons of Japheth, and the city-dwelling, conquering sons of Ham, the sons of Shem, too, adopt a unique lifestyle: "The conclusion is that *Ever*, the descendants of Shem, represents the sector of the world's population who wander from place to place, in contrast to societies that settle in one place."[27]

This theory is further supported by Noah's blessing to his sons, that Shem's descendants will live in tents. Tent dwellers are nomads, wandering shepherds with no true place, or, to cautiously anticipate one of the most central themes of Genesis, who have no true place *yet*. Their place will be granted by divine promise when Canaan become their servants, and they inherit his land.

The contrast between Ham and Shem is the contrast between Cain, the man of the earth, builder of the first city (4:17), and Abel, the wandering shepherd. Cain is powerful and productive, but his descendants

26. Nahmanides on Gen. 10:21.
27. Oded, "The Table of Nations," 22.

were wiped out from the face of the earth he once worked. God favored Abel's offering; God dwells in the tents of Shem, not the cities of Canaan.[28]

If so, it emerges that the dispersion of Noah's sons expresses their divergent lifestyles. Not only geographical distinctions result in their differences; their language, too, and their way of life, also set them apart. In the previous episode, the reader already learns that Shem's way of life is privileged above them all: Shem, the wandering shepherd, is more favored than Ham, the urban conqueror, or even the seafaring Japheth.

What, then, is the nationalistic view that emerges from this chapter? Biblical nationality is ethnic nationality, the approach that each person is born with a particular ethnic identity, just as he or she is born into a particular family. Additionally, the text views each nation as having an individual culture – but an "acquired culture" – that is, Ham and Canaan acted in a certain way out of their own free will, and this choice is reflected in the culture of their descendants, just as Shem's choice results in the particular culture of his descendants. Lifestyle, too, is theoretically a matter of choice, yet in this primal chapter of Genesis, three different lifestyles – nomads, seafarers, and city dwellers – are divided according to national identity.

Does this chapter express any approval or disapproval of the actual dispersal of the population and their separation into different nations? This is presented as the result of the Flood, as emphasized in the narrative framework of this chapter: "These are the generations of the sons of Noah, Shem, Ham, and Japheth; sons were born to them *after the Flood*" (10:1); "These are the families of Noah's sons, according to their generations, in their nations, and from these the nations spread out over the earth *after the Flood*" (10:32). In this sense, this new order of society may not be ideal. Nonetheless, it is hard to find actual disapproval of this new world order, of the population spreading out, in the text itself. On the contrary, there is certain elation at the prospect of the empty world filling up once more, of the newly growing population spreading out over the silent soil – why, from just these three, "the whole earth spread out"

28. It is interesting to note in context of this analogy that Cain was given the opportunity to lead the family, but he exploited his power for evil and murdered his brother. Cain's parallel, Ham/Canaan, is cursed with slavery to his brothers.

(9:19)! In this chapter, the spread of humanity is presented as a natural phenomenon. Children are born, and children are born to these children, and each family fills up their own corner of the world, naturally resulting in geographical and cultural segregation.

This can be presented in almost the opposite sense: chapter 10 presents the formation of nations as a way of preserving different ways of life. This is related to the aforementioned analogy between the sons of Noah and the sons of Adam. The contrast between Ham, the city builder, and Shem, the wandering shepherd, recalls the struggle between Cain and Abel, farmer and shepherd. There is no description of a violent struggle in this chapter, and certainly no echo of fratricide, but the description of the different nations is preceded by Ham's curse and Shem's blessing, which color the genealogy of each nation. Ham may be a mighty founder of empires for now, but he will be Shem and Japheth's servant in the future. On one hand, this should not come as a surprise for the reader, as this is the next stage in the broader comparison of these chapters of Genesis; the Flood narrative, as we saw, can be compared to the first Creation narrative, the story of Noah's drunkenness can be compared to the story of Eden, and now, the tension between Ham and Shem can be compared to the struggle between Cain and Abel. However, as is often the case, a comparison between the two episodes yields not only similarities, but differences. The patterns of the old world seem to repeat themselves in the new world, but there are crucial differences between the sagas. God is involved with Cain and Abel from beginning to end: the brothers' struggle begins with offerings to Him, God determines who will be the head of the family ("and you will rule over him"), and then God punishes the offender. The brothers' parents are not involved in their struggle at all; Adam and Eve only make an appearance at the beginning and end of the chapter to conceive, bear, and name their sons.

In contrast, the world after the Flood is a different world. We already saw how Noah takes initiative even before he leaves the ark – he sends out the raven and the dove, he plants a vineyard, he blesses and curses his sons. This pattern continues in chapter 10, with the dispersion of the nations. The struggle between Shem and Ham in the previous scene did not revolve around God, but around the question of their father's honor. And in the next chapter, unlike Cain and Abel, Ham does not seek out Shem's death. Each son sets out along his own path and builds his own culture within his own geographical borders. Why is Shem's life spared? How does humanity avoid the repetition of the old world's mistakes?

There are two intertwined answers to this question. The first is that this is precisely the power of a nation. Abel was alone and defenseless against his brother. In contrast, Shem's descendants are united, and there is strength in numbers; one purpose of a nation is to ensure its members' existence. Without this – as the history of chapter 4 proves – one form of life is liable to overcome another. Here, too, the transition between humanity's role in the old world and its role in the new world comes into play. In chapter 4, God Himself attempts to prevent Abel's murder: He hands the reins to Cain and warns him against succumbing to his sin – to no avail. Cain rises up against his shepherd brother and kills him. The founding of nations transfers responsibility to humanity itself, and to the political unions that become responsible for perpetuating the existence of its own way of life.

The individual clan's evolution into a nation can be connected to another aspect, which is also related to Shem's descendants' ability to defend themselves. Adam and Eve, like Noah, may have had three sons, but they first had two – Cain and Abel – and only after the death of Abel, they conceived and bore Seth, whose name testifies to his nature as an alternative son, as a replacement. In contrast, Noah has three sons at the same time. What is Japheth's role within the implied tension between Ham and Shem? From the story of Noah's drunkenness, it is evident that Japheth is seen as a friend and ally to Shem, but does this third wheel make any contribution to the struggle between Ham's urban conquerors and Shem's wandering nomads? Sara Daniel suggested to me that this third, seemingly superfluous line can be perceived as a neutral force that stabilizes the tension between the other two nations. As long as there are just two children – Cain and Abel, Cain and Seth, Isaac and Ishmael, Jacob and Esau – they are inherently defined against each other; if Abel's sacrifice is accepted, Cain automatically assumes he is rejected. This binary division is shattered as soon as there are more than two sons – from now on, there is room for all three of them to coexist.

One's life is not defined by the other's, because there is another presence that expands the family dynamics. If this is the case, then Japheth plays a key role in neutralizing the tension between the two nations descended from Shem and Ham. The broadening of Noah's family line from two binary dynasties to three allows room for each nation to bloom within its own boundaries, in its own culture, without being perpetually at odds with the alternative culture.

THE BIBLICAL CONCEPT OF NATIONALISM

The birth of nationhood in chapter 10 leads us to explore the concept of nationality in general and within biblical thought in particular.[29] Is a "nation" the product of a human decision, of a group of people declaring that they wish to govern their lives together for a common purpose, either pragmatic or ethical, or should this concept be perceived as a framework imposed upon human society, one that people are born into involuntarily?

Out of the three criteria that define each nation in this chapter – ethnicity, language, and geography – two are acquired, while one is "natural." A person is able to choose his or her place of residence, and his or her language, both of which constitute part of the definition of a "nation state," but a person is born with a certain ethnic identity, which is, of course, the main characteristic of a "natural state." That is, biblical discourse is rooted in a different sphere than what is accepted in modern philosophical thought, because if all three nations are presented as the expansion of three nuclear families, then the biblical notion of nationality and nationality is inherently, explicitly ethnic. However, the very fact that there is a biblical concept of a "nation" seems to be a new concept within the context of ancient Near Eastern thought.[30] As Daniel Gordis writes,

> The concept of nationhood – of a distinct group identity based on common language, culture, land, and blood ties – was not a modern European innovation, as some scholars proclaim it to

29. I discuss nationality at length in the context of the Abraham cycle in Grossman, *Abram to Abraham*, 43–68.

30. Wolfram von Soden, *The Ancient Orient: An Introduction to the Study of the Ancient Near East* (Grand Rapids, 1994), 13–14.

> be, but rather an integral part of the Jewish tradition from its very beginnings."[31]

Nonetheless, nationhood in the Bible is still considered an extension of family. This is evident from the presentation of humanity as the product of three distinct families – Shem, Ham, and Japheth: "These are the groupings of Noah's descendants, according to their origins, by their nations; and from these the nations branched out over the earth after the Flood" (6:32), which also seems to be reflected in the story of the Tower of Babel.[32] In fact, the very appellation, "the Children of Israel," illustrates that familial origin is what essentially defines a nation, and as Daniel Block emphasizes, the Bible considers all nations – and not just Israel – as extensions of family clans (such as Edom, Ammon, and Moab), even if it is not at all clear if these nations also perceived themselves in these terms.[33] Effectively, this perspective characterizes the Jewish people until this very day. As Blaise Pascal famously marveled:

> Advantages of the Jewish people – in this search the Jewish people at once attract my attention by the number of wonderful and singular facts which appear about them. I first see that they are a people wholly composed of brethren, and whereas all others are formed by the assemblage of an infinity of families, this, though so wonderfully fruitful, has all sprung from one man alone, and, being thus all one flesh, and members one of another, they constitute a powerful state of one family. This is unique.[34]

Perception of the nation as an extension of a family (not only in an ideal sense, as reflected in Aristotle, but when members of a nation are considered part of the same "clan") has broad implications in the context of mutual responsibility. This is prominent in biblical laws that

---

31. Daniel Gordis, "The Tower of Babel and the Birth of Nationhood," *Azure* 40 (2010): 19–36.
32. See, for example, Theodore Hiebert, "The Tower of Babel and the Origin of the World's Cultures," *JBL* 126 (2007): 29–58.
33. Daniel I. Block, "Nations/Nationality," *NIDOTTE* 4: 968.
34. Blaise Pascal, *Pensées*, trans. J. Ur (Jerusalem, 1976), 135–136.

require compassion for another member of the community because he is "your brother" (particularly evident in the laws of Lev. 25, Deut. 15, and Deut. 22–25). The law extends the concept of family responsibility to apply between every member of the nation.[35] In this respect, biblical nationalism is an extreme manifestation of the notion of a "natural nation," wherein membership is the automatic result of being born to a certain family. This is consistent with the biblical perception of Israel as a "nation of culture" – as a nation that is distinguished from other nations not merely by its political context, but through its covenant with God, by being "God's nation."[36] Moreover, this is also true, in at least some books of the Bible, in relation to other nations; the culture of Egypt or Amalek can also be traced over the course of the text,[37] among others.[38] This is evident from the story of Noah's drunkenness as an introduction to the dispersion of the nations – each branch of the family has its own behavioral norms, as defined by their ancestor's actions. Nonetheless,

35. For the notion of the nation as family as a basis for the moral guidelines of the Bible, see W. A. L. Elmslie, "Ethics," in *Record and Revelation*, ed. H. Wheeler Robinson (Oxford, 1938), 275–302, who even included the common covenant of the entire community as part of the moral guidelines.
36. On this point William Irwin is imprecise in his comprehensive essay on the Hebrews. He claims that the main point of connection with the people of Israel is spiritual and cultural, and a question of loyalty to the God of Israel, while the ethnic connection was pushed into a corner (William A. Irwin, "The Hebrews," in *The Intellectual Adventure of Ancient Man: An Essay of Speculative Thought in the Ancient Near East*, ed. H. Frankfort, H. A. Frankfort, J. A. Wilson, Th. Jacobsen and W. A. Irwin, [Chicago, 1946], 223–360, especially in the fourth chapter that discusses "Nation, Society, and Policy"). I believe that the Christian approach has skewed views of this issue. Israel's culture and covenant with God are indeed the foundation of the Israelite nation, but the premise is that even if this is a defined ethnic group which can be joined, the family connection is a fundamental part of this group, similar to Rabbi Judah HaLevi's perception of the Israelite *segula.*
37. Concerning Amalek, see, for example, Rabbi Yaakov Medan, "Amalek," in *On the Way of the Fathers*, ed. A. Bazak, S. Vigoda, and M. Munitz (Alon Shvut, 2001), 317–396; concerning Egypt, see, for example, Asher Weiser, "Egypt in the Bible," *Mahanaim* 105 (1961): 16–24.
38. It is debatable, however, whether this defines the nation according to its culture, or on a literary-symbolic level. Egypt, for example, represents human pride in several prophecies, but Egypt may merely be a *symbol* of pride; this was not necessarily the cultural factor that unified the Egyptian nation into a single political entity.

this must be stated with caution, as the "culture" that defines Israel is not derived from its nature, but from the events that befell its ancestors. Abraham was chosen as the father of a nation because of his morality (Gen. 18:19), while Amalek is characterized as God's enemy because it attacked the weak, newborn nation that had only just left Egypt.[39] That is, a biblical nation's culture is determined by its moral decisions.

The distinction between a nation as an extended family and a nation in a political sense is also reflected in the language of the biblical narrative. There are two common biblical expressions for the word nation: "*am*" and "*goy*." The word "*goy*" is usually translated as "nation," while the word "*am*" may be translated as "nation" or "people"; sometimes *am* is used, it seems, to differentiate it from the word *goy* if both are used in the same context (as in Is. 2, for example). E. A. Speiser claims that these terms actually have different meanings: the term *am* refers to an extended family that has evolved into a nation,[40] while the word *goy* represents a nation in the political sense.[41] The choice of a particular word often affects the connotations of a particular phrase: the term *am* is often accompanied by a possessive suffix ("My people," "your people," etc.), while such suffixes are rarely added to the word *goy*.

> This shows that *'am* is something subjective and personal, *goy* objective and impersonal. Note, "*Ure'eh ki emkha hagoy hazeh*" – "Consider, too, that this nation is Your people" (Ex. 33:13). The

39. See especially Medan, "Amalek." He shows how the fierce biblical enmity against Amalek does not stem from its ethnic identity, but is the result of its culture and immorality.
40. Sometimes the word simply means "family" (as in Gen. 32:8; 48:19; Lev. 21:1–4; Job 18:19). The expression "gathered unto his people" seems to be parallel to the phrase "gathered unto his forefathers" (Bern Alfrink, "L'expression *Ne'esaf El Amav*," *OTS* 5 [1948]: 118–131). The meaning of the word is not limited to the Bible, but appears in other Semite languages. At the end of a broad survey of different languages, Lipinski writes: "In summary, we can say that the West Semitic word *'amm* refers to agnates, both individually and collectively… The biblical usage of *'am* appropriates this double meaning without any difficulty" (E. Lipiński, "*'am*," *TDOT* 11: 169–170).
41. For a philological debate of these two terms, see also L. Rost, "Die Bezeichnungen fur Land und Volk im Alten Testament," in *Das kleine Credo und andere Studien zum Alten Testament* (Heidelberg, 1965), 76–101; Block, "Nations/Nationality," 966.

> same declaration with the two nouns interchanged would be unthinkable in a biblical context, though not in translation.[42]

This claim may seem somewhat exaggerated, as both terms sometimes appear in parallelisms, and the word *am* is sometimes used in the sense of a political nation.[43] Rather, this distinction should be drawn on a literary level, even if not on a semantic level:[44] the connotations of each word are different, and given that the word *am* is essentially associated with family, this meaning is present even when the word is used in the more general sense of "nation."

This distinction illuminates the verses that conclude each section in our chapter. Japheth's genealogy concludes thus: "From these the maritime nations spread out in their lands. Each had its own language for its *families in their nations* (*begoyehem*)" (10:5). Ham's genealogy concludes similarly: "These were the sons of Ham, by their *families* and languages, their lands and *nations* (*begoyehem*)" (v. 20), as well as Shem's: "These are the sons of Shem, by their *families* and languages, their lands and their *nations* (*legoyehem*)" (v. 31). This dichotomy – of family and nation – is repeated at the chapter's end, which sums up the history of all three branches: "These are the *families* of Noah's sons, according to their generations, in their *nations* (*begoyehem*), and from these the *nations* (*hagoyim*) spread out over the earth after the Flood" (v. 32). The text's insistence at referring to each branch as the head of both "family" and "nation" implies that each family began as a clan, which grew and grew until it became a nation – a political entity. At its heart, each nation has family roots, but its definition as a *goy* hints that each ethnic identity gradually evolves into a national, political group. This is implied through the narrative framework, which opens with focus on Noah's sons and the sons they themselves bore after the Flood: "These are the generations of the sons of Noah, Shem, Ham, and Japheth; sons were born to them

42. Ephraim A. Speiser, "'People' and 'Nation' of Israel," *JBL* 79 (1960): 157–163.

43. Jacob Licht, *Encyclopedia Biblica*, s.v. "*am*," vol. 6, 235–239; Lipinski, "*'am*," 174. See also Ronald E. Clements, "Goy," *TDOT* 2: 426–427.

44. Similar to the phrasing of Aelred Cody, "When Is the Chosen People Called a *Goy*?" *VT* 14 (1964): 1–6.

after the Flood" (v. 1) and concludes with the nations that spread all over the face of the earth: "These are the families of Noah's sons, according to their generations, in their nations, and from these the nations spread out over the earth after the Flood" (v. 32).

If so, it emerges that in biblical thought, a nation is essentially an extended family. This concept has wide implications, informing various moral mitzvot, and assuming that every citizen has a deep sense of connection with his or her own nation. In the context of the Abraham narrative cycle, I have shown that with very few exceptions, the word *goy* is not used in relation to Abraham's descendants; there is a clear preference to characterizing the nation of Israel as Abraham's children, as his family, rather than as a nation.[45]

This is salient, for example, in the aforementioned narrative of the Covenant between the Pieces. On one hand, there is a clear national dimension to this revelation. The covenant ends with a description of the borders of the land (including the eastern side of the Jordan), anticipating the nation that will inhabit this territory, which transpires in David and Solomon's time. This conclusion would serve well as the ending of a narrative of national-political character, but this is not the case. The chapter opens with Abraham's complaint that he has no "heir" (15:2–3); God promises him that he will be granted a son of his own, and that his descendants will one day be too numerous to count. The discussion of an "heir" connotes an intimate family atmosphere, and in this spirit the reader is also introduced to the subsequent discussion of inheritance of the land.[46] Indeed, the term "*yerusha*," "inheritance," with its striking familial connotations, is repeated in the chapter, mentioned in context of inheritance of the land. God promises "to assign this land to you as an inheritance *(lerishtah)*," whereupon Abram asks, "How shall I know that I am to inherit it (*irashenah*)?" (15:7–8).[47] Therefore, the

45. Grossman, *Abram to Abraham*, 43–64.

46. On the relationship between these two scenes see Ruth Fidler, "Genesis XV: Sequence and Unity," *VT* 57 (2007): 162–180; Grossman, *Abram to Abraham*, 95–112.

47. Note that the biblical law of inheritance (Num. 27:8–10) is given in the context of dividing the land into portions, so that "the Israelite law of inheritance originates in the division of land through tribal-familial organization." Samuel E. Loewenstamm, *Encyclopedia Biblica*, s.v. "*Yerusha*," vol. 3, 789.

aforementioned linguistic distinction is consistent with the general atmosphere of this chapter. The nation who will enslave Israel is referred to as a "nation," while Abraham's seed are his "offspring," the "fourth generation" of the head of the clan who will one day return to the land to inherit it.

The two exceptions to this rule – the two instances when the word *goy* is used in regard to Abraham's descendants in Abraham's narrative cycle – discuss the nation of Israel's place within the universal political sphere (12:2; 18:18). In these cases, there is profound importance in defining the sons of Abraham as a nation relevant to world politics. Within the inner Israelite narrative, however, Abraham's descendants are defined as a family, even when they are a family too numerous to number or count. Aelred Cody argues that the biblical reservations towards the term *goy* stem from the negative connotations of this word, as it is not used to present Israel as the chosen people, but rather lowers it to the level of other political nations (to the extent that the word *goy* became a post-exilic term for a non-Jew).[48] The Bible, however, often implements this word in a positive sense, as in the case of Genesis 12:2 and 18:18. It seems to me that even when Abraham's seed becomes a nation in the active political sphere – a "great nation" through which all nations shall be blessed – there is clear narrative intent to present this political entity in the context of its family ties, that is, as the product of its "forefathers." The Israelite nation is depicted as the natural, unified progeny of a single family, a "natural nation" (needless to say, the theory of social contract is not the basis of this kind of nationalism). This presentation of nationalism commissions more mutual commitment from its members, which in turn contributes to the members' emotional sense of belonging to their own nation.

This brings us to the unique approach of biblical-familial nationalism. Critics of natural-ethnic nationalism have claimed that this "natural" form of nationalism is liable to degenerate into fascism and negation of the Other – and history has proven them right. The premise of this criticism is clear: reinforcing the national sense of unity through emphasis on natural, unalterable factors constructs an insurmountable wall between members of the community, who were born into these circumstances, and outsiders.

48. Cody, "*Goy*."

The concept of nationalism presented in the book of Genesis, however, hardly seems to encourage such results; rather, this particular sense of belonging is calculated to encourage morality that emanates outside the community. It suffices to mention the father of the nation, Abraham, who is chiefly characterized by his moral quality, and this morality is what serves as the chosen nations' definitive cornerstone: "For I have singled him out, that he may instruct his children and his posterity to keep the way of the Lord by doing what is just and right" (18:19). This declaration is followed – and illustrated – by Abraham's efforts to prevent Sodom's obliteration. The description of Abraham's election presents the requirement for "doing what is just and right" as a requirement for all of Abraham's household, not just for the leader, the king.[49] A prevalent position in political philosophy attributes common ideals as a collective basis to the liberal definition of a nation, while the tribal-ethnic definition of a nation does not set moral objectives. The biblical ethnic nationalism shatters this dichotomy, however, at least in relation to Israel. It is not entirely clear whether the Bible holds that every nation has a definitive culture it must fulfill,[50] but this seems to be the case from the story of Noah' drunkenness and his sons' different attitudes towards him. In any case, the family-nation Abraham will establish is to be rooted upon moral values. In other words, although the nation in question evolves naturally, out of a single family, this "natural" nation is not solely characterized thus; rather, the narrative employs moral discourse about the nation's foundation upon divine values of righteousness and justice. The nation's morality is an immanent part of its character and purpose.[51]

---

49. Moshe Weinfeld, *'Justice and Righteousness' in Ancient Israel against the Background of 'Social Reforms' in the Ancient Near East* (Jerusalem, 1985), 125–126.

50. Some philosophers relied upon language differentiating between the nations as a gauge for difference in culture (Herder and Fichte). Even if they did not state this explicitly, this can be read in the story of the nations' dispersal (ch. 10) and the Tower of Babel (ch. 11). In these narratives, the narrator emphasizes the dispersion of the nations together with the development of their individual languages. According to this reading, the linguistic differentiation between nations hints that each nation has a culture it must fulfill.

51. A similar model appears in Hegel's *Grundlinien der Philosophie des Rechts* (in *Werke in zwanzig Bänden*, ed. E. Moldenhauer and K. M. Michel, vol. 7 [Frankfurt am Main: Suhrkamp Verlag, 1970]), even if it is only similar structurally. When he seeks to explore the "ethical life," he begins by presenting the family as every person's first

This seems to be possible because here, the "community's will" which serves as the basis for a "nation of culture" is replaced with divine will. Therefore, despite the "naturally" evolving depiction of the nation, it is not bound by a deterministic approach which creates the impression of a nation without moral value or purpose. The free will upon which the nation is based facilitates moral discourse; at the same time, however, because a single man is chosen as the father of the nation, the nation is still considered natural. Even though the nation is considered a naturally evolving entity, the culture of this nation is not imposed upon its members merely because they were born into it. The covenant with God is a moral and religious obligation more than a definition of national character.[52]

This biblical paradigm is connected to a key issue that touches upon the very formation of nationalism according to the Bible: Is God interested in national particularism, or is this an expression of human will that is not promoted as an independent goal in the Torah itself? The answer to this question is complex, and hinges upon understanding of the relationship between the dispersion of the nations in chapter 10, and the Tower of Babel narrative. To this end, let us gaze upon the Tower of Babel and determine whether or not its top indeed reaches the heavens.

social framework, and from this framework a person progresses to "civil society" and eventually encounters "the state," which in his opinion, is the fulfillment of the ethical ideal. He emphasizes that the ideal collective union (i.e., the "state") should not only be considered as if it were solely intended to safeguard the individual's property and individual freedom (which already occurs in "civil society"), but it should comprise the content and purpose of every individual in it, and only through the state can a person find ethical fulfillment (Hegel, Part 3, see especially #258). When Hegel refers to "general will" as something palpable, which surpasses individual will (even if the individual is not aware of it, he must submit to it), he already paves the way to the next step of God's will being an expression of general will.

52. This combination has several dramatic implications for the Abraham narrative cycle and his characterization as the father of the Israelite nation. See Grossman, *Abram to Abraham*, 43–68.

The Tower of Babel: Technology and Imperialism (11:1–9)

The Tower of Babel narrative poses an exceptional challenge: Was the construction of the tower a sin, and if so, what was it? The vast range of proposed readings illustrates that the answer is far from clear, and the text tolerates several interpretations.[1] The narrative should be read and analyzed not only as an isolated unit, but in its broader context, and especially in parallel with the Eden narrative. Moreover, beyond these two circles, the text should also be examined in dialogue with the Babylonian worldview, as the narrative presents the story of the Babylonian city's founding and even concludes with its naming – so there is room to explore the relationship between the biblical attitude

1. Ed Greenstein points out various reading approaches to this narrative and shows how each reader paves out his or her own reading through the questions he or she asks and the main components he or she focuses on (Edward Greenstein, "A Pragmatic Pedagogy of Bible," *Journal of Jewish Education* 75 (2009): 290–303).

towards the establishment of Babel and the Babylonians' perception of themselves. Not surprisingly, these three interpretive circles meet in the meta-objective of the narrative.

Beginning with an in-depth reading of the story itself, we will attempt to address the narrative's key issue: What was the builders' actual sin? There are too many opinions to address here, but I will list the central disputes here:

1. Some claim that the city and its tower were built as an act of some kind of sin (or even two separate sins, of both the city and the tower). Some even read this narrative as the classic biblical model that repeats itself throughout Genesis 1–11 of sin/punishment/divine compassion.[2] Throughout history, commentators have been divided regarding the nature of the sin itself, and their various suggestions can, perhaps, be divided into two main categories:
   a. The focus of their sin lies in the builders' fear "lest we be scattered over the face of the whole earth" (11:4) – that is, they were unwilling to spread out all over the world as God commanded Noah, and they preferred to remain in one place (Rashbam and Radak).
   b. Their sin can be traced to their aspirations to "make a name for themselves" (11:4). This is read as a statement of rebellion against God, whether idol worship or desire to seize control in the heavens themselves, or as an expression of pride, which undermines God's place in the world.
2. On the other hand, many claim that their actions were not an actual sin, but that the building of a city and a tower opposed God's will. Ibn Ezra, for example, emphasizes that the builders were not actually aware that they were acting against God's will:

2. Von Rad, *Genesis*, 148–150. In this context, Clines' reservations are interesting: he counters that there is no element of divine kindness (as there is after the sins of Eden, Cain, and the Flood). He therefore proposes seeing the election of Abram as God's appeasement after the punishment (David J. A. Clines, *The Theme of the Pentateuch* [JSOTSup 10: Sheffield, 1978], 61–79; see also H. Ringgern, "*Bavel*," *TDOT* 1: 467). As we will see later on, the Tower of Babel does, in a certain sense, serve as the introduction to Abraham's election.

"These builders thought that through their solution, they would not disperse. This was not God's will, but they did not know His thoughts."[3] I will return to this reading later.

Modern scholars are similarly divided, and for the sake of brevity, I will focus on an article written by Theodore Hiebert. He holds that there is no sin at all in the narrative; rather, it should be read as the story of the birth of multiple nations and cultures. He understands the description of the tower "whose top will reach heaven" as a figurative expression devoid of negative connotations (following Ibn Ezra). In general, he sees the construction of the tower itself as secondary to the building of the city, which, he holds, is the narrative focus.[4] He does not even perceive God's intervention as a punishment: "God is reacting not to pride, defiance, or imperial power, but to the cultural uniformity of humanity, and God's response is not an act of punishment or judgment, but an intervention to introduce cultural difference."[5] His reading received mixed responses, some of which championed the traditional reading that there is indeed an actual sin in the story. To mention some of the central points that challenge his interpretation:

- Is it really logical for the Bible to present Babylon as the cradle of universal culture, without any hint of criticism?[6]
- Unlike God, who usually reveals Himself on "mountains," and unlike Abraham, who builds altars on "mountains," the builders of Babel begin their task in the "valley." This contrast hints to criticism against the builders,[7] especially in relation to Abra-

3. Ibn Ezra on Gen. 11:4.
4. Through exploring the narrative structure, Radday reaches a similar conclusion (Radday, "Chiasmus," 100). See more later on.
5. Hiebert, "The Tower of Babel," 42.
6. André LaCocque, "Whatever Happened in the Valley of Shinar? A Response to Theodore Hiebert," *JBL* 128 (2009): 30.
7. LaCocque, "The Valley of Shinar," 32. He adds that "Shinar" has negative connotations itself in the Bible (he holds that the founder, Nimrod, is presented in a negative light; see also Gen. 14:1; Josh. 7:21; Is. 11:11; Zech. 5:11; Dan. 1:2). I believe there is room to debate the matter.

ham, who makes his appearance at the end of the same chapter. The builders, as I have discussed and will discuss further, wish to make a name for *themselves,* while Abraham seeks to glorify God's name; there may even be intentional wordplay between the "tower" (*migdal*) they build and the promise to Abraham that "I will make your name great (*ve'agadla shemekha*)"[8] – both are derived from the root G-D-L, "big" or "great." Moreover, the word "*sham,*" "there," though common, is a key word in both narratives. In the Tower of Babel narrative of chapter 11, it appears frequently (along with the word "*shem,*" "name"): "They found a valley in the land of Shinar and settled *there*.... Come, let us go down and *there* confuse their language.... From *there* the Lord scattered them over all the face of the earth.... For *there* the Lord turned the language of the whole earth into babble, and from *there* the Lord scattered them over all the face of the earth."[9] This word also accompanies the reader throughout Abram's journey to Canaan, and here, too, the word "name" also makes an appearance: "And they came to Haran and settled *there*.... And *there* he built an altar to the Lord who had appeared to him. From *there* he moved on to the hill country.... And *there* he built an altar to the Lord" (11:31–12:8).[10] The juxtaposition of "there" and "there" generates certain tension. The builders want to build their city *there,* while God wants Abraham to settle *there.*

- The phrase "and we will make a name for ourselves" mentioned here is charged with negative connotations. Abram, as

8. Hiang Chea Chew, "The Theme of 'Blessing for the Nations' in the Patriarchal Narratives of Genesis" (PhD diss., University of Sheffield, 1982), 154–155, 157. Jan Fokkelman has already noted that the term for tower, *migdal,* is related to the word "*gadol,*" great, and interprets this in a negative light, that the tower builders seek their own greatness.
9. It is interesting that he is also mentioned twice in the next verse: "These are the generations of Shem. When Shem was one hundred years old, he fathered Arpachshad" (11:10).
10. For a vast range of additional connections (some more convincing, others less so) see Chew, "Blessing for the Nations," ibid.

mentioned, does not wish to make a name for himself – he grows great by glorifying God's name (12:2). David's warriors, men of "name," do not achieve their fame by glorifying themselves: Abishai (in II Sam. 23:18) does not seek to make a name for himself, nor does Benaiah son of Jehoaida (II Sam. 23:22).[11]

- There is unmistakable irony between their reservations *against* being scattered all over the earth and God doing precisely that; this irony contributes to the reading of God's response as a punishment for some kind of offense.[12]

The confusion surrounding this episode is great indeed. Unlike the Eden narrative (or the story of Cain and Abel, or the story of Noah's drunkenness), there is no specific, obvious sin, and God's reaction is not presented as a punishment, but rather as a result of the fear that humanity will be able to do whatever it pleases: "Now nothing they intend to do will be impossible for them" (11:6). Their dispersion over the face of the earth is not necessarily a punishment, but an attempt to limit their power. On the other hand, the claim that Babylon is hardly an ideal setting for the world's cultural origins is justified. As we will see, the narrative structure hints to an actual conflict between humanity and God.

I wish to follow in the footsteps of Ibn Ezra – that while the builders are not strictly guilty of a specific sin, the whole narrative process takes place against God's will.

THE BEGINNING OF THE STORY

The first two verses, which serve as a kind of narrative exposition, provide important background information about the story and its nature. This background information is especially crucial as it is set to change over the course of the plot:

> And it was (*vayehi*) that the whole earth had one language and the same words.

11. A similar formulation is in Wenham, *Genesis*, 32.
12. John T. Strong, "Shattering the Image of God: A Response to Theodore Hiebert's Interpretation of the Story of the Tower of Babel," *JBL* 127 (2008): 626–627.

> And it was (*vayehi*) that as people journeyed from the east they found a valley in the land of Shinar and settled there. (11:1–2)

The anaphoric repetition of "*vayehi*," "and it was," points out two important aspects: the focus on language, "the whole earth had one language," and the geographical focus, "they settled there." These two aspects will be reversed by the story's end; the two opening verses will be paralleled with two concluding statements:

> That is why it was called Babel:
> for there the Lord turned the language of all the earth into babble,
> and from there the Lord scattered them over the face of all the earth. (11:9)

The repetition of "there" at the beginning of each phrase, and "all the earth" at its end, reinforces the sense of a double ending that corresponds with the first two lines of the story that takes place in Babel: the focus on language ("language of all the earth into babble"), and the geographical focus ("scattered them over the face of all the earth"). It is interesting that the two motifs are expressed through two similar words that are vocalized differently, "*sham*," "there," focuses on geographic location, while "*shem*," "name," is related to language and its construction. The connection between these words is rendered explicit in the builders' declaration: "Let us make a name for ourselves, lest we be scattered over the face of the whole earth" (11:4).[13]

The link between place of residence and language is obvious when discussing the dispersion of nations and the establishment of national boundaries. Nonetheless, unlike chapter 10, as I will discuss further below, the Tower of Babel narrative does not explicitly deal with the founding of "nations," but on the dispersion of humanity in every direction.

---

13. See further in Jan Fokkelman, *Narrative Art in Genesis* (Assen/Amsterdam, 1975), 16–18 (he adds that the word "*shamayim*," "heavens," also participates in this wordplay); Grossman, *Text and Subtext*, 109–110.

There are even more striking differences between chapters 10 and 11. First and foremost, how can we read the narrative opening that all people on earth lived in a single place and spoke a single language when the previous chapter describes how the three sons of Noah settled in different regions and spoke different languages? The simplest answer is that the Tower of Babel narrative takes place before this dispersion, that after the general, natural description of their migration and development, the text takes a step back and describes what triggered these events in the first place. A certain hint to this process can be found in Shem's genealogy: "To Eber two sons were born. The name of one was Peleg, *for in his time the earth was divided*" (10:25). The Tower of Babel narrative is thus anticipated in chapter 10, but not yet developed.[14]

Others have proposed to read this differently, through focusing on the different definitions of language in each chapter: chapter 10 discusses the "*lashon*," of each nation, while in the Tower of Babel narrative this word does not appear even once, and the term "*safa*" is used instead. Cassuto draws a significant distinction between the two terms:

> The use of the different terms "*lashon*" and "*safa*" [both rendered "language"] – the former in chapter 10 and the latter in chapter 11 – is not to be regarded, with the adherents of the documentary hypothesis, as an indication of exact quotation from two sources that differ from each other in their style and vocabulary.... [Rather,] Biblical Hebrew prefers the word *safa* if the reference is to a given language considered by itself, not in relation to other tongues, and the word *lashon*, when it is intended to express relationship and differentiation between languages.[15]

This easily explains why chapter 10 uses the word *lashon*, as it focuses on the difference between the nations and their languages, while chapter

14. Assuming that the division alluded to in Peleg's name refers to the dispersion of languages in the Tower of Babel narrative. His name could also be a hint to the shortening of the human lifespan by half in his lifetime, in which case there is no connection to the first nine verses of the chapter.

15. Cassuto, *From Noah to Abraham*, 144–145.

11 discusses the common tongue spoken by all the people of the world until this event took place, and therefore uses the word "*safa*."

Another proposal holds that while chapter 10 indeed describes the linguistic development of each and every nation as they settled in a different region, the human population was still able to communicate using a single universal language, a *lingua franca*. For a certain period in history, Sumerian was the common international language; later, it was replaced by Akkadian, Aramaic, and eventually Greek. Today, in most parts of the world, English is the default language that people from different places use to communicate with each other. This, too, might explain the disparity between "*safa*" and "*lashon*" – the latter is the term used for the local language, while the former refers to the *lingua franca*.[16] In this way, the two chapters can be read consecutively – even after the nations move apart, they can still communicate with each other through the universal language (which is consistent with Rashi's reading, "They said to one another – nation to nation, Egypt to Kush, and Put to Canaan"[17]). This suggestion is fascinating, but the Tower of Babel's clear association between geographical dispersion and linguistic dispersion seems to favor the first theory – that the chapters are not strictly arranged in chronological sequence. If this is the case, then the question arises as to why the narrative is presented in this particular order, and I will return to this point later.

"*Safa*" and "*lashon*" are not the only terms for language in these chapters. What kind of meaning is contained within the double description of the first line: "Now the whole earth had one language (*safa aḥat*) and the same words (*devarim aḥadim*)"? "One language" is clear, but what new information is conveyed by "the same words"? This could be a classic biblical parallelism,[18] or it could be indicative that this homogenous

16. Cyrus Gordon, "The Ebla Tablets and the World of the Bible," *HS* 22 (1981): 39–47 (and see his further studies). Hamilton also takes this direction (*Genesis*, 350–351). He claims that in light of this reading, it cannot be determined whether the Bible holds that there was one common language that branched out to different languages, or whether different languages developed in parallel (ibid., 357–358).
17. Rashi on Gen. 11:3.
18. For example, Westermann, *Genesis*, vol. 1, 543. In Bakhtinian terms, we have "dialogic words" at play (Kawashima, *Biblical Narrative*, 36).

people had a limited vocabulary.[19] Alternatively, it could be read as a sign that their thoughts were one and the same, that not only did they speak the same language, but they thought similar thoughts and expressed identical mind-sets.[20] There were no conflicts, no differences of opinion; all shared the same lifestyle, the same goals. Rashi's interpretation is based on the reading that they all shared a common goal – and a rebellious one at that: "The same words – they came with one scheme and said, 'He had no right to select for Himself the upper regions. Let us ascend to the sky and wage war with Him.'"[21] To interpret "words" as a "scheme" casts the narrative in a negative light from its very beginning. Nissan Ararat takes a step further and claims that this is also the meaning of the confusion of language:

> To this end, God – who watches over humankind – suggests an act that will prevent the "leaders" from executing their plot: He raises suspicions among the people regarding the point of building the city and tower: "Let us go down and confuse their language [i.e., their united opinions] so they will not understand one another's language [i.e., identify with their opinions]."[22]

This reading already raises the question of the value of cultural pluralism at the beginning of the narrative. If this is indeed the information provided in this opening verse, then this must be one of the themes that the narrative addresses.[23]

19. See especially in Cyrus Gordon, "*Aḥadim = iltênûtu* 'Pair,'" in *Sefer Segal: Studies in the Bible Presented to M. H. Segal*, ed. Y. M. Grintz and J. Liver (Jerusalem, 1964), 5–9. He claims that this word might mean "pairs" based on the Akkadian and Ezek. 37:17, and we should understand this as "limited," as in, a limited vocabulary. This is also favored by Hamilton, *Genesis*, 350–351.
20. As proposed by André LaCocque, *The Captivity of Innocence: Babel and the Yahwist* (Eugene, 2010), 26.
21. Rashi on Gen. 11:1.
22. Nissan Ararat, "The Tower of Babel as a Satiric Drama," *Beit Mikra* 39 (1994): 230.
23. Avraham Wolfensohn makes the interesting suggestion that this expression means that they shared items, implying that they were seeking to found a nation with organized economic implications (Wolfensohn, "Let Us Build a City [Genesis 11:1–9]," *Beit Mikra* 39 [1994]: 28–33). It does not seem that there is already political organization at the beginning of the narrative, however. On the contrary, the first political union will

The next verse also contributes to the narrative focus: "And it was that as people journeyed from the east they found a valley in the land of Shinar and settled there." I do not wish to address the somewhat surprising direction of their journey, "from the east," which many have discussed, but rather, I will focus on the importance of their actual journey. Why does the narrator begin by relating their journey to the valley in Shinar, rather than just describing what happened once they had settled there? The additional detail that "they found" this valley further contributes to the sense that a group of wanderers has finally found the perfect place to settle down and establish their civilization.[24]

The building of a city is a marked change from the nomadic lifestyle implied in the story's first verse – the same kind of contrast implied between the descendants of Ham and of Shem in the previous chapter. This reading is consistent with what is known about Babylon in the ancient world: "[Babylon] was considered the first city to be built by people, a vast metropolis whose abundant inhabitants and whose mighty edifices struck awe and fear in the hearts of nomads and the dwellers of strongholds and fortified villages."[25] This leads us to the main narrative objective, which we will trace through the narrative structure.

---

take place once they reach the Valley of Shinar – not that I am convinced that this was necessarily an organized political movement in the first place. I do not identify with Danna Fewell's proposal that the tower and the city were built for the king (Fewell, "Building Babel," in *Postmodern Interpretations of the Bible: A Reader,* ed. A. K. M. Adam [St. Louis: Chalice, 2001], 10). The expression "and they said to one another" suggests that it was a spontaneous move on the people's part (as held by Phillip M. Sherman, *Babel's Tower Translated: Genesis 11 and Ancient Jewish Interpretation* [Leiden and Boston, 2013], 27, for example).

24. See also Fokkelman, *Genesis,* 44. Miller compares this narrative with the story of the founding of the Sumerian city Eridu, and that both stories open with the people's wandering (Miller, "Eridu," 243). It may therefore be that this detail is a narrative convention that emphasizes the sense of stability the settlers experience when they build their city. In any case, Miller is correct that Eridu's construction is presented in a positive light (and is built at the gods' initiative) while our narrative does not approve of Babylon's establishment.

25. A. Leo Oppenheim, *Encyclopedia Biblica,* s.v. "Babel," vol. 2, 28.

The Narrative Structure: "Many Plans Are in a Man's Heart, But It Is the Lord's Plan That Will Endure" (Prov. 19:21)

While the narrative can be presented as two parallel halves,[26] the most stable structure is a chiastic arrangement:[27]

A. *Now the whole earth had one language* and the same words.

  B. And as they journeyed from the east they found a *valley in the land of Shinar and settled there.*

    C. And *they said to one another,* "Come, let us make bricks and burn them thoroughly." And they had brick for stone and bitumen for mortar.

      D. And they said, "*Come, let us build us a city and a tower* whose top will reach heaven, and let us make a name for ourselves, lest we be scattered over the face of the whole earth."

      D'. Then the Lord came down to see *the city and the tower* that the children of men had built.

    C'. And the Lord said, "Look, they are one people and with one language, and this is what they have begun to do. Now nothing they intend *to do* will be impossible for them. *Come, let us* go down and there **confuse** their *language,* so that they will not understand *one another's language.*"

  B'. *From there the Lord scattered them* over the face of *all the earth,* and they stopped building the city.

---

26. For example, Isaac M. Kikawada, "The Shape of Genesis 11:1–9," in *Rhetorical Criticism: Essays in Honor of James Muilenburg,* ed. J. J. Jackson and M. Kessler (Pittsburgh, 1974), 18–32; Wenham, *Genesis,* 235.

27. Fokkelman (*Genesis* 11–45) points out these two possibilities, and also develops the inverted structure (which he believes is a concentric structure). See these two possibilities in Frank Polak, *Biblical Narrative: Aspects of Art and Design,* 2nd ed. (Jerusalem, 1999), 228–230; Cotter, *Genesis,* 69–70; Day, *From Creation to Babel,* 168–170. Many have adopted the view that the narrative has a concentric structure, such as Miller, *Genesis,* 34–36; Radday, "Chiasmus," 100; Jacobs, *Measure for Measure,* 150–53; Blenkinsopp, *Creation,* 164; Mathews, *Genesis,* vol. 1, 468–469.

A'. That is why it was called Babel, for there the Lord *turned the language of all the earth into babble,* and from there the Lord scattered them over the face of *all the earth.*

The narrative is easily parted into two – the first half describes human action, and the second part God's reaction. The inverted structure of the two parts yields a neat chiastic structure.[28] At the beginning of the story, all humanity is united through a single language, but by its end, this language is reduced to babble (A-A'). At first, humanity settles in one place, but by the end, they are scattered (B-B'). At first, they communicate with one another and act as one, but by the end, they cannot understand one another and are unable to cooperate (C-C'). At the end of the first half they build a city and tower in order to stay together, but at the beginning of the second half God intervenes and goes down to see this city and tower, and things fall apart (D-D').[29]

This structure clearly reflects a struggle between human will and divine will, between the many plans in the human mind and God's own plans, but this is not necessarily an indication of actual sin.[30] Although human plans to settle in a certain place do not concur with God's intended course of history, the more subtle reading that this is not a story of crime and punishment still stands.

---

28. Cotter rightly emphasizes that there is a significant difference between the claim that the story is presented in a classic parallel structure and the claim that it is presented in a chiastic/concentric structure. These produce different reading effects: in a classic parallel structure, God is presented in parallel to the builders, whereas in a chiastic/concentric structure, God is contrasted with them and is presented as One who is against their plan (Cotter, *Genesis,* 69–70). On the difference between these structures and their reading experience, see also Grossman, *Text and Subtext,* 256–264.
29. Not only the structure creates tension between human action and divine action, but as Buber shows, this story makes special use of repetitive words that underscore this tension, such as: "all the earth"; "language"; "come, let us"; "city and tower"; "name"; "scatter" (Martin Buber, *Darko shel Mikra* [Jerusalem, 1964], 286–287). As Yitzhak Avishur has shown, the sages were keenly aware of the phenomenon of "measure for measure" expressed through this repetition (Yitzhak Avishur, "Stories of Genesis in Light of New Literary Science," *Beit Mikra* 21 [1976]: 613–618). See also Rashi on Gen. 11:8, and Jacobs, *Measure for Measure,* 150–153.
30. Unlike the aforementioned Strong, "Response," 626–627.

Human initiative and activity is emphasized even before the construction of the actual city through the catalyzing expression "*hava*," "come, let us," and the order of its appearance demands special attention:

- And they said to one another, "*Come, let us* make bricks and burn them thoroughly." And they had brick for stone and bitumen for mortar. (11:3)
- And they said, "*Come, let us* build us a city and a tower whose top will reach heaven, and let us make a name for ourselves, lest we be scattered over the face of the whole earth." (11:4)

Some have questioned the order of these actions (after all, why should the making of bricks be mentioned before the plan to build a city),[31] while others question the inclusion of the description of brick making at all: "True, the reference to bricks and mortar certainly adds nothing significant to the plot, and yet the narrator spends a good deal of time discussing the building materials. To what end?"[32] Indeed, we need to understand how the focus on building materials contributes to our understanding of the narrative, and why the technological prowess of the people of Shinar is given such attention in the narrative, even before its product is used for construction of the city and tower.[33]

This story, then, focuses on technological development in itself, and in the social organization expressed through technological development. In the land of Shinar, humanity learns how to harness natural resources for its own purposes; science is utilized for the fulfillment of desires. There is an act of social organization, of "one said to another," expressed independently of the plan to build a city, one that precedes the plan to build a city: "Come, let us make bricks and burn them thoroughly," and through this technological development, "they had brick for stone and bitumen for mortar" (11:3). Scholars wonder why the

31. Westermann, *Genesis*, vol. 1, 545.
32. Sherman, *Babel's Tower*, 28.
33. Wenham and von Rad saw this focus as a polemic against how the process of building differed in ancient Israel, in contrast to the ancient Babylonians (Wenham, *Genesis*, 239; von Rad, *Genesis*, 144).

making of bricks precedes the plan to build a city, assuming that these bricks are solely intended for the construction of the city, but this is not the case. The people of Shinar delight in their collective ability to create, to upgrade natural resources, to overcome the lack of stones with mere mud and straw – to develop technology.

The second statement conveyed by this sequence is that the people of Shinar decide to devote this technological development to the construction of a city and tower, but this is a separate stage with its own statement, with its own independent act of initiative: "And they said, 'Come, let us build us a city and a tower whose top will reach heaven'" (11:4).

This reading helps illuminate the narrative objective, and is even more salient in light of the structure: human initiative and ability to exploit natural resources, including human talent and skill, is what God objects to, what God seeks to limit. Component C' is mirrored by component C and not component D; that is, God's words in verse 6, which express the problematic nature of their actions, are not parallel to the construction of the tower and city, but to the very idea of human initiative rather than to a specific human initiative: "Look, they are one people and with one language, and this is what they have begun to do. Now nothing they intend to do will be impossible for them." Each half of the verse epiphorically ends with the word "to do" – God is opposed to doing, to exaggerated human production in itself, not just to any particular form it takes (in this case, a city and tower).[34]

God's apparent issue with human technology in itself brings us closer to understanding of the narrative objective (and the objective of the narrative design), but before drawing any conclusions, I wish to address the problematic nature of the city and the tower itself as proof that unbridled human initiative is dangerous. To this end – "come, let us" explore the relationship between the city and its tower.

---

34. I will cautiously propose that the text may be hinting to the fact that technology itself falls apart – that bricks and mortar are not as hardy as natural resources, and that humankind did not manage to overcome the lack of natural resources. Again, it may be that the city and tower do not endure because of the people's scattering, but perhaps they would have proved durable had this not been the case.

City and Tower

Some claim that the Tower of Babel and the city itself form two distinct narrative threads.[35] Some trace two entirely separate story lines through the various repeated details (such as God's double descent in verses 5 and 7), especially the conclusion that focuses solely on the city: "From *there* the Lord scattered them over all the face of earth, *and they stopped building the city*. That is why *it* was called Babel, for *there* the Lord turned the language of the whole earth into babble, and *from there* the Lord scattered them over all the face of earth" (vv. 8–9). This focus is surprising indeed – until this point, the city and tower are always mentioned together, when the people of the valley make their plans, and when God descends to see them. Why is the Tower of Babel completely overlooked at the story's end?[36] Why doesn't the verse say, "and they stopped building the city *and the tower*"? This omission continues through the end of the narrative, when the city is given a name, but there is no reference at all to the uncompleted tower. If there are two narrative threads, this is easily resolved – God is angry about the city and ceases construction, but there is no explicit criticism of the tower in this story.

One logical solution is that the city was supposed to be completed before the construction of the tower, so if the city was never finished, construction of the tower never even began, and there is therefore no reference to it at the narrative's end. Yet this reading is problematic, because God descends to see "the city *and* the tower," which implies that its construction had already begun. I also find Cassuto's claim that "it is unnecessary to add that… they gave up building the tower [as it is obvious],"[37] unconvincing, given, once again, that the city and tower are mentioned together during the first half of the narrative.

I believe that this detail supports the aforementioned idea that the narrative focus is on the city, rather than on the tower itself – despite

35. See, for example, Rabbi Yehuda Rock's proposal to split the narrative into two aspects, "An Analysis of 'The Same Words' of the Tower of Babel Narrative," *Megadim* 32 (2000): 9–20.
36. In the Septuagint and the Samaritan Pentateuch, this omission is filled in.
37. Cassuto, *From Noah to Abraham*, 248.

the misleading fact that these verses are usually referred to as the "Tower of Babel" narrative. The builders exclaim, "'Come, let us build us a city and a tower whose top will reach heaven, and let us make a name for ourselves, lest we be scattered over the face of the whole earth'" (v. 4), and logically, it is the city, not the tower, which will prevent the population from scattering – the tower will be part of the city, but it will not solve the problem of dispersion in itself. This view is rejected by many modern scholars, who identify the tower in the story with the Babylonian *ziggurat* – the towering, multilevel, terraced, pyramid-shaped structure that was part of the Babylonian temple compound. This particular tower is largely considered a reference to one of the most famous ziggurats, *Etemenanki,* which literally means "the house of the foundation of heaven and earth" – a lofty structure built in Marduk's temple in Babylon. As Cassuto writes, "There can be no doubt that the Biblical story refers specifically to the city of Babylon and to the ziqqurat *Etemenanki* therein."[38] This reading holds that the tower is related to the religious nature of the city, and it is clear why commentators ascribe it such a central place in the narrative.

However, it seems that the tower is only secondary to the city itself. Some, perhaps rightly, claim that the tower serves a technical purpose: the city's inhabitants will be able to see their home from afar, and safely make their way back (Radak),[39] while others reasonably claim that the city will gain renown and stability through its famous monument (Ralbag).[40]

The relationship between the tower and the city can be explained through a completely different, even more logical suggestion: a strong, well-defended city requires a wall with watchtowers.

38. Cassuto, *From Noah to Abraham,* 229. See also André Parrot, *The Tower of Babel,* trans. E. Hudson (London, 1955), 17; A. Leo Oppenheim, "The Mesopotamian Temple," *BA* 7 (1944): 54–63.

39. Radak on Gen. 11:4.

40. Ralbag on Gen. 11:4. Compare to the two possibilities raised by *Or HaḤayim* on Gen. 11:4: (1) so they would not lose their way, but always be able to find their way back through the tower; and (2) that their tower would be famous all over the world, so that they could always find their way back by asking how to reach their famous city. Bekhor Shor on Gen. 11:4 presents these two readings in a similar way.

Watchtowers feature throughout the Bible, especially in the context of war, as in Gideon's warning to the people of Penuel, who, confident in their strength, refuse to provide food for Gideon's warriors: "So he also retorted to the people of Penuel, saying, 'Upon my safe return, I shall smash down this tower'" (Judges 8:9, and see the continuation in v. 17). Similarly, the people of Tebez flee to their city's tower when Abimelekh attacks: "There was a stronghold in the town, where all the town's citizens, men and women, had fled; they locked themselves in and went up to the roof of the tower" (Judges 9:51). There are many further examples, and it is no wonder that Isaiah equates tower with strong wall in a poetic parallelism: "On every tall tower / and on every fortified wall" (Is. 2:15), or that Uzziah was praised for reinforcing the city's defenses by building towers: "And his fame reached up until Egypt, for he reinforced it all the way up. And Uzziah built towers in Jerusalem... and reinforced them" (II Chr. 26:8–9). The people of the valley (which is not a naturally defensible location, like as a hilltop would be) intend to build a powerful fortified city for themselves, a city with a mighty watchtower.[41] After all, in ancient times, Babylon was considered one of the strongest and most impenetrable cities – to the extent that its seven walls were considered one of the seven wonders of the world.[42]

In any case, the city, not its tower, seems to be the main narrative focus. Upon God's intervention, the narrator emphasizes that the city's construction ceases, and it is the city which receives a new name at the end of the story.[43] Once again, the fact that Gen 11:1–9 is generally referred to as the "Tower of Babel narrative," (especially in English), is misleading.

41. About the tower as a guard tower, see further in Christoph Uehlinger, *Weltreich und "eine Rede": Eine neue Deutung der sogenannten Turmbauerzählung (Gen 11, 1–9)* (Freiburg, 1990), 372–378. As for God's "fear" of the builders' fortifications, he refers to Job 42:2: "I know that You can do everything, that nothing You propose is impossible for You." There, Job states this about God; here, God fears the people's unlimited power. He is correct that Job, too, speaks of unlimited power.

42. Oppenheim, "Babel," 13. This is salient in Herodotus' description of the great walls of the city and its many fortifications. Sherman also holds that such a large or important city requires a tower (*Babel's Tower*, 31).

43. Compare to Cassuto, *From Noah to Abraham*, 226.

If we summarize the main narrative elements, we will be able to point out the central problem with the builders of the city, and thus determine the narrative objective. The people of the valley developed a new technology which allowed them to settle in the valley permanently, bringing their nomadic lifestyle to an end. The construction of their city is a fulfillment of their desire to settle down permanently, and if chapter 11 is read against chapter 10, the full significance of this change emerges: Ham's descendants are the ones who build cities, and if this chapter is read, in turn, in reference to the story of Noah's drunkenness, then there is clear preference for Shem's nomadic lifestyle over the urban development of Ham, the cursed son. Nimrod is the chief representative of Ham's descendants in this respect through his migration to Mesopotamia, his establishment of an empire, and his construction of cities (10:11). If the "beginning of his kingdom was Babylon... in the land of Shinar" (10:10), it is wholly consistent with our story, which begins with the settlement of a nomadic people in Shinar and their attempt to build the city that becomes known as Babylon. In both chapters, that is, Babylon is depicted as the cradle of political urban civilization. In ancient exegesis and rabbinic literature, Nimrod is repeatedly depicted as a central figure in Babylon's establishment and construction,[44] and indeed, a synchronic reading of these chapters invites the same conclusion.

The Italian commentator, Rabbi Obadiah Sforno, may be hinting to this connection in his commentary: "And they said, 'Come, let us build a city' – this was the counsel of the ministers of that generation, to appoint Nimrod king over the entire human race."[45] He sensed that the desire to build a city is a deep political statement, and suggests

44. Philo already associates Nimrod with the construction of the city and tower: Philo, *Questions and Answers on Genesis*, trans. R. Marcus (London and Cambridge, Mass, 1953), vol. 2, 81–82; Josephus, *Antiquities*, 1:113–119. Many midrashim also take this direction. However, see Pseudo-Jonathan's opposite view, that Nimrod actually opposed this construction, and thus managed to conquer Assyria and more. Pseudo-Jonathan translation of Gen. 10:11 states: "From that land went forth Nimrod, and reigned in Athur, because he would not be in the counsel of a divided generation. And he left those four cities; and the Lord thereupon gave him a place; and he builded four other cities, Nineveh and Pelatiath, Kartha and Parioth."

45. Sforno on Gen. 11:4.

that through the establishment of a royal metropolis, Nimrod was to rule over humanity.

In this narrative, however, the reservations towards the city and its tower are depicted as profoundly religious: human power must be limited, and God restricts this power by dividing humanity into different nations. There will not be a single omnipotent, unrivalled empire which is able to do as it pleases: "Look, they are one people and with one language, and this is what they have begun to do. Now nothing they intend to do will be impossible for them" (11:6). As I have already asserted, God is not concerned about the city itself, but rather about the potential problem of humanity's unrestrained power.

This is also expressed through the description of the tower as reaching the heavens. Some commentators, as early as Pseudo-Jonathan and Rashi, famously read this as a hint that the tower builders planned to "fight against the heavens," while others, such as Ibn Ezra and Radak, merely read this as an expression of the tower's great height (like Moses' figure of speech in Deut. 1:28, "fortified up to the heavens"). A further debate is whether their words should be understood literally or figuratively – did the builders actually believe that they could "reach the heavens" by building high enough,[46] or were they aware that this could simply not be achieved?[47]

I wish to focus on the literary aspect of this description. Whether their declaration is literal or figurative, this expression raises certain associations. Humanity seeks to reach beyond its allotted territory, beyond the earth, and break through to the heavens, even though "the heavens are the Lord's, but the earth He has given to humanity" (Ps. 115:16). Humankind seeks to build a city so strong and so mighty, with towers so tall that they encroach upon heaven itself. Whether literal or figurative, this declaration implies a breach of the boundaries between heaven and earth. Humanity must recognize its limits, and sometimes this limitation poses a challenge:

> Let me ask the following question: Is this Lurianic doctrine of *tzimtzum* just a Kabbalistic mystery, without any moral relevance

46. For example, Driver, *Genesis*, 135.

47. For example, von Rad, *Genesis*, 145. See also Sherman, *Babel's Tower*, 29–30.

> for us; or is it the very foundation of our morality? If God withdrew, and creation is a result of His withdrawal, then, guided by the principle of *imitatio Dei,* we are called upon to do the same. Jewish ethics, then, requires man, in certain situations, to withdraw. Man must not always be victor. From time to time triumph should turn into defeat. Man, in Judaism, was created for both victory and for defeat – he is both king and saint. He must know how to fight for victory and also how to suffer defeat. Modern man is frustrated and perplexed because he cannot take defeat. He is simply incapable of retreating humbly. Modern man boasts quite often that he has never lost a war. He forgets that defeat is built into the very structure of victory, that there is, in fact, no total victory; man is finite, so is his victory. Whatever is finite is imperfect; so is man's triumph.[48]

This sense is further reinforced through a comparison with the Eden narrative.

BABEL AND THE GARDEN OF EDEN

Nahmanides already hinted to a connection between the Tower of the Babel narrative and the first sin: "Their sin was similar to the sin of their ancestor." He traces this link to a midrash: "Perhaps it is for this reason they commented [in Genesis Rabba 38:9, on the verse] 'that the sons of Adam built,' R. Berekhya said, 'What, were they the sons of donkeys? The sons of camels? Rather, they were the sons of Adam, the first man.'"[49] Nahmanides points out that this midrash questions the rare use of the expression "*bnei adam,*" which literally means "sons of Adam," and answers that it hints to Adam himself. The builders of the first city are following in Adam's footsteps.

This reading has intriguing textual basis, especially given the linguistic connection I have already pointed out in my discussion of the story of Noah's drunkenness:[50]

48. Rabbi Joseph B. Soloveitchik, *Confrontation and Other Essays* (Jerusalem: Maggid Books, 2015).

49. Nahmanides on Gen. 11:2.

50. See especially Witte, *Die biblische Urgeschichte,* 87–89, and Rock, "The Same Words," who claims that the two aspects of the narrative are each in their own dialogue with the

Ada's Expulsion from Eden (3:22–23)	**The Tower Builders' Dispersion (11:6–8)**
And the Lord God said, "*Look*, man has now become *like one* of us, knowing good and evil. *Now*, he must not be allowed to reach out his hand and take also from the Tree of Life and eat, and live forever."	And the Lord said, "*Look*, they are *one* people and with one language, and this is what they have begun to do. *Now* nothing they intend to do will be impossible for them.
So the Lord God banished him from the Garden of Eden to work the earth *from where* (*misham*) he had been taken.	*From there* (*misham*) the Lord scattered them over all the face of earth.

This parallel is not merely linguistic; in both stories, God explicitly expresses unusual concern about the dangers of unlimited human power. In the Eden narrative, God fears that humans will live forever, and in the Tower of Babel narrative, God is concerned that "nothing they intend to do will be impossible for them." No such uncharacteristic divine statement can be found elsewhere in the Bible, and the solution to both problems is human displacement, scattering humanity elsewhere.

Moreover, Babylon was famous for its pride in its fertile rivers, the source of its strength and power.[51] Jeremiah, for example, describes Babylon: "O you who dwell by great waters, with vast treasuries" (Jer. 51:13); and Babylon, the most fertile of them all, controlled the famous "Fertile Crescent":

> The [Fertile Crescent region's] fertility was due to two factors: their levelness, and their abundant water supply, and this was especially true of the "land between the rivers," Mesopotamia

Eden narrative. Ginsberg has the interesting view that just as God separated between the woman and the serpent in Eden, now He is separating between humanity (Ginsberg, *Encyclopedia Judaica*, s.v. "Babel, Tower of: The Meaning of the Story," vol. 4, 20).

51. Herodotus also focuses on the rich, abundant produce of Babylon in his description. See Oppenheim, "Babel," 13.

> in Greek. This is the fat, rich part of the Fertile Crescent, whose vast plains were watered and kept fertile by the waters of the two great rivers – the Euphrates and the Tigris. The biblical "River" refers to "the Great River, the Euphrates."[52]

This description, of course, recalls God's fertile garden, which is watered by the four rivers that flow out of Eden.

Again, the fact that the people plan to build a tower that reaches the heavens is no coincidence; it is in dialogue with the human desire "to be like God." Even if this is not their main motive, it nonetheless contributes to their characterization:

> From a purely human viewpoint, building a tower as high as the sky is an audacious undertaking, but it seems likely that Genesis views it as a sacrilege. For the sky is also heaven, the home of God, and this ancient skyscraper may be another human effort to become like God.[53]

The connection with Eden is already hinted in the first words of the narrative, when the people journey "*mikedem,*" "from the east" (11:2). There have been various attempts to explain this surprising direction: Babylon, after all, is located in the east, so it would have been more appropriate to describe their journey as "from the west" rather than "from the east." The most straightforward explanation for this is that the settlers came from the east or northeast of Babylon (Mount Ararat, where Noah's ark lands, is located north of Babylon). It may also be that their wanderings took place within the eastern region in general. Some have even proposed that *mikedem* is a description of time, meaning "long ago," "in ancient times," rather than a geographic description.[54] I believe that this particular phrase has literary significance, as it forms a literary framework with

52. Aharoni, *Atlas Carta,* 12.

53. Wenham, *Genesis,* 239.

54. Christian Rose suggests that this (as well as Gen. 2:8) is an intentional ambiguity: *mikedem* can mean either one of the four points of the compass, or the past. Rose, "Nochmals: Der Turmbau zu Babel," *VT* 54 (2004): 225.

the Eden narrative. At the world's creation, God plants a garden *mikedem*, and places humanity inside: "The Lord God planted a garden in Eden in the east (*mikedem*), and placed there the human He had formed" (2:8). At the end of the story, humanity is driven out and replaced with the cherubim: "He drove out the human, and placed east (*mikedem*) of the Garden of Eden cherubim and the flaming, ever-turning sword to guard the way to the Tree of Life" (3:24). Given the charged meaning of the term, its use to describe the group of wanderers who attempt to build a city and tower can hardly be coincidental.[55]

It seems that the people of the valley seek to build an alternate Eden for themselves. Babel, lushly situated between two swelling rivers, is the people's answer to heaven on earth. The Garden of Eden, where God walks about freely in the cool of the day, is a meeting point between heaven and earth, and the people of the fertile plain attempt to build a tower whose top will reach the sky, joining heaven and earth once more.[56]

It emerges that just as humanity sought to "become like God" through eating in the Garden of Eden, the builders of the city stray from their proper place and seek to "become like God" – to stray beyond the proper boundaries of human power. I do not mean to claim that their sin is a rebellion against God. It is not at all clear that when they plan to build a tower that reaches the heavens, they imagine that they will build until they encounter God before them. The problem lies in the breaking of boundaries, in the sheer arrogance that their new technological capacity lends them.

If so, then the power of a person and of a nation, and the limits of such power, is the central theme of the Tower of Babel narrative. The power of a nation takes the form of a mighty city with a soaring watchtower – a royal metropolis confident in its own power, reaching out to touch the sky itself. Unrestricted individual power is presented in the Eden narrative, where God prevents human immortality; the unrestricted collective power of an empire is presented in the Tower of Babel narrative, in the figure of a city and tower that will make an eternal "name" for its empire. In Eden, the individual hoped for immortality; after the Flood, it is the nation, the kingdom, which aspires for collective immortality.

---

55. Compare to Blenkinsopp, *Creation*, 165; Sherman, *Babel's Tower*, 24–26.

56. Compare to LaCocque, *Babel*, 44.

The limits of human initiative bring us back to the story in its wider context. In the literary structure of the entire section, our story is parallel to Cain's construction of the world's first city and the technological prowess of his descendants (4:17–24, and see further in the introduction). Both stories explore the human ability to initiate and create, to build towers and to forge culture. Essentially, the connection between the narratives is yet deeper: in both episodes, the builders build a city as an alternative to their previous lifestyle, and, both Cain and the tower builders establish a city and begin anew after their departure from their previous place. Cain builds his city after he is forced to leave Eden and make his way to the east: "And Cain went out from the presence of the Lord and dwelled in the land of Nod *to the east* of Eden" (4:16), while the tower builders found Babel after "they journeyed from the *east*" (11:2). Human autonomy is emphasized in these journeys, which mark the transition from a nomadic lifestyle to a new urban culture in a new city. But the more crucial connection between them is that both episodes spark divine disapproval of unbridled human power. Cain and his family's creativity is intertwined with their murderous tendencies, while the initiative of the founders of Babel and the Babylonian Empire is presented as dangerous in this very respect: their homogeny threatens the freedom of the diversity of human culture.

The disparity between these narratives, however, reveals much about the inner development of chapters 1–11: the story of Cain and his descendants is the story of an individual family. Cain's city is named after his son Enoch, and his descendants are presented as private individuals who developed their own ideas for their own personal ends. The same is true of their murderous tendencies – their victims are individuals: Abel, and Lamech's nameless victim. The Tower of Babel, in contrast, symbolizes the powerful threat of a mighty empire that wishes to impose its authority over every living thing on earth. After the Flood, the discussion of the limits of human power becomes a discussion of nations and kingdoms.

In a certain sense, the Tower of Babel narrative is a necessary step after the changes that the human role undergoes after the Flood. Now that humanity is no longer the obvious ruler of the world, and it must prove itself worthy through taking responsibility, there is a need for a story that will define the boundaries of this power. The fortified city and tower, the human empire – Babel – is presented as a threat to divine rule, a theme that will recur again and again throughout the Bible. In this sense, the builders' motivation deviates from proper human boundaries: they wish to build an empire that will last forever – they wish to be like God – but God reestablishes the boundaries between heaven and earth.[57] It is no coincidence that this takes place in Babel; throughout the Bible, Babylon presents itself as an eternal empire, as a place where heaven and earth meet: "You thought, 'I shall be the mistress forever'" (Is. 47:7). Several prophecies are calculated to dispel this self-perception, such as: "Nevermore shall it be settled, nor dwelt in through all the ages. No Arab shall pitch his tent there, no shepherds make flocks lie down there" (Is. 13:20).[58] The Babylonians believed that the gods had an interest in Babylon's existence, that the city was established by the gods themselves, and therefore, Babylon would never be destroyed. The biblical account of Babel's creation, of course, counters this notion, presenting the city as a human initiative. God did not create Babel; on the contrary, divine intervention caused construction to cease, and scattered its builders in all directions.

Once again, I wish to emphasize that I am not stating that the city builders consciously intend to threaten heavenly rule, or to propose political atheism. They seek to remain together, and to build a kingdom that will last forever. However, human rule that is too confident in its own power clashes with divine rule, and God's plan to disperse the population and create nations. This reading is expanded in yet another exegetical circle of the narrative.

---

57. See especially Nahmanides there, and Jan Christian Gertz, "Babel im Rücken und das Land vor Augen: Anmerkungen zum Abschluss der Urgeschichte und zum Anfang der Erzählungen von den Erzeltern Israels," in *Die Erzväter in der biblischen Tradition, Festschrift für Matthias Köckert*, ed. A. Hagedorn and H. Pfeiffer (BZAW 400: Berlin/New York, 2009), 9–34.
58. See also A. L. H. M. van Wieringen, "Assur and Babel against Jerusalem: The Reader-Oriented Position of Babel and Assur within the Framework of Isaiah 1–39," in *'Enlarge the Site of Your Tent': The City as Unifying Theme in Isaiah*, ed. A. L. H. M. van Wieringen, and A. van der Woude (Leiden/Boston, 2011), 49–62.

BIBLICAL BABEL AND BABYLONIAN BABEL

The conclusion of the Tower of Babel narrative (Gen. 11:9) is generally read as a polemical etymology that mocks the inflated self-perception of the Babylonian Empire. While the Babylonians considered the name of Babel as being derived from the Akkadian "*bab-ilu*," "the gate of god" (or in its later form, "*bab-ilani*," "the gate of the gods"),[59] the biblical narrative names Babel as the site of the dispersion of the nations and the babbling confusion of languages. In the words of Cassuto, this narrative is taunting the early Babylonians: "How befitting for her is this name, which in our tongue is a designation signifying confusion!"[60]

However, even if the narrative's concluding verse mocks the name of the city and Babylonian tradition, this ridicule is not the main narrative objective.[61] There is no reason to assume that the name Babylon is so significant that an entire biblical episode should be devoted to its meaning.[62] At first glance, it seems that the city's name is mentioned as a *consequence* of the story, rather than as its central objective. Its objective lies in far more significant spheres.[63]

Nonetheless, I believe that this polemic tension is at play throughout the narrative and not merely in the city's naming at its end; it is related to the process of the city's founding and what that city represents.

59. Benno Landsberger, "Assyrische Königsliste und dunkles Zeitalter," *JCS* 8 (1954): 68.
60. Cassuto, *From Noah to Abraham*, 248.
61. Unlike Gunkel, *Genesis*, 99, and Wenham, *Genesis*, 241, who believe that the main narrative objective is to mock Babylon and its name.
62. As formulated by Frank Spina, who holds that it is unlikely that the biblical narrative would be an explicit polemic against Babylon, unless someone claims that the narrative was written by a Mesopotamian citizen who lived in a rival city (Spina, "Babel," *ABD* 1: 561).
63. Amit attempts to define the criteria for justifiably claiming that a narrative contains elements of covert polemics: "In order to ascertain that a conjectured hidden subject is in fact a cause of polemic, one needs first and foremost to examine whether he is dealing with a controversial subject – that is, whether there is a war of opinions relating to it in biblical literature – thereby making it possible to find other biblical texts in which the subject of the polemic is explicitly formulated" (Amit, *Hidden Polemics*, 94). Even if this criterion is too rigid, the reader will presumably agree with me that even a less stringent criterion is not consistent with our context.

First and foremost, this polemic is related to the process of Babylon's founding. The Babylonian version of Babel's founding is presented in *Enuma Elish,* the Babylonian creation epic, which describes how the gods themselves founded the city. In contrast, of course, the biblical account has humanity joining together to build the city, while divine intervention brings construction to a halt.[64] If the story should indeed be read as a foil to Babylonian tradition, there is room to explore whether its polemical nature undermines not just Babel's name, but all that it represents.

In *Enuma Elish,* Marduk, the head of the Babylonian pantheon, declares that he is about to establish a special place where the temple will be built, opposite the gods' heavenly abode.[65] In describing the construction, it states:

> The Anunnaki wielded the pick.
> For one year they made the needed bricks.
> When the second year arrived,
> They raised the peak of Esagil, a replica of the Apsu.
> They built the lofty temple tower of the Apsu
> And for Anu, Enlil, Ea and [Marduk] they established it as a dwelling.[66]

The location of the city of Babylon is crucial: built at the place where heaven meets earth so the gods can easily gather, it becomes the meeting point between heaven and earth. The Torah, of course, also describes the builders' ambition to build a tower that will reach the heavens, that will serve as a symbolic place of encounter between the upper world and the lower world. The connection between the clashing traditions is salient through the process of each edifice's construction: the Babylonians first spend a year making bricks for the temple's construction, and only then do they begin to build. Similarly, there is special focus on the separate

64. Miller points out the unique aspect of the concept that humans, not gods, founded a city upon their own initiative (Miller, "Eridu," 243).
65. *Enuma Elish,* Tablet V, lines 119–121.
66. *Enuma Elish,* Tablet VI, lines 59–64.

process of brick making before work on the actual Tower of Babel begins: "And they said to one another, 'Come, let us make bricks and burn them thoroughly.' And they had brick for stone and bitumen for mortar" (11:3). The unique biblical expression "to make bricks" creates the sense that our narrative is in dialogue with the Babylonian tradition of the city's founding. Moreover, the literal meaning of *e-sag-ila* is "a house whose head is raised up," so the description of the Esagila's construction: "They raised the peak (lit. "its head," "*ullu resisu*")," is at play with the literal meaning of the tower's name. This is also alluded to in the biblical description of "a tower whose top (lit. "head") will reach heaven."[67]

The etymology of the name Babel, or Babylon, is provided in *Enuma Elish* after the city's construction. Based on the city's designation as a gathering place for the gods – where the gods will ascend from *Apsu*, the watery underworld, and to there the gods will descend from the heavens – Marduk announces, "I shall call its name 'Babylon,' 'The Homes of the Great Gods' (*Babilim: bitat ilanim rabiutim*)."[68] As mentioned, this etymology is based on the reading that "Babel" means "*bab-ili*," "the gate of the gods," where the gods of the upper worlds and the gods of the underworld meet.

The polemic in Genesis challenges this tradition; for some reason it is crucial for the narrative, on the eve of Abraham's election, to dispel the notion that Babylon is the meeting place between heaven and earth, the home of the gods. On the contrary, Babylon is not a meeting place but the source of universal dispersion, the root of all divergence, the place where everyone was scattered.[69]

Reading the story against *Enuma Elish* also has the power to illuminate the surprising use of the verb root B-L-L. Many have noticed the discrepancy between the name of the city and the verb: "Clearly, verse 9 does not supply a literal etymology of Babylon. If it did, the name of

67. Compare to Ephraim A. Speiser, "Word Plays on the Creation Epic's Version of the Founding of Babylon," *Orientalia* 25 (1956): 317–323; Mathews, *Genesis*, vol. 1, 471–472.

68. *Enuma Elish*, Tablet V, line 129; Wilfred G. Lambert, *Babylonian Creation Myths* (Winona Lake, 2013), 105.

69. Marks may be correct that giving only one name to a city may be ironic, given that at the end of *Enuma Elish*, Marduk is given fifty different names (Marks, "Biblical Naming," 24).

the city would be *Balylon*, not *Babylon*."[70] Were the only discrepancy a consonantal difference (B-B-L and B-L-L), there would be no significant issue, as many etymologies play on phonetic similarity rather than identical root consonants:[71]

> Hebrew does not strictly adhere to this with naming, such as "*Shmuel*" from "for I asked him (*she'iltiv*) of the Lord" (I Sam. 1:20), as according to this etymology his name should have been "*Shaul*" but they are close enough.... Similarly, "*Yabetz*" comes from "*etzev*" (I Chr. 4:9), and so on.[72]

However, in this case, the very use of a verb from the root B-L-L is surprising. This verb usually appears in the Bible in the context of food,[73] meaning to blend or mix together. The meal offering must be "mixed (*belula*) with oil" – a dough made from mixing fine flour and oil. If we assume that the word "T-B-L", "perversion," which appears in Leviticus to describe sexual relations between a woman and an animal (Lev. 18:23), or a man and his daughter-in-law (20:12), is also derived from the root B-L-L,[74] then this meaning also comes into play: the word reflects a sexual

---

70. Victor Hamilton, "Babel," *NIDB*, vol. 1 (Nashville, 2006), 376.
71. Many have noted this. See, for example, Johannes Fichtner, "Die Etymologische Ätiologie in Den Namengebungen Der Geschichtlichen Bücher Des Alten Testaments," *VT* 6 (1956): 372–396; Andrew F. Key, "The Giving of Proper Names in the Old Testament," *JBL* 83 (1964): 55–59; Burke O. Long, *The Problem of Etiological Narrative in the Old Testament* (BZAW 108; Berlin: Topelmann, 1968); Andrzej Strus, *Nomen-omen: La Stylistique sonore des noms propres dans le Pentateuque* (AnBib 80; Rome, 1978); Allen Paul Ross, "Paronomasia and Popular Etymology in the Naming Narratives of the Old Testament" (PhD diss., Cambridge University, 1981); Garsiel, *Midrashic Names*; Russel T. Cheny, "Paronomasia and Proper Names in the Old Testament: Rhetorical Function and Literary Effect" (PhD diss., Southern Baptist Theological Seminary, 1988); Marks, "Biblical Naming"; Grossman, *Ambiguity*; Valérie Kabergs and Hans Ausloos, "Paronomasia or Wordplay? A Babel-Like Confusion: Toward a Definition of Hebrew Wordplay," *Biblica* 93 (2012): 1–20.
72. Radak on Gen. 5:29.
73. Hamilton, "Babel," 376. "...and always indicate a mixing of flour (or unleavened cakes) and oil that is presented as a grain offering" (W. A. Bailey, "*Balal*," *NIDOTTE* 1 [1997]: 663–664).
74. Bailey, "*Balal*," 664.

union between two entities who should not mix. If this is the case, it is strange to find this verb used to characterize a city in the sense of "scatter"; rather than blended or mixed, the people of the city are geographically scattered in every direction, and culturally-linguistically separated by language. Here, the verb *livlol* seems to function in an antithetical sense to its usual meaning, a sense which is also antithetical to the objective of the story; at the beginning, its people were fully integrated together, but by its end, the uniform mixture has been scattered and separated. This end is foreshadowed in verse 7, with the unusual verb "*navla,*" as in, "Let us go down, and confuse (*navla*) their language there," but this does not solve the problem; it merely transfers it to an earlier stage in the narrative. On a purely semantic level, the act of mixing can be extended to a mixing motion that leads to mess and confusion (and this sense is also reflected in the Akkadian verb *balalu*),[75] but given the fact that the plot focuses on scattering and dispersion, it is surprising that the narrative culminates with a verb used for the description of mixing things together.[76] A good example of a more typical use of the Akkadian verb *balalu,* in a context comparable to our story, can be found in a letter from Mari, wherein the king issues the following command: "Bring the deportees from A to the city of B and intermingle (*balālu*) them with the people of the city."[77] In this source, the people of city A are forcibly integrated with the people of city B. In the Tower of Babel narrative, the opposite transpires: the people of a single city are separated and scattered in every direction.

If the biblical narrative is calculated to undermine the perception that Babylon is the place where all the gods assemble, however, this very use of the verb root B-L-L may be ironic, where a verb, whose primary sense is "to mix together," is changed in the text to a sense of

75. Chicago Assyrian Dictionary, B, 39.

76. The latter ambivalence is evident in biblical dictionaries that use two separate entries for the definition of the root B-L-L, one referring to the sense of mixture, which appears throughout the Bible, and the second, which refers only to the Tower of Babel narrative: "There is a divine call for the mixing ("confuse" and "confused") of the languages." Bailey, "*Balal,*" 664.

77. J.-M. Durand, *Les documents epistolaires du Palais de Mari* (LAPO 17: Paris, 1998), 312. See also Marten Stol, *Women in the Ancient Near East,* trans. H. and M. Richardson (Boston/Berlin, 2016), 337.

scattering and dispersion, as a microcosm of the entire polemical subversion. While the Babylonians hold that their city and temple represent the place where the gods gather – where the three hundred gods of the heavenly pantheon convene with the six hundred gods of the underworld – the biblical narrator counters that Babylon was not a place of divine assembly but a place of human dispersion. The name is not based on a stirring motion that brings things together, but a frantic, chaotic stirring motion that drives them apart.

However, even if this etymology is plausible as part of the broader polemic subversion hinted to in the narrative, two troubling issues remain. Firstly, there is asymmetry between the subject of this subversion and the proposed etymology: Babylon is believed to be "the gate of the gods," while the biblical narrative proposes that it is the site of "the confusion of languages." There is no common denominator to these etymologies, and as a result, the irony of the effect is diminished; a more ironic counterpart to "the gate of the gods" might have been something along the lines of "the gate of death" or "the gate of demons." A more direct subversion of the Babylonian etymology would have been more cutting. For example, the name "Beth Aven" (Josh. 7:2; 18:12; Hos. 4:15; 5:8; 10:5; and more), whose literal translation is "House of Iniquity," is a subversion of the name Bethel ("House of God"), or, as some have proposed, of its former name, Beth Aben ("House of Stone").[78] In this case, the slight change results in strong yet subtle irony. This effect is lacking in our own narrative, where there is no clear dialogue with the name "the gate of the gods."

Another problem stems from the double etymology provided at the conclusion of the narrative. The first etymology echoes the name "Babel/Babylon," even if just phonetically: "Because there, the Lord confused (*balal*) the language of all the earth" (v. 9). The second phrase, however, bears no relation to the name "Babel" at all: "And from there, the Lord scattered them abroad over the face of all the earth" (v. 9). The anaphora that opens both phrases ("there, the Lord") and the epistrophe that concludes both phrases ("all the

78. Nadav Naaman, "Bethel and Beth-aven: The Location of the Early Israelite Sanctuaries," *Zion* 50 (1985): 15–25.

earth") emphasizes the duplication of the two etymologies; two separate statements that explain the source of the name "Babylon."[79] But how does the second statement, the description of the dispersion, function as an etymology of "Babylon," lacking as it is in phonetic similarity?

In light of these two problems, I wish to propose that the second statement also serves as an etymology of the word "Babylon," and, moreover, that this second etymology is the source of the expected irony. As mentioned, the etymology in *Enuma Elish* explains the name as a derivative of the phrase "gate of god";[80] there is, however, another clue in this work that hints to an additional meaning of the name "Babylon." While this meaning is only hinted to through wordplay, this wordplay seems intentional, and its appearance is not a coincidence. The fifth tablet describes how Marduk creates the world from Tiamat's body, and the creation of the rivers and dry land are described thus:[81]

> From her two eyes he let the Euphrates and Tigris flow,
> He blocked her nostrils, but left [...]
> He heaped up the distant [mountains] on her breasts,
> He bored wells to channel the springs.
> He twisted her tail and wove it into the Durmahu,
> [...] the Apsu beneath his feet.

Clearly, the world's creation revolves around Mesopotamia (the two rivers mentioned are the Euphrates and the Tigris): Mesopotamia is the fountainhead of creation, and the center point of the world. As Mircea Eliade notes, "Where heaven and earth meet is situated at the center of the world,"[82] and the peak of this mountain "is not only the highest point of the earth; it is also the earth's navel, the point at which the Creation began."[83] This presentation of Mesopotamia as the center

79. See especially Fokkelman, *Genesis*, 109–110; Grossman, *Text and Subtext*, 109–110.
80. *Enuma Elish*, Tablet VI, line 72.
81. *Enuma Elish*, Tablet V, lines 55–60; Lambert, *Babylonian Creation Myths*, 101.
82. Mircea Eliade, *The Myth of the Eternal Return, or, Cosmos and History* (Princeton, 1954), 12.
83. Eliade, *The Myth of the Eternal Return*, 16.

of the universe anticipates the construction of the temple in Babylon in the verses that follow.

As the "distant mountains" are set upon the gushing waters, the narrator relates that certain streams "channel the springs of water": "*namba uptallisa ana babalim kuppu.*"[84]

The verb *babalim* is a different form of the verb *abalu,* which in this context means "sweep away," "to carry water."[85] In *Enuma Elish,* the Akkadian name for "Babylon" is "*Babilim,*" which is very similar to the verb used to describe Marduk's channeling of the rivers, "*babalim,*" and this wordplay seems to be intentional. Various texts portray Babylon's pride in its nearby rivers, which are the source of its wealth and fertility, and the source of a city's wealth is a fitting source of inspiration for its name, at least as a popular etymology.[86]

This theory cannot be categorically proven, of course, but assuming that this implicit etymology of the city's name was well known in the ancient world, it may well be that this is the target of the biblical narrative's ironic conclusion. The verb *abalu* is not only used in relation to the channeling and movement of water; it also refers to the movement of animals or people from place to place.[87] If so, the biblical tale may be implying that Babylon is famous not for its redistribution of the rivers, but for its redistribution of humanity. With this reading, the city's new name mocks Mesopotamian tradition with an elegant ironic twist: the name Babylon is indeed derived from the verb root "to channel, to move," but this transportation does not refer to the movement of the waters that enrich the Babylonian soil. Rather, it refers to the movement of the people who were dislodged from their place and scattered to the ends of the earth.

According to this reading, the narrative's two concluding statements respectively refer to the two focal points of Babylon's name:

---

84. *Enuma Elish,* Tablet V, line 58.

85. Chicago Assyrian Dictionary, A, 10.

86. I have discussed this at length in "The Double Etymology of Babel in Genesis 11," *ZAW* 129 (2017): 1–13.

87. Ibid.

"Therefore it was called Babel, because:

- "There the Lord confused (*balal*) the language of all the earth." This is the *phonetic* similarity between Babel and *balal.*
- "There the Lord scattered them abroad over the face of all the earth." This is a new *semantic* understanding of the name Babel as a derivative of the Akkadian verb for "moving."

If this reading is correct, the etymology and its accompanying irony meld seamlessly with the narrative objective. The richness of the Babylonian soil, watered by the channeled rivers flowing around the city, symbolizes human power and belief that nature can be subjected to human control. In contrast, the dispersion of its population hints to the limits of human strength and their inability to build and maintain an invincible, interminable empire. If so, then the sudden movement of the population becomes the narrative's main motif: Babel is not named for the gathering of the gods in this site, nor for the rivers that have been channeled around it. Rather, Babylon is named for the upheaval and chaos there, which led to scattering and dispersion.

Here, in fact, may lie the source of the deep tension between the Tower of Babel narrative and the Babylonian text. Throughout history, Babylon is presented as a formidable empire that conquers and relocates its subjects through population transfer. Unlike the tolerant Persian Empire that rose in its wake, the Babylonians exiled the populations of the lands it conquered and led many captives to its own land, or to other conquered territories.[88] Babylon is famously characterized as a political monolith: they oppress and dominate their subjects – their "language" is forced upon everyone. This portrait of Babylon is undermined by the biblical portrait of Babylon's founding: rather than unite humanity under its own language and beliefs, Babylon is the source of universal dispersion and divergence.

---

88. See Bustenay Oded, "The Beginning of the Babylonian Diaspora – Organization and Economy," *Al HaPerek* 17 (2000): 101–113.

IS NATIONALISM A GOOD THING? CHAPTER 10 AND CHAPTER 11

Our conclusion so far is that even though the Tower of Babel narrative is not a story of actual sin, there is certainly dissonance between the people of the valley and divine plan. This dissonance is related to unbridled human ambition and power. But even if the builders' ambition to build an alternative Eden cannot be considered a sin, the impression created from this narrative is that the scattering of the nations and diverse languages is the negative result of God's anger, or at least, His dissatisfaction.

In light of this, what is the Torah's view of the existence of multiple nations and diverse languages? Is it a positive phenomenon, or was it a forced decision by God?

The complex answer to this question lies in the relationship between the two chapters that describe humanity's dispersal – chapters 10 and 11. Their order is surprising, as logically, chapter 11 seems to precede chapter 10.[89] After all, the name "Babel" is already mentioned in chapter 10, before God names the unfortunate city in chapter 11, so that it seems logical to read the Tower of Babel narrative before the story of the nations' dispersion in chapter 10.[90] Chapter 11, followed by chapter 10, would have formed a rational narrative sequence: God scatters the population gathered in the valley of Shinar, and the genealogical description of each family's line and where they settled follows immediately, logically, after.

I believe that the importance of the present order lies in the different atmosphere of each chapter.[91] As mentioned, chapter 10 describes the nations' dispersion as the natural course of events – as each family and clan grows, it naturally branches out. This natural growth saw each family's development into a nation. There is no criticism of the evolution of different nations, cultures, and languages in

89. The scholarly view that there are two different sources here cannot explain the strange redactive tendency here. It would have made more sense to place this narrative before chapter 10.

90. Hamilton, "Babel."

91. Roberto Tadiello, "La dispersione occasione positiva di crescita," *Bibbia e Oriente* 53 (2011): 129–148.

this chapter; even if the preceding story of Noah's drunkenness casts a negative light on Ham's line and a positive light on Shem's, this does not touch upon the actual divergence between the brothers. If anything, Noah's sons' distinction into separate family lines allows for individual evaluation according to the character of a particular nation. In this way, introducing chapter 10 before chapter 11 allows for a positive view of this dispersion, and informs the reader that the attempt to establish a single cosmopolitan kingdom in Shinar is doomed to failure before they ever begin. Chapter 10 asserts that God is interested in the dispersion of nations, in geographical and cultural diversity. As I already proposed, the expression "the same words" (11:1) hints to homogeny, to mental and cultural sameness, while dispersion encourages diversity.

If so, then the narrative model of this sequence closely echoes that of Eden. There, too, we learn that humanity will leave God's garden to work the earth before we are told why, and there, too, their punishment is presented, in a certain sense, as a necessary development. Similarly, the social evolution depicted in the Tower of Babel narrative is essentially a natural, necessary part of human development. Though it is presented as the result of excess human ambition and power, their failure, like the struggles of adolescence, is a necessary part of world progress. Chapter 10 conveys that this dispersion was intended all along and allows room for the conclusion of chapter 11 to be seen in a neutral or even positive light, rather than as the result of punishment.

APPENDIX: THOUGHTS ABOUT NATIONALISM AND MORALITY

As an afterword about the discussion of the founding of nationalism after the Flood, and the claim that the Bible does not see nationalism as a negative consequence, but rather a necessary step, I wish to express some thoughts about the challenge posed by the biblical view of nationalism, which is a natural ethnic view, and its relationship with the sphere of morality. The necessity to refrain from "too much" nationalism is almost a given in contemporary political thought; the trauma of the Holocaust is certainly a warning against all displays of extreme nationalism. However, marvelous things have been achieved in the name of nationality and nationalism. Lea Brilmayer eloquently articulates this ambivalence:

> One of the puzzling things about nationalism is that it sometimes seems to be a force for good, and sometimes a force for very great evil. At this particular time, we are more likely to think in terms of the evil nationalism brings about; this association is the legacy of the war in the former Yugoslavia, the killings in Rwanda, the ongoing fighting in Chechnya, and many other examples that all too easily come to mind. Nationalism now tends to be associated with barbarism, with genocide, ethnic cleansing, rape and wanton murder. But nationalism can also be a force for great good. When Armenians living in America contribute from their own limited resources to help Armenian earthquake victims, when Eritreans sacrifice their lives to liberate their country from a colonial power, or when Rigoberta Menchu commits herself to a life of personal hardship and danger to advance the human rights of Central American native peoples,[92] it is hard to deny that national sentiment can play a noble role in world events.[93]

The solidarity between members of the nations that Brilmayer mentions has been witnessed among Jews throughout history. This phenomenon has baffled cultural researchers, and still remains somewhat of a mystery. There are too many examples to mention, but one notable case is the reaction to the Damascus Affair; Jews across the world endangered their positions and sacrificed their time and resources for the Jews of Syria during the blood libels of February 1840. The Jews of Damascus suffered terribly at the hands of the government as a result of the libels. Different scholars point to the Damascus Affair as a climactic point of national solidarity: Jews from across the globe enlisted to help their brothers in a distant land.[94] The

92. Rigoberta Menchú Tum, who was born in 1959, is a human rights activist and winner of the Nobel Peace Prize.

93. Lea Brilmayer, "The Moral Significance of Nationalism," *Notre Dame Law Review* 71 (1995): 7.

94. Jonathan Frankel, *The Damascus Affair: "Ritual Murder," Politics, and the Jews in 1840* (Cambridge, 1997).

Jews who went to extremes to help the victims in Damascus – despite the heavy personal prices they were forced to pay – had never met their Syrian "brothers," nor is it even likely that had they met, they would have been able to communicate through the language barrier. Yet, belonging to the same nation served as sufficient motivation to leave their home for weeks on end in a desperate struggle to prevent injustice to their own people in Syria, while no such efforts were made by the victims' own Arab neighbors.

Of course, neither this story, nor the countless incidents similar to it, have the power to negate the grievous atrocities committed in the name of nationalism, nor was this my intention. Brilmayer, however, is correct in noting that national solidarity moves citizens to sacrifice themselves for the sake of their people.

In light of these ideas, I wish to take a step further and propose that what emerges from the sequence of chapters 10–11 is that nationalism itself is neutral, neither negative nor positive. It does, however, constitute a platform for positive, neutral, or negative actions, according to the nature of the relevant nation or its leaders.[95] The descendants of Shem have one culture, while the descendants of Ham have another; the land of Canaan can be characterized in one way and the land of Shinar in another; each should be evaluated individually. The same, however, is not true of imperialism: from the Tower of Babel narrative, it emerges that the Bible harbors reservations towards a single superpower that exercises its power over other nations.

This sheds important light on the role that the Bible assigns to different nations, and especially on Abraham's election. As I have proposed in another context, the question of Abraham's election is accompanied and explored through pairs of stories which examine his worth in different spheres: one of each pair clarifies his continuity from a national perspective, while the other does so from a moral perspective.[96] This is the case regarding a pair of narratives about Ishmael (chs. 16, 21);

95. Brilmayer writes similarly later on in her article: "Nationalism, itself, is morally transparent, and this fact accounts for its ability to coexist equally well with good and evil" ("Moral Significance," 7).

96. Grossman, *Abram to Abraham*, 155–173 (in relation to Isaac); 281–289 (Ishmael); 208–227 (Lot). See also the conclusion, 418–419.

about Lot (ch. 19 contains two narratives about his rescue from the ruined city); and about the birth of Isaac (Abraham is visited twice, in chs. 17 and 18). In each pair, one narrative presents the birth of a nation bound up in a covenant with God, while its parallel episode presents the birth of a nation as God's response as a moral God reacting to the characters' actions in terms of reward and punishment. Therefore, for example, Isaac's birth is justified in the Abraham cycle from a perspective of maintaining the covenant (ch. 17) and as a reward for Abraham and Sarah for their hospitality (ch. 18). This doubling – which recurs at every significant narrative junction – conveys the profound correlation between nationalism and morality, between Abraham's election as the founder of a nation and the founder of a moral movement. The focus on a nation's morality as its purpose and justification as a separate entity is a political revolution in the ancient world. Irwin is probably correct that this revolution stems from a deeper theological revolution: the uniquely moral God of Israel.[97] In any case, these chapters present the natural definition of (an ethnic) nation, its moral purpose planted deep within the roots of its very existence.

97. Irwin, "The Hebrews," 326–359.

From Noah to Abraham: Ten Generations (11:10–21)

In many ways, the genealogical list of Shem recalls the genealogical list of Seth (ch. 5). Ten generations, reported in a similar style and arrangement, transport the reader from one stage of history to the next. This similarity generates a connection between the two transitionary chapters. However, a comparison between them reveals that while in Seth's line, the age of each figure's death is reported as "X lived Y years, then he died," it does not explicitly state that Shem's descendants died – rather, calculation is required in order to determine their ages of death.[1] Some posit that this omission shows that the details of Shem's list are less important because its main purpose is to reach Abram,[2] but I believe that the opposite is true: Seth's line is almost entirely wiped out by the Flood. The fact that the text explicitly states that each of them died hints

1. The Septuagint adds the conclusion "and he died" in Shem's line as well, whereas the Samaritan Pentateuch also adds up the ages of death, such as: "And all the days of Arpachshad were 438 years, and he died" (its translation of Gen. 11:12 [manuscript 3 from Shechem synagogue, 33]. This addition is also found in the Or. 7562 manuscript).
2. Gunkel, *Genesis*, 154–155.

that these generations do not endure. This is not the case with Shem's line; a new age of hope begins after the Flood, especially in the wake of God's promise that there will never be such a Flood again. The ten generations from Noah to Terah will multiply and increase upon the earth, not like the first ten generations from Adam to Noah. Shem's line will become as numerous as the stars through Abraham, in whose birth his line culminates, but the descendants of his other branches will also endure and spread out.[3] This idea is consistent with the structure of these chapters as proposed in the introduction: the first half ends in sin, while the second part concludes with Shem's genealogical line, an expression of hope and continuity.

And yet this line is not as long-lived as their ancestors. Tracing the ages of each descendant reveals that this list can clearly be divided into two parts:

Shem – 600
Arpachshad – 438
Shelah – 433
Eber – 464

Peleg – 239
Reu – 239
Serug – 230
Nahor – 148
Terah – 205

Two facts can be gleaned from this list. First, that in general, human lifespan dwindles over the generations, fulfilling God's declaration on the eve of the Flood: "My spirit will not abide in man forever, since he is but flesh. His days will be a hundred and twenty years" (6:3). This is maintained in the rest of Genesis, and indeed, throughout the Bible – none of the patriarchs live past the age of 180, and Moses himself dies at the age of 120.

---

3. Compare to Harold A. Stigers, *A Commentary on Genesis* (Grand Rapids, 1976), 132; Mathews, *Genesis*, vol. 1, 490.

The second, more surprising datum is that rather than a gradual decrease in every generation, there is a sharp decline in Peleg's time – Peleg's life is almost half that of his father's (239 years to his father's 464) – to the extent that the nine generations can practically be divided into two separate parts. This steep drop does not repeat itself – the lifespans of the generations after Peleg continue to decrease in more gentle intervals. The list's division into two sections is also expressed through the slight increase of lifespan at the end of each section; despite the fact that the ages of each generation's death generally decrease, there are two exceptions: Eber, the final generation of the first section, lives 464 years while his father lives for 433 years, while similarly, Terah who marks the end of the second part of the line, lives for 205 years, longer than his father's 148. If so, the two halves of the list are separated by the drastic reduction of lifespan in the fifth generation. It is interesting to note that at this point, Shem's genealogy diverges from the list in chapter 10 – which concludes with the sons of Joktan, Peleg's brother – and introduces new figures who were not mentioned in the previous chapter. The division of Shem's line into two halves is also expressed in this sense – the first half refers to names that are mentioned in chapter 10, while the second half introduces new characters.

This, as Ibn Ezra notes, may be expressed in Peleg's very name: "The name of one was Peleg, for in his time the earth was divided (*niphliga*), and his brother's name was Joktan (*Yaktan*)" (10:25) – together their names hint that a new age began at this time, *dividing* the new generation from the previous generation, wherein human lives became "*katan*," "smaller," like the root of the name *Yaktan*.[4] But if this "division" hints to the dispersion of the Tower of Babel,

4. Ibn Ezra on Gen. 10:25. Radak, who interprets Peleg's name as related to the Tower of Babel narrative, sees Joktan's name as a hint to the shortening of the human lifespan: "Peleg was named for the division, and Joktan for the shortening of years" (on Gen. 10:25). For some reason, Radak writes that Peleg lived for 209 years, while the Masoretic text has 239 – this is presumably not a typo, as he later states that "he lived for *less* than half," which is logical according to his count, so he must have had access to a different manuscript with the number 209. Bekhor Shor mentions both possibilities, summarizing: "And for both reasons, he was called Peleg."

when the earth was divided into nations, then the shortening of the human lifespan in *this* particular generation closes an ironic circle. As we have already discussed, the connection between the Tower of Babel narrative and the Eden narrative is striking. One striking feature of the narrative is that the city builders seek a name for themselves, to touch eternity. Once again, just like Eden, the human desire to "be like God" results in the opposite. In Eden, eating of the Tree of Knowledge brings death into the world; here, too, their desire to make an eternal name for themselves results in the steep decline of their already ephemeral nature.

As I have already discussed, in Seth's genealogy in chapter 5, Noah is presented as Adam's replacement from a chronological perspective: Noah is the first person born after Adam's death, and this is expressed in his name. Does the birth of Terah's sons also mark the beginning of a new age?

A simple calculation reveals that Abram is born to Terah when Noah is 890. That is, while Noah is born after Adam's death, Abram is born when Noah is still alive. However, it seems that here, too, there is a hint that Abram's life marks a new stage in human history through God's revelation to him. When Abram leaves Ur of the Chaldeans, he is 75 years old (12:4) – that is, 965 years after Noah is born. As Noah lives until the age of 950, it emerges that God appears to Abram and commands him to leave Mesopotamia fifteen years after Noah's death.

Thus, while Noah is a replacement for Adam from the moment of his birth, Abram is the harbinger of a new era of divine revelation and instruction only when he makes a conscious choice to obey God's word and begin his journey to the land of Canaan. The Israelite nation is not born merely because its founding father is born; it is born when Abram determines to follow in God's path, when Abram begins to form a relationship with God. In a sense, Abram is born into the old world – Noah still lives. By the time he begins his journey, Noah has passed away, and a new age – a new world – has truly begun.

This also illuminates the surprising format of the ten generations of Shem's line.

IS ABRAHAM ACTUALLY THE TENTH GENERATION?

We have already seen how the ten-generation countdown to Abram does not strictly begin with Noah himself, but with his son, Shem; and indeed, this section begins with, "These are the generations of Shem" (11:10).[5] Yet this sequence can also be perceived differently: the ten generations that begin with Noah do not culminate in the birth of Abram, but in the birth of his father, Terah. This may sound strange, given the assumption that the whole purpose of this chapter is to introduce Abram, but nonetheless, Terah is presented as the end of the line. Cain's line, for example, concludes with Lamech and the report that he had three sons: Jabal, Jubal, and Tubal-cain. Seth's line concludes with Noah and the report that he had three sons: Shem, Ham, and Japheth. And now, Shem's line concludes with Terah and the report that he had three sons: Abram, Nahor, and Haran. While the recounting of the previous generations of Shem's line only mention the birth of one son (presumably the firstborn), all three of Terah's sons are mentioned in detail, which creates the impression that this is not the formulaic genealogical continuation of Shem's line but a description of Terah's family. The descriptions of Abram and his brothers are preceded with a new headline, marking the beginning of a new section: these are the generations of Terah. There are ten generations between Noah and Terah, not Abram, and now a new narrative section has begun.

Even if this may sound strange, the inner structure of Genesis supports this reading. As many have noted, the formula "*eleh toledot*" divides the book of Genesis into different sections of history.[6] After "the

5. Mathews claims that Abraham is thus the twentieth generation from Adam, and that this is the Torah's objective (Mathews, *Genesis*, vol. 1, 487–488). The Septuagint adds another generation: Arpachshad's son is "Kenan" and he begets Shelah, and Zipor assumes this is to place Abraham as the tenth generation since Shem (Zipor, *Septuagint*, 178), but this addition actually makes him the eleventh generation after Shem. According to the Masoretic text, Abraham is the tenth generation from Shem, but not according to the Septuagint. It is more likely, as Zipor cites from John Wevers, that the Septuagint wanted there to be exactly one thousand years between Arpachshad's birth and Terah's birth.
6. See, for example, Karl Fredreich Keil and Franz Delitzsch, *Biblical Commentary on the Old Testament: Volume I: The Pentateuch*, trans. J. Martin (Grand Rapids, MI, 1980), 35–37; Thomas Thompson, *The Origin Tradition of Ancient Israel: The Literary Formation of Genesis and Exodus 1–23* (JSOTSup 55: Sheffield, 1987), 167–172; David M. Carr, "'Biblos Geneseos' Revisited: A Synchronic Analysis of Patterns in

toledot of Seth" conclude with the birth of Noah, for example, the text shifts to the next protagonist: "These are the *toledot* of Noah. Noah was a righteous man, blameless in his time; Noah walked with God. Noah fathered three sons: Shem, Ham, and Japheth" (6:9–10). While the text has already reported that "when Noah was five hundred years old, he became the father of Shem, Ham, and Japheth" (5:32), this information is repeated in this new section as the beginning of Noah's own story.

A comparison with the genealogical list in chapter 11 reveals that the same is true of Terah. And the end of Shem's list, the reader learns, "When Terah had lived seventy years, he fathered Abram, Nahor, and Haran" (11:26). The very next verse, however, repeats this information: "And these are the generations of Terah. Terah fathered Abram, Nahor, and Haran" (v. 27). Many have questioned this stark repetition, and it suffices to mention that Radak proposed drawing a distinction between Terah's *toledot* to be in the sense of his sons, and his own *toledot* to be in the sense of history, events that befell him:

> 'And these are the *toledot* of Terah' – They have already been mentioned in the previous verse without adding any information except the birth of Lot. This is a description of the events that happened to him, for they, too, are called *toledot*, whereas the first *toledot* mentioned are his actual sons.[7]

I believe that the most straightforward reading is that this is the same pattern we saw in chapter 5. Shem's line concludes with Terah, and this repetition is not superfluous, but the opening of a new narrative: the fifth book of *toledot* in Genesis, the *toledot* of Terah.[8]

Genesis as Part of the Torah," *ZAW* 110, 2 (1998): 159–172, 3: 327–347; Klaus Koch, "Die Toledot-Formeln als Strukturprinzip des Buches Genesis," in *Recht und Ethos im Alten Testament – Gestalt und Wirkung*, ed. S. Beyerle, G. Mayer, and H. Strauss (Neukirchen-Vluyn, 1999), 183–191; Thomas Desmond Alexander, "A Literary Analysis of the Abraham Narrative in Genesis" (PhD diss., The Queen's University of Belfast, 1982).

7. Radak on Gen. 11:26–27.
8. Compare to Kiel, *Genesis*, 301. Even though he recognizes the new *toledot* book, the same as Noah, he holds that the repetition is for "reinforced emphasis." I believe that this repetition has more dramatic significance.

Assuming the "ten generations" model is intentional, there are two overlapping models in this section. On one hand, the list opens with Shem and concludes ten generations later with Abram, the hero and founding father of the Israelite nation, while on the other, beginning with Noah, the line ends with Terah.[9] There are nine definite members of this lineage, and to reach the tenth member, either the previous generation (Noah) or the next generation (Abram) can be counted.

This ambivalence reflects the tension concerning Noah's status: Does he symbolize the beginning of a new age, or the end of the old world? The genealogy in chapter 11 begins: "These are the generations of Shem. When Shem was one hundred years old, he fathered Arpachshad, two years after the Flood" (11:10). The emphasis that Arpachshad is born "two years after the Flood" gives the sense that this is a new era, a new world order, one that leads to Abraham's election and the founding of a nation that will form a covenant with God. Shem, like Abraham, gives birth to his son at the round, symbolic age of one hundred years old. In the context of Abraham's fatherhood, many have noted that this number symbolizes renewal and new beginnings, symbolism which can also be applied to the birth of Shem's son and which generates an interesting framework between the first and the last of this part of the dynasty, as both become fathers at the age of one hundred.

This ambivalent count of ten generations, therefore, is related to this very question: on one hand, Noah begins the world anew after the Flood – it is with him that God forms a covenant to maintain the world's existence, and he is the one who receives God's blessing of fertility in parallel to the first blessing at creation. On the other hand, Noah is still considered part of the old world – he is the final generation in the generations of Adam. Can he be a symbol of both old and new?

Ending the genealogical line with Terah encourages the reader to count back from Noah, while beginning with Shem encourages the reader to see Noah's sons as the harbingers of a new age (as we already

---

9. On the technique of double delineation that encourages simultaneous readings, see Grossman, *Text and Subtext*, 202–210 (where this phenomenon is coined "dynamic borders").

saw in the discussion of Noah's drunkenness), and from this perspective, Abraham is the tenth generation of this line.

At the same time, concluding the line with Terah, rather than Abraham, emphasizes that Abraham's election is not an automatic outcome, but the result of free choice. If Abraham is necessarily the tenth member of the line, this automatically assumes that he is the chosen one, that the world marches ahead according to a predetermined plan. This approach is reflected in the following midrash: "R. Yehoshua ben Karha said, '*Behibaram – Be'Avraham*,' [as if to say] 'with Abraham'; in the merit of Abraham, who was yet to be born."[10] He reads the word "*behibaram*," "when they were created" (Gen. 2:4), as an anagram of the name Abraham, stating that the heavens and earth were created in anticipation of Abraham's birth. Yet concluding the genealogical list in chapter 11 with Terah leaves Abraham out of the picture, leaving Abraham with the power of choice. Terah, like Noah, has three sons – who will prove, with his deeds, that he is the chosen one? Shem proves worthy through his treatment of his father. Will Abraham prove worthy and follow the command of his God in the next chapter, or will he decide to remain in Mesopotamia with his father's family?

The culmination of this family line with Terah is even more significant. In another context I already explored the profound tension throughout the Abraham cycle, between Abraham's separation from his family and the deep ties that remain between him and his Mesopotamian family. This is explicitly expressed through his son and grandson's marriage with his own brother's family, but is also subtly illuminated through the Abraham cycle being presented as "the *toledot* of Terah."[11] There is no section entitled "the *toledot* of Abraham" within the "*toledot*" formulae that shape the book of Genesis; Abraham's entire narrative cycle is named for his father Terah. Under this heading, the reader learns about Nahor's family (Gen. 22:20–24), how Haran, through his son Lot, is the founder of two nations himself (19:30–38), and, of course, how Abram-Abraham is granted his own descendants.

---

10. Genesis Rabba 12:9.

11. This issue troubled Bernard Eerdmans to the extent that he posited that the original formulation was "these are the *toledot* of Abram" rather than "of Terah" (Eerdmans, *Alttestamentliche Studien*, vol. 1 [Giessen, 1908], 28).

Therefore, even if Shem's genealogy begins with Shem himself and not with his father, thus culminating in Abraham as the peak of this line, its style and form show that it technically ends with Terah, not with Abraham. Only thus can the text continue on to "the *toledot* of Terah" and the story of his three sons. Why is it so important for the Torah that the story of Abraham is presented as part of his father's story? This is even more surprising, given that God's first revelation to Abraham lays emphasis on the need to detach himself from his family: "And the Lord said to Abram, 'Go forth from your land, your birthplace, and *your father's house* to the land that I will show you'" (12:1). This is profoundly connected to the narrative process of the first eleven chapters of Genesis, which portray the primordial, ideal picture of a single united humanity that serves God as one and calls on His name – and then present the shattering of this model, the failure of this model. Abraham's election is not presented in Genesis as the ideal option, but as the only possible way in a world where humanity has free choice and is liable to follow the evil inclinations of his heart. Abraham must disconnect from his family, but this is not a particularistic-nationalistic approach, but a nationalistic approach whose ultimate purpose is to correct the world in God's holy name. Thus, alongside the order to leave his father's house, Abraham is told that "through you will all the families of the earth be blessed" (12:3).

The transition between the primordial, universal narrative of how the world began and the focus on Abraham and his family line underscores one of the most profound themes of Genesis: Abraham's descendants are laden with the burden of correcting the world. Ideally, all of humanity would share this burden, but there is a need for a single family, especially suited for this purpose, to bring this message to the world: "For I have known him, so that he will instruct his children and his household after him to keep the way of the Lord by doing what is right and just" (18:19). There are ten generations from Noah to Terah, and from there, humanity begins a new journey: Abraham enters into a new covenant with God, but he will perpetuate his line through his connection to Terah's extended family. In one way or another, all three of Terah's sons become part of the long, winding journey of establishing the chosen people – the people whose ultimate purpose is to call on the name of God and lead the world by doing what is right and just.

Bibliography

Abramsky, Samuel. "Nimrod and the Land of Nimrod." *Beit Mikra* 25 (1980/81): 237–255 (Heb).

Adar, Zvi. *The Book of Genesis: An Introduction to the Biblical World*. Tel Aviv, 1967 (Heb).

Aharoni, Yohanan. *Carta Bible Atlas*. Jerusalem, 1964 (Heb).

Albright, W. F. "Was the Patriarch Terah a Canaanite Moon-God?" *BASOR* 71 (1938): 35–40.

Alexander, Thomas Desmond. "Genealogies, Seed and the Compositional Unity of Genesis." *Tyndale Bulletin* 44 (1993): 255–270.

Alexander, Thomas Desmond. "Genesis 22 and the Covenant of Circumcision." *JSOT* 25 (1983): 17–22.

Alexander, Thomas Desmond. "A Literary Analysis of the Abraham Narrative in Genesis." PhD diss., The Queen's University of Belfast, 1982.

Alfrink, Bern. "L'expression *Ne'esaf El Amav*." *OTS* 5 (1948): 118–131.

Alt, A. "Gedanken über das Königtum Jahwes." In vol. 1 of *Kleine Schriften zur Geschichte des Volkes Israel*, 345–357. Munich, 1953.

Alter, Robert. *Genesis: Translation and Commentary*. New York, 1996.

Alter, Robert. *The Art of Biblical Narrative*. New York, 1981.

Amit, Yairah. "Creation and the Calendar of Holiness." In *Tehillah le-Moshe: Biblical and Judaic Studies in Honor of Moshe Greenberg*, edited by M. Cogan, B. Eichler, and J. Tigay, 13–19. Winona Lake, IN, 1997 (Heb).

Amit, Yairah. *Hidden Polemics in Biblical Narrative*. Tel Aviv, 2003 (Heb).

Amit, Yairah. *Reading Biblical Narratives*. Tel Aviv, 2010 (Heb).

Amit, Yairah. "Biblical Utopianism: A Mapmaker's Guide to Eden." USQR 44 (1990): 11–17.

Anderson, Bernhard. "From Analysis to Synthesis: The Interpretation of Genesis 1–11." *JBL* 97 (1978): 23–39.

Ararat, Nissan. "The Story of Cain and Abel." *Beit Mikra* 30 (1985): 312–321.

Ararat, Nissan. "The Tower of Babel as a Satiric Drama." *Beit Mikra* 39 (1994): 224–231.

Arieli, Shemer. "Back to the Light – on the Temple as the Garden of Eden." *Parashat HaShavua* 957, *Ki Tetzeh,* Bar-Ilan University (2012) (Heb).

Arnold, Bill T. *Genesis.* NCBC: Cambridge, 2009.

Assmann, Jan. *Moses the Egyptian: The Memory of Egypt in Western Monotheism.* Cambridge, 1997.

Avishur, Yitzhak. "Stories of Genesis in Light of New Literary Science." *Beit Mikra* 21 (1976): 613–618 (Heb).

Bailey, W. A. "*Balal.*" *NIDOTTE* 1 (1997): 663–664.

Bailey, John A. "Initiation and the Primal Woman in Gilgamesh and Genesis 2–3." *JBL* 89 (1970): 137–150.

Baker, David W. "Tarshish." *ABD* 6: 331–333.

Balentine, Samuel E. "A Description of the Semantic Field of Hebrew Words for 'Hide.'" *VT* 30 (1980): 137–153.

Barr, James. "Was Everything That God Created Really Good? A Question in the First Verse of the Bible." In *God in the Fray: A Tribute to Walter Brueggemann,* edited by Tod Linafelt and Timothy K. Beal, 55–65. Minneapolis, 1998.

Barr, James. *The Garden of Eden and the Hope of Immortality.* London, 1992.

Barré, Lloyd M. "The Riddle of the Flood Chronology." *JSOT* 41 (1988): 3–20.

Bartelmus, Rüdiger. *Heroentum in Israel und seiner Umwelt: Eine traditionsgeschichtliche Untersuchung zu Gen. 6. 1–4 und verwandten Texten im Alten Testament und der altorientalischen Literatur.* AThANT 65: Zurich, 1979.

Barzel, Hillel. *New Interpretations of Literary Texts: From Theory to Method.* Ramat Gan, 1990.

Barzilai, Gabriel. *Meaningful Genesis.* Tel Aviv, 2012 (Heb).

Barzilai, Yoav et al. *Genesis-Exodus: Pages for Study and Teaching.* Herzog College: Alon Shvut, 1999 (Heb).

Bazak, Amnon. *Parallels Meet: Literary Parallels in the Book of Samuel.* Alon Shvut, 2006 (Heb).

Bechtel, Lyn M. "Genesis 2.4b–3.24: A Myth about Human Maturation." *JSOT* 67 (1995): 3–26.

Becking, Bob, and Marjo Korpel, C. A. "To Create, to Separate, or to Construct: An Alternative for a Recent Proposal as to the Interpretation of *Bara* in Genesis 1.1–2.4a." *JHS* 10 (2010): article 3.

Beentjes, Pancratius. "Partner-Partij-Paniek: De Bijbelse Notie 'Verbond' en zijn Problemen." *Collationes* 21 (1991): 287–300.

Bergsma, John, and Scott Hahn. "Noah's Nakedness and the Curse on Canaan." *JBL* 124 (2005): 25–40.

Berman, Joshua. "'Who in His Goodness Renews the Act of Creation' – Parallels and Differences between Bereshit Chapters 1 and 8." *Megadim* 9 (1989): 9–14.

Berman, Joshua. *Created Equal: How the Bible Broke with Ancient Political Thought*. New York/Oxford, 2008.

Bin-Nun, Yoel, and Bin-Nun, Eliad. "The Garden of Eden and the Earth – Adam's Sin." *Megadim* 54 (2013): 9–31 (Heb).

Birney, Leroy. "Exegetical Study of Genesis 6:1–4." *JETS* 13 (1970): 45–47

Blenkinsopp, Joseph. *Creation, Un-Creation, Re-Creation: A Discursive Commentary on Genesis 1–11*. London and New York, 2011.

Block, Daniel I. "Nations/Nationality." *NIDOTTE* 4: 966–972.

Bokovoy, David E. "Did Eve Acquire, Create, or Procreate with Yahweh? A Grammatical and Contextual Reassessment of K-N-H in Genesis 4:1." *VT* 63 (2013): 19–35.

Booth, Walter M. "Days of Genesis 1: Literal or Nonliteral?" *JATS* 14 (2003): 101–120.

Borger, Rykle. "Gen iv 1." *VT* 9 (1959): 85–86.

Brandscheidt, Renate. "Schöpfung im Bund: Die Schöpfungs und Bundeskonzeption in der priesterlichen Urgeschichte." *Trierer Theologische Zeitschrift* 123 (2014): 1–21.

Brettler, Marc Z. "The Bible as History." In *People of Faith and Biblical Criticism*, edited by Y. Brandes, T. Ganzel, and C. Deutsch, 211–223. Jerusalem, 2015 (Heb).

Breuer, Rabbi Mordechai. *Pirkei Bereshit*. 2 vols. Alon Shvut, 1998.

Brichto, Herbert C. *The Names of God: Poetic Readings in Biblical Beginnings*. New York, 1998.

Brilmayer, Lea. "The Moral Significance of Nationalism." *Notre Dame Law Review* 71 (1995): 7–33.

Brown, John P. "Peace Symbolism in Ancient Military Vocabulary." *VT* 21 (1971): 1–23.

Brown-Driver-Briggs. *A Hebrew and English Lexicon of the Old Testament*. Oxford, 1906.

Bryan, David T. "A Reevaluation of Gen 4 and 5 in Light of Recent Studies in Genealogical Fluidity." *ZAW* 99 (1987): 180–188.

Bryson, Bill. *Shakespeare: The World as a Stage*. London, 2007.

Buber, Martin. *Darko shel Mikra*. Jerusalem, 1964 (Heb).

Buchanan, George W. "The Old Testament Meaning of Good and Evil." *JBL* 75 (1956): 114–120.

Budde, Karl. *Die Biblische Urgeschichte (Gen. 1–12,5)*. Giessen, 1883.

Carr, David M. "'Biblos Geneseos' Revisited: A Synchronic Analysis of Patterns in Genesis as Part of the Torah." *ZAW* 110, 2 (1998): 159–172; 3: 327–347.

Carr, David M. "The Politics of Textual Subversion: A Diachronic Perspective on the Garden of Eden Story." *JBL* 112 (1993): 577–595.

Carr, David M. *Reading the Fractures of Genesis: Historical and Literary Approaches*. Louisville, 1996.

Cassuto, Umberto. *A Commentary on the Book of Genesis: From Adam to Noah*. Translated by Israel Abrahams. Jerusalem, 1961.

Cassuto, Umberto. *A Commentary on the Book of Genesis: From Noah to Abraham*. Translated by Israel Abrahams. Jerusalem, 1964.

Cassuto, Umberto. "The Sequence and Arrangement of the Biblical Sections." In *Biblical and Oriental Studies*, vol. 1, 7–16. Jerusalem, 1973.

Cassuto, Umberto. "The Episode of the Sons of God and the Daughters of Man." In *Biblical and Oriental Studies*, vol. 1, 17–28. Jerusalem, 1973.

Cassuto, Umberto. *Encyclopedia Biblica*, vol. 3, s.v. "*Ḥava*." Jerusalem, 1958 (Heb).

Cassuto, Umberto. *Encyclopedia Biblica*, vol. 6, s.v. "*Etz HaDaat*." Jerusalem, 1972 (Heb).

Cassuto, Umberto. *La Questione della Genesi*. Translated by M. E. Hartom. Jerusalem, 1990.

Castellino, G. R. "Genesis IV: 7." *VT* 10 (1960): 442–445.

Ceresko, Anthony R. "The Chiastic Word Pattern in Hebrew." *CBQ* 38 (1976): 303–311.

Charlesworth, James H. *The Good and Evil Serpent: How a Universal Symbol Became Christianized*. Anchor Yale Bible Reference Library: New Haven, 2010.

Cheny, Russel T. "Paronomasia and Proper Names in the Old Testament: Rhetorical Function and Literary Effect." PhD diss., Southern Baptist Theological Seminary, 1988.

Cherlow, Rabbi Yuval. *Song of Songs: 'Let Us Run After You.'* Tel Aviv, 2003.

Cherry, Shai. *Torah through Time: Understanding Bible Commentary from the Rabbinic Period to Modern Times*. Philadelphia, 2007.

Chew, Hiang Chea. "The Theme of 'Blessing for the Nations' in the Patriarchal Narratives of Genesis." PhD diss., University of Sheffield, 1982.

Childs, Brevard S. *Myth and Reality in the Old Testament*, 2nd ed. London, 1962.

Christensen, Duane. "Janus Parallelism in Genesis 6:3." *HS* 27 (1986): 20–24.

Clements, Ronald E. "Goy." *TDOT* 2: 426–433.

Clements, Ronald E. "*Yareaḥ*." *TDOT* 6: 355–362.

Clines, David J. A. "The Significance of the 'Sons of God' (Gen. 6,1–4) in the Context of Primeval History (Gen 1–11)." *JSOT* 13 (1979): 33–46.

Clines, David J. A. *The Theme of the Pentateuch*. JSOTSup 10: Sheffield, 1978.

Coats, George W. *Genesis*. FOTL: Grand Rapids, 1983.

Cody, Aelred. "When Is the Chosen People Called a *Goy*?" *VT* 14 (1964): 1–6.

Cohen, Gavriel Chaim. "Naming in the Book of Ruth." *Studies in Bible and Interpretation* 2 (1986): 151–160 (Heb).

Cohn, Robert L. "Narrative Structure and Canonical Perspective in Genesis." *JSOT* 25 (1983): 3–16.

Coleran, James E. "The Sons of God in Genesis 6,2." *Theological Studies* 2 (1941): 488–509.

Collins, John J. "The Sons of God and the Daughters of Man." In *Sacred Marriages: The Divine-Human Sexual Metaphor from Sumer to Early Christianity*, edited by M. Nissinen and R. Uro, 259–274. Winona Lake, 2008.

Coppens, Joseph. *La connaissance du bien et du mal et le péché du Paradis: contribution à l'interprétation de Gen., II–III*. Louvain, 1948.

Cornelius, I. "*Eden*." *NIDOTTE* 3: 331–332.

Cotter, David W. *Genesis*. Collegeville, MN, 2003.

Coxon, Peter W. "Another Look at Nebuchadnezzar's Madness." In *The Book of Daniel in the Light of New Findings*, edited by A. S. van der Woude, 211–222. BEThL 106: Leuven, 1993.

Cross, Frank Moore. *Canaanite Myth and Hebrew Epic*. Cambridge, 1973.

Crouch, Carly L. "*Ḥatat* as Interpolative Gloss: A Solution to Gen 4,7." *ZAW* 123 (2011): 250–258.

Cryer, Frederick H. "The Interrelationships of Gen 5,32; 11,10–11 and the Chronology of the Flood (Gen 6–9)." *Biblica* 66 (1985): 241–261.

Dan, Joseph. *Apocalypse Then and Now*. Tel Aviv, 2000 (Heb).

Darshan, Guy. "The Story of the Sons of God and the Daughters of Man (Gen. 6:1–4) in Light of the Hesiodic *Catalogue of Women*." *Shnaton* 23 (2014): 155–178.

Davidson, Richard M. "The Genesis Flood Narrative: Crucial Issues in the Current Debate." *Andrews University Seminary Studies* 42 (2004): 49–77.

Davidson, Robert. *Genesis 1–11*. CBC: Cambridge, 1973.

Davidson, Robert. *Genesis 12–50*. CBC: Cambridge, 1979.

Day, John. *From Creation to Babel: Studies in Genesis 1–11*. LHB/OTS 592; London: Bloomsbury, 2013.

De Moor, Johannes C. *New Year with Canaanites and Israelites*. 2 vols. Kampen, 1972.

De Moor, Johannes C. "*Baal*." *TDOT* 2: 181–192.

De Vries, Simon. "God's Provision for the Well-Being of Living Creatures in Genesis 9." In *Literary Encounters with the Reign of God*, edited by S. H. Ringe and H. C. Paul, 89–103. Atlanta, 2003.

Delitzsch, Franz. *A New Commentary on Genesis*, vol. 1. Translated by S. Taylor. Edinburgh, 1888.

Delitzsch, Franz. *Biblical Commentary on the Prophecies of Isaiah*, vol. 1. Translated by J. Martin. Edinburgh, 1890.

Deurloo, Karel A. "*Teshuka* – 'Dependency,' Gen 4:7." *ZAW* 99 (1987): 405–406.

Deutscher, Guy. *The Unfolding of Language: An Evolutionary Tour of Mankind's Greatest Invention*. New York, 2005.

Deutscher, Guy. *Through the Language Glass: How Words Colour Your World.* London, 2010.

Dewar, Canon Lindsay. "The Biblical Use of the Term 'Blood.'" *JTS* 4 (1953): 204–208.

DeWitt, Dale S. "The Generation of Genesis." *EvQ* 48 (1976): 196–211.

Dillmann, August. *Genesis: Critical and Exegetically Expounded.* Translated by B. Stevenson. 2 vols. Edinburgh, 1897.

Dinnur, Gali. "The Story of Cain and Abel (Gen. 4:1–16): The Supreme Value of Human Life." *Mo'ed* 18 (2008): 1–21 (Heb).

Dorsey, David A. *The Literary Structure of the Old Testament: A Commentary on Genesis-Malachi.* Grand Rapids, 1999.

Douglas, Mary. *Purity and Danger: An Analysis of Concepts of Pollution and Taboo.* London/New York, 1996.

Dragga, Sam. "Genesis 2–3: A Story of Liberation." *JSOT* 55 (1992): 3–13.

Driver, Godfrey R. "Theological and Philological Problems in the OT." *JTS* 47 (1946): 157–160.

Driver, Samuel R. *The Book of Genesis.* Westminster Commentaries, 10th ed. London, 1916.

Dumbrell, William J. *Covenant and Creation: A Theology of the Old Testament Covenants.* Exeter, 1984.

Durand, J.-M. *Les documents epistolaires du Palais de Mari.* LAPO 17: Paris, 1998.

Edenburg, Cynthia. "From Eden to Babylon: Reading Genesis 2–4 as a Paradigmatic Narrative." In *Pentateuch, Hexateuch, or Enneateuch: Identifying Literary Works in Genesis through Kings,* edited by T. Dozeman, T. Römer, and K. Schmid, 155–167. Atlanta, 2011.

Eerdmans, Bernard D. *Alttestamentliche Studien,* vol. 1. Giessen, 1908.

Eichrodt, Walther. *Theology of the Old Testament.* Translated by J. A. Baker. 2 vols. London/Philadelphia, 1961–67.

Eisler, Robert. "Joshua and the Sun." *The American Journal of Semitic Languages and Literatures* 42 (1926): 73–85.

Eliade, Mircea. *The Myth of the Eternal Return, or, Cosmos and History.* Princeton, 1954

Elmslie, W. A. L. "Ethics." In *Record and Revelation,* edited by H. Wheeler Robinson. 275–302. Oxford, 1938.

Emanueli, Yitzhak Moshe. *Genesis – Commentary and Insights.* Tel Aviv, 1978 (Heb).

Embry, Brad. "The 'Naked Narrative' from Noah to Leviticus: Reassessing Voyeurism in the Account of Noah's Nakedness in Genesis 9.22–24." *JSOT* 35 (2011): 417–433.

Emerton, John. A. "An Examination of Some Attempts to Defend the Unity of the Flood Narrative in Genesis." *VT* 37 (1987): 401–20 (part I); *VT* 38 (1988): 3–21 (part II).

Endo, Yoshinobu. "The Structure of the 'Genesis Flood Narrative' and the Documentary Hypothesis." *Exegetica* 10 (1999): 1–18.

Engnell, Ivan. "'Knowledge' and 'Life' in the Creation Story." In *Wisdom in Israel and the Ancient Near East Wisdom in Israel,* edited by M. Noth and D. Winton Thomas, 103–119. VTSup 3; Leiden: Brill, 1955.

Eslinger, Lyle. "A Contextual Identification of the *bene ha'elohim* and *benoth ha'adam* in Gen 6:1–4." *JSOT* 13 (1979): 65–73.

Farjun, Yoshi. "Wisdom and Science Are Yours: A Collection of Annotated Sources." In *People of Faith and Biblical Criticism,* edited by Y. Brandes, T. Ganzel, and C. Deutsch, 19–161. Jerusalem, 2015 (Heb).

Ferber, Michael. *A Dictionary of Literary Symbols,* 2nd ed. Cambridge, 2007.

Fewell, Danna Nolan. "Building Babel." In *Postmodern Interpretations of the Bible: A Reader,* edited by A. K. M. Adam, 1–15. St. Louis: Chalice, 2001.

Fichtner, Johannes. "Die Etymologische Ätiologie in Den Namengebungen Der Geschichtlichen Bücher Des Alten Testaments." *VT* 6 (1956): 372–396.

Fidler, Ruth. "Genesis XV: Sequence and Unity." *VT* 57 (2007): 162–180.

Fishman, Joshua A. *Reversing Language Shift: Theoretical and Empirical Foundations of Assistance to Threatened Languages.* Clevedon, 1991.

Fockner, Sven. "Reopening the Discussion: Another Contextual Look at the Sons of God." *JSOT* 32 (2008): 435–456.

Foh, Susan T. "What Is Woman's Desire?" *WTJ* 37 (1974–5): 376–383.

Fokkelman, Jan P. *Narrative Art in Genesis.* Assen/Amsterdam, 1975.

Fohrman, David. *The Ancient History of Good and Evil: Study of Adam and Eve and Cain and Abel.* 2011 (Heb).

Fox, Michael. "The Concept of Divinity in Didactic Wisdom Literature." *Beer Sheva* 1 (1973): 162–170.

Frankel, Jonathan. *The Damascus Affair: 'Ritual Murder', Politics, and the Jews in 1840.* Cambridge, 1997.

Fretheim, Terence. "Were the Days of Creation Twenty-Four Hours? Yes." In *The Genesis Debate: Persistent Questions about Creation and the Flood,* edited by R. Youngblood, 12–35. Nashville, 1986.

Freud, Sigmund. "Family Romances." In *Collected Papers,* vol. 5, edited by C. J. Strachey, 74–78. New York, 1959.

Freud, Sigmund. "Der Mann Moses und die monotheistische Religion." In *Selected Works in Hebrew.* Translated by R. Ginsburg, vol. 7. Tel Aviv, 2009.

Freud, Sigmund. *The Works of Sigmund Freud.* Translated by H. Isaac. Tel Aviv, 1966.

Friedman, Richard Elliott. *Who Wrote the Bible?* 2nd ed. New York, 1997.

Frisch, Amos. "'SH-M-A' and 'R-A-H' as a Pair of Leitwörter." *Proceeding of the Twelfth World Congress of Jewish Studies* (Division A: The Bible and Its World, Jerusalem: World Union of Jewish Studies, 1999): 89–98 (Heb).

Frisch, Amos. *The Toil of Your Hands: The Bible's View of Labor.* Tel Aviv, 1999 (Heb).

Frisch, Amos. "A Chapter in Nechama Leibowitz's Approach: On 'Repetition Structure' in Biblical Narrative." In *Pirkei Nechama: Prof. Nechama Leibowitz Memorial Volume*, edited by M. Ahrend, R. Ben-Meir and G. Cohn, 313–323. Jerusalem, 2001 (Heb).

Frymer-Kensky, Tikvah. "What the Babylonian Flood Stories Can and Cannot Teach Us about the Genesis Flood." *Biblical Archaeology Review* 4 (1978): 32–41.

Frymer-Kensky, Tikvah. "Biblical Cosmology." In *Backgrounds for the Bible*, edited by M. O. O'Connor and D. N. Freedman, 231–240. Winona Lake, 1987.

Fichte, Johann G. *Addresses to the German Nation*. Translated by R. F. Jones and G. H. Turnbull. Chicago, 1922.

Galpaz-Feller, Pnina. *VaYoled: Relations between Parents and Children in Biblical Stories and Laws*. Jerusalem, 2006 (Heb).

Garsiel, Moshe. *Midrashic Name Derivations in the Bible*. Ramat Gan, 1987 (Heb).

Gelander, Shammai. "The Story of Paradise: A Different Trial." *Beit Mikra* 39 (1994): 335–356 (Heb).

Gertz, Jan Christian. "Babel im Rücken und das Land vor Augen: Anmerkungen zum Abschluss der Urgeschichte und zum Anfang der Erzählungen von den Erzeltern Israels." In *Die Erzväter in der biblischen Tradition, Festschrift für Matthias Köckert*, edited by A. Hagedorn and H. Pfeiffer, 9–34. BZAW 400: Berlin/New York, 2009.

Gertz, Jan Christian. "'Im Schweisse deines Angesichts': Alttestamentliche Perspektiven zum Thema 'Sinn der Arbeit – Ethos der Arbeit.'" In *Alttestamentliche Wissenschaft und kirchliche Praxis*, edited by M. Oeming and W. Boës, 267–283. Münster, 2009.

Gesenius, Wilhelm. *Hebrew Grammar: As Edited and Enlarged by the Late E. Kautzsch*. Translated by A. E. Cowley, 2nd ed. Oxford, 1910.

Gilad, Chaim. "Cain and Abel." *Beit Mikra* 29 (1983): 14–28 (Heb).

Ginsberg, Harold Louis. *Encyclopedia Judaica*, s.v. "Babel, Tower of: The Meaning of the Story," vol. 4, 20.

Ginsberg, Harold Louis. *Encyclopedia Biblica*, s.v. "Nephilim," vol. 5, 896–897.

Ginzberg, Louis. *The Legends of the Jews*, vol. 1. Ramat Gan, 1966 (Heb).

Gordis, Daniel. "The Tower of Babel and the Birth of Nationhood." *Azure* 40 (2010): 19–36.

Gordis, Robert. "The Knowledge of Good and Evil in the Old Testament and the Kumran Scrolls." *JBL* 76 (1957): 123–138.

Gordis, Robert. "Commentary on the Text of Lamentations (Part Two)." *JQR* 58 (1967): 14–33.

Gordon, Cyrus H. "The Ebla Tablets and the World of the Bible." *HS* 22 (1981): 39–47.

Gordon, Cyrus H. "The Seventh Day." *UF* 11 (1979): 299–301.

Gordon, Cyrus H. "*Aḥadim = iltênûtu* 'Pair.'" In *Sefer Segal: Studies in the Bible Presented to M. H. Segal*, edited by Y. M. Grintz and J. Liver, 5–9. Jerusalem, 1964 (Heb).

Gordon, Cyrus H. "Notes on Proper Names in the Ebla Tablets." In *Archivi Reali di Ebla-Studi*, edited by A. Archi, vol. 1, 153–158. Rome, 1988.

Gordon, Robert P. "'Couch' or 'Crouch'? Genesis 4:7 and the Temptation of Cain." In *On Stone and Scroll*, edited by J. K. Aitken, K. J. Dell, and B. A. Mastin, 195–209. BZAW 420: Berlin, 2011.

Gosse, Bernard. "L'écriture de Gn 3, le serpent dualité de la femme et de l'homme." *Biblische Notizen* 98 (1999): 19–20.

Gottlieb, Hans, Knud Jeppesen, and Benedikt Otzen. *Myths in the Old Testament*. Translated by F. Cryer. London, 1980.

Gottlieb Zornberg, Avivah. *The Murmuring Deep: Reflections on the Biblical Unconscious*. New York, 2009.

Göttsberger, J. "*Yatzo VaShov* in Genesis 8,7." *BZ* 6 (1908): 113–116.

Granot, Tamir. "What Changed after the Flood?" *Virtual Beit Midrash of Yeshiva Har Etzion*. http://www.etzion.org.il/en/what-changed-after-flood.

Granot, Tamir. "Torah and Science according to Rav Kook, Letter 91." *HaMeir LaAretz* 65 (2007): 403–435 (Heb).

Graves, Robert, and Raphael Patai. *Hebrew Myths: The Book of Genesis*. London, 1963.

Green, Yosef. "When Does the Day Begin?" *JBQ* 36 (2008): 81–87.

Green, Barbara. *A Study of Field and Seed Symbolism in the Biblical Story of Ruth*. PhD diss., Michigan and London, 1982.

Greenberg, Moshe. "Some Postulates of Biblical Criminal Law." In *Torah Nidreshet: Three Interpretative Essays on the Bible*, edited by A. Shapira, 13–37. Tel Aviv, 1984 (Heb).

Greenstein, Edward L. "A Pragmatic Pedagogy of Bible." *Journal of Jewish Education* 75 (2009): 290–303.

Greenstein, Edward L. "Wordplay, Hebrew." *ABD* 6: 968–971.

Greenstein, Edward L. "God's Golem: The Creation of the Human in Genesis 2." In *Creation in Jewish and Christian Tradition*, edited by H. G. Reventlow and Y. Hoffman, 219–239. London and New York, 2002.

Grintz, Yehoshua. *The Book of Genesis: Its Uniqueness and Antiquity*. Jerusalem, 1983 (Heb).

Grossman, Avraham. *Pious and Rebellious: Jewish Women in Europe in the Middle Ages*. Jerusalem, 2001 (Heb).

Grossman, Avraham. *Rashi*. Translated by J. Linsider. Oxford, 2012.

Grossman, Jonathan, and Sara Daniel. "'Like Arrows in the Hand of the Warrior, So Are Youths': Reading Ishmael's Expulsion in Genesis 21 in light of Hermann Hesse's Siddhartha." *Hebrew Studies* 57 (2016): 73–91.

Grossman, Jonathan. "Different Dreams: Two Models of Interpretation for Three Pairs of Dreams (Genesis 37–50)." *JBL* 135 (2016): 717–732.

Grossman, Jonathan. "The Double Etymology of Babel in Genesis 11." *ZAW* 129 (2017): 1–13.

Grossman, Jonathan. "'Dynamic Analogies' in the Book of Esther." *VT* 59 (2009): 394–414.

Grossman, Jonathan. "Stability and Surprise in the Book of Ruth's Exposition." *Beit Mikra* 60 (2015): 202–237 (Heb).

Grossman, Jonathan. "The Expulsion of Ishmael Narrative – Boundaries, Structure, and Meaning." In *Doubling and Duplicating in the Book of Genesis: Literary and Stylistic Approaches to the Text*, edited by E. R. Hayes and K. Vermeulen, 27–37. Winona Lake, 2016.

Grossman, Jonathan. "Associative Meanings in the Character Evaluation of Lot's Daughters." *CBQ* 76 (2014): 40–57.

Grossman, Jonathan. "More on the Literary Structure of the Paradise Narrative (Gen. 2:4–3:24)." *Beit Mikra* 56 (2011): 5–39 (Heb).

Grossman, Jonathan. "'Structural Ambiguity' in Ezekiel 33–38." *Beit Mikra* 49 (2004): 194–224 (Heb).

Grossman, Jonathan. "The Structural Paradigm of the Ten Plagues Narrative and the Hardening of Pharaoh's Heart." *VT* 64 (2014): 588–610.

Grossman, Jonathan. *Abram to Abraham: A Literary Analysis of the Abraham Narrative.* Das Alte Testament im Dialog 11. Bern, 2016.

Grossman, Jonathan. "Ambiguity in the Biblical Narrative and Its Contribution to the Literary Formation." PhD diss., Bar-Ilan University, 2006.

Grossman, Jonathan. *Text and Subtext: On Exploring Biblical Narrative Design.* Tel Aviv, 2015 (Heb).

Gruppe, Otto. "War Genesis 6:1–4 ursprünglich mit der Sintflut verbunden?" *ZAW* 9 (1889): 135–155.

Gunkel, Hermann. *Genesis – Translated and Interpreted.* Translation by M. E. Biddle. Georgia, 1997.

Guterbock, Hans Gustav. "The Song of Ullikummi: Revised Text of the Hittite Version of a Hurrian Myth – part 2." *Journal of Cuneiform Studies* 6 (1952): 8–42.

Haag, Herbert. "*Ben.*" TDOT 2: 145–159.

Hack, M. *The Book of Adam and Eve.* In vol. 1 of *The Apocrypha*, edited by Abraham Kahana, 1–18. Jerusalem, 1940 (Heb).

Hagopian, David G. *The Genesis Debate: Three Views on the Days of Creation*, edited by David G. Hagopian. Mission Viejo, CA, 2001.

Hamilton, Victor P. "Babel." *NIDB*. Vol. 1. Nashville, 2006.

Hamilton, Victor P. *The Book of Genesis, Chapters 1–17*. NICOT. Grand Rapids, 1990.

Hanson, Paul D. "Rebellion in Heaven, Azazel, and Euhemeristic Heroes in 1 Enoch 6–11." *JBL* 96 (1977): 195–233.

Haran, Menachem. *Ages and Institutions in the Bible*. Tel Aviv, 1973 (Heb).

Haran, Menachem. "The Heavens and the Earth." *Olam HaTanakh: Genesis*. Tel Aviv, 1982, 16–17 (Heb).

Hart, Ian. "Genesis 1:1–2:3 as Prologue to the Book of Genesis." *Tyndale Bulletin* 46 (1995): 315–336.

Hartley, John E. "F-U-SH." *NIDOTTE* 3: 592.

Hartley, John E. *Genesis*. NIBC: Peabody, MA, 2000.

Hauret, Charles. "Réflexions pessimistes et optimistes sur Gen. IV, 17–24." In *Sacra Pagina Miscellanea Biblica Congressus Internationalis Cathohci de Re Biblica*, edited by J. Coppens et al., vol. 1, 358–365. Paris, 1959.

Hayes, Elizabeth R. "Whose World? Whose Time? A Text World Theory Examination of the Style and Message of Genesis 1:1–2:25." In *Doubling and Duplicating in the Book of Genesis: Literary and Stylistic Approaches to the Text*, edited by E. R. Hayes and K. Vermeulen, 145–165. Winona Lake, 2016.

Hayward, Robert. "What Did Cain Do Wrong? Jewish and Christian Exegesis of Genesis 4:3–6." In *The Exegetical Encounter between Jews and Christians in Late Antiquity*, edited by E. Grypeou and H. Spurling, 101–123. JCPS 18: Leiden, 2009.

Hegel, Georg Wilhelm Friedrich. *Grundlinien der Philosophie des Rechts*. In *Werke in zwanzig Bänden*, edited by E. Moldenhauer and K. M. Michel, vol. 7. Frankfurt am Main: Suhrkamp Verlag, 1970.

Heller, Jan. "Der Name Eva." *ArOr* 26 (1958): 636–656.

Hendel, Ron. "Other Edens." In *Exploring the Longue Durée: Essays in Honor of Lawrence E. Stager*, edited by D. Schloen, 185–189. Winona Lake, In: Eisenbrauns, 2008.

Hendel, Ron. "Of Demigods and the Deluge: Toward an Interpretation of Genesis 6:1–4." *JBL* 106 (1987): 13–26.

Hendel, Ron. "The Nephilim were on the Earth: Genesis 6:1–4 and Its Ancient Near Eastern Context." In *The Fall of the Angels*, edited by C. Auffarth and L. T. Stuckenbruck, 11–34. Leiden, 2004.

Hendel, Ron. *The Text of Genesis I-II: Textual Studies and Critical Edition*. New York, 1998.

Herodotus, *History*. Translated to Hebrew by B. Shimron and R. Zelnick-Abramovitz. Tel Aviv, 1998.

Herrmann, Wolfram. "die Gottessöhne." *ZRGG* 12 (1960): 242–251.

Hess, Richard S. "Cain." *ABD* 1: 806–807.

Hiebert, Theodore. "The Tower of Babel and the Origin of the World's Cultures." *JBL* 126 (2007): 29–58.

Hoffmann, Rabbi David Z. *Genesis.* 2 vols. Bnei Brak, 1969.

Horowitz, T. "The Garden of Eden Story (Genesis 3) – Reality or Parable? – An Interdisciplinary Debate." *Sha'anan* 9 (2004): 39–88.

Hutzli, Jürg. "Tradition and Interpretation in Gen 1:1– 2:4a." *JHS* 10, article 12.

Hvidberg, Flemming. "The Canaanitic Background of Gen i–iii." *VT* 10 (1960): 285–294.

Irwin, William A. "The Hebrews." In *The Intellectual Adventure of Ancient Man: An Essay of Speculative Thought in the Ancient Near East,* edited by H. Frankfort, H. A. Frankfort, J. A. Wilson, Th. Jacobsen and W. A. Irwin, 223–360. Chicago, 1946.

Isaac, Y., and A. Klein. "Introduction to the Book of Knowledge – the Thought of Maimonides against the Backdrop of General Jewish Thought." Chapter 5. http://www.daat.ac.il/daat/mahshevt/haguto/5–2.htm.

Jacob, Benno. *Das Erste Buch der Tora: Genesis.* Berlin, 1934.

Jacobs, Sandra. "Expendable Signs: The Covenant of the Rainbow and Circumcision at Qumran." In *The Dead Sea Scrolls in Context: Integrating the Dead Sea Scrolls in the Study of Ancient Texts, Languages, and Cultures,* edited by A. Lange, E. Tov and M. Weigold, 562–575. Leiden, 2011.

Jacobs, Jonathan. *Measure for Measure in the Storytelling Bible.* Alon Shvut, 2006 (Heb).

Jacobs-Hornig, B. "*Gan.*" *TDOT* 3: 34–39.

Janowski, Bernd. "Die lebendige Statue Gottes: Zur Anthropologie der priesterlichen Urgeschichte." In *Gott und Mensch im Dialog,* edited by M. Witte, 183–214. Berlin/New York, 2005.

Jobling, David. *The Sense of Biblical Narrative: Structural Analyses in the Hebrew Bible,* vol. 2. JSOTSup 39: Sheffield, 1986.

Joosten, Jan. "Réflexions théologiques sur Lévitique 17." *Revue d'Histoire et de Philosophie Religieuses* 93 (2013): 145–156.

Josephus, Flavius. *Antiquities of the Jews.* Shalit Edition: Jerusalem, 1944 (Heb).

Kabergs, Valérie, and Ausloos, Hans. "Paronomasia or Wordplay? A Babel-Like Confusion: Toward a Definition of Hebrew Wordplay." *Biblica* 93 (2012): 1–20.

Kahana, Menachem. "The Arrangement of the Orders of the Mishna." *Tarbiz* 76 (2006): 29–40 (Heb).

Kahana, A. "Why Was Eve Punished with 'In Sorrow You Will Bear Children'?" *Al HaPerek* 14 (1998): 20–22 (Heb).

Kahl, Brigitte. "And She Called His Name Seth (Gen 4:25): The Birth of Critical Knowledge and the Unread End of Eve's Story." *Union Seminary Quarterly Review* 53 (1999): 19–28.

Kaiser, Walter C. *Toward an Old Testament Theology.* Grand Rapids, 1978.

Kaminski, Carol M. "Beautiful Women or 'False Judgment'?: Interpreting Genesis 6:2 in the Context of the Primeval History." *JSOT* 32 (2008): 457–473.

Kant, Immanuel. *Religion and Rational Theology*. Translated and edited by A. W. Wood and G. Di Giovanni. Cambridge, 1996.

Kasher, Rimon. "II Kings 20:1–11 — Isaiah 38:1–22." *Shnaton* 7–8 (1983–4): 75–89 (Heb).

Kasher, Rimon. "Beliefs and Exegesis: Review on Israel Knohl, Biblical Beliefs." *Katharsis* 8 (2008): 82–103.

Kasher, Menachem Mendel. *Torah Shelema*. 45 vol. Jerusalem, 1992 (Heb).

Kass, Leon R. *The Beginning of Wisdom: Reading Genesis*. New York, 2003.

Katzir (Katz), T. "A Holiday Harvest." *The Academy for the Hebrew Language,* 2010. http://hebrew-academy.org.il.

Kaufmann, Yehezkel. *The Religion of Israel*. 8 vols. Jerusalem, 1953 (Heb).

Kawashima, Robert S. *Biblical Narrative and the Death of the Rhapsode*. Bloomington, 2004.

Kedar-Kopfstein, Benjamin. "*Eden*." *TDOT* 10: 481–490.

Kedourie, Elie. *Nationalism*. Oxford and Cambridge, MA, 1993.

Keil, Karl Fredreich, and Franz Delitzsch. *Biblical Commentary on the Old Testament: Volume I: The Pentateuch*. Translated by J. Martin. Grand Rapids, MI, 1980.

Key, Andrew F. "The Giving of Proper Names in the Old Testament." *JBL* 83 (1964): 55–59.

Kiel, Yehuda. "The Tabernacle, the Temple, and the Garden of Eden." *Shana Be-shanah* (1966): 225–255.

Kiel, Yehuda. *Daat Mikra: Genesis,* vol. 1. Jerusalem, 1997 (Heb).

Kikawada, Isaac M., and Arthur Quinn. *Before Abraham Was: The Unity of Genesis 1–11*. Nashville, 1985.

Kikawada, Isaac M. "The Shape of Genesis 11:1–9." In *Rhetorical Criticism: Essays in Honor of James Muilenburg,* edited by J. J. Jackson and M. Kessler, 18–32. Pittsburgh, 1974.

Kilmer, Anne D. "The Symbolism of the Flies in the Mesopotamian Flood Myth and Some Further Implications." In *Language, Literature, and History: Philological and Historical Studies Presented to Erica Reiner,* edited by F. Rochberg Halton, 175–180. AOS 67: Winona Lake, 1987.

Kimelman, Reuven. "The Seduction of Eve and Feminist Readings of the Garden of Eden." *Women in Judaism: A Multi-Disciplinary Journal* 1 (1998): 1–39.

Kissling, Paul J. "The Rainbow in Genesis 9:12–17: A Triple Entendre." *Stone Campbell Journal* 4 (2001): 249–261.

Klaus, Nathan. *Pivot Patterns in the Former Prophets*. Jerusalem, 1984 (Heb).

Klein, Jacob. "The 'Bane' of Humanity: A Lifespan of One Hundred and Twenty Years." *Acta Sumerologica* 12 (1990): 58–70.

Klein, Yehoshua. "Serpent in the Bible." In *Olam HaTanakh: Genesis*, 31–32. Tel Aviv, 1993 (Heb).

Kline, Meredith. "Divine Kingship and Genesis 6:1–4." *Westminster Theological Journal* 24 (1961): 187–204.

Klingbeil, Gerald A. "The Sabbath Law in the Decalogue(s): Creation and Liberation as a Paradigm for Community." *Revue biblique* 117 (2010): 491–509.

Knohl, Israel. *Biblical Beliefs*. Jerusalem, 2007.

Koch, Klaus. "Die Toledot-Formeln als Strukturprinzip des Buches Genesis." In *Recht und Ethos im Alten Testament – Gestalt und Wirkung*, edited by S. Beyerle, G. Mayer and H. Strauss, 183–191. Neukirchen-Vluyn, 1999.

Kohn, Hans. *The Idea of Nationalism*. New York: Collier-Macmillan, 1944.

Konkel, August H. "*Boker*." *NIDOTTE* 1: 710–720.

Kraeling, Emil G. "The Significance and Origin of Gen. 6.1–4." *JNES* 6 (1947): 193–208.

Kramer, Samuel Noah. "Dumuzi and Enkimdu: The Dispute between the Shepherd God and the Farmer-God." *ANET* 2 (1955): 41–42.

Kramer, Samuel Noah. "*Shomer*." *Encyclopedia Biblica*, vol. 7, 537–567 (Heb).

Kramsch, Claire. *Language and Culture*. Oxford, 1998.

Kübel, Paul. "Ein Wortspiel in Genesis 3 und sein Hintergrund: Die 'kluge' Schlange und die 'nackten' Menschen." *Biblische Notizen* 93 (1998): 11–22.

Kugel, James L. *How to Read the Bible: A Guide to Scripture, Then and Now*. New York, 2007.

Kugel, James L. *Traditions of the Bible: A Guide to the Bible as It Was at the Start of the Common Era*. London and Cambridge, MA, 1998.

Kvanvig, Helge S. "Gen 6:1–4 as an Antediluvian Event." *SJOT* 16 (2002): 79–112.

LaCocque, André. "Whatever Happened in the Valley of Shinar? A Response to Theodore Hiebert." *JBL* 128 (2009): 29–41.

Lacocque, André. *The Captivity of Innocence: Babel and the Yahwist*. Eugene, 2010.

LaCocque, André. *Trial of Innocence: Adam, Eve, and the Yahwist*. Eugene, 2006.

Lambert, Maurice. "A Study of the First Chapter of Genesis." *HUCA* 1 (1924): 3–12.

Lambert, Wilfred G. "A New Look at the Babylonian Background of Genesis." *JTS* 16 (1965): 287–300.

Lambert, Wilfred G. *Babylonian Creation Myths*, Winona Lake, 2013.

Landsberger, Benno. "Assyrische Königsliste und dunkles Zeitalter." *JCS* 8 (1954): 31–73.

Lanfer, Peter Thacher. *Remembering Eden: The Reception History of Genesis 3:22–24*. New York, 2012.

Lang, Bernhard. *Eugen Drewermann: interprète de la Bible*. Paris, 1994.

Larsson, Gerhard. "Remarks concerning the Noah-Flood Complex." *ZAW* 112 (2000): 75–77.

Leach, Edmund. *Genesis as Myth and Other Essays*. London, 1969.

Leibowitz, Nechama. *Studies in Bereshit – Genesis.* Translated by A. Newman. Jerusalem, 1983.

Leibowitz, Nechama. *Studies in Shemot – Exodus.* Translated by A. Newman. Jerusalem, 1983.

Leibtag, Menachem. "The Significance of Circumcision on the Eighth Day." *Alon Shvut* 130 (1991): 93–100 (Heb).

Levenson, Jon D. *Creation and the Persistence of Evil: The Jewish Drama of Divine Omnipotence.* New Jersey, 1994.

Levenson, Jon D. *The Love of God: Divine Gift, Human Gratitude, and Mutual Faithfulness in Judaism.* Princeton and Oxford, 2016.

Levinas, Emmanuel. *Difficile Liberté – Essais sur le judaisme.* Translated to Hebrew by Ido Bassok and S. Wygoda. Tel Aviv, 2007.

Levine, Etan. "The Syriac Version of Genesis IV 1–16." *VT* 26 (1976): 70–78.

Licht, Jacob. *Encyclopedia Biblica,* s.v. "*am,*" vol. 6, 235–239 (Heb).

Lipinski, E. "*'am*", *TDOT* 11: 163–177.

Lipton, Diana. "Legal Analogy in Deuteronomy and Fratricide in the Field." In *Studies on the Text and Versions of the Hebrew Bible in Honour of Robert Gordon,* edited by G. Khan and D. Lipton, 21–38. Leiden and Boston, 2012.

Loewenstamm, Samuel E. "*Yerusha.*" *Encyclopedia Biblica,* vol. 3, 788–791 (Heb).

Long, Burke O. *The Problem of Etiological Narrative in the Old Testament.* BZAW 108; Berlin: Topelmann, 1968.

Longacre, Robert E. "The Discourse Structure of the Flood Narrative." *Society of Biblical Literature: Seminar Papers* 10 (1976): 235–262.

Lorberbaum, Yair. "The Rainbow in the Cloud: An Anger-Management Device." *The Journal of Religion* 89 (2009): 498–540.

Lund, Nils Wilhelm. *Chiasmus in the New Testament: A Study in the Form and Function of Chiastic.* Chapel Hill, 1942.

Luria, B. Z. "The History of the Water Supply in Ancient Jerusalem." *Sinai* 28 (1951): 9–18.

Mann, Thomas W. "All the Families of the Earth: The Theological Unity of Genesis." *Interpretation* 45 (1991): 341–353.

Maori, Yeshayahu. *The Peshitta Version of the Pentateuch and Early Jewish Exegesis.* Jerusalem, 1995 (Heb).

Marks, Herbert. "Biblical Naming and Poetic Etymology." *JBL* 114 (1995): 21–42.

Marzel, Yitzchak. "The Sons of God and the Daughters of Man: Development and Annihilation." *Beit Mikra* 27 (1982): 203–219 (Heb).

Mason, Steven D. "Another Flood? Genesis 9 and Isaiah's Broken Eternal Covenant." *JSOT* 32 (2008): 177–198.

Mathews, Kenneth A. *Genesis.* 2 vols. NAC: Nashville, 1996.

Mazor, Lea. "The Correlation between the Garden of Eden and the Temple." *Shnaton* 13 (2002): 5–42.

McCarthy, Dennis J. *Treaty and Covenant: A Study in Form in the Ancient Oriental Documents and in the Old Testament.* Rome, 1978.

McClone, R. C. *The Genesis Debate: Persistent Questions about Creation and the Flood,* edited by R. Youngblood. Nashville, 1986.

McEvenue, Sean E. *The Narrative Style of the Priestly Writer.* AnBib 50: Rome, 1971.

McGuire, J. Amanda. "Evening or Morning: When Does the Biblical Day Begin?" *Andrews University Seminary Studies* 46 (2008): 201–214.

Medan, Rabbi Yaakov. "Amalek." In *On the Way of the Fathers,* edited by A. Bazak, S. Vigoda, and M. Munitz, 317–396. Alon Shvut, 2001 (Heb).

Medan, Rabbi Yaakov. "The Book of Bathsheba." *Megadim* 18–19 (1993): 67–167 (Heb).

Meek, Russell. "The Meaning of *Hevel* in Qohelet: An Intertextual Suggestion." In *The Words of the Wise Are Like Goads: Engaging Qohelet in the 21st Century,* edited by M. J. Boda et al., 241–256. Winona Lake, 2013.

Meigs, Anna S. "A Papuan Perspective on Pollution." *Manuscripta* 13 (1978): 304–318.

Meinhold, Johannes. *Die biblische Urgeschichte: Mose 1–12.* Bonn, 1904.

Meitlis, Yitzchak. *Parashat Derakhim: Archaeology and Geography in the Weekly Torah Reading.* Jerusalem, 2014 (Heb).

Mendenhall, George E. "Covenant Forms in Israelite Tradition." *BA* 17 (1954): 50–76.

Meyers, Carol. *Discovering Eve: Ancient Israelite Women in Context.* Oxford, 1988.

Mikaelsson, Lisbeth. "Sexual Polarity: An Aspect of the Ideological Structure in the Paradise Narrative, Gen 2:4–3:24." *Temenos* 16 (1980): 84–91.

Milgrom, Jacob. "A Prolegomenon to Lev. 17:11." *JBL* 90 (1971): 149–156.

Milgrom, Jacob. *Leviticus 1–16.* AB: New York, 1991.

Milgrom, Jacob. *Leviticus 17–22.* AB: New York, 2000.

Milgrom, Jacob. *Leviticus 23–27.* AB: New York, 2001.

Millard, A. R. "New Babylonian 'Genesis' Story." *Tyndale Bulletin* 18 (1967): 3–18.

Millard, A. R. "The Etymology of Eden." *VT* 34 (1984): 103–106.

Miller, Patrick D. *Genesis 1–11: Studies in Structure and Theme.* JSOTSup 8: Sheffield, 1978.

Miller, Patrick D. "Eridu, Dunnu, and Babel: A Study in Comparative Mythology." *Hebrew Annual Review* 9 (1985): 227–251.

Moberly, Robert Walter Lambert. "Did the Serpent Get It Right?" *Journal of Theological Studies* 39 (1988): 1–27.

Morgenstern, Julian. "The Sources of the Creation Story: Gen 1:1–2:4." *AJSL* 36 (1919/20): 169–212.

Morris, Leon. "The Biblical Use of the Term Blood." *JTS* 3 (1952): 216–226.

Mulder, M. J. "Baal in the OT." *TDOT* 2: 192–200.

Naaman, Nadav. "Bethel and Beth-aven: The Location of the Early Israelite Sanctuaries." *Zion* 50 (1985): 15–25 (Heb).

Nir, Elchanan. "The Mark of Cain: Derash." *Makor Rishon,* Motzash Supplement, 19 Tishrei 2017, 24 (Heb).

Noble, Paul R. "Esau, Tamar, and Joseph: Criteria for Identifying Inner-Biblical Allusion." *VT* 43 (2002): 219–252.

Noegel, Scott B. "The Significance of the Seventh Plague." *Biblica* 76 (1995): 532–539.

Oded, Bustenay. "The Table of Nations (Genesis 10) – a Socio-cultural Approach." *ZAW* 98 (1986): 14–31.

Oded, Bustenay. "The Beginning of the Babylonian Diaspora – Organization and Economy." *Al HaPerek* 17 (2000): 101–113 (Heb).

Oded, Bustenay. "Hezekiah's Illness and Isaiah's Wonders." In *Olam HaTanakh: II Kings,* 178–180. Tel Aviv, 1994 (Heb).

Oden, Robert A., Jr. "Divine Aspirations in Atrahasis and in Genesis 1–11." *ZAW* 93 (1981): 197–216.

Ofer, Yosef, and Jacobs, Jonathan. *Nahmanides' Torah Commentary Addenda Written in the Land of Israel.* Jerusalem/Alon Shvut, 2013 (Heb).

Olley, John. "Mixed Blessings for Animals: The Contrasts of Genesis 9." In *The Earth Story in Genesis,* edited by N. C. Habel and S. Wurst, 130–139. Sheffield, 2000.

Oppenheim, A. Leo. "The Mesopotamian Temple." *BA* 7 (1944): 54–63.

Oppenheim, A. Leo. "Babel." *Encyclopedia Biblica,* vol. 2, 10–28.

Oppenheim, A. Leo. *Ancient Mesopotamia: Portrait of a Dead Civilization.* Chicago, 1964.

Oppenheimer, Benjamin. "Cain and Abel: The Evolution of the Motif from the Ancient Near East, by Way of the Bible and on the Aggadic Literature and the Books of the Church Fathers." In *Gedaiyahu Alon Memorial Volume,* edited by S. Safrai and M. Stern, 27–68. Tel Aviv, 1970.

Ottosson, Magnus. "Eden and the Land of Promise." In *Congress Volume: Jerusalem 1986,* edited by J. A. Emerton et al., 177–188. VTSup 40: Leiden, 1986.

Parker, Simon B. *The Pre-Biblical Narrative Tradition: Essays on the Ugaritic Poems Keret and Aqhat.* SBL 24: Atlanta, 1989.

Parrot, André. *The Tower of Babel.* Translated by E. Hudson. London, 1955.

Pascal, Blaise. *Pensées.* Translated into Hebrew by J. Ur. Jerusalem, 1976.

Pedersen, Johannes. *Israel, Its Life and Culture,* vols. 1–2. Oxford, 1953.

Peleg, Yitzhak. "In the Beginning, God Created Water and Earth." *Beit Mikra* 41 (1996): 153–167 (Heb).

Penton, T. L. "Differing Approaches to the Theomachy Myth in Old Testament Writers." In *Studies in Bible and the Ancient Near East, Presented to Samuel E. Loewenstamm on His Seventieth Birthday,* edited by Y. Avishur and J. Blau, 337–381. Jerusalem, 1978 (Heb).

Perry, Theodore Anthony. "Cain's Sin in Genesis 4:1–7: Oracular Ambiguity and How to Avoid It." *Prooftexts* 25 (2005): 258–275.

Perry, Menachem. "Literary Dynamics: How the Order of a Text Creates Its Meaning." *Literature* 28 (1979): 6–46 (Heb).

Peterson, David L. "Gen. 6.1–4, Yahweh, and the Organization of the Cosmos." *JSOT* 13 (1979): 47–64.

Philo, *Questions and Answers on Genesis*. Translated by R. Marcus. London and Cambridge, MA, 1953.

Philo of Alexandria Writings (5 vols.), edited by S. Daniel-Nataf, Jerusalem, 1991–2012.

Pinker, Aron. "The Expulsion of Hagar and Ishmael (Gen 21:9–21)." *Women in Judaism* 6 (2009): 1–24.

Plessner, M., and Y. Licht. "*Yareaḥ*," *Encyclopedia Biblica*, vol. 3, 837–839 (Heb).

Polak, Frank. *Biblical Narrative: Aspects of Art and Design*, 2nd ed. Jerusalem, 1999.

Porten, Bezalel. "The Scroll of Ruth: A Rhetorical Study." *Gratz College Annual* 7 (1978): 23–49.

Posen, Rabbi Refael B. *Parshegen: Exegesis and Sources for Onkelos' Translation – Genesis*. Jerusalem, 2013 (Heb).

Prudky, Martin. "The Two Versions of the Sabbath-Commandment: Structural Similarities." In *Stimulation from Leiden*, edited by H. M. Niemann and M. Augustin, 239–255. BeAT 54: Frankfurt am Main, 2006.

Pullum, Geoffrey K. *The Great Eskimo Vocabulary Hoax and Other Irreverent Essays on the Study of Language*. Chicago and London, 1991.

Rabban, N. "The Problem of Eating Meat in Genesis." *Tarbiz* 21 (1949): 25–29.

Radday, Yehuda Thomas. "Chiasmus in Hebrew Biblical Narrative." In *Chiasmus in Antiquity*, edited by J. Welch, 50–115. Utah, 1981.

Rafeld, Meir. "The Figure of Cain in the Eyes of Rashi and Nahmanides." *Tallelei Orot* 9 (2000): 11–24 (Heb).

Rabbi Abraham Isaac Kook, *A Vision of Vegetarianism and Peace*. Jerusalem, 1965 (Heb).

Reinhold, Gotthard G. G. "Die Zahl Sieben als Zahl der Vollendung: Der Sabbat – Antworten auf die Frage nach seinem Ursprung." In *Die Zahl Sieben im Alten Orient*, edited by V. Golinets et al., 27–34. New York, 2009.

Reinhold, Gotthard G. G., ed. *Die Zahl Sieben im Alten Orient: Studien zur Zahlensymbolik in der Bibel und ihrer altorientalischen Umwelt*. Bern, 2008.

Reis, Pamela Tamarkin. "Genesis as Rashomon: The Creation as Told by God and by Man." *Bible Review* 17 (2001): 26–33.

Rendsburg, Gary A. "Alliteration in the Book of Genesis." In *Doubling and Duplicating in the Book of Genesis: Literary and Stylistic Approaches to the Text*, edited by E. R. Hayes and K. Vermeulen, 79–95. Winona Lake, 2016.

Rendsburg, Gary A. "Notes on Genesis XV." *VT* 42 (1992): 266–268.

Rendsburg, Gary A. "Wordplay in the Hebrew Bible: An Eclectic Collection." In *Puns and Pundits: Wordplay in the Hebrew Bible and Ancient Near Eastern Literature*, edited by S. B. Noegel, 137–162. Bethesda, MD, 2000.

Rendsburg, Gary A. *The Redaction of Genesis*. Winona Lake, 1986.

Reventlow, Henning Graf. "Sein Blut komme über sein Haupt." *VT* 10 (1960): 311–327.

Richelle, Matthieu. "La structure littéraire de l'Histoire Primitive (Genèse 1,1–11,26) en son état final." *Biblische Notizen* 151 (2011): 3–22.

Ringgern, H. "Bavel." *TDOT* 1: 466–469.

Risager, Karen. *Language and Culture Pedagogy: From a National to a Transnational Paradigm*. Languages for Intercultural Communication and Education 11: Clevedon, 2006.

Robinson, Robert B. "Literary Functions of the Genealogies of Genesis." *CBQ* 28 (1986): 595–608.

Rock, Rabbi Yehuda. "Knowledge and Labor in the Creation – Two Aspects of the Creation Story in Chapter 1." *Megadim* 25 (1996): 9–34 (Heb).

Rock, Rabbi Yehuda. "An Analysis of the 'The Same Words' of the Tower of Babel Narrative." *Megadim* 32 (2000): 9–20 (Heb).

Rofe, Alexander. *Angels in the Bible: Israelite Belief in Angels as Evidenced by Biblical Traditions*, 2nd ed. Jerusalem, 2012.

Rogerson, John W. "Genesis 1–11." *CR:BS* 5 (1997): 67–90.

Rose, Christian. "Nochmals: Der Turmbau zu Babel." *VT* 54 (2004): 223–238.

Rosenberg, Joel. *King and Kin*. Bloomington, 1986.

Ross, Allen Paul. "Paronomasia and Popular Etymology in the Naming Narratives of the Old Testament." PhD diss., Cambridge University, 1981.

Rost, L. "Die Bezeichnungen fur Land und Volk im Alten Testament." In *Das kleine Credo und andere Studien zum Alten Testament*, 76–101. Heidelberg, 1965.

Ruppert, Lothar. *Genesis I: Gen 1,1–11,26*. FzB 70: Würzburg, 1992.

Rüterswörden, Udo. "Der Bogen in Genesis 9, Militärhistorische und traditionsgeschichtliche Erwägungen zu einem biblischen Symbol." *Ugarit-Forschungen* 20 (1988): 247–263.

Ryle, Herbert Edward. *Genesis*. Cambridge Bible for Schools and Colleges: Cambridge, 1921.

Samet, Elchanan. *Studies in the Weekly Parasha*. Series 1. Jerusalem, 2002.

Samet, Elchanan. *Studies in the Weekly Parasha*. Series 2. Jerusalem, 2004.

Samet, Elchanan. *Studies in the Weekly Parasha*. Series 3. Jerusalem, 2013.

Sandmel, Samuel. "Parallelomania." *JBL* 81 (1962): 1–13.

Sarna, Nahum M. *Understanding Genesis*. The Heritage of Biblical Israel Series 1: New York, 1966.

Sasson, Jack M. "A Genealogical 'Convention' in Biblical Chronology?" *ZAW* 90 (1978): 171–185.

Sasson, Jack M. "The 'Tower of Babel' as a clue to the Redactional Structuring of the Primeval History (Gen 1–11:9)." In *The Bible World Essays in Honor of Cyrus H. Gordon*, edited by G. Rendsburg, 211–219. New York, 1980.

Saxegaard, Kristin Moen. *Character Complexity in the Book of Ruth*. Tübingen, 2010.

Sayce, Archibald H. *Early History of the Hebrews*. New York, 1897.

Scarlata, Mark W. *Outside of Eden: Cain in the Ancient Versions of Genesis 4.1–16*. LHB/OTS 573: New York and London, 2012.

Scharbert, J. "Traditions Redaktionsgeschichte von Gen. 6, 1–4." *BZ* 11 (1967): 66–78.

Schechterman, Deborah. "The Doctrine of Original Sin in the Jewish Philosophy of the Thirteenth and Fourteenth Centuries." *Daat* 20 (1988): 65–90 (Heb).

Schellenberg, Annette. "Humankind as the 'Image of God.'" *TZ* 65 (2009): 97–115.

Schlimm, Matthew Richard. *From Fratricide to Forgiveness: The Language and Ethics of Anger in Genesis*. Winona Lake, 2011.

Schrader, Malcolm. "God Rested on the Seventh Day." *JBQ* 41 (2013): 130–134.

Schweid, Eliezer. *The Cycle of Appointed Times: The Meaning of Jewish Holidays*. Tel Aviv, 1984 (Heb).

Seebass, Horst. *Genesis I: Urgeschichte (1,1–11,26)*, 3rd ed. Neukirchen-Vluyn, 2009.

Seeligmann, Isac Leo. "Etiological Elements in Biblical Historiography." *Zion* 26 (1961): 141–169 (Heb).

Shaked, Shaul. *Encyclopedia Biblica*, s.v. "*Peras – HaDat HaParsit*," vol. 6, 609–615 (Heb).

Shammah, Avraham. "*Parashot* of Revelation: Theological Studies and Reflections." In *People of Faith and Biblical Criticism*, edited by Y. Brandes, T. Ganzel, and C. Deutsch, 342–358. Jerusalem, 2015 (Heb).

Shaviv, Yehuda. "'Rule' in its Earliest Meaning." *Megadim* 22 (1994): 23–29 (Heb).

Shaviv, Yehuda. "*Zot HaPaam*." *Beit Mikra* 33 (1988): 129–130.

Shemesh, Yael. "Measure for Measure in Biblical Narrative." *Beit Mikra* 44 (1999): 261–277 (Heb).

Shemesh, Yael. *Mourning in the Bible: Coping with Loss in Biblical Literature*. Tel Aviv, 2015 (Heb).

Sherman, Phillip Michael. *Babel's Tower Translated: Genesis 11 and Ancient Jewish Interpretation*. Leiden and Boston, 2013.

Shifra, Shin, and Jacob Klein. *In Those Distant Days: Anthology of Mesopotamian Literature in Hebrew*. Tel Aviv, 1996 (Heb).

Shimon, Zvi. *Contrast in Biblical Narrative*. PhD diss., Bar-Ilan University, 2008.

Shimon, Zvi. *Human Choice Biblical Narrative and the Drama of Choice*. Jerusalem, 2015.

Ska, Jean-Louis. "The Story of the Flood: A Priestly Writer and Some Later Editorial Fragments." In *The Exegesis of the Pentateuch: Exegetical Studies and Basic Questions*, 1–22. FAT 66: Tübingen, 2009.

Skinner, John. *A Critical and Exegetical Commentary on Genesis*, 2nd ed. ICC: Edinburgh, 1930.

Smith, George Adam. "The Hebrew Genius as Exhibited in the Old Testament." In *The Legacy of Israel*, edited by E. R. Bevan and C. Singer, 1–28. Oxford, 1927.

Smith, Mark S. "Light in Genesis 1:3 – Created or Uncreated: A Question of Priestly Mysticism?" In *Birkat Shalom: Studies in the Bible, Ancient Near Eastern Literature, and Postbiblical Judaism Presented to Shalom M. Paul on the Occasion of His Seventieth Birthday*, edited by Ch. Cohen et al., vol. 1, 125–134. Winona Lake, 2008.

Smith, James Edward. *In the Beginning: Commentary on Genesis 1–3*. Morrisville, NC, 2016.

Smith, Anthony D. *The Nation in History: Historiographical Debates about Ethnicity and Nationalism*. Hanover, 2000.

Soggin, J. Alberto. "The Fall of Man in the Third Chapter of Genesis." In *Old Testament and Oriental Studies*, 88–111. Biblica et Orientalia 29: Rome, 1975.

Soloveitchik, Rabbi Joseph B. *Family Redeemed*. New York, 2000.

Soloveitchik, Rabbi Joseph B. *Confrontation and Other Essays*. Jerusalem, 2015.

Speiser, Ephraim Avigdor. *Genesis*. AB 1. New York, 1962.

Speiser, Ephraim Avigdor. "'People' and 'Nation' of Israel." *JBL* 79 (1960): 157–163.

Speiser, Ephraim Avigdor. "Word Plays on the Creation Epic's Version of the Founding of Babylon." *Orientalia* 25 (1956): 317–323.

Spina, Frank Anthony. "Babel." *ABD* 1: 561–563.

Stade, Bernhard. *Geschichte des Volkes Israel*. Berlin, 1887–1889.

Stager, Lawrence E. "Jerusalem and the Garden of Eden." *Eretz-Israel* 26 (1999): 183–194.

Steck, Odil Hannes. *Der Schöpfungsbericht der Priesterschrift*. FRLANT 115: Göttingen, 1975.

Steinmetz, Devora. "Vineyard, Farm, and Garden: The Drunkenness of Noah in the Context of Primeval History." *JBL* 113 (1994): 193–207.

Sternberg, Meir. "Repetition Structure in Biblical Narratives: Strategies of Informational Redundancy." *Literature* 25 (1977), 109–150 (Heb).

Stigers, Harold G. *A Commentary on Genesis*. Grand Rapids, 1976.

Stol, Marten. *Women in the Ancient Near East*. Translated by H. and M. Richardson. Boston/Berlin, 2016.

Stordalen, Terje. *Echoes of Eden: Genesis 2–3 and Symbolism of the Eden Garden in Biblical Hebrew Literature*. Contributions to Biblical Exegesis and Theology 25: Leuven, 2000.

Stratton, Beverly J. *Out of Eden: Reading, Rhetoric, and Ideology in Genesis 2–3*. JSOTSup 208: Sheffield, 1995.

Strauss, Gilad. "Three Wise Women in the Book of Samuel." *Megadim* 21 (1994): 55–60 (Heb).

Strong, John T. "Shattering the Image of God: A Response to Theodore Hiebert's Interpretation of the Story of the Tower of Babel." *JBL* 127 (2008): 625–634.

Strus, Andrzej. *Nomen-omen: La Stylistique sonore des noms propres dans le Pentateuque*. AnBib 80; Rome, 1978.

Sussman, Max. "Sickness and Disease." *ABD* 6: 6–15.

Sutskover, Talia. "Name Giving in Genesis and Establishing Authority." *Beit Mikra* 57 (2012): 33–51 (Heb).

Sweeney, Deborah, and Julia M. Asher-Greve. "On Nakedness, Nudity, and Gender in Egyptian and Mesopotamian Art." In *Images and Gender: Contributions to the Hermeneutics of Reading Ancient Art*, edited by S. Schroer, 125–176. OBO 220: Fribourg and Göttingen, 2006.

Tadiello, Roberto. "La dispersione occasione positiva di crescita." *Bibbia e Oriente* 53 (2011): 129–148.

Tal, Abraham. *The Samaritan Targum of the Pentateuch: A Critical Edition*. Part 1: Genesis-Exodus. Tel Aviv, 1980 (Heb).

Talshir, Zipora. "The Unity of Structure in Genesis I–XI – Research on the Verge of Midrash." *Shnaton* 11 (1987): 131–138 (Heb).

Taylor, R. A. "G-Y-Ḥ," *NIDOTTE* 1: 853.

Taylor, J. Glen. *Yahweh and the Sun: Biblical and Archaeological Evidence for Sun Worship in Ancient Israel*. Sheffield, 1993.

Tengstrom, Sven. *Die Toledotformel und die literarische Struktur der priesterlichen Erweiterungsschicht im Pentateuch*. ConBot 17: Lund, 1982.

The New Dictionary – the Combined Version in Five Volumes. Tel Aviv, 2000.

Thomas, Matthew A. *These Are the Generations: Identity, Covenant and the 'Toledot' Formula*. LHBOTS 551: New York, 2011.

Thompson, Thomas L. *The Origin Tradition of Ancient Israel: The Literary Formation of Genesis and Exodus 1–23*. JSOTSup 55: Sheffield, 1987.

Titus, Joseph P. *The Second Story of Creation (Gen 2:4–3:24): A Prologue to the Concept of the Enneateuch?* Frankfurt, 2011.

Towner, Sibley W. "Genesis 9:8–17." *Interpretation* 63 (2009): 168–171.

Trible, Phyllis. *God and the Rhetoric of Sexuality*. Philadelphia, 1978.

Tsevat, Mattitiahu. "The Two Trees That Were in the Garden." *Eretz Yisrael* 12 (1975): 40–43 (Heb).

Tsumura, David Toshio. *The Earth and the Waters in Genesis 1 and 2: A Linguistic Investigation*. JSOTSup 83: Sheffield, 1989.

Turner, Laurence A. "The Rainbow as the Sign of the Covenant in Genesis ix 11–13." *VT* 43 (1993): 119–124.

Turner, Laurence A. *Announcements of Plot in Genesis.* JSOTSup 96: Sheffield, 1990.

Tur-Sinai, Naftali Herz. *Language and the Book.* Jerusalem, 1950 (Heb).

Theological Wordbook of the Old Testament, edited by R. L. Harris. Chicago, 1980.

Tyndale House Publishers. *Genesis 1–12.* NLT Study Bible: Illinois, 2008.

Uehlinger, Christoph. *Weltreich und "eine Rede": Eine neue Deutung der sogenannten Turmbauerzählung (Gen 11, 1–9).* Freiburg, 1990.

Urbach, Ephraim E. *The Sages: Their Concepts and Beliefs,* 2nd ed. Jerusalem, 1971.

van der Toorn, Karel. "Sun." *ABD* 6: 237–239.

van der Toorn, Karel, and Pieter W. van der Horst. "Nimrod before and after the Bible." *HTR* 83 (1990): 1–29.

Van Leeuwen, Raymond C. "*Bara.*" *NIDOTTE* 1: 728–735.

van Wieringen, A. L. H. M. "Assur and Babel against Jerusalem: The Reader-Oriented Position of Babel and Assur within the Framework of Isaiah 1–39." In *'Enlarge the Site of Your Tent': The City as. Unifying Theme in Isaiah,* edited by A. L. H. M. van Wieringen, and A. van der Woude, 49–62. Leiden/Boston, 2011.

van Wolde, Ellen. "One Bow or Another? A Study of the Bow in Genesis 9:8–17." *VT* 63 (2013): 124–149.

van Wolde, Ellen. *Reframing Biblical Studies: When Language and Text Meet Culture, Cognition, and Context.* Winona Lake, 2009.

van Wolde, Ellen. *Stories of the Beginning: Genesis 1–11 and Other Creation Stories.* Translated by J. Bowden. London, 1996.

van Wolde, Ellen. *Words Become Worlds: Semantic Studies of Genesis 1–11.* Leiden, 1994.

Vawter, Bruce. *On Genesis: A New Reading.* Garden City, 1977.

Vermeulen, Karolien. "The Art of Blessing and Cursing in Genesis 1–11: Stylistic Patterns and Their Ideological Motivation." In *Doubling and Duplicating in the Book of Genesis: Literary and Stylistic Approaches to the Text,* edited by E. R. Hayes and K. Vermeulen, 113–128. Winona Lake, 2016.

Vogels, Walter. "'And God Created the Great Tanninim' (Gn 1:21)." *Science et esprit* 63 (2011): 349–365.

von Herder, Johann Gottfried. *Vom Geist der Ebräischen Poesie: Eine Anleitung für die Liebhaber derselben, und der ältesten Geschichte des menschlichen Geistes.* Deßau, 1782.

von Rad, Gerhard. *Genesis.* Translated by J. H. Marks, 2nd ed. OTL: London, 1963.

von Soden, Wolfram. *The Ancient Orient: An Introduction to the Study of the Ancient Near East.* Grand Rapids, 1994.

Waldman, Nahum M. "The Breaking of the Bow." *JQR* 69 (1978–9): 82–88.

Wallace, Howard N. "Eden, Garden of." *ABD* 2: 281–283.

Wallace, Howard N. *The Eden Narrative.* Atlanta, 1985.

Walsh, Jerome T. "Genesis 2:4b–3:24: A Synchronic Approach." *JBL* 96 (1977): 161–177.

Walsh, Jerome T. *Style and Structure in Biblical Hebrew Narrative.* Collegeville, 2001.

Waltke, Bruce K. "The Literary Genre of Genesis, Chapter One." *Crux* 27 (1991): 2–10.

Walton, John H. "Joshua 10:12–15 and Mesopotamian Celestial Omen Texts." In *Faith, Tradition, and History: Old Testament Historiography in Its Near Eastern Context,* edited by A. R. Millard et al., 181–190. Winona Lake, 1994.

Walton, John H. "The Sons of God in Genesis 6:1–4." In *The Genesis Debate,* edited by R. Youngblood, 184–209. Nelson, 1986.

Weinfeld, Moshe. "The Covenant of Grant in the Old Testament and in the Ancient Near East." *JAOS* 90 (1970): 184–203.

Weinfeld, Moshe. "God the Creator in Genesis 1 and in the Prophecy of Second Isaiah." *Tarbiz* 37 (1968): 105–132 (Heb).

Weinfeld, Moshe, ed. *Olam HaTanakh: Genesis.* Tel Aviv, 1993 (Heb).

Weinfeld, Moshe. *"Justice and Righteousness" in Ancient Israel against the Background of "Social Reforms" in the Ancient Near East.* Jerusalem, 1985 (Heb).

Weiser, Asher. "Egypt in the Bible." *Mahanaim* 105 (1961): 16–24.

Weitman, Rabbi Zev. "The New Creation." *Alon Shvut* 78 (1980): 27–38 (Heb).

Wellhausen, Julius. *Die Composition Des Hexateuchs Und Der Historischen Bucher Des Alten Testaments,* 3rd ed. Berlin, 1899.

Wellhausen, Julius. *Reste arabischen Heidentums.* Berlin, 1897.

Wenham, Gordon J. "The Coherence of the Flood Narrative." *VT* 28 (1978): 336–348.

Wenham, Gordon J. "Method in Pentateuchal Source Criticism." *VT* 41 (1991): 84–109.

Wenham, Gordon J. "Sanctuary Symbolism in the Garden of Eden Story." In *Proceedings of the Ninth World Congress of Jewish Studies, Division A,* 19–25. Jerusalem: World Union of Jewish Studies, 1986.

Wenham, Gordon J. *Genesis 1–15.* WBC: Waco, 1987.

Wenham, Gordon J. *Leviticus.* NICOT: Michigan, 1979.

Wénin, André. "Adam et Eve: la jalousie de Cain, 'semence' du serpent: Un aspect du récit mythique de Genèse 1–4." *Revue des sciences religieuses* 73 (1999): 3–16.

Westermann, Claus. *Genesis: A Continental Commentary.* 3 vols. Translated by J. J. Scullion. Minneapolis, 1985–1994.

Williams, W. C. "*Ava.*" *NIDOTTE* 1: 304–306.

Williamson, Paul. *Abraham, Israel and the Nations: The Patriarchal Promise and Its Covenantal Development in Genesis.* JSOTSup 315; Sheffield, 2001.

Wiseman, Percy John. *New Discoveries in Babylonia about Genesis.* London, 1936.

Witte, Markus. *Die biblische Urgeschichte: Redaktions und theologiegeschichtliche Beobachtungen zu Genesis 1,1–11,26.* Berlin, 1998.

Wolfensohn, Avraham. "Let Us Build a City (Genesis 11:1–9)." *Beit Mikra* 39 (1994): 28–33 (Heb).

Wyatt, Nicolas. "Interpreting the Creation and Fall Story in Genesis 2–3." *ZAW* 93 (1981): 10–21.

Yaniv, Iris. "From What Kind of Tree Did Adam Eat?" *Al HaPerek* 14 (1998): 8–15 (Heb).

Younger, K. L. "*Keshet*." *NIDOTTE* 3: 1004–1006.

Zakovitch, Yair. *The Song of Songs: Introduction and Commentary*. Mikra Leyisra'el: Jerusalem/Tel Aviv, 1992 (Heb).

Zipor, Moshe A. "The Flood Chronology: Too Many an Accident." *Dead Sea Discoveries* 4 (1997): 207–210.

Zipor, Moshe A. *The Septuagint Version of the Book of Genesis*. Ramat Gan, 2005 (Heb).

The fonts used in this book are from the Arno family

Maggid Books
The best of contemporary Jewish thought from
Koren Publishers Jerusalem Ltd.